INTRODUCTION TO
MACROECONOMICS

SIXTH EDITION

Edwin G. Dolan
PhD Yale University

Introduction to Macroeconomics

SIXTH EDITION

Publisher and Director of Business Development: Richard Schofield
Business Development and Ancillary Manager: Shannon Conley
Graphic Designer/Typesetter: Esther Scannell
Typesetting Manager: Rhonda Minnema
Managing Editor: Anne Schofield
Production and Fulfillment Manager: Janai Bryand
Proofreader: Tara Joffe

Photo Credits: Front cover and chapter openers (Shutterstock).

Some ancillaries, including electronic and print components, may not be available to customers outside the United States.

eBook^Plus ISBN: 978-1-62751-629-7

Loose-Leaf ISBN: 978-1-62751-630-3

Softcover ISBN: 978-1-62751-633-4

Textbook^Plus (Loose-Leaf Bundle): 978-1-62751-631-0

ABOUT THE AUTHOR

Edwin G. Dolan, economist and educator, holds a PhD from Yale University. Early in his career, he was a member of the economics faculty at Dartmouth College, the University of Chicago, and George Mason University. From 1990 to 2001, he taught in Moscow, Russia, where he and his wife founded the American Institute of Business and Economics (AIBEc), an independent, not-for-profit MBA program. Since 2001, he has taught at several universities in Europe, including Central European University in Budapest, the University of Economics in Prague, and the Stockholm School of Economics in Riga. During breaks in his teaching career, he worked in Washington, DC, as an economist for the Antitrust Division of the Department of Justice and as a regulatory analyst for the Interstate Commerce Commission. He later served a stint in Almaty as an adviser to the National Bank of Kazakhstan. When not lecturing abroad, he makes his home in northwest Michigan.

Brief Contents

Detailed Contents

PART 1   Introduction to Economics

SIXTH EDITION REVIEWERS

PREFACE

The spread of instant electronic communication has changed not only the economy itself but also the way students learn economics and the way instructors teach the subject. A textbook, perhaps supplemented by a few photocopied handouts, used to be almost the only source of information for students. A blackboard was often the instructor's only teaching tool. All this has changed.

Today, both students and instructors rely on the internet as their primary source of information about current economic events. They still need a good textbook to provide a framework for organizing all the information that is available, but that textbook needs to mesh with the material available from online news sources, blogs, and social media. This sixth edition of *Introduction to Macroeconomics* from BVT Publishing includes several changes that integrate it more smoothly into the world of e-learning.

One change is a new design with more prominent headings that will make the electronic version of the book more readable on screen. Readers will also find sections that provide direct links from chapters in the text to related material on my blog.

In addition to a more inviting presentation, there are extensive revisions of the content. It will hardly come as a surprise to say that much has happened since the fifth edition was written (as the US and global economies were beginning to recover from the Great Recession).

Here are some of the other key changes:

- There have been many changes in the financial system and monetary policy. Chapter 7 reviews problems of banking and finance that led up to the 2008 crisis, and explains structural and regulatory changes since that time. Chapter 8 is completely redone to present monetary theory in a way that is more consistent with the way modern central banks actually carry out monetary policy.

- Chapter 9 deals with exchange rates, currency areas, and international monetary policy. It includes extended case studies on the euro area and its problems, and on China's currency policy and the reasons for its slowing growth.

- The two chapters on fiscal policy contain much new material. Chapter 12 covers the short-run perspective on fiscal policy and the business cycle, including discretionary fiscal stimulus, automatic stabilizers, the budget process, and the risks of procyclical fiscal policy. Chapter 13 takes the long-term perspective on sustainability of government deficits and debts, and fiscal policy rules.

- Fortunately, the US economy has not fallen into either deflation or hyperinflation, but issues related to the price level continue to be a focus of macroeconomic policy. Chapter 14 covers the latest developments, including reasons why inflation in major economies has continued to fall below central bank targets.

There are new case studies and examples in every chapter and, in addition, many more for which there is no room in the book itself. Every week, Ed Dolan's Econ Blog provides new material to both students and instructors. The blog's Resource Center for Teaching Economics, found at dolanecon.blogspot.com, brings regular posts on micro- and macroeconomic topics. Students and instructors can also follow @DolanEcon on Twitter® to keep up with the latest economic news. I also invite instructors and students to suggest topics for blog posts or submit guest posts of their own on favorite subjects.

Finally, this edition recognizes the fact that instructors no longer rely solely on blackboards and photocopied handouts as teaching aids. Most instructors now regularly use slideshows, smartboards, and videos in class, and course websites to help students with their studying between classes.

One important aid to e-teaching and e-learning is a complete set of PowerPoint™ slides, which include all of the graphs and tables from each chapter, plus other relevant material that is available as a supplement to *Introduction to Macroeconomics* from BVT. Beyond the basic slides for each chapter, Ed Dolan's Econ Blog provides additional content in PowerPoint format.

Acknowledgments

As always, I thank the entire publishing and editorial staff of BVT Publishing for their highly professional support. They are a pleasure to work with, and I hope that all students and instructors who use this book benefit as much as I have from their unique and innovative approach to textbook publishing. Enjoy your teaching and learning!

SUPPLEMENTS & RESOURCES

Instructors Supplements

A complete teaching package is available for instructors who adopt this book. This package includes an online lab, instructor's manual, test bank, course management software, and PowerPoint™ slides.

BVTLab	An online lab is available for this textbook at www.BVTLab.com, as described in the BVTLab section below.
Instructor's Manual	The instructor's manual helps first-time instructors develop the course, while offering seasoned instructors a new perspective on the material. Each section of the instructor's manual coincides with a chapter in the textbook. The user-friendly format begins by providing learning objectives and detailed outlines for each chapter. Then, the manual presents lecture discussions, class activities, and sample answers to the end-of-chapter review questions. Lastly, additional resources—books, articles, websites—are listed to help instructors review the materials covered in each chapter.
Test Bank	An extensive test bank is available to instructors in both hard copy and electronic form. Each chapter has approximately 200 multiple choice, 100 true/false, 50 short answer, and 10 essay questions ranked by difficulty and style. Each question is referenced to the appropriate section of the text to make test creation quick and easy.
Course Management Software	BVT's course management software, Respondus, allows for the creation of tests and quizzes that can be downloaded directly into a wide variety of course management environments such as Blackboard®, WebCT™, Desire2Learn®, Canvas™, and others.
PowerPoint Slides	A set of PowerPoint slides for each chapter, comprise a chapter overview, learning objectives, slides covering all key topics, key figures and charts, as well as summary and conclusion slides.

Student Resources

Student resources are available for this textbook at www.BVTLab.com. These resources are geared toward students needing additional assistance, as well as those seeking complete mastery of the content. The following resources are available:

Practice Questions	Students can work through hundreds of practice questions online. Questions are multiple choice or true/false in format and are graded instantly for immediate feedback.
Flashcards	BVTLab includes sets of flashcards that reinforce the key terms and concepts from each chapter.
Chapter Summaries	A convenient and concise chapter summary is available as a study aid.
PowerPoint Slides	All instructor PowerPoints are available for convenient lecture preparation and for students to view online for a study recap.

BVT LAB

BVTLab is an affordable online lab for instructors and their students. It includes an online classroom with a grade book and chat room, a homework grading system, extensive test banks for quizzes and exams, and a host of student study resources. Even if a class is not taught in the lab, students can still utilize the resources described below.

Course Setup	BVTLab has an easy-to-use, intuitive interface that allows instructors to quickly set up their courses and grade books, and to replicate them from section to section and semester to semester.
Grade Book	Using an assigned passcode, students register for the grade book, which automatically grades and records all homework, quizzes, and tests.
Chat Room	Instructors can post discussion threads to a class forum and then monitor and moderate student replies.
Student Resources	All student resources for this textbook are available in BVTLab in digital form.
eBook	Students who have purchased a product that includes an eBook can download the eBook from a link in the lab. A web-based eBook is also available within the lab for easy reference during online classes, homework, and study sessions.

CUSTOMIZATION

BVT's Custom Publishing Division can help you modify this book's content to satisfy your specific instructional needs. The following are examples of customization:

- Rearrangement of chapters to follow the order of your syllabus
- Deletion of chapters not covered in your course
- Addition of paragraphs, sections, or chapters you or your colleagues have written for this course
- Editing of the existing content, down to the word level
- Customization of the accompanying student resources and online lab
- Addition of handouts, lecture notes, syllabus, etc.
- Incorporation of student worksheets into the textbook

All of these customizations will be professionally typeset to produce a seamless textbook of the highest quality, with an updated table of contents and index to reflect the customized content.

PART 1

Introduction
to
Economics

CHAPTER 1

HOW ECONOMISTS THINK

AFTER READING THIS CHAPTER,
you will understand the following:

1. What economics is really about

2. Four fundamental economic choices

3. The coordination of economic choices

4. How economists use theory, graphs, and data

CHAPTER
Outline

What do you consider the most important economic issue today? Inequality of income and wealth? (Increasing for the United States, but decreasing for the world as a whole.) The high cost of college? (Rising faster than inflation for years.) The federal budget deficit? (Dramatically lower than its peak, but likely to increase in coming years.) The high price of gasoline? (Down for the month as I write this, but maybe back up again by the time you read it.) How can we understand these complex, yet interrelated, issues?

There are many ways to understand what goes on in the world around us. Sociologists, poets, and religious leaders each have a contribution to make. So do economists. Although reading this book will not make you an economist, it should give you a good overview of how economists think about things. By adding the economic perspective to others, you will better understand the world around you.

This chapter will take the first steps toward explaining the economic way of thinking by introducing a few big ideas that apply everywhere, in all countries, at all times. The most important of them is **scarcity**. Scarcity means any situation in which there is not enough of something to fill everyone's wants. For example corn grown in the US Midwest is scarce because there is not enough of it to meet all the competing needs of Chinese consumers, who want to eat more corn-fed pork as they become wealthier, and of US drivers, who are burning more corn-based ethanol in their cars. The scarcity of corn affects people's choices about how to use not only corn but also other goods like wheat and gasoline. Any change in the scarcity of corn can have indirect effects on exchange rates and stock markets that may not be quite so easy to trace, but are no less important.

Scarcity and the way people deal with it are defining concepts of **economics**, the social science that seeks to understand the choices people make in using scarce resources to meet their wants. As this definition makes clear, economics is a study not of things, money, or wealth, but of *people*. Economics is about people because scarcity itself is a human phenomenon. Wild strains of corn grew for millions of years and deposits of crude oil lay undisturbed in the ground long before they became the objects of human wants. Only after humans deemed them desirable did they become scarce, at least in the sense that economists understand the term.

The focus on the human dimension of scarcity and choice is part of what makes economics a social science. Economics is a social science also because people do not deal with scarcity in isolation. Instead they can stretch scarce resources to meet their wants more effectively by trading with one another. As people trade, each person gives up something of value to others so that everyone gains from the exchange. Some economists think exchange is even more important than scarcity as a defining characteristic of economics.

We can divide the wide range of topics covered by economics into two main branches. Understanding what determines corn prices belongs to the branch known as **microeconomics**. The prefix *micro*, meaning "small," indicates that this branch of economics deals with the choices of small economic units such as households, firms, and government agencies. Although microeconomics studies individual behavior, its scope can be worldwide, as when it focuses on global trade in goods such as food and energy.

Economics also has another branch, known as **macroeconomics**. The prefix *macro*, meaning "large," indicates that it deals with larger-scale phenomena. Typical problems in macroeconomics include the causes of unemployment, inflation, and changes in living standards. Macroeconomics and microeconomics are not really separate. Because macroeconomic phenomena like inflation represent the result of millions of individual choices about the prices of particular goods and services, macroeconomics ultimately rests on a microeconomic foundation.

Scarcity

A situation in which there is not enough of a resource to meet all of everyone's wants

Economics

The social science that seeks to understand the choices people make in using scarce resources to meet their wants

Microeconomics

The branch of economics that studies the choices of individual units—including households, business firms, and government agencies

Macroeconomics

The branch of economics that studies large-scale economic phenomena, particularly inflation, unemployment, and economic growth

1.1 WHAT? HOW? WHO? FOR WHOM?

Among the most important economic choices people make are what goods will be produced, how people will produce them, who will do which jobs, and who will benefit from the goods and services that the economy produces. Scarcity makes each of these choices necessary. We can use each of them to introduce a key aspect of how economists think.

1.1a Deciding What to Produce: Opportunity Cost

The first choice is what goods to produce. In a real economy there are more distinct goods and services than we can count, but we can illustrate some basic principles with an economy that produces just two goods: cars and education. Both goods are scarce. Going without a car (or driving a used car instead of a new one) is a sacrifice many students must make to get a college education. The economy as a whole faces the same trade-off that individual students face. It is not possible to give everyone all the cars and education they want or just the kind and quality they would like. Somehow, someone must make choices.

No economy can produce as much of everything as everyone wants because the resources used to make things are, themselves, scarce. For example making a car requires steel, glass, paint, welding machines, land for factories, and the labor of autoworkers. Economists traditionally group all the various resources used in production into three basic categories called **factors of production**: labor, capital, and natural resources. **Labor** includes all of the productive contributions made by people working with their minds and hands. **Capital** includes all the productive inputs created by people, including tools, machinery, buildings, and intangible items like computer software. **Natural resources** include anything that people can use as a productive input in its natural state—for example, farmland, building sites, forests, and mineral deposits.

We cannot use factors of production to satisfy two wants at the same time. We cannot use the same steel, concrete, and building sites both for automobile factories and for classrooms. People who work as teachers cannot spend the same time working on an automobile assembly line. Students could spend part of their time working in an auto plant to earn money to pay for college, but if they did, that would take time away from studying. Whenever scarce inputs have more than one possible use, using them to produce one good means giving up the opportunity to produce something else instead. Economists express this basic truth by saying that everything has an **opportunity cost.** The opportunity cost of a good or service is its cost in terms of the forgone opportunity to pursue the best possible alternative activity with the same time or resources.

In our two-good economy, the opportunity cost of producing a college graduate can be expressed as the number of cars that could have been produced by using the same labor, capital, and natural resources. Suppose that

Many students must go without a car (or drive a used car instead of a new one) in order to get a college education. (Shutterstock)

Factors of production

The basic inputs of labor, capital, and natural resources used in producing all goods and services

Labor

The contributions to production made by people working with their minds and their hands

Capital

All means of production that are created by people, including tools, industrial equipment, and structures

Natural resources

Anything that people can use as a productive input in its natural state, such as farmland, building sites, forests, and mineral deposits

Opportunity cost

The cost of a good or service measured in terms of the forgone opportunity to pursue the best possible alternative activity with the same time or resources

the opportunity cost of educating a college graduate is four Toyota® Camrys®. That ratio (graduates per car or cars per graduate) would be a useful way to express opportunity cost in an economy with just two goods; more typically, though, we deal with situations in which there are many goods. Having more of one means giving up a little bit of many others.

In an economy with many goods, we can express opportunity costs in terms of a common unit of measurement: money. For example rather than saying that a college education is worth four Camrys, or that a Camry is worth one-fourth of a college education, we could say that the opportunity cost of a car is $30,000 and that of a college education is $120,000.

Useful as it is to have a common unit of measurement, we must take great care when expressing opportunity costs in terms of money because not all out-of-pocket money expenditures represent the sacrifice of opportunities to do something else. At the same time, not all forgone opportunities take the form of money spent. *Applying Economic Ideas 1.1,* which analyzes both the out-of-pocket expenditures and the opportunity costs of a college education, shows why.

We will stress the importance of opportunity cost repeatedly in this book. The habit of looking for opportunity costs is one of the distinguishing features of the economic way of thinking.

Applying Economic Ideas 1.1

The Opportunity Cost of a College Education

How much does it cost you to go to college? If you are a resident student at a typical four-year college in the United States, you can answer this question by making up a budget like the one shown in Part A of the table. We can call this a budget of out-of-pocket costs because it includes all the items—and only those items—that you or your parents must actually pay for in a year.

Part A: Budget of Out-of-Pocket Costs		Part B: Budget of Opportunity Costs	
Item	Amount	Item	Amount
Tuition and fees	$14,000	Tuition and fees	$14,000
Books and supplies	1,200	Books and supplies	1,200
Transportation to and from home	1,100	Transportation to and from home	1,100
Room and board	7,000	Forgone income	16,000
Personal expenses	1,400		
Total out-of-pocket costs	**$24,700**	**Total opportunity costs**	**$32,300**

Your own out-of-pocket costs may be much higher or lower than those given in the table, but chances are these are the main categories that first come to mind when you think about the costs of college. As you begin to think more like an economist, you may find it useful to restate your college budget in terms of opportunity costs. Which of the items in Part A represent opportunities that you have forgone in order to go to college? Are any forgone opportunities missing? To answer these questions, compare Part A with Part B, which shows a budget of opportunity costs.

Some items are both opportunity costs and out-of-pocket costs. The first three items in Part A show up again in Part B. To spend $14,000 on tuition and fees and $1,200 on books and supplies, you must give up the opportunity to buy other goods and services—maybe to buy a car or rent a ski condo. To spend $1,100 getting to and from school, you may have to pass up the opportunity to travel somewhere else or to spend the money on something other than travel. Not all out-of-pocket costs are also opportunity costs, however. Consider the last two items in the out-of-pocket budget. By spending $8,400 on room, board, and personal expenses during the year, you are not really giving up the opportunity to do something else. Whether or not you were going to college, you would have to eat, live somewhere, and buy clothes. Because you would have those expenses in any case, they do not count as opportunity costs of going to college.

Income that could have been earned with time spent studying is an opportunity cost of getting a college education. (iStock)

Finally, some items are opportunity costs without being out-of-pocket costs. Think about what you would be doing if you were not going to college. If you were not going to college, you probably would have taken a job and started earning money soon after leaving high school. As a high-school graduate, your earnings would be about $16,000 during the nine months of the school year. (You can work during the summer even if you are attending college.) Because this potential income is something that you must forgo for the sake of college, it is an opportunity cost even though it does not involve an outlay of money.

Which budget you use depends on the kind of decision you are making. If you have already decided to go to college and are doing your financial planning, the out-of-pocket budget will tell you how much you have to raise from savings, money earned, parents' contributions, loans, and scholarships to make ends meet. But if you are making the more basic choice between going to college and pursuing a career that does not require a college degree, the opportunity cost of college is what counts.

1.1b Deciding How to Produce: Efficiency and Entrepreneurship

How to produce is a second basic economic choice. There is more than one way to make almost anything. Auto firms can, for example, make cars in highly automated factories, using a lot of capital equipment and relatively little labor, or build them one by one in smaller shops, using a lot of labor and only a few general-purpose machines. Toyota builds its Camrys the first way; Lamborghini builds its Huracán (priced at a thrifty $237,000) the second way. We could say the same about education. A professor can teach a course directly to twenty students in a small classroom using only a whiteboard, or teach the same course online to hundreds of students.

Some cars come from highly automated factories, while others use lots of hand labor. (Dreamstime)

Economic efficiency

A state of affairs in which it is impossible to make any change that satisfies one person's wants more fully without causing some other person's wants to be satisfied less fully

Efficiency in production

A situation in which it is not possible, given available knowledge and productive resources, to produce more of one good without forgoing the opportunity to produce some of another good

Efficiency   Efficiency is one of the most important things to keep in mind when deciding how to produce something. In everyday language, efficiency means producing with a minimum of expense, effort, and waste. Economists use a more precise definition. **Economic efficiency**, they say, refers to a state of affairs in which it is impossible to make any change that satisfies one person's wants more fully without causing some other person's wants to be satisfied less fully.[1]

This formal definition of economic efficiency does not differ greatly from the everyday notion. If there is some way to make you better off without making me worse off, it is wasteful to pass up the opportunity. If I have a red pen that I am not using, and you need one just for a minute, it would be wasteful for you to buy a red pen of your own. It is more efficient for me to lend you my pen; it makes you better off and me no worse off. If there is a way to make us both better off, it would be all the more wasteful not to take advantage of the opportunity. You lend me your bicycle for the afternoon, and I will lend you my volleyball. If I do not ride a bicycle very often and you do not play volleyball very often, it would be inefficient for us both to own one of each.

The examples of the pen, the bicycle, and the volleyball all concerned goods that already existed, but many applications of efficiency concern the production of new goods. **Efficiency in production** refers to a situation in which it is not possible, given available productive resources and existing knowledge, to produce more of one good without forgoing the opportunity to produce some of another good. Like the broader concept of economic efficiency, efficiency in production has its roots in the everyday notion of avoiding waste. For example a grower of apples finds that, beyond some certain quantity, using more water per tree does not increase the yield of apples; so using more than that amount would be wasteful. Better to transfer the extra water to the production of, say, peaches. That way the grower can get more peaches without reducing the apple crop.

The economist's definition also includes more subtle possibilities for improving the efficiency of production. For example it is possible to grow apples in Georgia. It is also possible, by selecting the right tree varieties and using winter protection, to grow peaches in Vermont. Some hobbyists do grow both fruits in both states. However, growing them commercially would be inefficient even if growers in both states followed best practices and avoided any obvious waste.

An example will show why. Suppose that, to start with, growers plant equal numbers of apple and peach trees in each state. Then compare a situation with five hundred fewer struggling peach trees growing in Vermont, with their place taken by five hundred thriving apple trees. At the same time, suppose growers plant five hundred fewer heat-stressed apple trees in Georgia, and peaches take their place. The second situation would increase the output of both fruits without increasing the total land, labor, and capital used in fruit production, showing that the original distribution of trees was inefficient.

How to Increase Production Potential

Once the economy is producing efficiently, we can get more of one good only by giving up the opportunity to produce something else—assuming we hold productive resources and knowledge constant. Over time, though, we can find new resources or new ways to use existing resources.

At one time population growth and the discovery of new supplies of natural resources were the most important ways of increasing production potential. However, as we deplete the most easily tapped supplies of natural resources and as population growth slows in most parts of the world, capital will increasingly be the factor of production that contributes most to the expansion of production potential.

Economists use the term **investment** to refer to the act of increasing the economy's stock of capital—that is, its supply of productive inputs made by people. Investment involves a trade-off of present consumption for future consumption. To build more factories, roads, and computers, we have to divert resources from the production of bread, movies, haircuts, and other things that satisfy immediate wants. In return we put ourselves in a better position to satisfy our future wants.

It is more efficient to grow apples in Vermont than in Georgia. (Shutterstock)

Increases in the quantities of labor, capital, and natural resources are not the only sources of economic growth. Even more important are improvements in knowledge—the invention of new technology, new forms of organization, and new ways of satisfying wants. **Entrepreneurship** is the process of looking for new possibilities, making use of new ways of doing things, being alert to new opportunities, and overcoming old limits. It is a dynamic process that breaks down the constraints imposed by existing knowledge and limited supplies of factors of production.

Entrepreneurship does not have to mean inventing something or starting a new business, although it often does. It may mean finding a new market for an existing product—for example, convincing people in Germany that Japanese sushi makes a quick and tasty lunch. It may mean taking advantage of price differences between one market and another—for example, buying hay at a low price in Pennsylvania, where growing conditions have been good in the past year, and reselling it in Virginia, where the weather has been too dry.

We can be entrepreneurs in our roles as consumers and workers, too. We do not just repeat the same patterns of work and leisure every day. We seek variety—new jobs, new foods, and new places to visit. Each time we try something new, we are taking a step into the unknown. In that sense, we are all entrepreneurs.

Some people call entrepreneurship the fourth factor of production, but it differs from the three classical factors of production in important ways. Unlike labor, capital, and natural resources, we cannot measure entrepreneurship because it is intangible. Although entrepreneurs earn incomes reflecting the value that the market places on their accomplishments, we cannot speak of a price per unit of entrepreneurship; there are no such units. Also, unlike human resources (which grow old), machines (which wear out), and natural resources (which can be used up), the inventions and discoveries of entrepreneurs are not depleted as they are used. Once someone invents a new product or concept—lithium battery power for cars, taking pictures with cell phones, or hedge funds as a form of financial investment—the required knowledge does not have to be created again, although it may be supplanted by even better ideas. All in all, it is more helpful to think of entrepreneurship as a process of learning better ways of using the three basic factors of production than as a separate factor of production.

Investment

The act of increasing the economy's stock of capital—that is, its supply of productive inputs made by people

Entrepreneurship

The process of looking for new possibilities, making use of new ways of doing things, being alert to new opportunities, and overcoming old limits

1.1c Deciding Who Will Do Which Work: The Division of Labor

Even a person living in complete isolation would have to choose what to produce and how to produce it. The fictional castaway Robinson Crusoe had to decide whether to fish or hunt birds. If he decided to fish, he had to decide whether to do so with a net or with a hook and line. Other important economic choices, including who will do which work and who will get the resulting output, exist only for people living in society. That is another reason economics is one of the social sciences.

Working as a team, two people can get a job done more easily.
(Dreamstime)

Deciding who will do which work is a matter of organizing the social division of labor. Will everyone work independently—be a farmer in the morning, a tailor in the afternoon, and a poet in the evening? Or will people cooperate by specializing in one particular job, coordinating their work with other specialists, and trading the resulting goods and services? Economists have long argued that specialization and cooperation are the best strategies. Three things make cooperation pay off: teamwork, learning by doing, and comparative advantage.

First, consider *teamwork*. In a classic paper on this subject, Armen Alchian and Harold Demsetz used the example of workers unloading bulky crates from a truck.[2] The crates are so large that one worker alone cannot move them at all without unpacking them. Two people, each working independently, would take hours to unload the truck. However, if they work as a team, they can easily pick up the crates and stack them on the loading dock. This example shows that even when everyone is doing the same work, and even when little skill is involved, teamwork pays.

A second reason for cooperation applies when there are different jobs to do and different skills to learn. In a furniture plant, for instance, some workers operate production equipment, others use office equipment, and still others buy materials. Even if all the workers start out with equal abilities, each gets better at a particular job by doing it repeatedly. *Learning by doing* turns workers of average productivity into specialists, thereby creating a more productive team.

Comparative advantage

The ability to produce a good or service at a lower opportunity cost than someone else

A third reason for cooperation comes into play when the differing skills of workers give them a *comparative advantage* in particular tasks. **Comparative advantage** is the ability to do a job or produce a good at a lower opportunity cost than someone else. An example will show how two people can use comparative advantage to improve the efficiency of the division of labor.

Suppose two clerical workers, Bill and Jim, are working at the job of getting out a batch of invoices to clients. The invoices include both a personalized text and a table with data. Jim is very good at working with both text and data. He can prepare the text section of an invoice in five minutes and do the data table in one minute. Working alone, he can finish ten invoices in an hour. Bill is not so good at either task. It takes him ten minutes to do the text for an invoice and five minutes to prepare the data. Alone, he can do only four invoices an hour. In summary form:

Jim: Prepare one text, five minutes

   Prepare one data table, one minute

Bill: Prepare one text, ten minutes

   Prepare one data table, five minutes

INVOICE

Fieldcom Inc.

Dear Mr. Gupta:

We were glad to learn that the P622.2 replacement modules for your Model A41 smartphone continue to perform well. If you would like any further technical assistance or advice, please contact Ms. Ivana Pleschko at ext. 517. As your firm grows, we hope that you will visit our website frequently (www. fieldcom.biz) to learn of our latest product releases.

Below please find your account activity for the month. If you have any questions regarding your account, please feel free to contact me directly at ext. 032.

Yours truly,
Andrea Martin

Part No.	Quantity	Item	Price per Unit	Total
P622.2	8	Replacement module	$56.27	$450.16
A41	2	Smartphone	$798.00	$1,596.00
Subtotal				$2,046.16
Preferred customer discount				−$204.62
Total due 30 days after receipt				$1,841.54

Without cooperation, the two workers' limit is fourteen invoices per hour between them. Could they do better by cooperating? It depends on who does which job. One way of cooperating would be for Jim to prepare all the text while Bill does all the data; with this division of labor, they can just keep up with one another. That turns out to not be such a good idea. At five minutes per invoice, that kind of cooperation cuts their combined output to only twelve invoices per hour, which is worse than when they weren't cooperating at all.

Instead they should divide the work according to the principle of *comparative advantage*. Even though Bill is slower at preparing the text, he has a comparative advantage in text preparation because the opportunity cost of that part of the work is lower for him: The ten minutes he takes to do the text for one invoice is equal to the time he needs to do two data tables. Jim could use the five minutes he takes to prepare text for one invoice to do the data for five invoices. For Bill, then, the opportunity cost of preparing one text is to forgo two data tables, whereas for Jim the opportunity cost of preparing one text is to forgo five data tables.

Because Bill gives up fewer data tables per text than Jim, the principle of comparative advantage says that Bill should spend all his time preparing text. If he does, he can produce the text for six invoices per hour. Meanwhile Jim can spend forty-five minutes of each hour preparing the text for nine invoices, and the last fifteen minutes of each hour doing the data for all fifteen invoices. By specializing according to comparative advantage, the two workers can increase their total output to fifteen invoices per hour—which is the best they can possibly do.

In this example, two people working side-by-side use comparative advantage to work out the efficient division of labor, but the principle also has broader implications. It can apply to a division of labor between individuals or business firms working far apart—even in different countries. In fact the earliest application of the principle was to international trade (see *Who Said It? Who Did It? 1.1*). Comparative advantage remains one of the primary principles of mutually beneficial cooperation, whether on the scale of the workplace or on that of the world as a whole.

Whatever the context, comparative advantage arises from opportunity cost. Suppose there are two tasks, A and B, and two parties, X and Y (individuals, firms, or countries), each capable of doing both tasks but not equally well. First ask what the opportunity cost is for X doing a unit of task A, measured in terms of how many units of task B could be done with the same time or resources. Then ask the same question for Y. The party with the lower opportunity cost for doing a unit of task A has the comparative advantage in doing that task. To check, ask what the opportunity cost is for each party doing a unit of task B, measured in terms how many units of task A could be done with the same time or resources. The party with the lower opportunity cost for doing a unit of task B has the comparative advantage in doing that task. Both X and Y will be better off if each specializes according to comparative advantage.

Who Said It? Who Did It? **1.1**

David Ricardo
and the
Theory of Comparative Advantage

(Wikimedia Commons)

David Ricardo was born in London in 1772, the son of an immigrant who was a member of the London stock exchange. Ricardo's education was rather haphazard, and he entered his father's business at the age of 14. In 1793, he married and went into business on his own. These were years of war and financial turmoil. The young Ricardo developed a reputation for remarkable astuteness and quickly made a large fortune.

In 1799, Ricardo read Adam Smith's *The Wealth of Nations* and developed an interest in political economy (as people at that time called the field we now call economics). In 1809, Ricardo published his first writings on economics— a series of newspaper articles on "The High Price of Bullion." Several other short works added to his reputation in this area. In 1814, he retired from business to devote all his time to political economy.

Ricardo's major work was *On the Principles of Political Economy and Taxation*, first published in 1817. This work contains, among other things, a pioneering statement of comparative advantage as applied to international trade. Using a simple numerical example, Ricardo showed why—even though Portugal could produce both wine and wool with fewer labor hours than England—it was to the advantage of both countries for England to export wool to Portugal and to import wine in return because the comparative cost was less in England.

International trade is only one topic in Ricardo's *Principles*. The book covers the whole field of economics, as it then existed, beginning with value theory and progressing to a theory of economic growth and evolution. Ricardo held that the economy was growing toward a future "steady state." At that point, economic growth would come to a halt, and the wage rate would fall to the subsistence level. This gloomy view and the equally pessimistic views of Ricardo's contemporary, Thomas Malthus, gave political economy a reputation as "the dismal science."

Ricardo's book was extremely influential. For more than half a century thereafter, much of the writing on economic theory published in England consisted of expansions of and commentaries on Ricardo's work. Economists as different as Karl Marx, the revolutionary socialist, and John Stuart Mill, a defender of liberal capitalism, took Ricardo's theories as their starting point. Even today there are "neo-Ricardian" and "new classical" economists who look to Ricardo's works for inspiration.

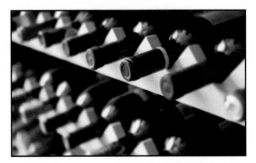

Ricardo's pioneering book on political economy applied the concept of comparative advantage to trade in wine and wool between England and Portugal. (Wikimedia Commons)

1.1d Deciding for Whom Goods Will Be Produced

Together, the advantages of team production, learning by doing, and comparative advantage mean that people can produce more efficiently by cooperating than if each person worked in isolation. Cooperation raises a new issue, however: Who will benefit from the goods that the economy has produced? The question of the distribution of output among members of society matters for both efficiency and fairness.

Efficiency in Distribution

Suppose, first, that people have already produced a fixed supply of goods. For example imagine that thirty students get on a bus to go to a football game. The driver hands out bag lunches. Half the bags contain a ham sandwich and a root beer; the others, a tuna sandwich and a cola. What happens when the students open their bags? They do not just eat whatever they find—they start trading. Some swap sandwiches; others swap drinks. Maybe there is not enough of everything to give each person his or her first choice. Nevertheless, the trading makes at least some people better off than they were when they started. Moreover, no one ends up worse off. If some of the students do not want to trade, they can always eat what they got in the first place.

This example shows one sense in which the "for whom" question is partly about efficiency: Starting with any given quantity of goods, we can improve the distribution through trades that better satisfy preferences. Doing so permits some people to satisfy their wants more fully without making others worse off. That improves **efficiency in distribution** even while the total quantity of goods remains fixed.

So far we have considered efficiency in distribution and efficiency in production in isolation. In practice, however, there is a close link between the two because rules for distribution affect patterns of production. For example suppose wages of home health-care workers increase relative to the wages of clothing workers. If so, two things will happen. One is that health-care workers will receive a bigger share of total goods and services produced by the economy. Another is that the pattern of output will change, with more health-care services produced, and less clothing. By the same token, the way output is distributed affects incentives for entrepreneurship. If there are great rewards for discovering new ways of doing things, people will make greater efforts to improve products, methods of production, and means of distribution.

Fairness in Distribution

Efficiency is not the whole story when it comes to distributing goods and services. We also need to ask whether a given distribution is fair. Questions of fairness often dominate discussions of distribution.

One widely held view judges fairness in distribution in terms of equality. That concept of fairness follows from the idea that all people, by virtue of their shared humanity, deserve a portion of the goods and services turned out by the economy. There are many versions of this concept. Some people think that people have a right to an equal share of all income and wealth. Others think that people have an equal right to a "safety net" level of income, but that inequality in distributing any surplus beyond that level is not unfair. Still others think that the economy should distribute certain goods equally (for example, health-care or education) but that it is fair to distribute other goods less equally.

An alternative view, which also has many adherents, judges fairness not in terms of how much each person receives but in terms of the process through which goods are distributed. In this view, fairness requires the observation of certain rules and procedures, such as respect for property or nondiscrimination on grounds of race and gender. As long as people follow those rules, any resulting distribution of income is acceptable. This view emphasizes equality of opportunity more than equality of outcome.

Efficiency in distribution

A situation in which it is not possible, by redistributing existing supplies of goods, to satisfy one person's wants more fully without causing some other person's wants to be satisfied less fully

Positive and Normative Economics   Some economists make a sharp distinction between questions of efficiency and fairness. Discussions of efficiency are seen as part of **positive economics**, or the area of economics that is concerned with facts and the relationships among them. Discussions of fairness, in contrast, are seen as part of **normative economics**, or the area of economics that is devoted to judgments about whether particular economic policies and conditions are good or bad.

Normative economics extends beyond the question of fairness in the distribution of output. Value judgments also arise about the fairness of the other three basic choices faced by every economy. In choosing what to produce, is it fair to permit production of alcohol and tobacco but to outlaw production of marijuana? In choosing how to produce, is it fair to allow people to work under dangerous or unhealthy conditions, or should the government prohibit work under such conditions? In choosing who does which work, is it fair to limit access to specific jobs according to age, gender, race, or union membership? As you can see, normative issues extend to every corner of economics.

Positive economics, rather than offering value judgments about outcomes, focuses on understanding the processes by which we can answer the four basic economic questions. It analyzes the way economies operate—or would operate if there were changes in certain institutions or policies. It traces relationships between facts, often looking for regularities and patterns that we can measure statistically.

Most economists consider positive economics their primary area of expertise, but normative considerations do influence the conduct of positive economics in several ways. The most significant of those influences is the selection of topics to investigate. An economist who sees excessive unemployment as a glaring injustice may study that problem; one who sympathizes with victims of job discrimination may take up a different line of research. Also, normative views are likely to affect the ways in which data are collected, ideas about which facts can be considered true, and so on.

Some economists think that it is possible to formulate a purely positive economics, untouched by normative considerations of values and fairness. Within its framework, they could resolve all disputes using objective facts. Not everyone agrees that positive and normative notions can be so neatly separated. Whichever point of view you take, be aware that most major economic controversies—especially those that have to do with government policy—have normative as well as positive components, each of which shapes the way we think about those controversies.

1.2 COORDINATING ECONOMIC CHOICES

Every economy must have some way of coordinating the choices of millions of people about what to produce, how to produce it, who will do each job, and who will get the output. This section discusses how to accomplish the needed coordination.

1.2a A Noneconomic Example

You, like almost everyone, have probably had the experience of shopping at a supermarket where there are several long checkout lines. You and other shoppers want to get through checkout as fast as possible. The store, too, would like to avoid a situation in which customers in some lines have a long wait, while the cashiers in other lines stand idle; but how to do it?

One way would be to have an employee on duty to direct people to the line with the shortest wait. Busy airports and government offices sometimes use that method, but supermarkets do not usually work that way. Instead, supermarkets leave you to decide for yourself

Positive economics

The area of economics that is concerned with facts and the relationships among them

Normative economics

The area of economics that is devoted to judgments about whether economic policies or conditions are good or bad

Shoppers' choice of which checkout aisle to use is an example of coordination by spontaneous order. (Shutterstock)

which line to join, based on your own observations. As you approach the checkout area, you first look to see which lines are the shortest. You then make allowance for the possibility that some shoppers have heaped their carts full, while others have only a few items. Using your own judgment, you head for the line you think will be fastest.

The coordination system in which an airport employee directs customers to the shortest line is an example of **hierarchy**. Hierarchy is a way of achieving coordination in which a central authority issues instructions to guide individual actions. The approach used in supermarkets is an example of coordination by **spontaneous order**. Coordination comes about as people adjust their own actions as they see fit in response to cues received from their immediate environment. This method is *orderly* because it achieves an approximately equal waiting time in each check-out line. It is *spontaneous* in that coordination takes place without central direction. Even though no shopper has the specific goal of equalizing the lines, the result is approximate equalization.

1.2b Spontaneous Order in Markets

In economics, *markets* are the most important example of coordination through spontaneous order. A **market** is any arrangement people have for trading with one another. Some markets have formal rules and carry out trading all in one place, such as an auction house that sells works of art. Other markets are more informal, such as the word-of-mouth networks through which domestic workers get in touch with people who need their services. Despite their variety of forms, all markets have one thing in common: They provide the information and incentives people need to coordinate their decisions.

Above all, people need information about the scarcity and opportunity costs of goods and factors of production. Markets use prices to transmit such information. If a good or factor of production becomes scarcer, people bid up its price. The rising price tells people it is worth more and signals producers to make greater efforts to increase supplies. For example, when automakers first began to use catalytic converters with platinum to reduce exhaust pollution, new buyers entered the market. As automakers began to compete with makers of jewelry and other traditional users, platinum became harder to acquire. Competition for available supplies bid up the price. That gave buyers a cue that the value of platinum had increased and an incentive to use it more carefully. At the same time, producers got a cue to look for ways to increase the quantity of platinum mined.

On another occasion a new technology might reduce the cost of producing platinum. For example it might become possible to extract platinum from wastes that miners had discarded in earlier periods when the metal was less valuable. Markets would transmit information about the new technology in the form of a lower price. People could then consider using more platinum.

Hierarchy

A way of achieving coordination in which individual actions are guided by instructions from a central authority

Spontaneous order

A way of achieving coordination in which individuals adjust their actions in response to cues from their immediate environment

Market

Any arrangement people have for trading with one another

At the same time markets provide information, they also provide incentives to act on it. Markets provide incentives to sell goods and services where they will bring the highest prices and to buy them where the price is lowest. Profits motivate business managers to improve production methods and to design goods that match consumer needs. Workers who stay alert to opportunities and work where they are most productive receive the highest wages. Consumers are motivated to use less expensive substitutes where feasible.

Adam Smith, often considered the father of economics, saw coordination through markets as the foundation of prosperity and progress. In a famous passage in *The Wealth of Nations*, he called markets an "invisible hand" that nudges people into the economic roles they can play best (see *Who Said It? Who Did It? 1.2*). To this day, an appreciation of markets as a means of coordinating choices remains a central feature of the economic way of thinking.

Who Said It? Who Did It? **1.2**

Adam Smith
on the
Invisible Hand

(Wikimedia Commons)

Economists consider Adam Smith to be the founder of their field, even though he wrote only one book on the subject: *The Wealth of Nations,* published in 1776. Smith was 53 years old at the time. His friend David Hume found the book such hard going that he doubted that many people would read it. Hume was wrong—people have been reading it for more than two hundred years.

The wealth of a nation, in Smith's view, is not a result of the accumulation of gold or silver in its treasury, as many thought at the time. Rather it is the outcome of working and trading by ordinary people in free markets. To Smith, the remarkable thing about a market economy is that it produces wealth not as a result of any organized plan, but rather as the unintended outcome of the actions of many people, each of whom is pursuing his or her own interests. As he put it, "It is not from the benevolence of the butcher, the brewer, or the baker that we expect our dinner, but from their regard to their own interest." In another passage he wrote that "every individual is continually exerting himself to find out the most advantageous employment for whatever capital he can command. ... He is in this, as in many other cases, led by an invisible hand to promote an end which was no part of his intention."

Much of the discipline of economics, as it has developed over the past two centuries, consists of elaborations on ideas found in Smith's work. The idea of the "invisible hand" of market incentives that channels people's efforts in directions that are beneficial to their neighbors remains the most durable of Smith's contributions to economics.

Sources: Adam Smith, *The Wealth of Nations* (1776), Book 1, Chapter 2; Adam Smith, *The Wealth of Nations* (1776), Book 4, Chapter 2.

1.2c The Role of Hierarchy

Important as markets are, they are not the only way to coordinate economic activity. Hierarchy within formal organizations is a widely used alternative. Government agencies are one example. Government agencies do not usually make decisions through the spontaneous choices of individuals, but according to directives issued by a central authority. The directives tell people to submit tax forms by a certain date, to monitor pollution according to certain standards, to pay fines if they do not follow the rules, and so on.

Farmers decide how much corn to plant based on the price they expect at the time of harvest. (Shutterstock)

Business firms, especially large corporations, also use hierarchical forms of organization. For example a company like Toyota uses directives from a central authority to make many important decisions, such as building a new hybrid version of its popular Camry in Kentucky rather than in Japan.

Although governments and corporations use hierarchies to make choices internally, they deal with one another and with consumers through markets. Markets and hierarchies play complementary roles. Some economies rely more on markets; others, on government or corporate planning. At one extreme, the centrally planned economy of North Korea places heavy emphasis on government authority. Economies like that of the United States make greater use of markets. No economy uses one means of coordination to the exclusion of the other. Government regulatory agencies in the United States establish laws to control pollution or protect worker safety; North Korea permits small-scale street markets for some goods. Large corporations use commands from higher authorities to make many decisions, but they often also subcontract with outside suppliers through markets or encourage their own divisions to deal with one another on a market basis.

1.3 ECONOMIC METHOD

We have seen that when economists think about the world around them, they use concepts like scarcity, choice, and exchange. In doing so, they also have distinctive methods of approaching problems and expressing conclusions. We will conclude the chapter with a few comments about method.

1.3a Theories and Models

Theory

A representation of the relationships among facts

Model

A synonym for *theory*; in economics, often applied to theories that take the form of graphs or equations

Economists try to understand the choices people make in terms of the context in which they make them. They call the relationships between choices and context **theories** or **models**. The terms mean almost the same thing, although economists tend to use the term *theory* to refer to more general statements about economic relationships and the term *model* to refer to more particular statements, especially those that take the form of graphs or equations.

Economics needs theories and models because facts do not speak for themselves. Take, for example, the fact that in recent years, US farmers have planted more acres in corn than ever before. Economists have a theory for why this happened: They relate the change in crop patterns to higher prices for corn, in part due to the increased use of corn to produce ethanol for motor fuel. The link between the price of corn and the choice of what crop to grow is an example of a broader theory according to which an increase in the price of any good, other things being equal, leads producers to increase output of the good.

The theory, as stated, is a simple one. It relates crop choices to just one other fact: the price of corn. A more complete theory would bring in other influences—such as the price of gasoline, for which corn-based ethanol is a substitute; the price of soybeans, which can be grown on the same land as corn; tax advantages provided by Congress to producers of biofuels; and so on. Where does one draw the line? How much detail does it take to make a good theory?

There are no simple answers to these questions. Adding detail to a theory involves a trade-off. On the one hand, if a theory leaves out essential details, it may fail altogether to fit the facts. On the other hand, adding too much detail defeats the purpose of understanding because key relationships may become lost in a cloud of complexity. The only real guideline is that a theory should have just enough detail to suit its purpose, and no more.

By analogy consider the models that aircraft designers use. A scaled-down wind-tunnel model made to test the aerodynamics of a new design would need to represent the shapes of the wings, fuselage, and control surfaces accurately. It would not need to include tiny seats with tiny tables and magazine pockets. On the other hand, a full-scale model built to train flight crews would need seats and magazine pockets, but it would not need wings.

Extending the same analogy, the theories and models presented in this book are helpful in understanding economics in the same way that playing a flight simulation game on a laptop computer is helpful in understanding the basics of flying. Professional economists use more detailed models, just as professional pilots train with complex flight simulators rather than with simple computer games. Still the basic principles of the simple models should not contradict those of the more complex ones. In the simple flight simulator games, just as in the complex professional version, adjusting the rudder makes the plane turn and adjusting the elevators makes it climb or dive.

1.3b Using Graphs

So far all of the theories we have introduced have been stated in words. Words are a powerful tool for developing understanding, but they can be even more powerful when we add pictures. An example will illustrate how economists use graphs together with words to represent theories.[3]

The Production Possibility Frontier
Earlier in the chapter, we discussed a trade-off between education and cars. Figure 1–1 shows that trade-off in graphical form for an economy that produces only those two goods. The horizontal axis measures the quantity of education in terms of the number of college graduates produced per year; the vertical axis measures the production of cars. Any combination of education and cars corresponds to a point in the space between the two axes. For example, point E represents production of ten million graduates and five million cars.

BVT *Lab*

Visit **www.BVTLab.com** to explore the student resources available for this chapter.

FIGURE 1–1

Production Possibility Frontier

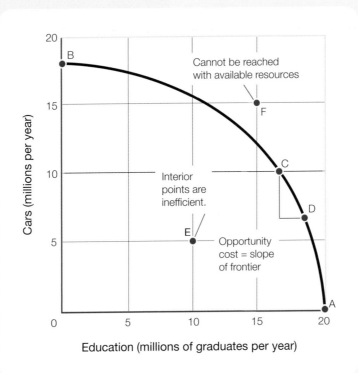

This figure shows combinations of cars and education that are possible for a simple economy in which these are the only two products. We assume that quantities of available factors of production and technologies are fixed. If we devote all factors to education, we can produce twenty million college graduates each year (point A). If we use all factors for making cars, we can produce eighteen million cars each year (point B). Combinations of the two goods that we can produce when the available factors are used efficiently—for example, points C and D—lie along a curve called a production possibility frontier. The slope of the frontier indicates the opportunity cost of education in terms of cars. Interior points, such as E, represent inefficient use of resources. Beginning from such a point, we can produce more of one good without producing less of the other. We cannot reach points outside the frontier, such as F, using available factors of production and technology.

Production possibility frontier

A graph that shows possible combinations of goods that an economy can produce given available technology and factors of production

In drawing this graph, we assume that supplies of productive resources and technology remain constant. Even if all available resources go to education, the limit to the number of graduates that the economy can produce in a year is twenty million. The extreme possibility of producing twenty million graduates and no cars is shown by point A. Likewise point B shows that the maximum number of cars the economy can produce is eighteen million if no resources go to education. Between those two extremes is a whole range of possible combinations of education and cars. Points such as C and D along the curve between A and B show points the economy can produce that include some cars and some graduates. We call that curve a **production possibility frontier**.

Efficiency and Economic Growth   A production possibility frontier based on given technology and productive resources serves nicely to illustrate efficiency in production. Points inside the frontier, such as point E, represent inefficient production. Beginning from such a point, we can make more cars without cutting the output of education (shown by a vertical move toward the frontier); we can produce more education without cutting the output of cars (a horizontal move toward the frontier); or we can increase the output of both goods (a move up and to the right toward the frontier).

Points like A, B, C, and D that are on the frontier represent efficient production. Starting from any of them, it is not possible to produce more of one good without producing less of the other. For example, in moving from C to D, we increase output of education but decrease output of cars. In contrast we cannot reach points like F that lie outside the frontier even when we use available knowledge and resources with complete efficiency.

Over time economic growth can stretch the production possibility frontier outward so that points like F become possible. As mentioned earlier, the discovery of new ways of using available factors of production is one source of growth. So are additions to the total stock of factors of production—for example, through growth of the labor force. Over time the educational process itself improves the quality of the labor force, thus making a given number of people capable of producing more.

Opportunity Cost and Comparative Advantage   We can also use the production possibility frontier to illustrate opportunity cost. As we have seen, once the economy is producing efficiently at a point on the frontier, choosing to make more of one good means making less of the other. For example, suppose we start at point C, representing sixteen million graduates and ten million cars. If we want to increase the output of graduates to eighteen million per year, we must give up some cars and use the labor, capital, and natural resources freed in this way to build and staff classrooms. In moving from point C to point D, we trade off production of four million cars for the extra two million graduates. Over that range of the frontier, the opportunity cost of each extra graduate is about two cars. The slope of the frontier shows the opportunity cost of graduates, measured in terms of cars.

As more students graduate and we move down and to the right along the frontier, the frontier becomes steeper and the opportunity cost of producing graduates increases. A major reason is that not all factors of production—especially not all workers—are alike. Suppose we start all the way up at point B, with no graduates, and then transfer enough resources to education to open one small college. The first people we would pull off the assembly line to staff the classrooms would be those who have a comparative advantage in teaching. By the time enough resources move to education from the auto industry to reach point D, we will begin to run out of the most suitable recruits for academic life. Increasingly, to produce still more education, we have to take some of the best production workers, with no assurance that they will be good teachers. The opportunity cost of increasing the output of education (shown by the slope of the frontier) is correspondingly greater.

1.3c Theory and Evidence

Theories are of no use in explaining relationships among facts unless they fit those facts. Theory building is a matter of constantly comparing proposed explanations with evidence gleaned from observations of the actual choices people make—that is, with *empirical* evidence. When **empirical** evidence is consistent with the relationships proposed in a theory, our confidence in the validity of the theory increases. When evidence is not consistent with the theory, we need to reexamine the theory. The relationships proposed in it may be invalid, or they may be valid only under different circumstances. We then need to modify the theory by changing the proposed relationships or adding detail.

Empirical

Based on experience or observation

Government agencies and private firms generate mountains of empirical data on economic activity. Economists constantly examine that data in an effort to confirm theories or find inconsistencies that point the way to better theories. Statistical analysis of empirical economic data is known as **econometrics**—the science of economic measurement.

1.3d Theories and Forecasts

Economic theories can help us understand things that happened in the past—trends in crop patterns over the past decade, the effects of new communication technologies, and so on—but understanding the past is not always enough. People also want forecasts of future economic events.

Within limits, economic theory can be useful here, too. Any theory that purports to explain a relationship between past events can help predict what will happen under similar circumstances in the future. To put it more precisely, economic theory can be used to make **conditional forecasts** of the form "If A, then B, other things being equal." Thus an economist might say, "If gasoline prices rise, and if at the same time consumer incomes and the prices of other goods do not change, purchases of SUVs will fall."

Thousands of economists make a living from forecasting. Decision makers in business and government use economic forecasts extensively. Forecasts are not perfect, however; and forecasters sometimes make conspicuous mistakes. There are at least three reasons for these mistakes.

First, people sometimes pay insufficient attention to the conditional nature of forecasts. For example the news might report, "Economists predict a drop in SUV sales." Yet people keep right on buying big vehicles. In such a case, the news report may have failed to note the forecasters' cautionary comments. The forecasters may have said that SUV sales would drop in response to a gas price increase if consumer incomes and technology remained the same; but consumers got richer and new technology made SUVs less gas-hungry, so SUV sales did not fall, after all.

Second, a forecast may be invalid because the theory behind it is incorrect or incomplete. Economists do not always agree on what theory best fits the facts. Some theories give more weight to one fact; others, to different facts. The competing theories may imply conflicting forecasts under some conditions. At least one of the forecasts will then turn out to be wrong. Finding out which theories yield better forecasts than others is an important part of the process through which economists distinguish valid theories from inadequate ones.

A forecast of a drop in SUV sales should include the forecaster's precautionary comments. (iStock)

Third, economic forecasts can go wrong because some of the things that business managers and government officials most want to know are among the hardest to predict. For example a competent economist could produce a fairly accurate forecast of car sales based on certain assumptions about incomes and the prices of gasoline and other goods. However, what the marketing people at General Motors would like to know is what will happen to the social image of SUVs: Will they continue to be a symbol of high status, or will they become an embarrassment in a more environmentally conscious society? Social attitudes are not among the variables that economists can forecast accurately.

Econometrics

The statistical analysis of empirical economic data

Conditional forecast

A prediction of future economic events in the form "If A, then B, other things being equal"

Despite these limitations, most economists take the view that well-founded conditional forecasts, for all their limitations, are a better basis for business and public policy decisions than whims and guesswork. Still, they caution against relying too heavily on forecasts.

1.3e Theory and Policy

People often ask economists to use their theories to analyze the effects of public policies or forecast the effects of policy changes. The government may, for example, be considering new measures to aid unemployed workers, new responses to climate change, or new measures to regulate international trade. How will the effects of such policies spread through the economy? How will they affect people's lives?

Economists have their own characteristic way of thinking about public policy, just as they have their own way of thinking about other topics. In particular, economists want to understand not just the direct effects of policy but also the indirect effects, some of which may be completely unintended. Here are some examples:

- Unemployment compensation has the intended effect of aiding unemployed workers, but it also has the unintended effect of increasing the number of workers who are unemployed. The reason is that workers who receive compensation can afford to take their time finding just the right new job. In some ways that is bad. In the short run, more people out of work means fewer goods and services produced. In other ways, it may be good. When people have more time to find jobs that match their skills, they can produce more goods and services in the long run.

- Regulations intended to improve the fuel efficiency of automobiles encourage production of cars that weigh less, but the lighter cars are somewhat less safe. Increased highway deaths may be an unintended consequence.

- After widespread banking failures in the 1980s, US regulators made rule changes intended to stabilize the banking system by strengthening the balance sheets of commercial banks. Those regulations also raised the cost of bank loans relative to loans from sources outside the banking system. As an unintended consequence, much lending activity—including home mortgage lending—moved to an emerging "shadow banking system" consisting of mortgage brokers, securitized loans, and special purpose financial vehicles. When a new crisis came in 2008, the new financial system turned out, in some ways, to be less stable than the old one.

It would be wrong to conclude that the government should never act simply because its policies may do some harm as well as some good. Sometimes the harm may outweigh the good, and sometimes not. What is important, economists say, is that policymakers look at the whole picture, not just part of it, before they make a decision. Henry Hazlitt seized on this idea to reduce the whole of economics to a single lesson:

> The art of economics consists in looking not merely at the immediate but at the longer effects of any act or policy; it consists in tracing the consequences of that policy not merely for one group but for all groups.[4]

As you progress through your study of economics—both macro and micro—you will repeatedly encounter examples of the ways economic theory can help you understand the choices people make and the complex effects of policies intended to regulate those choices.

Summary

1. What is the subject matter of economics?

Economics is a social science that seeks to understand the choices people make in using scarce resources to meet their wants. Scarcity is a situation in which there is not enough of something to meet everyone's wants. *Microeconomics* is the branch of economics that studies choices that involve individual households, firms, and markets. *Macroeconomics* is the branch of economics that deals with large-scale economic phenomena, such as inflation, unemployment, and economic growth.

2. What considerations underlie the choice of what an economy will produce?

Producing more of one good requires producing less of something else because productive resources that go into producing one good cannot produce another at the same time. Productive resources fall into three groups called *factors of production. Labor* means the productive contributions made by people working with their hands and minds. *Capital* means the productive inputs created by people. *Natural resources* include anything useful in its natural state as a productive input. The *opportunity cost* of a good or service is its cost in terms of the forgone opportunity to pursue the best possible alternative activity with the same time or resources.

3. What considerations underlie the choice of how to produce?

The economy can produce goods and services in many different ways, some of which are more efficient than others. *Economic efficiency* means a state of affairs in which it is impossible to make any change that satisfies one person's wants more fully without causing some other person's wants to be satisfied less fully. *Efficiency in production* means a situation in which it is not possible, given the available productive resources and existing knowledge, to produce more of one good or service without forgoing the opportunity to produce some of another good or service. Once an economy achieves efficiency, it can expand production potential by increasing the availability of resources or by improving knowledge. The term *investment* refers to the process of increasing the economy's stock of capital. Entrepreneurship is the process of looking for new possibilities—making use of new ways of doing things, being alert to new opportunities, and overcoming old limits.

4. What considerations underlie the choice of who will do which work?

Cooperation can greatly enhance economic efficiency. Three things make cooperation worthwhile: teamwork, learning by doing, and comparative advantage. Teamwork can enhance productivity even when there is no specialization. Learning by doing improves productivity even when all workers start with equal talents and abilities. Comparative advantage comes into play when people have different abilities or, after learning by doing, have developed specialized skills. Having a comparative advantage in producing a particular good or service means being able to produce it at a relatively lower opportunity cost than someone else.

Summary

5. **What considerations underlie the choice of who will benefit from goods and services that the economy produces?**

    In part, deciding who will benefit revolves around issues of efficiency. *Efficiency in distribution* refers to a state of affairs in which, with a given quantity of goods and services, it is impossible to satisfy one person's wants more fully without satisfying someone else's less fully. In addition, the choice of how we distribute goods depends on judgments about fairness.

6. **What mechanisms are used to coordinate economic choices?**

    The two principle methods of coordinating choices are *hierarchy* and *spontaneous order*. Markets are an example of spontaneous order. The internal decisions of large corporations and units of government are examples of hierarchy.

7. **How do economists use theories, graphs, and evidence in their work?**

    A theory or *model* is a representation of the relationships among facts. Economists use graphs to display data and make visual representations of theories and models. For example, a *production possibility frontier* is a graph that uses available factors of production and knowledge to show the boundary between combinations of goods that are possible to produce and those that are not. Economists refine theories in the light of *empirical* evidence—that is, evidence gleaned from observation of actual economic decisions. *Econometrics* means the economic analysis of empirical evidence. Economic models are a way to make *conditional forecasts* of the form "If A, then B, other things being equal."

KEY TERMS

Capital	5	Macroeconomics	4
Comparative advantage	10	Market	16
Conditional forecast	22	Microeconomics	4
Direct relationship	32	Model	18
Econometrics	22	Natural resources	5
Economic efficiency	8	Negative slope	33
Economics	4	Normative economics	15
Efficiency in distribution	14	Opportunity cost	5
Efficiency in production	8	Positive economics	15
Empirical	21	Positive slope	32
Entrepreneurship	9	Production possibility frontier	20
Factors of production	5	Scarcity	4
Hierarchy	16	Slope	31
Inverse relationship	33	Spontaneous order	16
Investment	9	Tangent	33
Labor	5	Theory	18

PROBLEMS AND TOPICS FOR DISCUSSION

1. **Opportunity cost**   Gasoline, insurance, depreciation, and repairs are all costs of owning a car. Which of these are opportunity costs in the context of each of the following decisions?

    a. You own a car and are deciding whether to drive one hundred miles for a weekend visit to a friend at another university.

    b. You do not own a car but are considering buying one so that you can get a part-time job located five miles from where you live.

    In general, why does the context in which you decide to do something affect the opportunity cost of doing it?

2. **Comparative advantage in international trade**   Suppose that companies in the United States can produce a car with 200 labor hours and a ton of rice with 20 labor hours. In China it takes 250 labor hours to make a car and 50 labor hours to grow a ton of rice. What is the opportunity cost of producing rice in each country, stated in terms of cars? What is the opportunity cost of cars, stated in terms of rice? Which country has a comparative advantage in cars? Which in rice?

PROBLEMS AND TOPICS FOR DISCUSSION

3.   **Efficiency in distribution and the food stamp program**   The federal Supplemental Nutrition Assistance Program (SNAP), formerly known as food stamps, could have been designed so that every low-income family would receive a ration consisting of so much bread, so much milk, and so on. Instead SNAP gives the family an allowance to spend on almost any kind of food the family prefers. For a given cost to the federal government, which plan do you think would better serve the goal of efficiency in distribution? Why?

Now consider a program that would allow families to trade their SNAP credits for cash (some gray-market trading does occur, but it is restricted by law) or one in which poor families are given cash with which they can buy whatever they want. Compare these alternatives with the existing program in terms of both positive and normative economics.

4.   **Spontaneous order in the cafeteria**   Suppose that your college cafeteria does not have enough room for all the students to sit down to eat at once. It stays open for lunch from 11:30 a.m. to 1:30 p.m. Consider the following three methods of distributing diners over the two-hour lunch period in such a way that everyone can have a seat.

- The administration sets a rule: First-year students must eat between 11:30 and 12:00, sophomores between 12:00 and 12:30, and so on for juniors and seniors.

- The lunch period is broken up into half-hour segments with green tickets for the first shift, blue tickets for the second, and so on. There is an equal number of tickets of each color. At the beginning of each semester, the cafeteria holds an auction in which students bid for the ticket color of their choice.

- Students can come to the cafeteria whenever they want. If there are no empty seats, they have to stand in line.

Compare the three schemes in terms of the concepts of (1) spontaneous order and hierarchy, (2) information and incentives, and (3) efficiency.

5.   **A production possibility frontier**   Bill Schwartz has four fields spread out over a hillside. He can grow either wheat or potatoes in any of the fields, but the low fields are better for potatoes and the high ones are better for wheat. Here are some combinations of wheat and potatoes that he could produce:

Number of Fields Used for Potatoes	Total Tons of Potatoes	Total Tons of Wheat
All 4	1,000	0
Lowest 3	900	400
Lowest 2	600	700
Lowest 1	300	900
None	0	1,000

Use these data to draw a production possibility frontier for wheat and potatoes. What is the opportunity cost of wheat, stated in terms of potatoes, when the farmer converts the highest field to wheat production? What happens to the opportunity cost of wheat as Schwartz switches more and more fields to wheat?

CASE *for* DISCUSSION

Cow Power

As natural resources go, it doesn't have much glamour; but, unlike oil, the United States has plenty of it. We're talking about cow manure. The average cow puts out about thirty gallons a day. Multiply that by something like eight million cows on the nation's sixty-five thousand dairy farms, and you have—well, what do you have? A big problem or a big opportunity?

In the past manure was a problem. True, it makes good fertilizer, but with big drawbacks. Most dairy farms stored it in open lagoons before spreading it on fields. The smelly lagoons created a nuisance to neighbors. What is more, the lagoons were a big source of methane, a greenhouse gas that, pound for pound, contributes ten times more to global warming than carbon dioxide.

Methane burns, however; and that's where cow manure becomes an opportunity. If farmers pump manure into an anaerobic digester instead of into an open lagoon, it produces a purified gas that the farm itself can burn to produce electricity or sell to a company that will transport it by pipeline to other customers.

Marie and Earl Audet's dairy farm in Bridport, Vermont, was one of the earliest farms to go on line with cow power. Already in 2006, they were expecting to sell $200,000 worth of cow power a year to Central Vermont Public Service, the local electric utility. In addition they expected to benefit from a clear liquid by-product that could serve as fertilizer and to save another $50,000 by using the dry, odorless fluff that remains from the digester as bedding for the cows, in place of expensive sawdust.[5]

In addition to the Audet's early project, another larger digester has come on line on the Jordan Dairy Farm in Rutland, Vermont. That digester supplies enough electricity for three hundred homes. In addition to cow manure, the Jordan digester uses food scraps from four local food companies, making use of biomass that previously went to disposal. Working together with the Massachusetts energy company, National Grid, four neighboring dairy farms expect to add digesters soon.

Cow power has now spread far beyond Vermont. The Environmental Protection Agency reported that, as of the end of 2013, more than 220 farms throughout the country had installed equipment to produce gas from manure.[6]

Cow power, like other forms of alternative energy, is not a "free lunch." It requires expensive capital investments. In many locations, electric companies encourage such investment by paying a premium rate for energy from biomass and other renewable resources.

Questions

1. Based on the information given in the case, do you think the out-of-pocket costs of producing electricity from cow manure are greater than, less than, or about the same as the cost of conventional power sources? On what information in the case do you base your answer?

2. Anaerobic digestion of cow manure reduces harm to neighbors (less smell) and harm to the environment (less greenhouse gas). How do these benefits enter into the calculation of the opportunity cost of producing cow power? Do these benefits tend to make the opportunity cost greater than or less than the out-of-pocket costs?

3. Based on information in the case, do you think the growth of the cow power industry illustrates the principle of spontaneous order or that of hierarchy? Or is it a little bit of both? Explain your reasoning.

From Ed Dolan's Econ Blog

Ed Dolan's econ blog offers a wide selection of case studies in slideshow format. For example, the slideshow "By One Measure, the Cost of Driving Is Lower than Ever Before" uses minutes worked per mile driven to show how the opportunity cost of driving a car has fallen over the years, taking into account wage rates, the price of gasoline, and increases in fuel efficiency. You can access it by scanning the QR code or by visiting http://bvtlab.com/p7Tg8.

You can browse a complete index of slideshows at http://bvtlab.com/A7467 or by scanning the QR code.

SLIDESHOW

By One Measure, the Cost of Driving Is Now Lower than Ever Before

RESOURCE CENTER

Index of Slideshows

Endnotes

1. Economists sometimes call efficiency, defined this way, *Pareto efficiency* after the Italian economist Vilfredo Pareto.

2. Armen A. Alchian and Harold Demsetz, "Production, Information Cost, and Economic Organization," *American Economic Review* (December 1972): 777–795.

3. The appendix to this chapter provides a review of basic graphical concepts, including axes, points and number pairs, slopes, and tangencies.

4. Henry Hazlitt, *Economics in One Lesson* (New York: Arlington House, 1979), 17.

5. Martha T. Moore, "Cows Power Plan for Alternative Fuel," *USA Today,* Dec. 6, 2006, http://www.usatoday.com/news/nation/2006-12-03-cow-power_x.htm.

6. See Emily Atkin, "How Farms Across America Are Using Cow Manure for Renewable Energy," Climate Progress, Dec. 9, 2013, http://thinkprogress.org/climate/2013/12/09/3040781/farms-cow-manure-renewable-energy/.

Appendix to Chapter 1

Working with Graphs

Which is smarter, a computer or the human brain? The computer certainly does some things faster and more accurately—say, dividing one twenty-digit number by another. The human brain, however, has the ability to solve other kinds of problems with speed and accuracy beyond the ability of most computers. Although computers are making progress, working with pictures is still one of the areas in which the human brain excels. Three key abilities give the brain a comparative advantage where pictures are involved.

1. An ability to store and retrieve a vast number of images quickly and accurately (think of how many people's faces you can recognize)

2. An ability to discard irrelevant detail while highlighting essentials (think of how easily you can recognize a politician's face in a political cartoon that has just a few lines)

3. An ability to see key similarities between patterns that are not exactly the same (that is why you can usually connect two pictures of a person taken twenty years apart)

Graphs are an aid to learning economics precisely because they make use of those three special abilities of the human brain. Economists use graphs to make their theories easier to understand, not harder. All it takes to use graphs effectively as a learning tool is your inborn human skill in working with pictures plus knowledge of a few simple rules for extracting the information that graphs contain. This appendix outlines those rules in brief.

Pairs of Numbers and Points

The first thing to master is how to use points on a graph to represent pairs of numbers. The table in Figure 1A–1 presents five pairs of numbers. The two columns are labeled "x" and "y." The first number in each pair is called the x value, and the second, the y value. Each pair of numbers is labeled with a capital letter. Pair A has an x value of 2 and a y value of 3, pair B has an x value of 4 and a y value of 4, and so on.

The diagram in Figure 1A–1 contains two lines that meet at the lower left-hand corner; we call them *coordinate axes*. The horizontal axis is marked off into units representing the x value and the vertical axis into units representing the y value. Each pair of numbers from the table corresponds to a point in the space between the two axes. For example we find point A by going two units to the right along the horizontal axis and then three units straight up, parallel to the vertical axis. That point represents the x value of 2 and the y value of 3. The other points are located in the same way.

We can often improve the visual effect of a graph by connecting the points with a line or a curve. That makes it possible to see the relationship between x values and y values at a glance: As the x value increases, the y value also increases.

FIGURE 1A–1

Number Pairs and Points

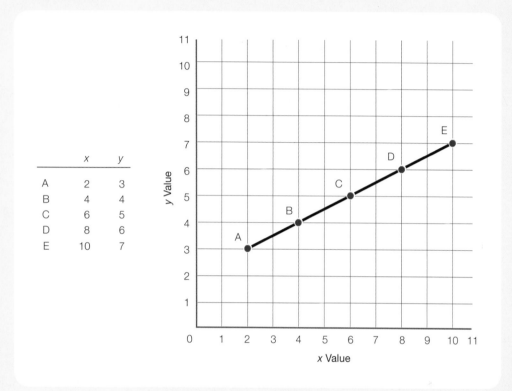

	x	y
A	2	3
B	4	4
C	6	5
D	8	6
E	10	7

Each lettered pair of numbers in the table corresponds to a lettered point on the graph. The x value of each point corresponds to the horizontal distance of the point from the vertical axis; the y value corresponds to its vertical distance from the horizontal axis.

Slopes and Tangencies

Every line or curve in a graph has a slope. The **slope** of a straight line between two points is the ratio of the change in the y value to the change in the x value between the two points. In Figure 1A–2, for example, the slope of the line between points A and B is 2. The y value changes by six units between these two points, whereas the x value changes by only three units. The slope is the ratio 6/3 = 2.

We can express the slope of a line between the points (x_1, y_1) and (x_2, y_2) in terms of a simple formula that is derived from the definition just given:

$$\text{Slope} = \frac{(y_2 - y_1)}{(x_2 - x_1)}$$

Slope

For a straight line, the ratio of the change in the y value to the change in the x value between any two points on the line

FIGURE 1A–2

Slopes of Lines

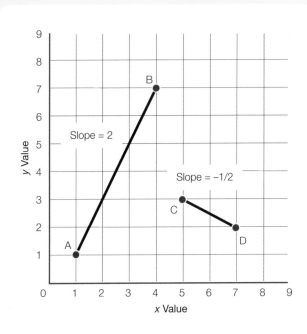

The slope of a straight line drawn between two points is defined as the ratio of the change in the y value to the change in the x value as one moves from one point to the other. For example the line between points A and B in this figure has a slope of +2, whereas the line between points C and D has a slope of –1/2.

Applied to the line between points A and B in Figure 1A–2, the formula gives the following result:

$$\text{Slope} = \frac{(7-1)}{(4-1)} = \frac{6}{3} = 2$$

Positive slope

A slope having a value greater than zero

Direct relationship

A relationship between two variables in which an increase in the value of one variable is associated with an increase in the value of the other

A line such as that between A and B in Figure 1A–2, which slopes upward from left to right, is said to have a **positive slope** because the value of its slope is a positive number. A positively sloped line represents a **direct relationship** between the variable represented on the x axis and that represented on the y axis—that is, a relationship in which an increase in one variable is associated with an increase in the other. The relationship of the age of a tree to its height is an example of a direct relationship. An example from economics is the relationship between family income and expenditures on housing.

When a line slants downward from left to right, like the one between points C and D in Figure 1A–2, the x and y values change in opposite directions. Going from point C to point D, the y value changes by –1 (that is, decreases by one unit) and the x value changes by +2 (that is, increases by two units). The slope of this line is the ratio –1/2.

When the slope of a line has a negative value, we say it has a **negative slope**. Such a line represents an **inverse relationship** between the x variable and the y variable—that is, a relationship in which an increase in the value of one variable is associated with a decrease in the value of the other variable. The relationship between the temperature in the room and the time it takes the ice in your lemonade to melt is an example of an inverse relationship. In economics, the relationship between the price of gasoline and the quantity that consumers purchase, other things being equal, is an inverse relationship.

The concepts of positive and negative slopes, and of direct and inverse relationships, apply to curves as well as to straight lines. However, the slope of a curve, unlike that of a straight line, varies from one point to the next.[1] We cannot speak of the slope of a curve in general, but only of its slope at a given point. The slope of a curve at any given point is the slope of a straight line drawn tangent to the curve at that point. (A **tangent** line is one that just touches the curve without crossing it.) In Figure 1A–3, the slope of the curve at point A is 1, and the slope at point B is –2.

---

[1] Economists try to be consistent; yet in talking about lines and curves, they fail. They have no qualms about calling something a "curve" that is a straight line. For example, later we will encounter "demand curves," which are as straight as a stretched string. Less frequently, economists may call something a line that has a curved shape.

Negative slope

A slope having a value less than zero

Inverse relationship

A relationship between two variables in which an increase in the value of one variable is associated with a decrease in the value of the other

Tangent

A straight line that touches a curve at a given point without intersecting it

FIGURE 1A–3

Slopes of Curves

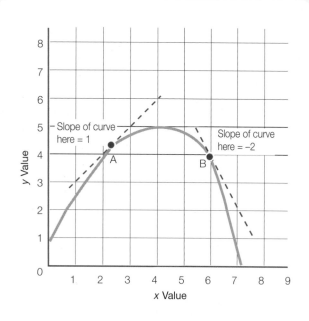

The slope of a curve at any point is the slope of a straight line drawn tangent to the curve at that point. A tangent line is one that just touches the curve without crossing it. In this figure, the slope of the curve at point A is 1, and the slope at point B is –2.

Using Graphs to Display Data

Economists use graphs for two primary purposes: for displaying data and for representing economic relationships. Some graphs serve one purpose; some, the other; and some, a little of both. We begin with some common kinds of graphs whose purpose is to display data.

Figure 1A–4 shows three kinds of graphs that display data. Part (a) is a *pie chart*. We use pie charts to show the relative size of various quantities that add up to a total of 100 percent. In this case, the quantities are the percentages of US foreign trade accounted for by various trading partners. In the original source, the graph illustrated a discussion of US trade with Canada, Japan, and Western Europe. The author wanted to make the point that trade with these countries is very important. Note how the graph highlights Canadian, Japanese, and Western European trade with the United States and, at the same time, omits details not relevant to the discussion by lumping together the rest of Europe, Africa, the rest of Asia, and many other countries under the heading "Rest of the World." In reading graphs, do not just look at the numbers; ask yourself, "What point is the graph trying to make?"

Part (b) of Figure 1A–4 is a *bar chart*. Bar charts, like pie charts, can display numerical data (in this case, unemployment rates) in relationship to a nonnumerical category (in this case, education). Bar charts are not subject to the restriction that data displayed must total 100 percent. What point do you think the author of this graph was trying to make?

Part (c) of Figure 1A–4 is an example of a data display graph very common in economics—the *time-series graph*. A time-series graph shows the values of one or more economic quantities on the vertical axis and time (years, months, or whatever) on the horizontal axis. This graph shows the ups and downs of the US unemployment rate by month from 2008 to 2014.

Note one feature of this time-series graph: The scale on the vertical axis begins from 2 percent rather than from 0. By spreading out the data points in the range 2 percent to 12 percent, one can show the trend of unemployment in greater detail. The advantage of greater detail has an offsetting danger, however. Careless reading of the graph could cause one to exaggerate the amount by which unemployment rose during the 2007–2009 recession. For example the unemployment line is almost three times higher above the horizontal axis in mid-2009 as at the beginning of 2008. However, careful reading of the graph shows that the unemployment rate was actually only twice as high (10 percent versus 5 percent). The moral of the story: Always examine the vertical and horizontal axes of a graph carefully.

FIGURE 1A–4

Using Graphs to Display Data

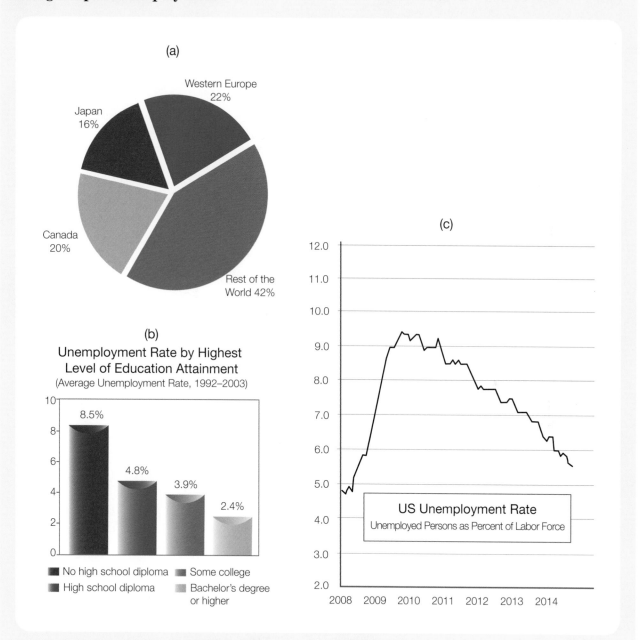

(a)

Western Europe
22%

Japan
16%

Canada
20%

Rest of the
World 42%

(b)
Unemployment Rate by Highest
Level of Education Attainment
(Average Unemployment Rate, 1992–2003)

8.5%

4.8%

3.9%

2.4%

■ No high school diploma ■ Some college
■ High school diploma ■ Bachelor's degree
or higher

(c)

US Unemployment Rate
Unemployed Persons as Percent of Labor Force

2008 2009 2010 2011 2012 2013 2014

This figure shows three common kinds of data display graphs. The pie chart in part (a) is appropriate when the data items sum to 100 percent. The bar chart in part (b), like the pie chart, is good for reporting numerical data that are associated with nonnumerical categories (in this case, educational attainment). The bar chart does not require data items to sum to 100 percent. The time-series graph in part (c) shows the values of one or more economic quantities on the vertical axis and time on the horizontal axis.

Sources: Part (a), US Council of Economic Advisers, *Economic Report of the President* (Washington, DC: Government Printing Office, 2002), Table B-105, 397; part (b), Bureau of Labor Statistics, *Current Population Survey;* and part (c), Bureau of Labor Statistics, *The Employment Situation*.

Using Graphs to Show Relationships

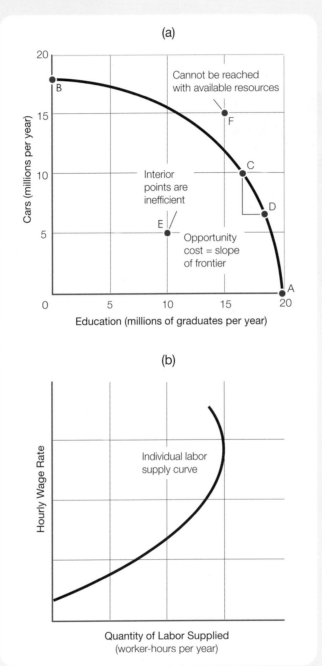

Relational graphs are visual representations of theories—that is, of relationships among facts. This figure shows two typical relational graphs. Part (a) is the production possibility frontier discussed in Chapter 1. It relates quantities of cars to quantities of education the economy can produce with given factors of production and knowledge. Part (b) represents a theory of individual labor supply, according to which an increase in the hourly wage rate, after a point, will cause a person to reduce the quantity of labor supplied. Part (b) is an abstract graph in that it shows only the general nature of the relationship, with no numbers on either axis.

Using Graphs to Display Relationships

Some graphs, rather than simply recording observed facts, represent theories and models. Instead of simply presenting facts, they highlight the relationships among facts. Figure 1A–5 shows two typical graphs whose primary purpose is to display relationships.

Part (a) of Figure 1A–5 is the production possibility frontier that we encountered in Chapter 1. The graph represents the inverse relationship between the quantities of cars and education that the economy can produce, given available knowledge and productive resources.

Part (b) of Figure 1A–5 represents a relationship between the number of hours per year a person is willing to work and the wage rate. The graph shows that raising the wage rate will, up to a point, induce a person to work more hours; beyond a certain point, however, a further increase in the wage will cause the person to work fewer hours. Why? According to the theory represented by the graph, once a person's income reaches a certain level, he or she tends to prefer "spending" some of the higher income by taking more leisure time instead of earning money to buy more material goods.

Note one distinctive feature of the graph in part (b): There are no numbers on the axes. It is an abstract graph that represents only the qualitative relationships between the hours of labor per year and the wage rate. It makes no quantitative statements regarding how the change in hours worked is associated with any given change in wage rate. In reality, the point where people prefer more leisure to additional income is different for different people, and many people never reach that point. We often use abstract graphs to represent theories that apply in a general way to many cases, regardless of differences in detail from one case to another.

Packing Three Variables into Two Dimensions

Anything drawn on a flat piece of paper is limited to two dimensions. The relationships discussed so far fit a two-dimensional graph easily because they involve just two variables. In the case of the production possibility frontier, they are the quantity of education (horizontal axis) and the quantity of cars (vertical axis). In the case of labor supply, they are hours of work per year (horizontal axis) and wage rate (vertical axis). However, two-variable relationships often oversimplify the reality we are trying to understand. When that happens, we must find a way to represent three or more variables in two dimensions.

There are a number of ways to represent relationships among three or more variables on a flat piece of paper. For example a map of the United States might use coordinates of latitude and longitude to indicate position, contour lines to indicate altitude, and colors to indicate vegetation. An architect might use a perspective drawing to give the illusion of three dimensions—height, width, and depth. This section deals with still another way of packing three variables into two dimensions. Although the method is a favorite of economists—we will use it often in this book—we will show its generality by beginning with a noneconomic example.

A Noneconomic Example

The example concerns heart disease, the leading cause of death in the United States. There is a close link between the risk of heart disease and the quantity of cholesterol in a person's blood. Studies have indicated, for example, that a 25 percent reduction in cholesterol can cut the risk of death from heart attack by nearly 50 percent. Knowing this, millions of people order tests of their cholesterol levels; and, if results are high, they use diet, exercise, or medications to reduce their risk of heart disease.

Important though cholesterol is, just knowing your cholesterol level is not enough to tell you your risk of dying of a heart attack in the coming year. Other variables also matter, including age. For men aged 20 with average cholesterol levels, the mortality rate from heart disease is only about three per one hundred thousand. For men aged 60, the mortality rate rises to over five hundred per one hundred thousand (still assuming average cholesterol). Thus we have three variables with which to deal—mortality, cholesterol, and age. How can we represent these three variables using a two-dimensional graph?

A possible approach would be to draw two separate graphs. One would show the relationship between age and heart disease for the male population as a whole, without regard to cholesterol levels. The other would show the relationship between cholesterol and heart disease for the male population as a whole, without regard to age. By looking from one diagram to the other, we could get an idea of the three-variable relationship. However, such a side-by-side pair of graphs would be clumsy.

A better way, shown in Figure 1A–6, is to use cholesterol and mortality as the x and y axes and to take age into account by plotting separate lines for men of various ages. That chart is far easier to interpret than the side-by-side pair would be. If you are a man and know your age and cholesterol count, you just pick out the appropriate line and read off your risk. If you do not like what you see, you go on a diet.[2]

The multicurve graph is a lovely invention. One of the great things about it is that it works for more than three variables. For example, we could add a fourth variable, gender, to the graph by drawing a new set of lines in a different color to show mortality rates for women of various ages. Each line for women would have a positive slope similar to the men's lines, but it would lie below the corresponding line for men of the same age because women, other things being equal, experience lower mortality from heart disease.

Shifts in Curves and Movements Along Curves

Now that it is clear how to read three-variable graphs, we can turn our attention to some special terminology. How can we best describe what happens to a man as he ages, given the relationship shown in Figure 1A–6?

---

[2] *We could have started, instead, with an age-mortality chart and drawn separate lines for men with different cholesterol levels. Such a chart would show exactly the same information. We could even draw a chart with cholesterol and age on the axes and separate contour lines to represent various levels of mortality. The choice often depends on what one wants to emphasize. Here, we emphasize the cholesterol-mortality relationship because cholesterol is something you can do something about. You cannot do anything about your age, so we give age slightly less emphasis by not placing it on one of the two axes.*

FIGURE 1A–6

Three Variables in Two Dimensions

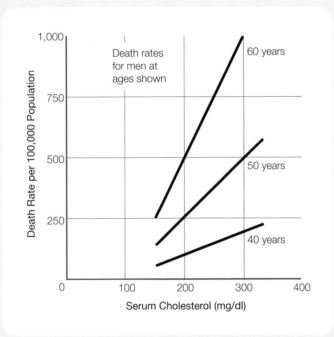

This graph shows a common way of representing a three-variable relationship on a two-dimensional graph. The three variables in this case are serum cholesterol (a measure of the amount of cholesterol in the blood), age, and death rate from heart disease for the US male population. We can most easily interpret the relationship among the three variables if we represent all of them on one graph by drawing separate cholesterol–death rate lines for each age group. As a man ages, his cholesterol–death rate line shifts upward.

One way to describe the effects of aging would be to say, "As a man ages, he moves from one curve to the next higher one on the chart." There is nothing at all wrong with saying that, but an economist would tend to phrase it a bit differently; an economist would say, instead, "As a man ages, his cholesterol-mortality curve shifts upward." The two ways of expressing the effects of aging have exactly the same meaning. Preferring one or the other is just a matter of habit.

If we express the effects of aging in terms of a shift of the cholesterol-mortality curve, how should we express the effects of a reduction in cholesterol for a man of a given age? An economist would say it this way: "Cutting a man's cholesterol count through diet or exercise will move him down and to the left along his cholesterol-mortality curve."

Before you finish this book, you will see the phrases "shift in a curve" and "movement along a curve" a great many times. How can you keep them straight? Nothing could be easier.

- If you are talking about the effect of a change in a variable that appears on one of the coordinate axes of the diagram, the effect will appear as a movement along one of the curves. For example the effect of a change in cholesterol (horizontal axis) on mortality (vertical axis) appears as a movement along the curve for a given age.

- If you are talking about the effect of a change in a variable that does not appear on one of the coordinate axes of the diagram, the effect appears as a shift in one of the curves. For example, the effect of a change in age (not the unit for either axis) on mortality (vertical axis) appears as a shift in the curve relating cholesterol to mortality.

Study Hints

So much for the basic rules of graphs. Once you master them, how should you study a chapter that is full of graphs?

The first—and most important—rule is to *avoid trying to memorize graphs as patterns of lines.* In every economics course, at least one student comes to the instructor after failing an exam and exclaims, "But I learned every one of those graphs! What happened?" The reply is that the student should have learned economics instead of memorizing graphs. Following are some hints for working with graphs.

After reading through a chapter that contains several graphs, go back through the graphs one at a time. Cover the caption accompanying each graph, and try to express the graph's "picture" in words. If you cannot say as much about the graph as the caption does, reread the text. Once you can translate the graph into words, you have won half the battle.

Next, cover each graph and use the caption as a guide. Try to sketch the graph on a piece of scratch paper. What are the labels on the graph's axes? On the curves? What are the slopes of various curves? Are there important points of intersection or tangencies? If you can go back and forth between the caption and the graph, you will find that the two together are much easier to remember than either one separately.

Finally, try going beyond the graph that appears in the book. If the graph illustrates the effect of an increase in the price of butter, try sketching a similar diagram that shows the effect of a decrease in the price of butter. If the graph shows what happens to the economy during a period of rising unemployment, try drawing a similar graph that shows what happens during a period of falling unemployment. Doing practice exercises of this kind will give you an edge on your next exam.

Making Your Own Graphs

For some students, the hardest test questions to answer are ones that require original graphs as part of an essay. Suppose the question is, "How does a change in the number of students attending a university affect the cost per student of providing an education?" Here are some hints for making your own graph.

1. Write down the answer to the question in words. If you cannot, you might as well skip to the next question. Underline the most important quantities in your answer, such as "The larger the *number of students* who attend a college, the lower the *cost per student* of providing them with an education because it is not necessary to duplicate fixed facilities, such as libraries."

2. Decide how you want to label the axes. In our example, the vertical axis could be labeled "cost per student," and the horizontal axis, "number of students."

3. Do you have specific numbers to work with? If so, the next step is to construct a table showing what you know, and use that table to sketch your graph. If you have no numbers, you must draw an abstract graph. In this case all you know is that the cost per student goes down when the number of students goes up. Your graph would thus be a negatively sloped line.

4. If your graph involves more than one relationship between quantities, repeat steps 1 through 3 for each relationship you wish to show. When constructing a graph with more than one curve, pay special attention to points at which you think the curves should intersect. (Intersections occur whenever both the x and y values of the two relationships are equal.) Also note the points at which you think two curves ought to be tangent (which requires that their slopes be equal), the points of maximum or minimum value, if any, and so on.

5. When your graph is finished, try to translate it back into words. Does it really say what you want it to?

A Reminder

As you read this book and encounter various kinds of graphs, turn back to this appendix now and then. Do not memorize graphs as patterns of lines; if you do, you will get lost. If you can alternate between graphs and words, the underlying point will be clearer than if you rely on either one alone. Keep in mind that the primary focus of economics is not graphs; it is people and the ways in which they deal with the challenge of scarcity.

CHAPTER 2

SUPPLY AND DEMAND: THE BASICS

AFTER READING THIS CHAPTER,
you will understand the following:

1. How the price of a good or service affects the quantity demanded by buyers
2. How other market conditions affect demand
3. How the price of a good affects the quantity supplied by sellers
4. How other market conditions affect supply
5. How supply and demand interact to determine the market price of a good or service
6. Why market prices and quantities change in response to changes in market conditions
7. What the unintended consequences are of price floors and price ceilings

BEFORE READING THIS CHAPTER,
make sure you know the following concepts:

Spontaneous order

Markets

Opportunity cost

Law of unintended consequences

CHAPTER
Outline

Olive oil is the flavorful centerpiece of the healthful and popular Mediterranean diet. Its price can rise or fall sharply from year to year. Although it may not be featured on the nightly news as often as the price of gasoline, it, along with millions of other prices, affects the way we live—our jobs, our incomes, the things we buy, and the things we sell. What determines prices? The short answer is supply and demand.

Economists use the term **supply** to refer to sellers' willingness and ability to provide goods for sale in a market. **Demand** refers to buyers' willingness and ability to purchase goods. This chapter will show how supply and demand work together to determine prices.

2.1 DEMAND

Supply

The willingness and ability of sellers to provide goods for sale in a market

Demand

The willingness and ability of buyers to purchase goods

Law of demand

The principle that an inverse relationship exists between the price of a good and the quantity of that good that buyers demand, other things being equal

Demand curve

A graphical representation of the relationship between the price of a good and the quantity of that good that buyers demand

According to the **law of demand**, there is an inverse relationship between the quantity of a good that buyers demand and its price. The quantity demanded tends to rise as the price falls and to fall as the price rises. We expect that to happen for two reasons. First, if the price of one good falls while the prices of other goods stay the same, people are likely to substitute the cheaper good. Second, when the price of one good falls while incomes stay the same, people feel a little richer. They use their added buying power to buy a bit more of many things—including, in most cases, a little more of the good whose price went down.

The terms *demand* and *quantity demanded*, as used in economics, are not the same as want or need. For example I think a Porsche® is a beautiful car. Sometimes when I see one on the street, I think, "Hey, I want one of those!" Alas, my income is limited. Although in the abstract I might want a Porsche, there are other things I want more. As a result, the quantity of Porsches I demand at the going price is zero.

On the other hand I might *need* dental surgery to avoid losing my teeth. However, suppose I am poor. If I cannot pay for the surgery or find someone to pay for it on my behalf, I am out of luck. The quantity of dental surgery I demand, therefore, would be zero, however great my need.

Demand, then, combines both willingness and ability to buy. It is not desire in the abstract, but desire backed by the means and the intent to buy.

2.1a The Demand Curve

The law of demand defines a relationship between the quantity of a good that people are willing and able to buy, other things being equal, and the price of that good. Figure 2–1 represents this relationship for a familiar consumer good: chicken. It would be possible to discuss a single consumer's demand for chicken; but, more frequently, we focus on the total demand for the good by all buyers in the market (as in this figure).

The figure shows the demand relationship in two different ways. Start with Part (a). The first row of the table shows that when the price of chicken is $3.00 a pound, the quantity demanded per year is 1.0 billion pounds. Reading down the table, we see that as the price falls, the quantity demanded rises. At $2.50 per pound, buyers are willing and able to purchase 1.5 billion pounds per year; at $1.50, 2.5 billion pounds; and so on.

Part (b) of Figure 2–1 uses a graph, which we call the **demand curve** for chicken, to show the same information in a different way. To use the demand curve to find out what quantity buyers will demand at a price of $2.00 per pound, start at $2.00 on the vertical axis and move across, as shown by the arrow, until you reach the demand curve at point A. Then, still

The demand curve shows a relationship between the price of a good, such as chicken, and the amount that people are willing and able to buy. (iStock)

FIGURE 2–1

A Demand Curve for Chicken

(a)

Price of Chicken (dollars per pound)	Quantity of Chicken Demanded (billions of pounds per year)
	$3.50	0.5
	$3.00	1.0
	$2.50	1.5
A	$2.00	2.0
	$1.50	2.5
B	$1.00	3.0
	$0.50	3.5

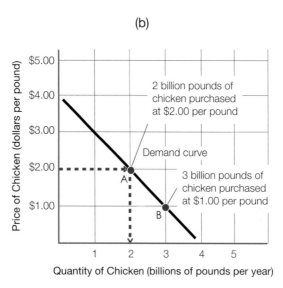

(b)

2 billion pounds of chicken purchased at $2.00 per pound

Demand curve

3 billion pounds of chicken purchased at $1.00 per pound

Both the table and the chart show the quantity of chicken demanded at various prices. For example, at a price of $2.00 per pound, buyers are willing and able to purchase two billion pounds of chicken per year. Row A in Part (a) and point A in Part (b) show this price-quantity combination.

following the arrow, drop down to the horizontal axis. Reading from the scale on that axis, you can see that the quantity demanded at a price of $2.00 per pound is 2.0 billion pounds per year. That is the same as the quantity demanded in row A of the table in Part (a).

The effect of a change in the price of chicken, other things being equal, takes the form of a movement from one point to another along the demand curve. Suppose that the price drops from $2.00 to $1.00 per pound. In response, the quantity that buyers plan to buy increases. The point corresponding to the quantity demanded at the new, lower price is point B, which corresponds to row B of the table. Because there is an inverse relationship between price and quantity demanded, the demand curve has a negative slope.

Economists speak of a movement along a demand curve as a **change in quantity demanded**. Such a movement represents buyers' reactions to a change in the price of the good, other things being equal.

2.1b Shifts in the Demand Curve

The demand curve[1] in Figure 2–1 shows a relationship between two variables: the price of chicken and the quantity of chicken demanded. Changes in other variables can also affect people's buying decisions. For example the prices of beef and pork would affect the demand for chicken. So would changes in consumer incomes. Changes in expectations about the future and changes in consumer tastes are still other factors that affect

Change in quantity demanded

A change in the quantity of a good that buyers are willing and able to purchase that is caused by a change in the price of a good, other things being equal; shown by a movement from one point to another along a demand curve

how much chicken people will buy. We could make a similar list for any good or service—the weather affects the demand for ice, the birthrate affects the demand for diapers, the won-lost record of the home team affects the demand for baseball tickets, and so on.

How do we handle all these other variables graphically? In brief, two rules apply.

1. When we draw a single demand curve for a good, such as the one in Figure 2–1, we treat all conditions other than the price of chicken as constant, following the "other things being equal" clause of the law of demand. As long as that clause is in force, the only two variables at work are quantity demanded (on the horizontal axis) and the price of chicken (on the vertical axis). The effect of a change in price on quantity demanded takes the form of a movement along the demand curve.

2. When we look beyond the "other things being equal" clause to discuss the effect of a change in any variable that does not appear on one of the axes, the situation changes. We show the effect of any other variable, such as a change in consumer income or the price of another good, as a shift in the demand curve. In its new position, the demand curve still represents a relationship between the price of chicken and the quantity demanded, but it is a slightly different relationship than before because one of the "other things" is no longer equal.

These two rules for demand curves are crucial to understanding the theory of supply and demand. Let's look at some examples.

Changes in the Price of Another Good

We already know that the demand for chicken depends on the price of beef as well as the price of chicken. Figure 2–2, which shows demand curves for both goods, provides a closer look at how the two prices interact.

Suppose that the price of beef starts at $3.00 per pound and then increases to $4.50. The effect of this change on the quantity of beef demanded appears in Part (a) of Figure 2–2 as a movement along the beef demand curve from point A to point B. Part (b) shows the effect on the demand for chicken. With the price of beef higher than before, people will tend to buy more chicken *even if the price of chicken does not change.* Suppose the price of chicken is steady at $2.00 per pound. When beef was selling at $3.00, consumers bought 2.0 billion pounds of chicken a year (point A′ on demand curve D_1). After the price of beef goes up to $4.50, they will buy 3.5 billion pounds (point B′ on demand curve D_2).

An increase in the price of beef would cause consumers to buy more chicken regardless of the price of chicken. If the price of chicken had started at $3.00 and remained there while the price of beef went up, people would have increased their chicken consumption from 1.0 billion pounds a year to 2.5 billion pounds a year. If the price of chicken were $1.00 a pound, the quantity bought would have increased from 3.0 billion pounds to 4.5 billion, and so on. An economist would say that a change in the price of beef causes the entire demand curve for chicken to shift. The chicken demand curve shifts because one of the "other things," this time the price of beef, is no longer equal. For the new demand curve, D_2, the price of beef is $4.50 a pound, rather than the $3.00 we assumed in drawing demand curve D_1.

If we call a movement along a demand curve a "change in quantity demanded," what do we call a shift in the curve? Economists call a shift in a demand curve a **change in demand**. A change in quantity demanded (a movement along the curve) is the result of a change in the price of the good in question—in our example, that means the price of chicken, which is the

Change in demand

A change in the quantity of a good that the buyers are willing and able to purchase that is caused by a change in some condition other than the price of that good; a shift in the demand curve

A change in the price of gasoline will affect consumer choice between economy cars and SUVs. *(Shutterstock)*

FIGURE 2–2

Effects of an Increase in the Price of Beef on the Demand for Chicken

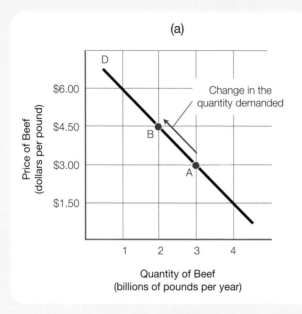

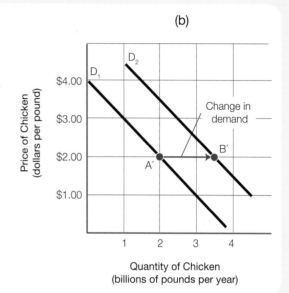

(a)

(b)

An increase in the price of beef from $3.00 to $4.50 per pound, other things being equal, causes a movement from point A to point B on the beef demand curve—a decrease in the quantity of beef demanded. With the price of chicken unchanged at $2.00 per pound, consumers will substitute chicken for beef. That will cause an increase in the demand for chicken, which takes the form of a shift in the chicken demand curve from D_1 to D_2.

variable on the vertical axis. In contrast, a change in demand (a shift in the demand curve) is the result of a change in some variable other than the price of the good in question. In our example, it was the price of beef, a variable that does not appear on either axis.

In the example in Figure 2–2, people bought more chicken when the price of beef went up, replacing one meat with the other in their dinners. Economists call such pairs of goods **substitutes** because an increase in the price of one increases the demand for the other—a rightward shift in the demand curve.

A different situation arises when consumers tend to use two goods together. One example is cars and gasoline. An increase in the price of gasoline affects people's selection of cars. For example, they buy fewer low-mileage, large SUVs—even if the price of SUVs does not change. An increase in the price of gasoline thus causes a movement upward along the gasoline demand curve and a *leftward shift* in the demand curve for SUVs. We call pairs of goods that have this relationship to one another **complements**.

One more point regarding the effects of changes in the prices of other goods: It is the price of a good *relative to the prices of other goods* that counts for demand. During periods of inflation, when the average level of all prices rises, it is especially important to distinguish between changes in *relative prices* and changes in *nominal prices* (the number of dollars actually paid per unit of a good). During a time of inflation, a good can become relatively less expensive, even though its nominal price rises, if the prices of other goods rise even faster.

Substitute goods

A pair of goods for which an increase in the price of one causes an increase in demand for the other

Complementary goods

A pair of goods for which an increase in the price of one causes a decrease in demand for the other

For example between 1950 and 2005 the average retail price of broiler chicken rose by almost 40 percent, from $0.59 per pound to $1.05 per pound. Over the same period, the average price of all goods and services rose by about 600 percent. Thus the relative price of chicken fell during the period even though its nominal price rose. The drop in the relative price of chicken had a lot to do with its growing popularity on the dinner table.

Changes in Consumer Incomes
Changes in consumer incomes also affect demand. People tend to buy larger quantities of many goods when their incomes rise, assuming that prices do not change.

Figure 2–3 shows the effect of an increase in consumer income on the demand for chicken. Demand curve D_1 is the same one shown in Figure 2–1. Suppose, now, that consumer income rises. With higher incomes, people throughout the world tend to eat more meat. Increasing income was another factor that made chicken increasingly popular in the decades after World War II.

Suppose that, after their incomes rise, people want to buy 2.5 billion pounds of chicken instead of 1.0 billion at $3.00 per pound. Figure 2–3 shows the change as an arrow drawn from point A to point B. If the price of chicken were instead $2.00, consumers would buy even more chicken at any level of income. When income was at its original low level, consumers would buy 2.0 billion pounds, as shown by point C. After their incomes went up, buyers would want 3.5 billion pounds, shown by point D.

The same reasoning applies for any given price of chicken. As a result, rising income tends to shift the entire demand curve to the right. Later, if consumer incomes stay at the new, higher level but the price changes, the effects would appear as movements along the new demand curve. There is a chicken demand curve for every possible income level. Each represents a one-to-one relationship between price and quantity demanded for that income.

In the example we have just given, an increase in income causes an increase in demand. Because that is what happens for most goods, economists call goods like chicken **normal goods**.

Not all goods are normal, however. People buy less of some goods when their incomes rise, other things being equal. For example, as the economy slipped into a deep recession in 2008, sales of new shoes fell, but demand for shoe repair services increased sharply. Hormel Foods Corp. reported a surge in sales of staple products like Spam® and Dinty Moore® beef stew, even while demand for its upscale, single-serving microwaveable foods fell. We call goods like shoe repair services and Spam, for which demand increases as income falls, **inferior goods**. An increase in income shifts the demand curve for an inferior good to the left instead of to the right.

Changes in Expectations
Changes in buyers' expectations can also shift demand curves. If people expect the price of something to go up, they may hurry to buy more before it is too late.

For example, suppose that in May consumers hear that airline prices will go up after June 1. Some of them may be planning to travel late in the summer and would have waited several weeks before booking a flight, but instead, they will book early. The expectation of higher prices later produces a temporary rightward shift in the demand curve before the increase takes effect.

The same thing can happen if people expect something other than a price increase to raise the opportunity cost of the good. For example, in June 2009, a change in rules required US citizens visiting Canada to show a passport—an increase in opportunity cost for people who did not already have one. Some of those people moved their planned Canadian vacations forward to avoid the extra hassle. The result was a temporary surge in demand for Canadian travel.

Normal good

A good for which an increase in consumer income results in an increase in demand

Inferior good

A good for which an increase in consumer incomes results in a decrease in demand

FIGURE 2–3

Effects of an Increase in Consumer Income on the Demand for Chicken

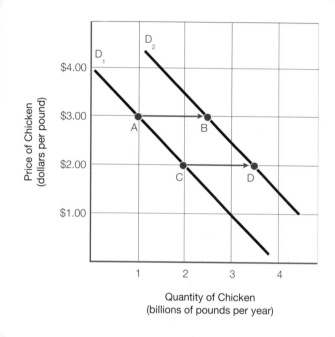

Demand curve D_1 assumes a given level of consumer income. If incomes increase, consumers will want to buy more chicken at any given price, other things being equal. That will shift the demand curve rightward to, say, D_2. If the prevailing market price at the time of the demand shift is $3.00 per pound, the quantity demanded increases to 2.5 billion pounds (B) from 1.0 billion (A); if the prevailing price is $2.00 per pound, the quantity demanded will increase to 3.5 billion pounds (D) from 2.0 billion (C); and so on.

Changes in Tastes   Changes in tastes can also cause an increase or decrease in demand. Sometimes these changes occur rapidly, such as with popular music, clothing styles, and fast foods. In other cases, changes in tastes take longer but are more permanent. For example, over the years, US consumers have been more health conscious. As that has happened, demand has fallen for cigarettes and fatty foods, while demand for fish, organic vegetables, and gym memberships has risen.

2.2 SUPPLY

Let's turn now to the supply side of the market. To continue our earlier example, we change our focus from the quantity that consumers are willing and able to buy under given market conditions to the quantity that producers are willing and able to sell.

As US consumers have become more health conscious, demand for fish, organic vegetables, and gym memberships has increased. (Wikimedia Commons)

As in the case of consumers, we will see that the choices made by producers depend both on the price of the good in question and on other relevant conditions.

2.2a The Supply Curve

We begin with Figure 2–4, which shows the relationship between the price of chicken and the quantity that suppliers are willing and able to sell. We call the relationship shown in the figure a **supply curve** for chicken. The supply curve has a positive slope because the quantity supplied increases when the price goes up. Like demand curves, supply curves are based on an "other things being equal" condition. The supply curve shows how sellers respond to a change in the price of chicken, assuming no changes in the prices of other goods, production techniques, input prices, expectations, or other relevant conditions.

Supply curve

A graphical representation of the relationship between the price of a good and the quantity of that good that sellers are willing to supply

Why do sellers, other things being equal, plan to supply more chicken when the price is higher? Before developing a detailed theory, we can consider some commonsense explanations.

One is that the positive slope of the supply curve represents *producers' responses to market incentives.* When the price of chicken goes up, farmers have a reason to expand their capacity. Some who raise chickens as a sideline may decide to make chickens their main business. Other people may enter the chicken business for the first time. The same

FIGURE 2–4

A Supply Curve for Chicken

(a)

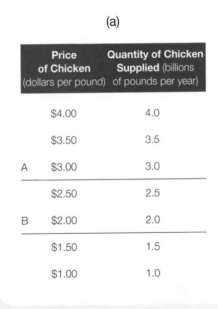

Price of Chicken (dollars per pound)	Quantity of Chicken Supplied (billions of pounds per year)
$4.00	4.0
$3.50	3.5
A $3.00	3.0
$2.50	2.5
B $2.00	2.0
$1.50	1.5
$1.00	1.0

(b)

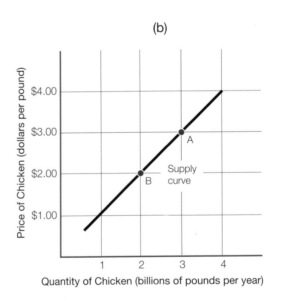

Parts (a) and (b) of this figure show the quantity of chicken supplied at various prices. As the price rises, the quantity supplied increases, other things being equal. The higher price gives farmers an incentive to raise more chickens, but the rising opportunity cost of doing so limits the supply produced in response to any given price increase.

reasoning applies in every market. If parents are finding it hard to get babysitters, what do they do? They offer a bigger incentive in the form of a higher hourly rate. If a sawmill cannot buy enough timber, it raises the price it offers to loggers, and so on. Exceptions to the rule that a higher price causes a greater quantity supplied are rare.

Instead, we could explain the positive slope of the supply curve in terms of the *rising cost of producing additional output in facilities of a fixed size.* A furniture factory with a fixed amount of machinery might be able to produce more chairs only by adding shifts or paying overtime. A farmer trying to grow more wheat on a fixed amount of land could increase the use of fertilizer; but beyond a point, each added ton of fertilizer would yield less additional output.

Finally, we can explain the positive slope of the supply curve in terms of *comparative advantage and opportunity cost.* Part (a) of Figure 2–5 shows a production possibility frontier for an economy that produces tomatoes and chicken. Some farmers have a

FIGURE 2–5

The Production Possibility Curve and the Supply Curve

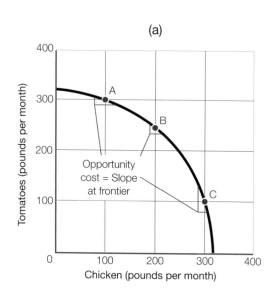 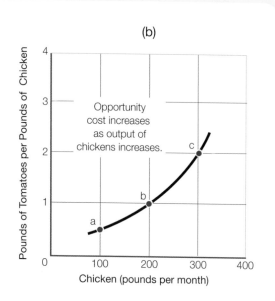

This figure offers an interpretation of the supply curve in terms of the production possibility frontier for an economy that produces two goods: tomatoes and chicken. Part (a) shows a production possibility frontier. The slope of the frontier, at any point, shows the opportunity cost of producing an additional pound of chicken measured in terms of the quantity of tomatoes that farmers could have produced using the same factors of production. The frontier curves because some farmers have a comparative advantage in producing tomatoes and others have a comparative advantage in producing chicken. As farmers raise more chicken, those with the greatest comparative advantage are the first to stop producing tomatoes. Because the frontier gets steeper as the quantity of chicken increases, the opportunity cost rises, as shown in Part (b). We can interpret the curve in Part (b) as a supply curve, in the sense that an incentive, in the form of a higher price, will cause producers to shift factors from tomatoes to chicken despite the rising opportunity cost of chicken.

comparative advantage in one product; some, in the other. Suppose we start from a point where farmers produce only tomatoes and then introduce chicken. The first farmers to switch to chicken will be those with the strongest comparative advantage—that is, those able to produce chicken at the lowest opportunity cost relative to tomatoes. They will be willing to switch from tomatoes to chicken even if the price of chicken is low. As farmers add more and more chicken, the point of production moves down and to the right along the frontier. After each adjustment, the price of chicken must rise further to give the needed incentive for farmers with higher opportunity costs to make the switch.

The slope of the frontier at any point represents the price of chicken, relative to the price of tomatoes, that will cause one more farmer to switch. Part (b) of Figure 2–5 uses information on opportunity costs, based on the slope of the frontier at points like A, B, and C, to construct a supply curve for chicken. That curve shows how the price of chicken must rise relative to the price of tomatoes to induce more farmers to switch from one product to the other.

Each of these commonsense explanations fits certain circumstances. Together, they provide an intuitive basis for the positive slope of the supply curve.

2.2b Shifts in the Supply Curve

We call the effects of a change in the price of chicken, other things being equal, a **change in quantity supplied**, shown as a movement along the supply curve. The effects of a change in a condition other than the price of chicken are known as a **change in supply**, shown as a shift in the supply curve. Four sources of change in supply are worth noting. Each of them reflects a change in the opportunity cost of producing the good or service in question.

Changes in Technology   A given supply curve is based on a given technology. Entrepreneurs are constantly looking for new ways of doing things that lower costs. When production costs fall, it becomes worthwhile to sell more of the good at any given price. Figure 2–6 shows how new technology affects the supply curve for chicken.

Supply curve S_1 is the same as the one shown in Figure 2–4. It indicates that farmers will plan to supply 3.0 billion pounds of chicken per year at a price of $3.00 per pound (point A). Now suppose that the development of a faster-growing bird reduces feed requirements. With lower costs per unit, farmers will be willing to supply more chicken at any given price. They may, for example, be willing to supply 4.0 billion pounds of chicken at $3.00 (point B). The move from A to B is part of a shift in the entire supply curve from S_1 to S_2. Once the new methods of production are established, any increase or decrease in the price of chicken, other things being equal, will cause a movement along the new supply curve.

Changes in Input Prices   Changes in input prices are a second item that can cause supply curves to shift. An increase in input prices, other things being equal, increases the cost of producing the good in question and reduces quantity supplied at any given price. Refer again to Figure 2–6. Suppose that, starting from point A on supply curve S_1, the price of chicken feed increases and no offsetting changes occur. Now, instead of supplying 3.0 billion pounds of chicken at $3.00 per pound, farmers will supply just 2.0 billion pounds (point C). The move from A to C is part of a leftward shift in the supply curve, from S_1 to S_3.

If the price of feed remains at the new level, changes in the price of chicken will cause movements along the new supply curve. For example farmers could be induced to supply the original quantity of chicken—3.0 billion pounds—if the price of chicken were raised enough to cover the increased cost of feed. As you can see in Figure 2–6, that would require a price of $4.00 per pound for chicken (point D).

Change in quantity supplied

A change in the quantity of a good that suppliers are willing and able to sell that is caused by a change in the good's price, other things being equal; shown by a movement along a supply curve

Change in supply

A change in the quantity of a good that suppliers are willing and able to sell that is caused by a change in some condition other than the good's price; shown by a shift in the supply curve

FIGURE 2–6

Shifts in the Supply Curve for Chicken

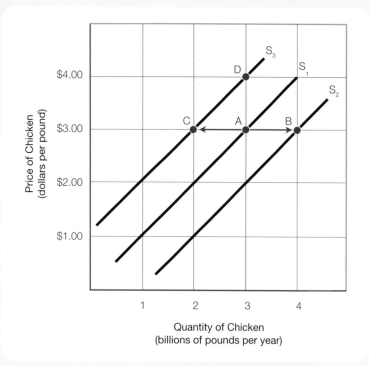

Several kinds of changes can cause the supply of chicken to increase or decrease. For example a new production method that lowers costs will shift the curve to the right, from S_1 to S_2, because producers will be willing to supply more at any given price. An increase in the price of inputs, other things being equal, will shift the curve to the left, from S_1 to S_3. Changes in sellers' expectations or in the prices of competing goods can also cause the supply curve to shift.

Changes in the Prices of Other Goods

Changes in the prices of other goods that producers could make using the same factors of production can also shift the supply curve. In our earlier example, farmers could use available resources for either chickens or tomatoes. Suppose that the price of tomatoes rises while the price of chicken stays at $3.00. The higher price of tomatoes gives some farmers who would otherwise have produced chickens an incentive to shift to tomatoes. The result would be a leftward shift in the chicken supply curve.

Changes in Expectations

Changes in producers' expectations are a fourth factor that can cause supply curves to shift. For example a farmer's selection of crops depends less on the price at planting time than on that expected at harvest. Expectations over a time span also matter. Each crop requires special equipment and know-how. We have just seen that an increase in the price of tomatoes gives farmers an incentive to shift from chicken to tomatoes. The incentive will be stronger if they expect the price of tomatoes to remain high, making it worthwhile to buy special equipment and learn the necessary production techniques.

2.3 THE INTERACTION OF SUPPLY AND DEMAND

Markets transmit information, in the form of prices, to people who buy and sell. Buyers and sellers take those prices into account, along with other knowledge they have, when making the plans that shape the supply and demand curves.[2]

Nothing guarantees that all of the buyers and sellers in a market will be able to carry out their plans, as hoped, when they meet to trade. Perhaps the quantity of a good that buyers want is greater than the quantity suppliers are willing to sell at the prevailing price. In that case, some of the would-be buyers will be disappointed and must change their plans. Perhaps planned sales exceed planned purchases. In that case, some would-be sellers will have to adjust their plans. Sometimes, though, buyers' and sellers' plans will exactly mesh when they meet in the marketplace; no one is disappointed or needs to change plans. In that case, the market is in **equilibrium**.

Equilibrium

A condition in which buyers' and sellers' plans exactly mesh in the marketplace, so that the quantity supplied exactly equals the quantity demanded at a given price

2.3a Market Equilibrium

We can illustrate a state of market equilibrium by drawing both the supply and demand curves for a good on one diagram. Figure 2–7 does that for the chicken market. If we compare the quantity of planned sales at each price with the quantity of planned purchases, we can see that there is only one price where the two sets of plans mesh. (We can use either the table or the graph to make the comparison.) That price—$2.00 per pound—is the equilibrium price. If all buyers and sellers make their plans with the expectation of a price of $2.00, no one will be surprised and no one will have to change their plans.

Excess quantity demanded (shortage)

A condition in which the quantity of a good demanded at a given price exceeds the quantity supplied

2.3b Shortages

What would happen if people were to base their plans on a price other than $2.00 a pound?[3] Suppose, for example, that they plan for a price of $1.00. As Figure 2–7 shows, planned purchases at that price are 3.0 billion pounds per year, but farmers plan to supply only 1.0 billion. When the quantity demanded exceeds the quantity supplied, the difference is an **excess quantity demanded** or, more simply, a shortage. In Figure 2–7, the **shortage** at a price of $1.00 is 2.0 billion pounds per year.

Inventory

A stock of a good awaiting sale or use

In most markets, the first sign of a shortage is a decrease in **inventories**—that is, in previously produced stocks of a good that are ready for sale or use. Sellers normally plan to hold a certain level of inventory to allow for minor changes in demand. When they see inventories dropping below the planned level, they change their plans. Some sellers may try to rebuild their inventories by increasing their output. Others may take advantage of strong demand to raise prices. Many are likely to do a little of both. As sellers adjust their plans, they will move upward and to the right along the supply curve.

As the price begins to change, buyers, too, adjust their plans. They cut back on their planned purchases, moving up and to the left along the demand curve. As both buyers and sellers adjust, the market moves toward equilibrium. When the price reaches $2.00, the shortage disappears, along with the pressure to make further adjustments in plans.

In the markets for services—knee surgery, tax preparation, lawn care, and the like—the adjustment process is a little different because there are no inventories of services produced but not yet sold. The same is true of goods like custom-built houses and custom-designed machine tools, where producers do not begin work until they have a contract with a buyer.

A line of people waiting to buy something is a sign of shortage. (Dreamstime)

FIGURE 2–7

Equilibrium in the Chicken Market

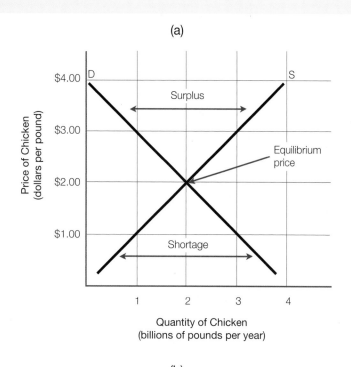

(a)

Quantity of Chicken
(billions of pounds per year)

(b)

Price (per pound)	Quantity Demanded (billions of pounds)	Quantity Supplied (billions of pounds)	Shortage (billions of pounds)	Surplus (billions of pounds)	Direction of Pressure on Rice
$3.50	0.5	3.5	—	3.0	Downward
$3.00	1.0	3.0	—	2.0	Downward
$2.50	1.5	2.5	—	1.0	Downward
$2.00	2.0	2.0	—	—	Equilibrium
$1.50	2.5	1.5	1.0	—	Upward
$1.00	3.0	1.0	2.0	—	Upward
$0.50	3.5	0.5	3.0	—	Upward

This figure shows the supply and demand curves for chicken presented earlier in graphical and numerical form. The demand curve shows how much buyers plan to purchase at a given price. The supply curve shows how much producers plan to sell at a given price. At only one price ($2.00 per pound) do buyers' and sellers' plans exactly match. That is the equilibrium price. A higher price causes a surplus of chicken and puts downward pressure on price. A lower price causes a shortage and puts upward pressure on price.

In markets where there are no inventories, the first sign of a shortage is a queue of buyers. The queue may take the form of a line of people waiting for service or a list of names in an order book. The queue is a sign that, at the prevailing price, people would like to buy more of the good than is being supplied. In that case, buyers cannot carry out all of their plans—at least not right away.

The formation of a queue of buyers has the same effect on the market as a decrease in inventories. Sellers react by increasing output, raising prices, or both. Buyers react by reducing purchases or by offering higher prices. The market moves up and to the right along the supply curve and, at the same time, up and to the left along the demand curve until it reaches equilibrium.

2.3c Surpluses

Suppose, instead, that buyers and sellers expect a price that is above the equilibrium. For example, in Figure 2–7, if the expected price is $2.50 per pound, farmers will plan to supply 2.5 billion pounds of chicken, but their customers will plan to buy only 1.5 billion pounds. When that happens, there is an **excess quantity supplied**, or a **surplus**. Here, the surplus at $2.50 per pound is 1.0 billion pounds per year.

Taxi queues indicate a surplus of sellers looking for customers. (Wikimedia Commons)

If there is a surplus, suppliers will not be able to sell all they had hoped at the expected price. Inventories will start to grow. Suppliers will react to the inventory buildup by changing their plans. Some will cut back their output. Others will lower their prices in the hope of getting customers to buy more. Still others will do a little of both. Those changes in plans will cause a movement down and to the left along the supply curve.

As unplanned inventory buildup puts downward pressure on the price, buyers change their plans, too. Finding that chicken costs less than they had expected, they buy more of it. Figure 2-7 shows that reaction as a movement down and to the right along the demand curve. Taken together, buyers' and sellers' reactions to the surplus bring the market into equilibrium.

In markets in which there are no inventories, surpluses lead to queues of sellers looking for customers. Taxi queues at airports are a case in point. At some times of the day, the fare for taxi service from the airport to downtown is more than high enough to attract all the taxis needed to meet demand. A queue of cabs waiting for passengers then forms. If there are rules against fare cutting, as there are in many traditional taxi services, the queue continues to grow until the next peak period when a surge in demand shortens it. In contrast, nontraditional ride services like Uber adjust prices flexibly as weather, traffic, and other conditions change.

2.3d Changes in Market Conditions

Finding the equilibrium price and quantity looks easy enough in our examples, but in real life, it is a moving target. The market conditions that fall under the "other things being equal" proviso change frequently. When they do, both buyers and sellers must revise their plans, and the equilibrium price and quantity change.

Response to a Shift in Demand   Let's start by looking at how a market responds to a shift in demand. Suppose you hear on Twitter that there has been an outbreak of food poisoning linked to chicken. As the news spreads, the demand for chicken decreases. Part (a) of Figure 2–8 shows that as a leftward shift of the demand curve.

After the decrease in demand, there will be a surplus at the original price of $3.00. The price will not stay at that level for long, though. As soon as inventories start to rise, producers begin to revise their plans. They cut their prices and reduce quantities supplied. Suppliers' reactions appear as a movement along the supply curve, not as a shift in the curve, because

Excess quantity supplied (surplus)

A condition in which the quantity of a good supplied at a given price exceeds the quantity demanded

FIGURE 2–8

Effects of Changing Conditions in the Chicken Market

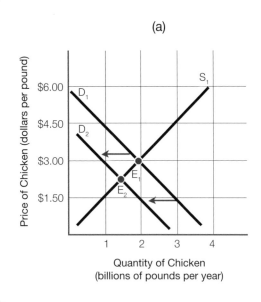

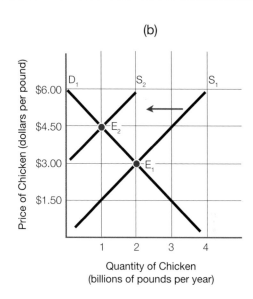

Part (a) of this figure shows the effects of a decrease in demand for chicken caused by reports linking food poisoning to eating chicken. Initially the market is in equilibrium at E_1. The report shifts the demand curve. At the original equilibrium price of $3.00, there is a temporary surplus of chicken. That causes inventories to rise and puts downward pressure on the price. As the price falls, producers move down along the supply curve to a new equilibrium at E_2. There, both the price and quantity of chicken are lower than before the shift in demand. Part (b) shows the effects of a decrease in supply caused by an increase in the price of chicken feed. The shift in the supply curve causes a shortage at the initial price of $3.00 per pound. The shortage puts upward pressure on price. As the price rises, buyers move up and to the left along the demand curve until they reach a new equilibrium at E_2. In each case, note that only one curve needs to shift to bring about the new equilibrium.

the producers are responding to a change in the price of chicken—the variable shown on the vertical axis. Nothing has happened to change the "other things being equal" conditions, such as technology or input prices, which could cause the supply curve to shift.

Adjustments continue until the plans of suppliers once again mesh with those of consumers. That happens at point E_2 in Part (a) of Figure 2–8, where the price has fallen to $2.25 and the quantity sold to 1.5 billion pounds. Later, if the conditions that caused the health warning disappear, the demand curve will shift back to D_1, and the market will return to its original equilibrium.

Response to a Shift in Supply   In another case, the market equilibrium might be upset by a change in supply rather than demand. For example, suppose that increased use of corn to make ethanol pushes up the price of chicken feed. That would shift the supply curve for chicken to the left, while the demand curve remains unchanged, as shown in Part (b) of Figure 2–8.

The shift in the supply curve would cause a shortage if the price of chicken remained unchanged at $3.00 per pound. Inventories would fall, putting upward pressure on the price. Producers would increase the amount they planned to sell, moving upward and to the right along the new supply curve. Buyers would move upward and to the left along the demand curve. A new equilibrium would be established when the price reached $4.50.

A Shift in One Curve or Both?   One of the most common mistakes people make in using supply and demand is to think that *both* curves always must shift in order to restore equilibrium. The examples given in Figure 2–8 show why they do not. As Part (a) shows, after the demand curve shifts, the market moves along the supply curve to reach the new equilibrium. The supply curve does not need to shift. Similarly, in Part (b), where the supply curve shifts, the market moves along the demand curve to reach the new equilibrium.

However, in the turmoil of real-world markets, it is easy to find cases where two separate changes occur at the same time, one acting on supply and the other on demand. *Economics in the News 2.1* provides an example: the way both demand and supply conditions affect prices for cocoa. In that market, a steady rightward shift in the demand curve has led to a long-term trend toward higher prices. Superimposed on the long-term demand-driven trend are short-term changes in supply caused by changes in other conditions.

No central authority has to plan the process of adjustment. Equilibrium is not a compromise negotiated by a committee of consumers and producers. Just as shoppers manage to equalize the length of supermarket checkout lines without the guidance of a central authority, markets like that for cocoa move toward equilibrium spontaneously through the small, local adjustments that people make in their efforts to serve their own interests. As Adam Smith might have put it, we have not the benevolence of the International Cocoa Organization to thank for our dessert; instead it is self-interest that puts that box of chocolates on the table.

Economics in the News 2.1

Chocolate Lovers Keep Nervous Eye on Cocoa Prices

Supply and demand have driven the prices of cocoa, the main ingredient in chocolate, to record highs in recent years. Prices have not only been high but also increasingly volatile.

Changing demand conditions are responsible for much of the upward trend in prices in recent decades. Since chocolate is a normal good, the hundreds of millions of new middle-class consumers in developing countries buy more chocolate as their incomes rise. Changing tastes also play a role. For example until recently, chocolate was not especially popular in China, even among those who could afford it. Per capita consumption was some one hundred times less than in Europe and the United States—a far bigger difference than income alone could explain. Now Chinese consumers are starting to see chocolate as trendy. Consumption has been growing by more than 10 percent per year.

Both rising incomes and changing tastes have shifted the chocolate demand curve to the right. Even if supply conditions had remained unchanged, the shift in demand by itself would be enough to push the price of cocoa steadily higher.

In practice, though, supply conditions do change, often more rapidly than demand. Political conflicts are one source of change. For example in 2010, a disputed election in Ivory Coast, the world's largest cocoa producer, threw the market into turmoil. A spiraling civil war disrupted exports, shifting the world supply curve to the left and causing a spike in world prices. When the crisis was finally resolved in April 2011, normal supply conditions returned and prices fell again.

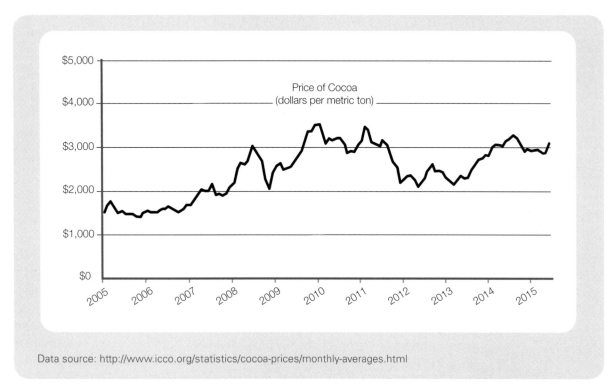

Data source: http://www.icco.org/statistics/cocoa-prices/monthly-averages.html

Also the cocoa supply, like that of any farm product, is subject to changes in growing conditions. Cocoa crops throughout West Africa suffer from periodic outbreaks of swollen shoot disease. The leaves of affected trees turn red, and the cocoa pods are ruined. In the summer of 2011, just as a return of political calm allowed the cocoa price to fall a bit, a new outbreak of swollen shoot disease shifted the supply curve to the left once again, pushing the price back up.

In 2014, a new disaster struck West Africa, this time in the form of an Ebola epidemic. To prevent the spread of the disease from neighboring Liberia and Guinea, Ivory Coast closed its borders, cutting off an important supply of labor to harvest its cocoa crop. The labor shortage and fear of contagion sent prices higher again.

The bottom line? You may have to get ready to pay more for your chocolate—or you may not. Any way you look at it, the complexities of supply and demand are likely to keep chocolate prices volatile. But look at the bright side. If high chocolate prices depress you, just remember that chocolate itself is a reliable cure for depression!

Source: http://www.icco.org/statistics/cocoa-prices/monthly-averages.html

2.4 PRICE FLOORS AND CEILINGS

The previous section discussed how temporary surpluses and shortages cause prices and output to change when market conditions change. Sometimes, however, government regulations impose price floors or ceilings that interfere with free adjustment of prices. Surpluses and shortages then become persistent, often resulting in unintended consequences for producers, consumers, and taxpayers. This section uses the supply and demand model to analyze the effects of government-imposed price floors and ceilings and provides some examples.

2.4a Price Supports: The Market for Milk

In our earlier example of the market for chicken, a decrease in demand caused a surplus that, in turn, caused the price to decrease until the surplus disappeared. Markets have not always been free to respond by adjusting prices, however. The market for milk is one such case.

Figure 2–9 shows the market for milk in terms of supply and demand curves. The horizontal axis shows the quantity of milk in hundredweight, the unit used for bulk milk sales, equal to roughly twelve gallons. Suppose that, initially, the market is in equilibrium at point E_1. The wholesale price of milk is $13 per hundredweight, and the output is 110 million hundredweight per year. Then suppose that a trend in taste away from high-cholesterol foods shifts the demand curve for milk to the left. The result would be a surplus of milk at the $13 price, as shown by the arrow in Figure 2–9.

If the price of milk were free to fall in response to a surplus, the market would quickly reach a new equilibrium at $10 per hundredweight. However, suppose that the government sets a minimum price of $13 and enforces it by agreeing to buy all of the milk that farmers cannot sell at that price. With the demand curve in its original position, D_1, there was no surplus, and the government did not need to buy any milk. However, with the demand curve in position D_2, there is a surplus of forty million hundredweight per year. The result is a persistent surplus.

In effect, the price floor sends conflicting signals to producers and consumers. To consumers, the price of $13 says, "Milk is scarce. Its opportunity cost is high. Hold your consumption down." To producers, it says, "All is well. Incentives are unchanged. Feel free to continue using scarce resources to produce milk." Without the price supports, a drop in the price to $10 would send a different set of messages. Consumers would hear, "Milk is cheaper and more abundant. Although it is not cholesterol free, give in to temptation! Drink more of it!" Producers would hear, "The milk market is not what it once was. Look at your opportunity costs. Is there perhaps some better use for your labor, capital, and natural resources?"

Congress established the original milk price support program in 1949. For most of its first fifty years, the price floor was consistently higher than the equilibrium price. By the 1990s, the program became very expensive—more than $1,000 per US family by some estimates, enough to buy each family its own cow. From time to time, Congress attempted to control program costs without harming dairy interests.

One idea was to shift the supply curve to the left so that it would intersect the demand curve near the support price by encouraging farmers to sell their cows for slaughter. However, that and other supply-side efforts failed to eliminate the milk surplus. That was, in part, because a high milk price encouraged entrepreneurial efforts by dairy farmers in the form of improved breeding, use of hormones and antibiotics, and automated farm management practices, all of which increased milk output per cow.

FIGURE 2–9

Price Supports for Milk

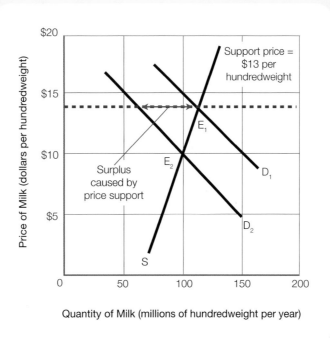

The market for milk is in equilibrium at E_1. A change in tastes away from high-cholesterol foods then shifts the demand curve to D_2. If the price were free to fall, a temporary surplus would push the price down to a new equilibrium at $10 per hundredweight. Instead suppose that the government maintains a support price for milk at a level higher than the equilibrium price, as it did for many years ($13 per hundredweight in this example). The government would then need to buy the surplus milk and store it in the form of powdered milk, butter, and cheese to keep the price from falling.

Then, during the early years of the twenty-first century, conditions in the milk market changed. Increasing demand from emerging-market countries and rising feed costs caused shifts in both supply and demand curves. By 2005, the support price had fallen below the market price, and the surplus had disappeared. By 2014, changing market conditions plus renewed political pressure to cut government spending finally led to the end of milk price supports. Dairy interests did not come away entirely empty-handed. Farmers received the opportunity to buy into a program that protects their profit margins against any squeeze from a simultaneous fall in milk prices and rise in feed prices. However, it appears that artificially high prices and persistent surpluses have become a thing of the past.

2.4b Price Ceilings: The Case of Rent Control

Milk price controls established a price floor that was higher than the market equilibrium. In other markets policy has, instead, imposed a price ceiling below the equilibrium. Consider the case of rent control in housing markets.

Several cities, including New York, Los Angeles, San Francisco, and Washington, DC, have used rent control in one form. The ostensible aim is to aid tenants by preventing landlords from charging "unreasonably high" rents. However, what should be considered unreasonably high is determined by the relative political strength of landlords and tenants rather than by the forces of supply and demand.

Intended Effects   Figure 2–10 interprets the effects of rent control in terms of supply and demand. (For simplicity, we assume that housing units have equal size and rental value.) Part (a) of the figure shows the effects of rent control in the short run. Here the short run means a period that is too short to permit significant increases or decreases in the supply of rental housing, making the short-run supply curve a vertical line.

FIGURE 2–10

Effects of Rent Control

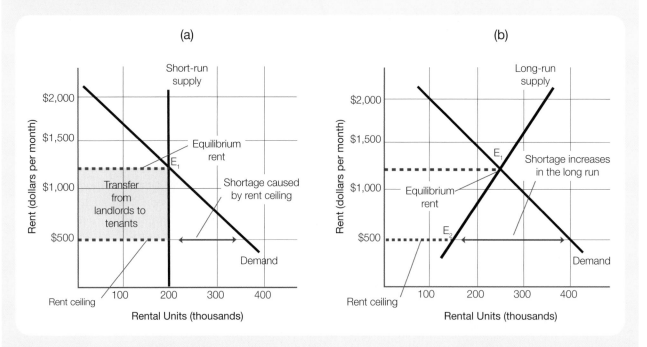

Part (a) shows the short-run effects of rent control. In the short run the supply of rental apartments is fixed. The equilibrium rent is $1,250 per month. Authorities then impose a rent ceiling of $500 per month. One possible outcome is that landlords will charge disguised rent increases, which will bring the true price back to $1,250 per month. If regulations prohibit such disguised increases, there will be a shortage of 350,000 units at the ceiling price. Part (b) shows the long-run effects, when there is time to adjust the number of units in response to the price. With the ceiling in effect, landlords move down their supply curve to E_2. The shortage then becomes even more severe than in the short run.

Under the conditions shown, the equilibrium rent per standard housing unit is $1,250 per month for each of the two hundred thousand units in the city. Now suppose that authorities impose a rent ceiling of $500. At that price, tenants would save $750 per unit per month. The total sum transferred to tenants in the form of below-market rents is $750 multiplied by two hundred thousand units, or $150 million, equal to the area of the shaded rectangle.

Unintended Effects

Unfortunately for tenants, rent control also produces unintended consequences. In the short run, when the stock of apartments is fixed, the unintended consequences stem from the apartment shortage created because the quantity demanded is greater at the lower ceiling price than at the higher equilibrium price. Quantity demanded increases, in part, because some people who would otherwise own a house or condominium might prefer to seek rent-controlled units in the city instead of living in suburbs without rent control.

The shortage creates a problem for both landlords and tenants: How will the limited supply of apartments be rationed among those who want them? Both landlords and tenants devise a number of creative responses—*entrepreneurial* responses, as an economist would say.

One response on the part of landlords is to seek disguised rent increases—for example requiring large, nonrefundable deposits, selling used furniture or appliances at inflated prices as a condition for renting the apartment, or overcharging for maintenance or security services. Tenants, too, may get into the act. When they decide to move, they may sublet their apartments to other tenants rather than give up their leases. Now it is the tenant who collects the deposits or sells the old furniture to the subtenant. The original tenant may have moved to a distant city but maintains a bank account and a post office box for use in paying the rent. The subtenant is instructed to play the role of a "guest" if the landlord telephones.

Advocates of rent control view these responses as cheating and often try to outlaw them. If prohibitions are enforced, the landlord will find that there are many applicants for each vacant apartment. In that case the landlord must decide to whom to rent the apartment. The result will often be discrimination against renters who are from minority groups, who have children, or who have unconventional lifestyles.

In the long run, rent control has other unintended effects. The long run in this case means enough time for the number of rental units to grow through construction of new units or shrink through abandonment of old ones (or their conversion to condominiums). Other things being equal, the higher the rent, the greater the rate of construction; the lower the rent, the greater the rate of abandonment or conversion. Those effects produce the positively sloped long-run supply curve in Part (b) of Figure 2–10.

If landlords enforce rent controls in such a way that there are no disguised charges, the number of rental units shrinks, and the market moves from E_1 to E_2. At E_2, the unintended effects that appeared in the short run become more pronounced. The intensity of housing discrimination increases relative to the short-run case because the difference between the number of units available and the number sought by renters increases. That difference shows up as a horizontal gap between the supply and demand curves at the ceiling price. In the short run, there is a shortage of fifty thousand units; in the long run, the shortage increases to seventy-five thousand units.

Advocates of rent controls often defend them as beneficial to the poor; but when all of the unintended effects of rent control are taken into account, one may question whether that is really true. In cases in which disguised rent increases are possible, the true cost of rental housing does not really fall. Further, it is hard to believe that the tendency of landlords to discriminate against minority group members, single-parent families, and tenants with irregular work histories will benefit the poor. The most likely beneficiaries of rent control are stable middle-class families who work at the same jobs and live in the same apartments for long periods.

Why does rent control persist as a policy, given its many unintended consequences? Some economists explain the popularity of rent control in terms of the political power of the middle-class tenants, who are most likely to benefit from rent controls and who see "helping the poor" as nothing more than a convenient cover for their own self-interest. Some explain the popularity in terms of the short time horizon of government officials: The adverse effect on tenants of ending rent control would appear very quickly, whereas such benefits as increased construction of new apartments would materialize only long after the next election. Others attribute the popularity of rent control to the simple fact that many voters do not give much thought to the policy's unintended consequences.

Whatever the reason, it appears that rent control is very gradually weakening its hold. In New York and elsewhere, strict rent ceilings are gradually giving way to more flexible forms of "rent stabilization" that limit increases for sitting tenants but allow larger increases for new tenants and make it easier to pass cost increases through to higher rents.

2.4c Equilibrium as Spontaneous Order

The way that markets adjust to change is an example of economic coordination through spontaneous order. Consider, again, the market for cocoa. Adjustments to changes in income, consumer tastes, political events, and growing conditions involve decisions made by thousands of farmers, wholesalers, and retailers, as well as millions of consumers. Somehow their action must all be coordinated. But how?

A market economy needs no central planning agency or regulatory bureaucracy. The required changes in the use of scarce resources take place in response to information and incentives transmitted by changing market prices. As prices rise, farmers plant new cocoa trees where possible. At the same time researchers redouble their efforts to breed disease-resistant trees. Meanwhile candy makers in Europe and the United States employ new marketing strategies—like introducing vintage, estate-grown chocolates in an attempt to maintain the product's appeal as its price rises.

2.5 SOME CLOSING THOUGHTS

This chapter has covered the basics of the supply and demand model and described a few of its applications. There are many more applications in both macro- and microeconomics. In macroeconomics, supply and demand apply to financial markets, labor markets, and the problem of determining the rate of inflation and real output for the economy as a whole. In microeconomics, the model applies to product markets, markets for labor and natural resources, and policy issues ranging from pollution to farm policy to international trade. As the great economist Alfred Marshall once put it, nearly all of the major problems of economics have a "kernel" that reflects the workings of supply and demand (see *Who Said It? Who Did It? 2.1*).

When we turn from the general outline presented in this chapter to some of the finer details, we will see that the supply and demand model fits some markets more closely than others. The fit is best for markets in which there are many buyers and many sellers, the goods offered by one seller are much like those sold by others, and all buyers and sellers have good information on market conditions. Markets for farm commodities, such as wheat and corn, and some financial markets, such as the New York Stock Exchange, meet these standards reasonably well.

However, not all markets display all of these features. Chocolate is an example. Cocoa, the basic commodity, fits the supply and demand model closely. Markets for high-end chocolate confections do not. In those markets, the products of different producers are not alike, and just a few specialist firms dominate some segments of the market. Even in markets like those, however, the notions of supply and demand provide a useful framework to which we can add refinements and extensions.

Who Said It? Who Did It? **2.1**

Alfred Marshall
on
Supply and Demand

(Wikimedia Commons)

Alfred Marshall, who many think was the greatest economist of his day, was born in London in 1842. His father was a Bank of England cashier who hoped the boy would enter the ministry. Young Marshall had other ideas, however. He turned down a theological scholarship at Oxford to study mathematics, receiving his MA from Cambridge in 1865.

While at Cambridge, Marshall joined a philosophical discussion group. There he became interested in promoting the broad development of the human mind. He was soon told that harsh economic realities would prevent the realization of his ideas. Britain's economic potential as a country could, supposedly, never allow the masses enough leisure for education. This disillusioning episode appears to have triggered Marshall's fascination with economics.

At the time, the classical school founded by Adam Smith and David Ricardo dominated British economics. Marshall had great respect for the classical writers. At first he saw his own work as simply applying his mathematical training to refine the classical system. Before long, however, he was breaking new ground and developing a system of his own. By 1890, when he brought out his famous *Principles of Economics*, he had laid the foundation of what we now call the neoclassical school.

In an attempt to explain the essence of his approach, Marshall included the following passage in the second edition of his *Principles*:

> In spite of a great variety in detail, nearly all the chief problems of economics agree in that they have a kernel of the same kind. This kernel is an inquiry as to the balancing of two opposed classes of motives, the one consisting of desires to acquire certain new goods, and thus satisfy wants; while the other consists of desires to avoid certain efforts or retain certain immediate enjoyment … in other words, it is an inquiry into the balancing of the forces of demand and supply.

Marshall's influence on economics—at least in the English-speaking world—was enormous. His *Principles* was the leading economics text for several decades, and modern students can still learn much from it. As a professor at Cambridge, Marshall taught a great many of the next generation's leading economists. Today his neoclassical school continues to dominate the profession. Many have challenged it, but it lives on.

Summary

1. How does the price of a good or service affect the quantity that buyers demand?

The term *demand* means the willingness and ability of buyers to purchase goods and services. According to the *law of demand*, there is an inverse relationship between the price of a good and the quantity demanded. The *quantity demanded* is the amount buyers will purchase at a given price. We can represent the law of demand with a negatively sloped *demand curve*. A movement along the demand curve shows a change in the quantity demanded.

2. How do other market conditions affect demand?

A change in any of the variables covered by the "other things being equal" clause of the law of demand causes a shift in the demand curve, known as a *change in demand*. Examples include changes in the prices of goods that are *substitutes or complements* of the good in question, as well as changes in consumer incomes, expectations, and tastes.

3. How does the price of a good affect the quantity supplied by sellers?

The term *supply* means sellers' willingness and ability to offer products for sale in a market. In most markets, an increase in the price of a good will increase the quantity of the good that sellers are willing to supply. This relationship can be expressed by a positively sloped *supply curve*. The higher price gives producers an incentive to supply more, but rising opportunity costs set a limit on the amount they will supply at any given price.

4. How do changes in other market conditions affect supply?

A change in any of the items covered by the "other things being equal" clause of the supply curve will shift the curve. Examples include changes in technology, changes in the prices of inputs, changes in the prices of other goods that producers could make with the same resources, and changes in expectations.

5. How do supply and demand interact to determine the market price of a good or service?

In a market with a positively sloped supply curve and a negatively sloped demand curve, there is only one price at which the quantity of a good that sellers plan to supply will exactly match the quantity that buyers plan to purchase. We call that the *equilibrium* price. At any higher price, there will be a surplus; and at any lower price, there will be a shortage.

6. Why do market prices and quantities change in response to changes in market conditions?

A change in any market condition that shifts the supply or demand curve will change the equilibrium price and quantity in a market. For example, for a normal good, the demand curve will shift to the right if consumer incomes increase. That causes a shortage at the old price, and the price begins to rise. As the price rises, suppliers move up along the supply curve to a new equilibrium. Instead, an improvement in technology would shift the supply curve to the right. In that case there is a surplus at the old price, and the price will fall. As the price decreases, buyers will move down along their demand curve to a new equilibrium. No shift in the demand curve is required.

7. What are the unintended consequences of price floors and price ceilings?

Price floors, like those long imposed on milk and other farm products, are intended to help producers, but they lead to persistent surpluses. To prevent prices from falling, the government must buy surplus output and either store it or give it away. Price ceilings, like those on rent-controlled apartments, are intended to help low-income tenants, but they lead to persistent shortages. In the long run, construction slows and abandonments increase, so the shortages become more severe over time. Price ceilings and floors can still be found for some goods and services, but their unintended consequences have led many of them to be phased out over time.

KEY TERMS

PROBLEMS AND TOPICS FOR DISCUSSION

1.   **A shifting demand curve**   A vending machine company has studied the demand for soft drinks sold from machines. On a 70° day consumers in the firm's territory will buy about 2,000 cans at a price of $0.75. For each $0.05 rise in price, the quantity sold falls by 200 cans per day; for each 5° rise in temperature, the quantity sold rises by 150 cans per day. The same relationships hold for decreases in price or temperature. Using this information, draw a set of curves showing the demand for soft drinks on days when the temperature is 60°, 70°, and 85°. Then draw a separate diagram with temperature on the vertical axis and quantity on the horizontal axis. Draw a line representing the relationship between temperature and quantity when the price is $0.75. Next, draw additional temperature-quantity lines for prices of $0.50 and $1.00. Do the two diagrams give the same information? Discuss. (Note: If you have any trouble with this exercise, review the appendix to Chapter 1, "Working with Graphs," especially the section entitled "Packing Three Variables into Two Dimensions.")

2.   **Demand and the price of motor fuel**   From 2007 to 2008, the price of gasoline in the United States rose from $2.76 per gallon to $3.20 per gallon. The quantity used decreased from 3,389 million barrels to 3,290 million barrels. In 2009, the price fell to $2.30 per gallon, yet the quantity used continued to decline, to 3,283 million barrels. After-tax personal income increased from 2007 to 2008, but it fell from 2008 to 2009.

     Which one or more of the following hypotheses do you think best explain(s) the pattern of gasoline sales? Illustrate your chosen hypothesis with an appropriate diagram.

     a.   In 2008, the demand curve for gasoline had the usual negative slope. However, in 2009, the demand curve shifted to a positively sloped position.

     b.   The demand curve had a negative slope at all times, but because gasoline is a normal good, the demand curve shifted to the right in 2008 and then to the left in 2009.

3.   **Shortages, price controls, and queues**   During the late 1980s and early 1990s, economic reforms initiated by Soviet president Mikhail Gorbachev began to raise consumer incomes; however, the Soviet government continued to impose price ceilings on basic goods like food, clothing, and household goods. As higher income led to increased demand, severe shortages of many goods and long lines at all kinds of stores became common. Finally, in January 1992, a new Russian government under president Boris Yeltsin removed retail price controls on most goods. Within a month, prices more than doubled on average, and lines disappeared. Analyze these events using the supply and demand model. First draw a supply and demand diagram for some normal good such as butter. Show the market in equilibrium at a price of 1 ruble per kilo before the beginning of the Gorbachev reforms. Draw a horizontal line at that level to represent the price ceiling; no butter can be sold for more than 1 ruble per kilo. Next show the effect of rising income. Does it shift the supply curve? Does it shift the demand curve? What is the shortage or surplus at the controlled price? After the price control ends, assuming no further shift in the supply and demand curve, what happens to the price? What happens to the shortage or surplus?

PROBLEMS AND TOPICS FOR DISCUSSION

4.　**Flexible pricing for rides**　　In most cities taxi fares stay the same every day and in every kind of weather. In contrast, ride services like Uber change prices more frequently. On a recent Halloween, some riders were shocked when they were charged far more than usual for a late evening ride from Uber. Do you think higher prices for rides on Halloween make sense from the point of view of supply and demand? Do you think it is ethical to charge a much higher price during a high-demand period like the evening of Halloween? (Uber says it always gives riders an estimate of the fare before they agree to the service.) Discuss in terms of efficiency and fairness.

5.　**The market for olive oil**　　The chapter began by using olive oil as an example of a good whose price varies greatly from year to year. Using supply and demand diagrams, explain how each of the following would affect the market:

　　a.　A severe drought hits Spain, the world's largest olive oil producer. Would the supply curve shift? What about the demand curve? What will happen to the price?

　　b.　Medical research proves that the Mediterranean diet, which includes abundant use of olive oil, is not just a fad but is really good for you. In response, millions of consumers start following the diet. Would the supply curve shift? What about the demand curve? What will happen to the price?

CASE *for* DISCUSSION

Will CNG Power Your Next Car?

There has been a lot of talk in the United States about the automotive fuel of the future. Most of it has centered on ethanol, electricity, and, to some extent, hydrogen. Yet the real fuel of the future may turn out to be compressed natural gas, or CNG.

CNG as an automotive fuel is not new technology. Thousands of buses and delivery vehicles use it every day in the United States. So do millions of passenger cars in other countries. Now market forces favor CNG as an automotive fuel in the United States. As recently as 2005, natural gas actually cost more than gasoline on an energy-equivalent basis. By 2012, it cost only a quarter as much—a record gap between the two fuels.

What is behind the radical change in relative price? On the supply side, the main change is new technologies that allow greater production of nonconventional gas from shales, coal beds, and other sources. On the demand side, the change arises from greater environmental awareness on the part of consumers, regulations that encourage alternative fuels, and, yes, the rising price of oil.

So what is holding back widespread use of CNG, an off-the-shelf technology already in wide use elsewhere, for cars here in the United States? The main factor seems to be what economists call a *network problem*—in everyday terms, a chicken-and-egg issue. There are not enough filling stations that dispense natural gas. With the right kind of pump, filling you car's tank with CNG is just as quick and easy as using gasoline; however, it is not worth it for gas stations to install the pumps until there are lots of CNG-powered cars on the road. A few CNG cars, including a CNG-powered Honda, are already on the market, but demand will be limited until there are more filling stations.

However, the situation may be changing. One thing that helps is the availability of dual-fuel cars that will run on natural gas if it is available, but can switch to gasoline when it is not. Another is the increasing popularity of natural gas among long-haul truck drivers. Truck stops have found it worthwhile to invest in natural gas pumps even if neighborhood filling stations have not yet done so. A CNG-powered eighteen-wheeler can now make it coast to coast by following a chain of gas-dispensing truck stops. That will hasten the day when passenger cars will be able to do the same.

Sources: Ed Dolan's Econ Blog (http://dolanecon.blogspot.com), "Technology, Environment, and the Future of Natural Gas," Feb. 27, 2010, "Move Over Ethanol: Market Forces Favor CNG," March 16, 2011, and "What Is Holding Back Natural Gas as the Fuel of the Future?" Jan. 7, 2013. Used by permission of author.

Questions

1. Beginning from a position of equilibrium, use supply and demand curves to show how new technologies that reduce the cost of producing gas from unconventional deposits affect the market. Does the supply curve shift? The demand curve? Both? Explain.

2. Starting from the end point of your answer to Question 1, show the effects of increased consumer preference for alternative fuels. Does the supply curve shift? The demand curve? Both? Explain.

3. Environmentalists are concerned that producing natural gas by fracking may damage the environment. How would stricter regulations on fracking affect the market for natural gas? Would the supply curve shift? The demand curve? Both? Explain.

From Ed Dolan's Econ Blog

Ed Dolan's econ blog offers a wide selection of case studies in slideshow format. Each discusses recent events in a real-world market (chocolate, olive oil, CNG, and more) and shows how supply and demand curves can explain their effects. A list of available slideshows can be found at http://bvtlab.com/b998U, or scan the QR code.

CASE STUDIES

Index of Slideshows

Endnotes

1. Before continuing, you may want to review the Chapter 1 appendix, "Working with Graphs," especially the section entitled "Packing Three Variables into Two Dimensions."

2. The "plans" referred to need not be formal, or thought out in detail, and are subject to change. A consumer might, for example, make out a shopping list for the supermarket based on the usual prices for various foods, but then revise it to take into account unexpected price increases or sales on certain items. On specific occasions, consumer decisions may even be completely impulsive, with little basis in rational calculation. The model of supply and demand does not require people to base every decision on precise analysis; only that consumer intentions, on the average, are influenced by prices and other economic considerations.

3. Why might buyers and sellers enter the market expecting a price other than the one that permits equilibrium? It may be, for example, that market conditions have caused the supply or demand curve to shift unexpectedly, so that a price that formerly permitted equilibrium no longer does so; it may be that buyers or sellers expect conditions to change, but they do not change after all; or it may be that government policy has established a legal maximum or minimum price that differs from the equilibrium price. Later sections of the chapter will explore some of these possibilities.

CHAPTER 3

SUPPLY, DEMAND, AND ELASTICITY

AFTER READING THIS CHAPTER,
you will understand the following:

1. What economists mean by elasticity
2. The relationship of demand to revenue
3. How economists apply the concept of elasticity to changes in market conditions
4. How elasticity helps in understanding issues of public policy

BEFORE READING THIS CHAPTER,
make sure you know the following concepts:

Supply and demand

Demand, quantity demanded

Supply, quantity supplied

Substitutes and complements

Normal and inferior goods

CHAPTER
Outline

How much did you pay for this textbook? Did it cost more or less than the books you buy for other courses? As a student, you probably have a strong desire to pay less for your books if you can. Have you ever wondered why your professors sometimes choose books that cost so much?

This chapter will help you understand the effect of price on choices that people make among goods like textbooks, foods, or medical services. It will focus on *elasticity*, a concept economists use to describe how sensitive buyers are to prices. If you, like many students, pay for your own textbooks, you are probably highly sensitive to price—your demand is elastic, to use the economist's term. However, your professor, who does not personally pay for the books, may care less about how much they cost. Your professor's demand may be *inelastic*. In the following pages, you will learn how to define, measure, and apply the concept of elasticity.

3.1 ELASTICITY

We can express the responsiveness of quantity demanded to a change in price in many ways. Take demand for chicken, for example. If you read a discussion of the choices made by a typical American household, you might learn that an increase of $0.10 per pound would decrease consumption by one pound per month. A study done in France might show that a price increase of €1.00 per kilogram would decrease consumption of all consumers in the city of Lille by twenty-five thousand kilos per month. Are the findings of these studies similar? It is hard to tell, not just because the currencies and units of weight are different, but also because we don't know the starting points for the prices or quantities. Ten cents a pound is not a very large increase if it refers to premium organic, boneless chicken breasts that initially cost $5.49 a pound; but that same increase would be much more significant for commercial-grade chicken backs and necks intended for use in soup.

(iStock)

To cut through the confusion of different units of measurement and different starting points for changes, economists standardize by expressing all changes as percentages. For example it might turn out that the studies of both American and French consumers found that a 20 percent increase in price was associated with a 10 percent decrease in quantity demanded. It would then make no difference whether we recorded individual observations in dollars per pound, euros per kilo, or whatever.

Economists use the term **elasticity** to refer to the ratio of a change in one variable to a change in another, expressed as a percentage. This chapter introduces several applications of elasticity in economics.

3.1a Price Elasticity of Demand

The **price elasticity of demand** is the ratio of the percentage change in the quantity of a good demanded to a given percentage change in its price. Figure 3–1 presents five demand curves showing different degrees of price elasticity of demand. Notice that elasticity affects not only the shape of the curves but also the way a change in price affects the **revenue** that sellers earn from the good in question. (Revenue means the price of a good times the quantity sold.)

Elasticity

A measure of the ratio of a change in one variable to a change in another, expressed as a percentage

Price elasticity of demand

The ratio of the percentage change in the quantity of a good demanded to a given percentage change in its price, other things being equal

Revenue

Price multiplied by quantity sold

FIGURE 3–1

Price Elasticity of Demand

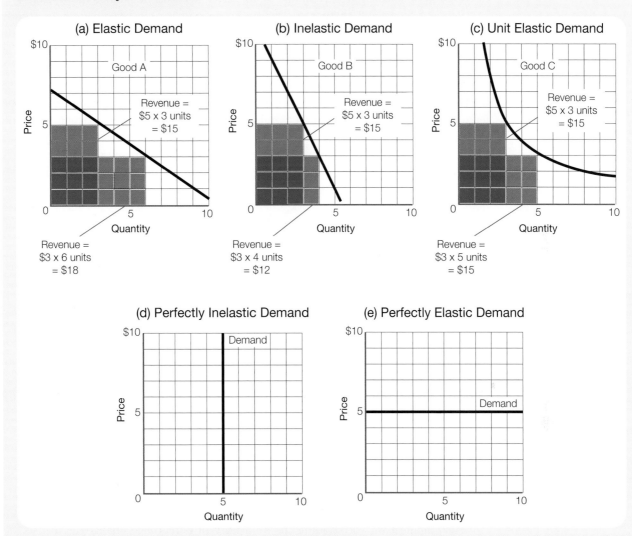

This figure shows five examples of demand curves with various degrees of elasticity over the indicated range of variation of price and quantity. The examples illustrate elastic, inelastic, unit elastic, perfectly inelastic, and perfectly elastic demand. The first three cases show the revenue change associated with a change in price. When demand is elastic, a price decrease causes revenue to increase. When demand is inelastic, a price decrease causes revenue to decrease. When demand is unit elastic, revenue does not change when price changes.

In Part (a) of Figure 3–1, the percentage change in quantity demanded is greater than the percentage change in price. In such a case we say that demand is **elastic**. Revenue before and after the changes in price is shown as the area of a rectangle drawn under the demand curve, with a height equal to price and a width equal to quantity demanded. When demand is elastic, a decrease in price causes revenue to increase: The seller's revenue after the price reduction ($3 per unit for 6 units = $18) is greater than it was before ($5 per unit for 3 units = $15).

Elastic demand

A situation in which quantity demanded changes by a larger percentage than price, so that total revenue increases as price decreases

In contrast, Part (b) of Figure 3–1 shows a case in which quantity demanded is only weakly responsive to a change in price. There, a $2 decrease in price, from $5 to $3 per unit, causes the quantity demanded to increase by just one unit—from three to four. Now the percentage change in quantity demanded is less than the change in price, so a decrease in price causes total revenue to fall. In such a case, demand is **inelastic**.

Part (c) shows still another possibility. There, a change in price causes an exactly proportional change in quantity demanded, so that total revenue does not change at all. When the percentage change in quantity demanded equals the percentage change in price, demand is **unit elastic**.

The final two parts of Figure 3–1 show two extreme cases. Part (d) shows a vertical demand curve. Regardless of the price, the quantity demanded is five units—no more, no less. Such a demand curve is **perfectly inelastic**. Part (e) shows a horizontal demand curve. Above a price of $5, the quantity demanded is zero; but as soon as the price drops to $5, there is no limit to how much buyers will purchase. A horizontal demand curve is **perfectly elastic**. The law of demand, which describes an inverse relationship between price and quantity, does not encompass the cases of perfectly elastic and inelastic demand, and we do not expect market demand curves for ordinary goods and services to fit these extremes. Nonetheless, perfectly elastic and inelastic curves sometimes provide useful reference points even if we rarely see them in the real world.

3.1b Calculating Elasticity of Demand

Inelastic demand

A situation in which quantity demanded changes by a smaller percentage than price, so that total revenue decreases as price decreases

Unit elastic demand

A situation in which price and quantity demanded change by the same percentage, so that total revenue remains unchanged as price changes

Perfectly inelastic demand

A situation in which the demand curve is a vertical line

Perfectly elastic demand

A situation in which the demand curve is a horizontal line

Sometimes it is enough to say that demand is elastic or inelastic, without being more precise. At other times, it is useful to give a numerical value for elasticity. This section outlines one of the most common ways to calculate the value of elasticity of demand.

The first step in turning the definition of elasticity into a formula is to specify a way of measuring percentage changes. The everyday method for calculating a percentage change is to use the initial value of the variable as the denominator and the change in the value as the numerator. For example suppose the quantity of California lettuce demanded in the national market is initially twelve thousand tons per week and then decreases to eight thousand tons per week. We then say there has been a 33 percent decrease ($4{,}000/12{,}000 = 0.33$) in quantity. The trouble with this convention is that the same change in the opposite direction gives a different percentage. Using the same everyday approach, an increase in the quantity of lettuce demanded from eight thousand tons per week to twelve thousand tons per week is a 50 percent increase ($4{,}000/8{,}000 = 0.5$).

The standard way of avoiding the ambiguity of percentage changes is to use the midpoint, rather than the beginning or end point, as the denominator. To find the midpoint, take the sum of the value before the change and the value after and then divide by two. In our example the midpoint of the quantity range is ten thousand ($[8{,}000 + 12{,}000]/2 = 10{,}000$). When we use that value as the denominator, a change of four thousand units, whether as an increase or a decrease, becomes a 40 percent change ($4{,}000/10{,}000 = 0.4$).

Using Q_1 to represent the quantity before the change and Q_2 to represent the quantity after the change, the midpoint formula for the percentage change in quantity is

$$\text{Percentage change in quantity} = \frac{Q_2 - Q_1}{(Q_1 + Q_2)/2}$$

We can use the same approach for price. Suppose that the price of lettuce increases by $200, from $700 per ton to $900 per ton. Using the midpoint of the range, or $800, as the denominator ([700 + 900]/2 = 800), we see that the price increases by 25 percent (200/800 = 0.25). The midpoint formula for the percentage change in price is

$$\text{Percentage change in price} = \frac{P_2 - P_1}{(P_1 + P_2)/2}$$

The Midpoint Formula for Elasticity Expressing both changes in price and quantity in this way allows us to write a complete midpoint formula for price elasticity of demand. Simplifying by omitting the terms "/2", which cancel out, the midpoint formula is

$$\text{Price elasticity of demand} = \frac{(Q_2 - Q_1)/(Q_1 + Q_2)}{(P_2 - P_1)/(P_1 + P_2)}$$

$$= \frac{\text{Percentage change in quantity}}{\text{Percentage change in price}}$$

If an increase in price from $700 per ton to $900 per ton causes the quantity of lettuce demanded to fall from twelve thousand tons to eight thousand tons, the complete calculations for the elasticity of demand are as follows:[1]

P_1 = price before change = $700

P_2 = price after change = $900

Q_1 = quantity before change = 12,000 tons

Q_2 = quantity after change = 8,000 tons

$$\text{Elasticity} = \frac{(8,000 - 12,000)/(8,000 + 12,000)}{(\$900 - \$700)/(\$700 + \$900)}$$

$$= \frac{-4,000/20,000}{200/1,600}$$

$$= \frac{-0.2}{0.125}$$

$$= -1.6$$

Because demand curves have negative slopes, price and quantity change in opposite directions. As a result, the midpoint formula gives a negative value for elasticity. When the price decreases, the term $(P_2 - P_1)$, which appears in the denominator of the formula, is negative, whereas the term $(Q_2 - Q_1)$, which appears in the numerator, is positive. When the price increases, the numerator is negative, and the denominator is positive. Sometimes economists use the minus sign when reporting price elasticity of demand, and sometimes they do not. In this book, we follow the common practice of dropping the minus sign when there is no ambiguity. We will use the minus sign only where there is a particular reason to call attention to the inverse relationship between price and quantity demanded.

Elasticity Numbers and Terminology   Earlier in the chapter, we defined *elastic, inelastic, unit elastic, perfectly elastic,* and *perfectly inelastic* demand. Each of those terms corresponds to a value or range of values of elasticity. A perfectly inelastic demand curve has a value of zero. There is no change in quantity demanded regardless of how great the change in price. *Inelastic demand* (but not perfectly inelastic) corresponds to values from zero up to, but not including, one. Unit elasticity means a numerical value of exactly one; the percentage change in quantity equals the percentage change in price. *Elastic demand* means any value for elasticity that is greater than one. *Perfectly elastic* demand, represented by a horizontal demand curve, is numerically undefined; as the demand curve approaches horizontal, the denominator of the elasticity formula approaches zero, and the measured value of elasticity increases without limit.

3.1c Varying- and Constant-Elasticity Demand Curves

The midpoint formula shows elasticity of demand over a certain range of prices and quantities. Measured over some other range, the elasticity of demand for the same good may be the same or different, depending on the shape of the demand curve, as shown in Figure 3–2.

Part (a) of Figure 3–2 shows a demand curve that, like most of those in this book, is a straight line. The elasticity of demand is not constant for all points along the curve. For example, over the price range $8 to $9, elasticity is 5.66, but over the range $2 to $3, it is 0.33. (The figure shows the calculations.)

The calculations illustrate the general rule that elasticity decreases as one moves down and to the right along a straight-line demand curve. It is easy to see why. When the demand curve is a straight line, a $1 reduction in price always causes the same absolute increase in quantity demanded. At the upper end of the curve, a $1 change is a small percentage of the relatively high price, while the change in quantity is a large percentage of the relatively low quantity demanded. At the lower end, the situation is reversed: A $1 change is a large percentage of the relatively low price, while the increase in quantity is smaller in relation to the relatively larger quantity demanded.

Demand curves do not always have to be straight lines. There is an important special case in which the demand curve has just the shape needed to keep elasticity constant over its entire length. Part (b) of Figure 3–2 shows such a curve. As the figure shows, elasticity is 1.0 at every point on that curve. It is possible to construct demand curves with constant elasticities of any value. Statistical studies of demand elasticity often use constant-elasticity demand curves as a simplifying approximation.

3.1d Determinants of Elasticity of Demand

The fact that elasticity may vary along the demand curve means that we must take care in making general statements about the elasticity of demand for a good. In practice what such statements usually refer to is the elasticity, measured by the midpoint formula or some other method, over the range of price variation that is usual in the normal course of business. With that understanding, we can generalize about what makes the demand for some goods elastic and the demand for others inelastic.

Substitutes, Complements, and Elasticity   One important determinant of elasticity of demand is the availability of substitutes. When a good has close substitutes, the demand for it tends to be elastic because people willingly switch to the substitutes when the price of the good goes up. For example the demand for corn oil is elastic because consumers can easily substitute other cooking oils. On the other hand the demand for cigarettes is inelastic because, for a habitual smoker, there is no good substitute.

FIGURE 3–2

Elasticity at Various Points Along a Demand Curve

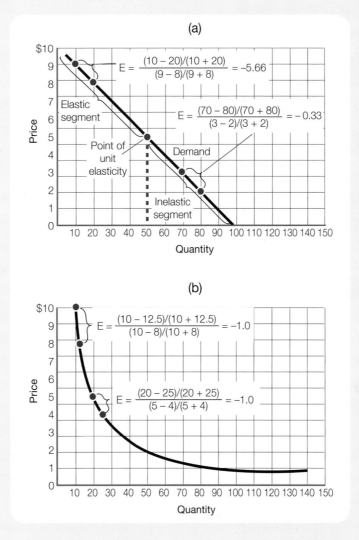

(a)

$$E = \frac{(10-20)/(10+20)}{(9-8)/(9+8)} = -5.66$$

$$E = \frac{(70-80)/(70+80)}{(3-2)/(3+2)} = -0.33$$

Elastic segment

Point of unit elasticity

Demand

Inelastic segment

(b)

$$E = \frac{(10-12.5)/(10+12.5)}{(10-8)/(10+8)} = -1.0$$

$$E = \frac{(20-25)/(20+25)}{(5-4)/(5+4)} = -1.0$$

Elasticity varies along a straight-line demand curve, as Part (a) of this figure illustrates. At the upper end of the curve, where the price is relatively high, a $1 change in price is a relatively small percentage change. Because the quantity demanded is low, the corresponding percentage change in quantity is relatively large. That makes demand elastic near the top of the demand curve. At the lower end of the curve, the opposite is true: A $1 change in price is now a relatively large percentage change, and the corresponding percentage change in quantity is smaller. Demand is inelastic. As Part (b) shows, we can also draw a demand curve with such a shape that elasticity is constant at all prices and quantities.

This principle has two corollaries. One is that the demand for a good tends to be more elastic the narrower the definition of the good. For example the demand for coffee, as a whole, is inelastic. However, the demand for Colombian coffee is likely to be elastic because, if the price of that particular type rises, people can switch to similar coffee from Nicaragua or Sumatra.

The other corollary is that demand for the product of a single firm tends to be more elastic than the demand for the output of all producers operating in the market. As one example, as a whole, the demand for soap will be less elastic than the demand for any particular brand. The reason is that consumers can substitute one brand for another when the price of a brand changes.

The complements of a good can also play a role in determining its elasticity. If something is a minor complement to a good that accounts for a large share of consumers' budgets, demand for it tends to be inelastic. For example the demand for motor oil tends to be inelastic because it is a complement to a more important good, gasoline. The price of gasoline has a greater effect on the amount of driving a person does than the price of motor oil.

Textbook prices are opportunity costs for students. (Dreamstime)

Price Versus Opportunity Cost   Elasticity measures the responsiveness of quantity demanded to the price of a good. In most cases the price, in money, is an accurate indicator of opportunity cost; but that is not always the case. We mentioned one example at the beginning of the chapter: The price of a textbook is an opportunity cost to the student who buys it, but it is not an opportunity cost to the professor who assigns it. The reason is that the students pay for the book, not the professor. As a result publishers have traditionally assumed that professors will pay little attention to the price of the text, and demand will be highly inelastic. However, in recent years students have increasingly been making their influence felt, so the price elasticity of demand for textbooks may be increasing.

Medical care is another market where the responsibility for choice does not lie with the party who bears the opportunity cost. Doctors choose what drug to offer to patients, but either the patient or the patient's insurance company pays for the drug. That sometimes leads doctors to prescribe expensive brand-name drugs when cheaper generic drugs are available to do the same job. The separation between the party who makes the decision and the one who bears the opportunity cost is one factor that makes the demand for many drugs highly inelastic.

Business travel is still another example of the separation of price and opportunity cost. Business travelers do not pay for their own airline tickets, hotels, and meals. As a result, their demand for these services tends to be inelastic. When vacationers purchase the same services, they bear the full opportunity cost. Not surprisingly, business travelers often choose more expensive options, such as first-class seats. Often airlines and hotels take advantage of the separation of price and opportunity cost by charging different rates to business and vacation travelers.

Time Horizon and Elasticity   Still another determinant of elasticity of demand is the time horizon within which buyers make their decisions. For several reasons, demand is typically less elastic in the short run, when consumers have less time to adapt to a change in the price of a good, than in the long run, when they have time to adjust their behavior more fully.

One reason is that full adjustment to a change in the price of one good may require changes in the kind or quantity of other goods that a consumer buys. For example, when the price of gasoline rises, people can cut out some nonessential driving; but the total quantity of gasoline demanded is only slightly affected. Econometricians have estimated short-run demand elasticity for gasoline at about 0.25. Over time, though, consumers can adjust to a higher price in several ways. They can buy fewer fuel-hungry SUVs and more higher-mileage hybrid cars. They can change their jobs or move in order to shorten their daily commute. They can switch to public transportation, if it is available. Estimates for the long-run demand for gasoline are in the range of about 0.6 to 0.8, considerably higher than the short-run elasticity.

Another reason elasticity tends to be greater in the long run is that an increase in the price of one good encourages entrepreneurs to develop substitutes. The availability of substitutes, in turn, makes demand more elastic. Consider the response to what some people call America's first energy crisis. In the early nineteenth century, whale oil was widely used as lamp fuel. As heavy hunting reduced the whale population, the price of whale oil rose. Over time the high price of whale oil spurred entrepreneurs to develop a better substitute, kerosene. Once kerosene came onto the market, the quantity of whale oil demanded for lamp fuel dropped to zero. Today market forces are spurring the development of many alternative forms of energy, ranging from compressed natural gas as a motor fuel to wind, wave, and solar energy for generating electricity.

A final reason for greater long-run elasticity of demand is the slow adjustment of consumer tastes. The case of beef and chicken, featured in the preceding chapter, provides an example. Chicken, originally the more expensive meat, achieved a price advantage over beef many years ago, but eating lots of beef was a habit. Gradually, as chicken developed an image as a healthy, versatile food, it overtook beef as the number-one meat in the United States.

3.1e Income Elasticity of Demand

The relationship of quantity demanded to price is the most common application of elasticity, but by no means the only one. We can also use elasticity to express the response of demand to changes in any of the conditions covered by the "other things being equal" assumption that underlies a demand curve. The response of demand to changes in consumer income is an important example.

The **income elasticity of demand** for a good is the ratio of the percentage change in the quantity demanded to a percentage change in income, assuming no change in price. Using Q_1 and Q_2 to represent quantities before and after the change in income and y_1 and y_2 to represent income before and after the change, we can write the midpoint formula for income elasticity of demand as follows:

$$\text{Income elasticity of demand} = \frac{(Q_2 - Q_1)/(Q_1 + Q_2)}{(y_2 - y_1)/(y_1 + y_2)}$$

$$= \frac{\text{Percentage change in quantity}}{\text{Percentage change in income}}$$

For a normal good, an increase in income causes demand to increase. Because income and demand change in the same direction, the income elasticity of demand for a normal good is positive. For an inferior good, an increase in income causes demand to decrease. Because income and demand change in opposite directions, the income elasticity of demand for an inferior good is negative.

Income elasticity of demand

The ratio of the percentage change in the quantity of a good demanded to a given percentage change in consumer incomes, other things being equal

Some of the considerations that determine price elasticity also affect income elasticity. In particular, whether a good is normal or inferior depends on how narrowly we define it and on the availability of substitutes. For example one group of researchers looked at the demand for frozen orange juice.[2] Orange juice, considered as a broad category, is a normal good; people tend to consume more of it as their incomes rise. However, when the definition is narrowed so that house-brand and national-brand frozen orange juice are treated as separate products, the house-brand product turns out to be an inferior good. As their incomes rise, consumers substitute the higher-quality national brands, which have a positive income elasticity of demand.

3.1f Cross Elasticity of Demand

Another condition that can cause a change in the demand for a good is a change in the price of some other good. Changes in the price of beef affect the demand for chicken, changes in the price of gasoline affect the demand for SUVs, and so on. The **cross elasticity of demand** for a good is the ratio of the percentage change in the quantity demanded of that good to a given percentage change in the price of another good. The midpoint formula for cross elasticity of demand looks just like the one for price elasticity of demand, except that the numerator shows the percentage change in the quantity of one good while the denominator shows the percentage change in the price of some other good.

Cross elasticity of demand provides a way of measuring the relationships of substitutes and complements. Because lettuce and cabbage are substitutes, an increase in the price of cabbage causes an increase in the quantity of lettuce demanded; the cross elasticity of demand is positive. Because SUVs and gasoline are complements, an increase in the price of gasoline causes a decrease in the quantity of SUVs demanded; the cross elasticity of demand is negative. The previously mentioned study of frozen orange juice found a positive cross elasticity of demand between house-brand and national-brand juices, indicating that the two are substitutes.

3.1g Price Elasticity of Supply

Elasticity applies to supply as well as demand. The **price elasticity of supply** of a good is the percentage change in the quantity of the good supplied divided by the percentage change in its price. The midpoint formula for calculating price elasticity of supply looks like the one for determining price elasticity of demand, but the Qs in the numerator of the formula now refer to quantity *supplied* rather than quantity *demanded*. Because price and quantity change in the same direction along a positively sloped supply curve, the formula gives a positive value for the elasticity of supply. Figure 3–3 applies the elasticity formula to two supply curves, one with constant elasticity and the other with variable elasticity.

As in the case of demand, several considerations can affect elasticity of supply, including the time horizon allowed for the adjustment of supply. In recent years the development of oil fields in North Dakota has increased the demand for transportation facilities. In the short run the supply of trucks to haul oil is elastic, since the oil industry can bid trucks and drivers away from other uses. The supply of pipelines is much less elastic, at least in the short run; but over a period of years, the regional pipeline network is slowly growing.

Cross elasticity of demand

The ratio of the percentage change in the quantity of a good demanded to a given percentage change in the price of some other good, other things being equal

Price elasticity of supply

The ratio of the percentage change in the quantity of a good supplied to a given percentage change in its price, other things being equal

Development of North Dakota oil fields has increased demand for transportation both by truck and by pipeline.
(Shutterstock)

FIGURE 3–3

Calculating Price Elasticity of Supply

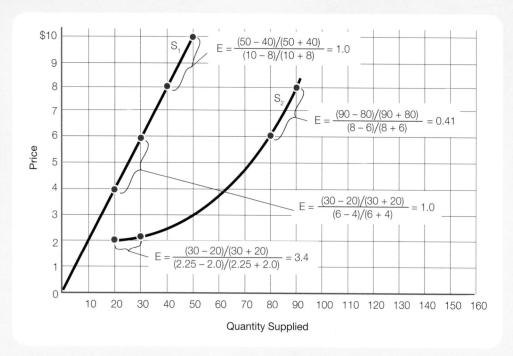

This figure gives four examples of the way price elasticity of supply is calculated. The figure gives price elasticity of supply for two ranges on each of the two supply curves. Supply curve S_1, which is a straight line passing through the origin, has a constant elasticity of 1.0. Supply curve S_2, which is not a straight line, is elastic for small quantities and inelastic for larger ones.

3.2 APPLICATIONS OF ELASTICITY

Elasticity has many applications in both macro- and microeconomics. In macroeconomics it applies to financial markets, to the aggregate supply and demand for all goods and services, and to foreign-exchange markets, to name just a few. In microeconomics elasticity plays a role in discussions of consumer behavior, business behavior, and government policy. We conclude this chapter with two examples.

3.2a Gas Tax or Mileage Standards?

For many years, the US government has gradually been increasing its Corporate Average Fuel Economy standard (CAFE standard) for passenger cars. The standard is currently scheduled to reach 54.0 miles per gallon (mpg) by 2025. The new standard will be almost double the 27.5 mpg in force in the 1990s and early 2000s.

Many economists agree that some government policy to discourage excessive fuel consumption is a good idea. Using gasoline and diesel fuel on the highway has many undesirable spillover effects. Pollution, both in the form of local smog and global climate change, is one concern. National security problems stemming from dependence on oil

The US government's Corporate Average Fuel Economy standard for passenger cars is scheduled to rise to 54.0 mpg by 2025. (Shutterstock)

from unstable and unfriendly countries are another. Highway congestion and wear and tear on roads and bridges are still others. But are CAFE standards the best way to reduce fuel consumption? Or would an increase in the federal gasoline tax work better? It turns out that the answer depends, in part, on the price elasticity of demand for motor fuel.

The fundamental problem with CAFE standards is that they attack the spillover effects of fuel use only partially and indirectly. As a result, the cost of achieving a given reduction in fuel use via CAFE standards is higher than the cost of reaching the same goal through a tax increase.

To understand why, we need to consider the various ways consumers can cut back on fuel use. In the short run they can buy an efficient hybrid instead of a gas-guzzling SUV; they can reduce discretionary driving; or they can shift some trips from their Ford F-250® to their Honda®, if they happen to have one of each in the driveway. Given more time to adjust, they can make work and lifestyle changes, such as moving closer to public transportation, work, and shopping; changing jobs; or working at home.

Higher fuel prices directly affect all of these choices. They encourage people to make the marginal adjustments that best suit their circumstances. CAFE standards, in contrast, encourage fuel saving only with regard to the choice of what car to buy. Once a consumer buys a low-mileage vehicle, the cost of driving an extra mile goes down. That actually reduces the incentive for fuel-saving measures like moving closer to work, working at home, riding the bus to work, or consolidating errands.

Economists call the tendency of more fuel-efficient vehicles to induce additional driving the "rebound effect." The size of the rebound effect depends directly on the elasticity of demand for driving. For example suppose that the elasticity of demand based on fuel-cost per mile is 0.3. If so, a 10 percent decrease in the price of gasoline would cause a 3 percent increase in miles driven—but so would a 10 percent increase in fuel efficiency, assuming no change in fuel prices. The increased miles driven would partly offset the increase in miles per gallon, so that total fuel consumption would decrease by only about 7 percent in response to a 10 percent increase in fuel efficiency.

Even taking the rebound effect into account, higher CAFE standards are still somewhat helpful in reducing spillover effects that are proportional to the quantities of fuel consumed, including pollution and national security concerns. However, the rebound effect causes an increase in those externalities that are proportional to miles driven, including road congestion, traffic accidents, and road maintenance.

What is more, the very fuel-saving strategies that CAFE standards discourage, like moving closer to work or consolidating errands, are often the ones that have the lowest costs. That is why the total cost of reaching a given national fuel-saving target will be greater when achieved through CAFE standards than through fuel taxes. A 2004 study from the Congressional Budget Office concluded that an increase in the federal gasoline tax would achieve a given reduction in fuel economy at a cost 27 percent less than that of an equivalent tightening of CAFE standards. Furthermore its effects would come more quickly because they would not have to wait for the gradual turnover of the national motor vehicle fleet. Over the fourteen-year time horizon of the CBO study, the gas tax increase would save 42 percent more total fuel.

We see, then, that the relative merits of CAFE standards versus fuel taxes depend critically on the price elasticity of demand for fuel. Studies indicate that the short-run elasticity of demand for gasoline is probably around 0.3 and the long-run elasticity lies in a range of –0.4 to –0.8. These estimates imply that the rebound effect is strong, especially in the long run—a finding that weakens the case for CAFE standards.[3]

All this leaves one last question: If the economics of elasticity show that CAFE standards are a bad idea, why do they remain so popular? If you are an economist, choosing higher fuel taxes over CAFE standards looks like a no-brainer; but if you are a politician, fuel taxes have an obvious drawback. Fuel taxes make the cost of reducing consumption highly visible. You see the big dollars-per-gallon number right there in front of you every time you drive up to the pump. CAFE standards, in contrast, hide the cost. You pay the price of a higher-mileage car only when you buy a new one; and, even then, the part of the price attributable to the mileage-enhancing features is not broken out as a separate item on the sticker. You may notice that your new car costs more than your old one did, but there are lots of other reasons for that besides fuel economy.

It is a classic case of the TANSTAAFL principle—There Ain't No Such Thing As A Free Lunch. If you try to make something look like it is free, it only ends up costing more in the long run. If you are a politician, you may well prefer a big hidden cost to a small visible cost. If you are a friend of the environment, you should know better.

3.2b Elasticity and Prohibition

The previous case showed how a tax or regulation could reduce the use of a product whose consumption has undesired spillover effects. Prohibition is a more extreme policy to accomplish the same end. The ultimate goal of prohibition is to reduce the quantity sold to zero. Alcoholic beverages were subject to prohibition in the United States during the 1920s; drugs like heroin and cocaine are subject to prohibition today. Environmental regulations sometimes also rely on prohibition. For example, regulations do not just tax the use of the pesticide DDT and lead additives for gasoline—they completely prohibit them.

On the surface, a policy of prohibition may seem very different from a tax. However, a closer economic analysis reveals similarities as well as differences between taxation and prohibition.

First, passage of a law prohibiting production and sale of a good does not make it impossible to supply the good—it simply makes it more expensive to do so. After the prohibition is in effect, the supplier must consider not only the direct costs of production but also the extra costs of covert transportation and distribution systems, the risk of fines or jail terms, the costs of hiring armed gangsters to protect illegal laboratories, and so on. From the lawbreaking supplier's point of view, these costs are an implicit tax. If the price rises by enough to cover them, lawbreakers will still supply the good. Thus the effect of prohibition of a good is to shift its supply curve to the left until each point on the new supply curve lies above the corresponding point on the old curve by a distance equal to the extra costs associated with evading the prohibition.

Second, the effects of the prohibition, like those of a tax, depend on the elasticities of demand and supply. Figure 3–4 illustrates this point by comparing the effects of prohibition on the US markets for DDT and cocaine. The demand for DDT is shown as elastic because effective substitutes are available at a price only a little higher than the banned pesticide. The demand for cocaine is inelastic—in part because once people become addicted, they will find it hard to cut back on their use of the drug even if its price rises sharply.

In the case of elastic demand for DDT (Part (a) of Figure 3–4), even a weakly enforced prohibition, which raises costs of illegal supply only a little, will sharply reduce the quantity sold. Such a weak prohibition, represented by a shift in the supply curve from S_1 to S_2, is already enough to reduce the total revenue earned by producers (price multiplied by quantity sold) from \$14,000 per week to \$8,500 per week. A more vigorously enforced prohibition, as represented by supply curve S_3, raises the cost of supply by enough to eliminate use of the product altogether. In practice, the DDT prohibition in the

FIGURE 3–4

Elasticity and the Effects of Prohibition

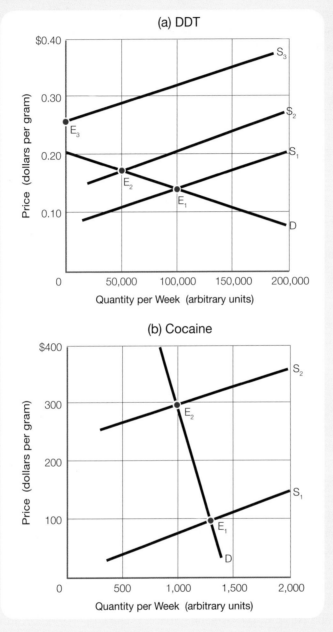

A law prohibiting production and sale of a good, like a tax on the good, shifts its supply curve to the left. The new supply curve will lie above the old supply curve at any given quantity by a distance equal to the cost of evading the prohibition. The effects on price, quantity, and revenue depend on the elasticity of demand. Part (a) uses DDT to illustrate prohibition of a good with elastic demand. A weakly enforced prohibition (S_2) raises the price, reduces the quantity, and reduces total revenue earned by producers from sale of the product. A strongly enforced prohibition reduces quantity and revenue to zero (S_3). Part (b) uses cocaine to illustrate prohibition of a good with inelastic demand. In this case even strong efforts to enforce prohibition do not reduce quantity sold to zero. Because quantity sold increases by a smaller percentage than price increases, there is an increased total revenue and expenditure on the good.

United States is almost 100 percent effective, although one hears scattered reports of a tiny black market, fueled partly by people who think it is effective in combating bedbugs.

In the case of cocaine, even a strongly enforced prohibition has a small effect on quantity sold. By the nature of the market, it is hard to get accurate price and quantity data for illegal drugs; however, the few studies that have been done suggest a short-run price elasticity of about 0.5 to 0.7. Accordingly, in Part (b) of Figure 3–4, as prohibition shifts the supply curve to S_2, total revenue from the sale of cocaine rises sharply—from $130,000 per week at equilibrium E_1 to $300,000 per week at equilibrium E_2. As long as demand is inelastic, increasing strictness of enforcement, which drives the supply curve still higher, will make the sales revenue of drug suppliers increase still further.

Drugs like heroin and cocaine are subject to prohibition in the United States. (Wikimedia Commons)

Elasticity of demand is important in understanding the intended and unintended consequences of prohibition. The intended consequence, of course, is to reduce or eliminate use of the product. As we can see, the more elastic the demand for the product, the more successful the policy of prohibition is in achieving its intended effects. The unintended effects of prohibition are those associated with the change in revenue that the policy produces. These are very different in the case of elastic and inelastic demand.

Where demand is elastic, there is a moderate loss of revenue to DDT producers and a small rise in the cost of growing crops as farmers switch to more expensive pesticides. Neither has major social consequences. Chemical companies offset the loss of revenue from producing DDT by increased revenue from production of substitutes. The benefits of a cleaner environment offset the increased cost of growing crops.

On the other hand, where demand is inelastic, the intended consequences are smaller and the unintended consequences greater. With inelastic demand, prohibition increases total expenditure on the banned product. The social consequences may be severe. First, users of cocaine must spend more to sustain their habit. At best this means impoverishing themselves and their families; at worst it means an increase in muggings and armed robberies by users desperate for cash. Second, we must also consider the impact of the prohibition on suppliers. For suppliers, the increase in revenue does not just mean an increase in profit (although profits may increase) but also an increase in expenditures devoted to evading prohibition. In part the result is simply wasteful, as when drug suppliers build special submersible boats that they discard after a single one-way smuggling voyage rather than shipping their product cheaply by normal transportation methods. Worse, some of suppliers' increased expenditures take the form of hiring armies of thugs to battle the police and other suppliers, further raising the level of violence on city streets, or bribing government officials, thereby corrupting the quality of government.

The issue of drug prohibition, of course, involves many normative issues that reach far beyond the concept of elasticity. One such issue is whether people have a right to harm themselves through consumption of substances like tobacco, alcohol, or cocaine, or whether, instead, the government has a duty to act paternalistically to prevent such harm. Another concerns the relative emphasis that should be placed on prohibition versus treatment in allocating resources to reduce drug use. The analysis given here cannot answer such questions. However, it does suggest that the law of unintended consequences applies in the area of drug policy, and that elasticity of demand is important in shaping those consequences.

Summary

1. **What do economists mean by elasticity?**

   Elasticity is the responsiveness of quantity demanded or supplied to changes in the price of a good (or changes in other factors), measured as a ratio of the percentage change in quantity to the percentage change in price (or another factor causing the change in quantity). The *price elasticity of demand* between two points on a demand curve is the percentage change in quantity demanded divided by the percentage change in the good's price.

2. **What is the relationship of demand to revenue?**

   If the demand for a good is elastic, a decrease in its price will increase total revenue. If it is inelastic, an increase in its price will increase total revenue. When the demand for a good is unit elastic, revenue will remain constant as the price varies.

3. **How do economists apply elasticity to changes in market conditions?**

   We can apply the concept of elasticity to many situations besides movements along demand curves. The *income elasticity of demand* for a good is the ratio of the percentage change in quantity demanded to a given percentage change in income. The *cross elasticity of demand* between goods A and B is the ratio of the percentage change in the quantity of good A demanded to a given percentage change in the price of good B. The *price elasticity of supply* is the ratio of the percentage change in the quantity of a good supplied to a given change in its price.

4. **How does elasticity help in understanding changes in public policy?**

   Many issues of public policy depend on how responsive demand or supply is to changes in price. One example is the choice of mileage standards or higher fuel prices as a means of decreasing motor fuel use. Higher elasticity of demand would favor price mechanisms; lower elasticity would favor mileage standards. Prohibition is another example where elasticity is important. Prohibition is more likely to have harmful unexpected consequences when demand is inelastic.

Key Terms

PROBLEMS AND TOPICS FOR DISCUSSION

1. **Time horizon and elasticity**   Suppose a virus infects the California lettuce crop, cutting production by half. Consider three time horizons: (a) The "very short" run means a period that is too short to allow farmers to change the amount of lettuce that they plant. No matter what happens to the price, the quantity supplied will be the amount already planted, less the amount destroyed by the virus. (b) The "intermediate" run means a period that is long enough to allow farmers to plant more fields in lettuce, but not long enough to permit them to develop new varieties of lettuce, introduce new methods of cultivation, or acquire new specialized equipment. (c) The "long" run means a period that is long enough to allow farmers to develop new varieties of virus-resistant lettuce and improve cultivation techniques. Discuss these three time horizons in terms of the price elasticity of supply. Sketch a figure showing supply curves for each time horizon.

2. **Calculating elasticity**   Draw a set of coordinate axes on a piece of graph paper. Label the horizontal axis from 0 to 50 units and the vertical axis from $0 to $20 per unit. Draw a demand curve that intersects the vertical axis at $10 and the horizontal axis at 40 units. Draw a supply curve that intersects the vertical axis at $4 and has a slope of 1. Make the following calculations for these curves, using the midpoint formula:

    a.   What is the price elasticity of demand over the price range $5 to $7?

    b.   What is the price elasticity of demand over the price range $1 to $3?

    c.   What is the price elasticity of supply over the price range $10 to $15?

    d.   What is the price elasticity of supply over the price range $15 to $17?

3. **Elasticity and revenue**   Look at the demand curve given in Figure 2–1 of the preceding chapter. Make a third column in the table that gives revenue for each price-quantity combination shown. Draw a set of axes on a piece of graph paper. Label the horizontal axis as in Figure 2–1, and label the vertical axis from $0 to $5 billion of revenue in increments of $1 billion. Graph the relationship between quantity and revenue using the column you added to the table. Discuss the relationship of your revenue graph to the demand curve, keeping in mind what you know about elasticity and revenue and about variation in elasticity along the demand curve.

4. **Elasticity of demand and revenue**   Assume that you are an officer of your campus theater club. You are at a meeting called to discuss ticket prices. One member says, "What I hate to see most of all is empty seats in the theater. We sell out every weekend performance, but there are always empty seats on Wednesdays. If we cut our Wednesday night prices by enough to fill up the theater, we'd bring in more money." Would this tactic really bring in more revenue? What would you need to know in order to be sure? Draw diagrams to illustrate some of the possibilities.

5. **Cross elasticity of demand**   In recent years the price of natural gas in the United States has fallen to a record low relative to the prices of fossil fuels, including coal. Over the same period the share of US electricity output generated by gas has increased and output generated by coal has fallen. What do these facts suggest to you about the cross elasticity of demand between coal and gas? Illustrate your answer with a pair of diagrams showing the market for coal and that for natural gas. Which supply curves would have needed to shift to produce results consistent with the reported facts? Which demand curves? Why?

CASE *for* DISCUSSION

Does a Higher Price Promote Energy Efficiency? Results from a Natural Experiment in New York City

What does the demand curve for electricity look like? If we ask the question in the abstract, not everyone would agree.

Some people might say, "It's obvious. If the price goes up, people use less; if it goes down, they use more. Like this." Then they grab a pencil and draw a negatively sloped straight line that looks just like the demand curves they remember from their college econ textbook.

No, not so fast! Other people might say, "I agree that people are going to use more when the price is lower, but I'm not so sure about that straight line. It seems to me that if the price gets really low—for example, if electricity were completely free—there would be no limit to how much they would use. The demand curve is more likely to look like this." Then they would take their own pencil and draw a curved line that flattens out as it approaches the horizontal axis—one that looks like what economists call a constant elasticity demand curve.

"Nonsense," still other people might say. "Electricity is a necessity in the modern world. Raising the price wouldn't do any good for promoting conservation. Rich people can afford to use as much as they want no matter what it costs, and poor people would still need electricity to run refrigerators and other necessities of life. Raising the price would just make them even poorer." Someone from this third group would draw the demand curve as a vertical line.

Who is right? Fortunately, in this case, we don't have to guess. We have a natural experiment based on the experience of New York City apartments. About 1.75 million apartments in New York have electric meters. The average rate per kilowatt-hour is about $0.21. Yet about 250,000 apartments have no electric meters. People who live in those apartments have unlimited electric power included in the rent. The price for them is effectively zero.

The people who live in unmetered apartments do use more electricity than those with meters. "My A.C. is pretty much running 24/7," says a 28-year-old TV producer with no meter, who likes to keep a cool apartment for his cat. In another unmetered apartment, a young couple recently left their A.C. on for four days in July when they left town for a funeral. They wanted to come home to a cool apartment.

Still, there is a limit to wasteful use. Total electric consumption in unmetered apartments is only about 30 percent greater than use in metered apartments.

Source: Based in part on "A Natural Experiment in Demand Elasticity: Metered vs. Unmetered Electricity," Ed Dolan's Econ Blog, Aug. 17, 2010 (http://dolanecon.blogspot.com/2010/08/natural-experiment-in-demand-elasticity.html). Used by permission of author. Quotations and data from Sam Dolnick, "Air-Conditioners That Run When Nobody's Home," *New York Times*, Aug. 16, 2010, p. A13.

Questions

1. What value of price elasticity of demand for electricity is assumed by people who draw the vertical demand curve? What evidence from the New York "experiment" is consistent with this hypothesis? What evidence is inconsistent?

2. What is assumed about price elasticity of demand by the people who draw the negatively sloped straight-line demand curve? Does the elasticity of demand increase, decrease, or remain the same as the price approaches zero? What evidence from the New York "experiment" is consistent with this hypothesis? What evidence is inconsistent?

3. What is assumed about price elasticity of demand by the people who draw the curved demand curve that does not intersect the horizontal axis? What evidence from the New York "experiment" is consistent with this hypothesis? What evidence is inconsistent?

4. On balance, which of the three hypotheses about electricity demand does the New York "experiment" best support?

From Ed Dolan's Econ Blog

Ed Dolan's econ blog offers several slideshows that use the concept of elasticity to help explain what is happening in real-world markets. One of them examines the effects of legalization of marijuana in Colorado, Washington, and other states: http://bvtlab.com/79bG8.

Another looks at the market for guar, a strange substance that, surprisingly, is a key ingredient both for ice cream and for the fluids used in fracking for oil and gas: http://bvtlab.com/FmUh9.

And a third discusses China's near-monopoly on rare earth metals, which are essential ingredients in many high-tech products: http://bvtlab.com/6g34t.

SLIDESHOWS

The Economics of Legal Marijuana Markets

Supply and Demand: Will Fracking Enrich India's Guar Farmers?

China's Fragile Rare Earth Monopoly

Endnotes

1. The midpoint formula (also sometimes called arc elasticity) is not the only one for calculating elasticity. A drawback of that formula is that it can give misleading elasticity values if applied over too wide a range of price or quantity. Because of that limitation, the midpoint formula works best over small ranges of price or quantity. A more precise approach gives a value for elasticity for a single point on the demand curve. For a linear demand curve having the formula $q = a - bp$ (with q representing quantity demanded, p the price, and a and b constants), the point formula for elasticity of demand (stated, as elsewhere, as a positive number) is

$$\text{Elasticity} = \frac{bp}{(a - bp)}$$

2. Jonq-Ying Lee, Mark G. Brown, and Brooke Schwartz, "The Demand for National Brand and Private Label Frozen Concentrated Orange Juice: A Switching Regression Analysis," *Western Journal of Agricultural Economics* (July 1986): 1–7.

3. For more estimates and sources related to elasticity and CAFE standards, see Ed Dolan, "Is a 56.4 Fuel Economy Standard Really a Good Idea?" *Ed Dolan's Econ Blog*, July 15, 2011. http://bvtlab.com/vP58D

PART 2

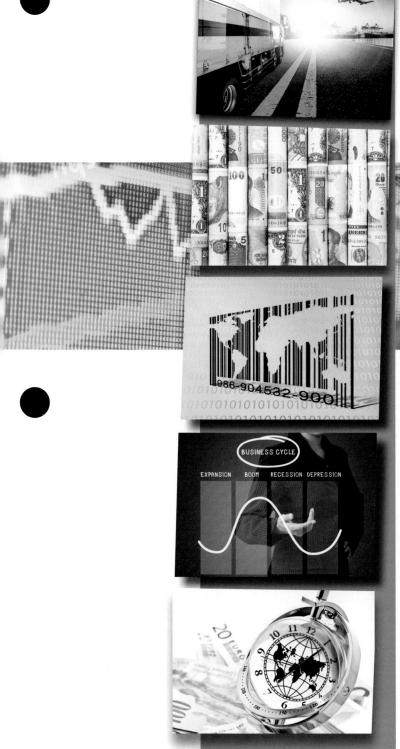

An Overview of Macroeconomics

CHAPTER 4

IN SEARCH OF PROSPERITY AND STABILITY

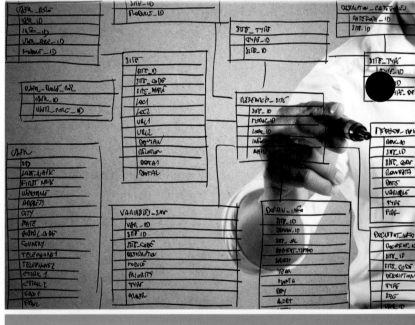

AFTER READING THIS CHAPTER,
you will understand the following:

1. The meaning and origins of economic growth
2. The nature of the business cycle
3. The meaning of unemployment and its importance for economic policy
4. The meaning of inflation and its impact on the economy

BEFORE READING THIS CHAPTER,
make sure you know the following concepts:

Production possibility frontier   **Factors of production**

CHAPTER
Outline

Many economists date the beginning of their discipline from the publication, in 1776, of Adam Smith's book *The Wealth of Nations* (see *Who Said It? Who Did It? 1.2*). The question that Smith raises—why some nations prosper while others lag behind—remains a central focus of macroeconomic policy.

In the early 2000s, prosperity was widespread. A booming financial sector powered growth and job creation in the United States. China's export-led economy grew by more than 10 percent per year. Energy producers like Russia and the Persian Gulf states piled up large surpluses. Then, beginning in 2007, things started to go wrong. A downturn that began in the financial and construction sectors of the US economy spread rapidly through much of the world. As the economies of the leading industrialized countries slowed down, demand for Chinese manufactured goods and Middle Eastern oil collapsed. As output fell, unemployment rose. The downturn has come to be known as the **Great Recession**. Since that time, prosperity has become more elusive. The US economy gradually recovered to pre-recession levels of output and employment, but much of Europe has failed to do so. China's growth has slowed, although it still remains faster than that of the world's advanced economies. A collapse in the prices of oil and other basic commodities has brought instability to countries ranging from Russia to Venezuela to Saudi Arabia.

This chapter begins the exploration of macroeconomics by looking at the forces that shape prosperity and stability in the long run and those that cause short-run, cyclical disturbances like the recent global crisis.

4.1 MACROECONOMICS IN THE LONG RUN: ECONOMIC GROWTH

Great Recession

An informal term for the period of low economic activity that began in December 2007

Gross domestic product (GDP)

A measure of the value of total output of goods and services produced within a nation's borders

Real

In economics, a term that refers to data that have been adjusted for the effects of inflation

Nominal

In economics, a term that refers to data that have not been adjusted for the effects of inflation

Real output

A synonym for real gross domestic product

No country becomes wealthy overnight. Nations that are prosperous have become so as the result of steady growth over periods of decades and even centuries. On the whole, as Figure 4–1 shows, emerging and developing economies have grown more rapidly in recent years than those that are already developed. Poorer countries (like India, China, and Brazil) have caught up with more developed ones (such as the United States, Japan, and those in Western Europe). As they have done so, the world distribution of income has become more equal, and hundreds of millions have escaped from extreme poverty. Not all the news is good, however. Even as global income inequality has fallen, income distribution within countries—including the United States and China, among others—has become less equal.

4.1a Measuring Economic Growth

Economic growth is most often expressed in terms of **gross domestic product (GDP)**, a measure of the value of total output of goods and services produced within a nation's borders.[1] If GDP is to provide a meaningful measure of growth over time, it must be expressed in **real** terms; that is, it must be adjusted for the effects of changes in the average price level. For example, during the period of prosperity from the last quarter of 2001 to the last quarter of 2007, US **nominal** GDP (that is, GDP measured according to prices at which goods were actually sold in the given year) grew from $10,373 billion to $14,253 billion, or 37 percent. However, part of the increase in nominal GDP was due to an increase of roughly 20 percent in the average price level during the period. Adjusted for inflation and expressed in constant dollars, real GDP increased by only 17 percent. The term **real output** is a synonym for real gross domestic product.

FIGURE 4–1

World Economic Growth, Actual and Forecast, 2005–2016

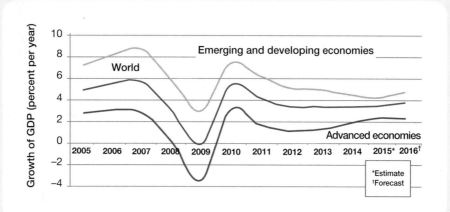

Emerging and developed economies have consistently grown faster than advanced economies, although recently the gap has narrowed. As a result, the world distribution of income has become more equal. Paradoxically, however, income distribution within many countries, including the United States and China, has become less equal. Growth rate for 2015 is estimated; growth rate for 2016 is forecast.

Source: International Monetary Fund, World Economic Outlook Database, April 2015.

4.1b Sources of Economic Growth

We can divide the sources of economic growth into two main components: the growth of total labor inputs and the growth of output per unit of labor (labor productivity).

The growth of total labor inputs depends on social and demographic factors that differ from one country to another, but that do not change rapidly within any one country. One source of growth of labor inputs is population growth. Population in the United States is now growing at about 1 percent per year or less. Most of the growth is due to immigration. Population in most other advanced countries is stable or slowly declining. Another possible source of increased labor input is increased labor force participation. In the United States, the **labor force participation rate** increased from about 59 percent in the 1950s to a peak of more than 67 percent in 2000. Much of that increase was due to an increase in labor force participation by women, from 37 percent to 57 percent. Since 2000, labor force participation has begun to decrease again. This time, half or more of the increase is due to retirement of workers of the baby boom generation. By 2015, the rate had fallen to around 62 percent, which is still well above the rates of the 1950s and 1960s. Increases in population and labor force participation have been partly offset by a decrease of about three hours in the average hours worked per week.

Labor force participation rate

The percentage of the adult population that is working or looking for work

Largely due to immigration, the US population is growing about 1 percent a year. (Shutterstock)

In contrast to the slow changes in hours worked, output per worker (productivity) has experienced considerable volatility over the past fifty years, as shown in Figure 4–2. To show trends more clearly, the chart shows both quarterly rates of productivity growth and averages over a five-year period. The simple average rate of productivity growth over the whole period was 2.2 percent. During the 1970s and early 1980s, productivity growth suffered a prolonged slowdown, in part due to the entry into the labor force of many women with little previous work experience. From the mid-1990s to mid-2000s, productivity growth grew more strongly again. However, since 2005, output per worker has fallen back to levels seen in the mid-1980s.

FIGURE 4–2

US Annual Productivity Growth, Nonfarm Business Sector

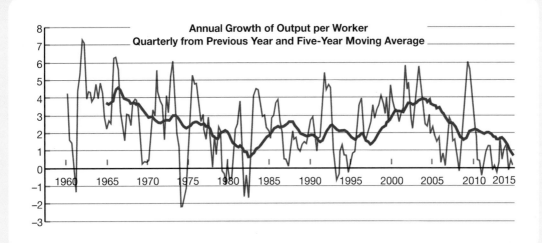

This chart depicts output per worker in the business sector of the US economy from 1960 to 2015. Quarterly data (blue line) move irregularly. To show trends more clearly, the chart also includes a five-year moving average of productivity growth (red line).

Data source: Federal Reserve Bank of St. Louis

Since hours worked per capita tend to fall as countries get richer, productivity growth holds the key to prosperity in the long run. What determines whether productivity grows rapidly or slowly?

Increases in capital per worker are one important source of productivity growth. Capital includes industrial equipment like bulldozers and assembly robots, capital used in service jobs like hospital equipment and office information systems, and infrastructure capital like roads and communications systems. Economists use the term **total factor productivity** to refer to any increase in output per worker that they cannot attribute to changes in capital per worker.

Capital includes industrial equipment like bulldozers and assembly robots. (Shutterstock)

Sources of growth in total factor productivity include technological innovation, better organization of production, better education of the labor force (sometimes called human capital), and improvements in political institutions that reduce corruption and conflict. All of these play a role in year-to-year and longer-term variations in productivity growth.

4.1c The Benefits and Costs of Economic Growth

Economic growth has many benefits. First and foremost, it provides consumers with a higher standard of living in the form of more goods and services. Growth also means new opportunities to choose between work and leisure. If more people choose to work, or if people want to work longer hours, growth makes possible the capital investment needed to create jobs for them. Over a longer span of US history, however, people have opted for more leisure with fewer hours per week and more days off.

Finally, many people see economic growth as a necessary condition for reducing poverty and economic injustice. Growth is not a sufficient condition, as it is not always the case that a rising tide lifts all boats. For example, in the United States, the yachts of the rich have risen significantly more rapidly than the rafts of the poor, at least in recent years. From 1979 to 2007, the share of total income going to the highest-earning 1 percent of US households roughly doubled—from about 9 percent to about 18 percent.[2] Still, there is little dispute that issues of social equality are even harder to resolve in countries where the tide is going out.

Despite its obvious benefits, economic growth has had its critics. More than a century ago the English economist John Stuart Mill worried that growth might cause the loss of "a great portion of the earth's pleasantries" (see *Who Said It? Who Did It? 4.1*).

Today, too, critics continue to raise doubts about the benefits of growth. Some point to adverse environmental effects, including both the air and water pollution that plague the cities of many developing countries and greenhouse gas emissions that raise the possibility of global climate disaster. Others think people work too hard and enjoy too little leisure. Still others point out that growth of GDP does not guarantee improved health or human rights. Economists have made many attempts to develop broader measures of well-being that include factors not accounted for in GDP.

Total factor productivity

A measurement of improvements in technology and organization that allow increases in the output produced by given quantities of labor and capital

Who Said It? Who Did It? **4.1**

John Stuart Mill
on the
Stationary State

(Wikimedia Commons)

Economic growth was a major concern of the classical economists of the nineteenth century. Then, as now, most of the leading economists were inclined to view economic growth as a good thing. However, some of them feared that the pressure of growing populations on limited natural resources would sooner or later bring economic growth to a halt. Economists portrayed the "stationary state" toward which society was moving as one of poverty and over-population, causing one critic to dub economics the "dismal science."

John Stuart Mill thought otherwise. Mill was one of the most remarkable figures of the nineteenth century. Eldest son of the prominent economist James Mill, John Stuart Mill began studying Greek at age three, was tutoring the younger members of his family in Latin at age eight, and first read Smith's *Wealth of Nations* at age thirteen. His *Principles of Political Economy*, published in 1848, was the standard text on the subject until Alfred Marshall transformed "political economy" into "economics" at the end of the century.

Mill agreed with earlier classical economists that the economy would sooner or later reach a stationary state, but he did not view the prospect as entirely gloomy:

> I cannot … regard the stationary state of capital and wealth with the unaffected aversion so generally manifested towards it by political economists of the old school. I am inclined to believe that it would be, on the whole, a very considerable improvement on our present condition. I confess I am not charmed with the ideal of life held out by those who think that the normal state of human beings is that of struggling to get on; that the trampling, crushing, elbowing, and treading on each other's heels, which form the existing type of social life, are the most desirable lot of human kind, or anything but the disagreeable symptoms of one of the phases of our industrial progress …

> If the earth must lose that great portion of its pleasantries which it owes to things that the unlimited increase of wealth and population would extricate from it, for the mere purpose of enabling it to support a larger, but not a better or happier population, I sincerely hope, for the sake of posterity, that they will be content to be stationary long before necessity compels them to.

Today many writers who are concerned about problems of population, pollution, and resource depletion echo Mill's sentiments.

One of the most ambitious efforts to measure noneconomic aspects of human welfare is the Social Progress Index (SPI), developed by a group of economists led by Michael Porter of the Harvard Business School.[3] The SPI combines data for three groups of factors that contribute to human well-being: basic human needs (nutrition, medical care, sanitation, safety), foundations of well-being (access to knowledge and information, health, and environment), and opportunity (personal rights, freedom, tolerance, and education).

Figure 4–3 shows the relationship between the SPI and GDP per capita. Clearly, the overall relationship is positive, but it is not simple. Three features stand out.

FIGURE 4–3

Human Well-being and GDP per Capita

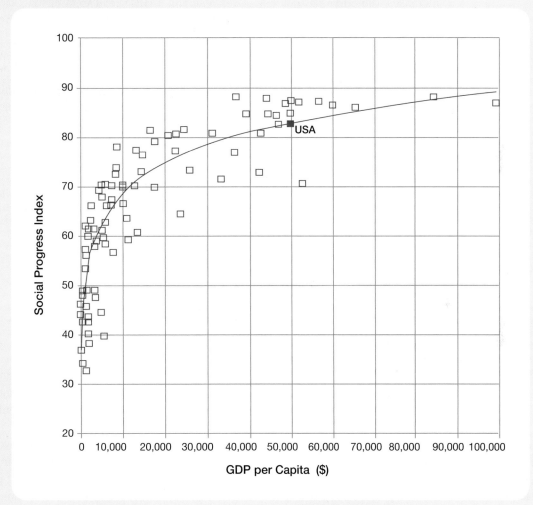

This figure shows the relationship between a measure of human well-being known as the Social Progress Index and GDP per capita. Growth of GDP provides a strong boost to well-being for low-income countries, but for wealthier countries, further growth of GDP matters much less than factors like access to health care and education, freedom of information, and human rights.

Data sources: 2015 Social Progress Index (Social Progress Imperative, http://www.socialprogressimperative.org/); GDP data are from the International Monetary Fund.

First, the positive slope of the trend line shows that material production, as measured by GDP per capita, really is a springboard to human flourishing as measured by the SPI, but there are many outliers. The biggest outliers on the downside—wealthy countries with SPI scores far below the trend line—are Kuwait, the United Arab Emirates, and Saudi Arabia. The biggest outlier on the upside is New Zealand, which manages to achieve the top SPI score of any country, even though its real GDP per capita of $31,000 is only twenty-fourth in the world and just two-thirds that of the United States.

Second, the relationship of GDP to the SPI is far from linear. For poor countries, even modest gains in GDP have a big payoff in terms of the quality of life. As income increases, the curve flattens out. After reaching a GDP per capita of $20,000 (that is, about the level of Portugal or South Korea), improvements in the SPI from further GDP growth alone are modest.

Third, the relationship of GDP to SPI not only flattens as countries grow wealthier, it also becomes significantly less tight. For poorer countries, GDP explains about two-thirds of differences in SPIs, but for the wealthier countries, only about one-third.

The bottom line? Policies that improve human welfare always make sense. Policies that sacrifice human welfare to achieve growth for its own sake never do. Yes, there is a positive correlation between growth of real GDP per capita and broad measures of human welfare, but the relationship is much weaker for rich countries than for poor ones. For high-income countries, strategies that focus on using GDP directly to improve well-being are far more attractive than policies that focus on growth and hope that well-being will take care of itself.

4.2 SHORT-RUN MACROECONOMICS AND THE BUSINESS CYCLE

The first section of this chapter focused on prosperity—economic growth and its causes in the long run. In this section, we turn to issues of stability—that is, to short-run variations around the long-run trends of real GDP, inflation, and employment.

Figure 4–4 shows growth of the US economy since 1991. Because of increasing labor inputs, capital accumulation, and technological and organizational improvements, the economy's production capacity, known as its **natural** or **potential level of real output** (natural or potential real GDP), has risen steadily.

Natural (potential) level of real output

The trend of real GDP growth over time, also known as potential

Output gap

The economy's current level of real output minus its natural level of real output

As the chart shows, until the onset of the Great Recession, real GDP moved sometimes above and sometimes below the long-term trend line, but never far from it. Economists call the difference between the current level of real output and potential real output the **output gap**. A positive output gap indicates that real output is above its natural level; a negative output, that it is below the natural level. After 2008, real GDP dropped much farther below the long-term trend of potential GDP than at any time since the Great Depression of the 1930s. Also, the impact of the recession—plus the effects of an aging population and other factors—has reduced the estimated growth rate of potential GDP. It now seems unlikely that the US economy will return to the pre-recession growth trend.

FIGURE 4–4

Actual and Potential Real Output in the United States, 1990–2015

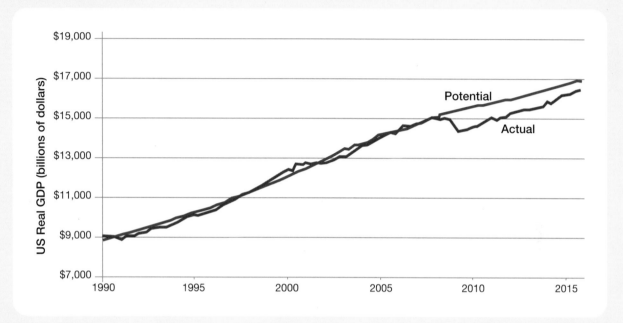

This chart shows US actual and natural, or potential, real GDP. Potential GDP represents the estimated long-term trend of growth for the economy. In any given year, actual real GDP may fall below or rise above the trend. The difference between actual and natural real GDP in any year is the output gap.

Source: Federal Reserve Bank of St. Louis.

4.2a Phases of the Business Cycle

Economists use the term **business cycle** to refer to the alternating periods of growth of GDP above and below its long-term trend. The chronology of the business cycle for the US economy is maintained by the Business Cycle Dating Committee of the National Bureau of Economic Research. Figure 4–5 shows an idealized business cycle. Economists commonly divide the cycle into four, and sometimes five, phases. The peak of the cycle is the point at which real output reaches a maximum. At that point, there is a positive output gap. The period during which real output falls is a contraction. The dating committee typically applies the term **recession** to any contraction lasting six months or more. At the end of the *contraction*, real output reaches a minimum known as the *trough* of the cycle, at which point the output gap is negative. After the trough, real output begins to grow again, and the economy enters an expansion that lasts until a new peak is reached. Some economists use the term *recovery* to refer to the first part of the expansion, before the economy returns to its previous peak of output or before the output gap once again becomes positive.

Business cycle

A pattern of irregular but repeated expansion and contraction of aggregate economic activity

Recession

A cyclical economic contraction that lasts six months or more

FIGURE 4–5

An Idealized Business Cycle

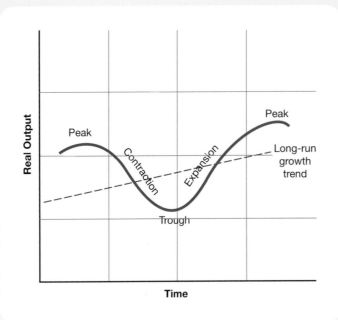

This figure shows an idealized business cycle. The cycle begins from a peak and then enters a contraction. A contraction lasting six months or more is called a recession. The low point of the cycle is its trough. Following the trough, the economy enters an expansion until it reaches a new peak. Because real GDP varies about an upward trend, each cyclical peak tends to carry the economy to a higher level of real GDP than the previous one.

Popular discussions of the business cycle do not always follow the terminology preferred by economists. For example, although the most recent recession, which began in late 2007, officially lasted only until the trough of mid-2009, commentators continued to speak of the "Great Recession" as an ongoing phenomenon far into the early phase of the subsequent expansion. Even this long-lasting downturn, the worst of the post–World War II period, was less severe than many cyclical contractions of the nineteenth and early twentieth centuries, which were known as depressions. The most spectacular of these was the Great Depression of the 1930s, which actually consisted of two contractionary periods separated by an incomplete recovery. During this episode, real output fell by one-third, the price level fell by one-quarter, and the unemployment rate climbed to 24 percent of the labor force. Because no succeeding contraction has come close to it in severity, the term *depression* has passed out of use in all but historical contexts.

4.2b Employment and the Business Cycle

As real output rises and falls over the business cycle, employment also varies. Changes in employment tend to get even more public attention than changes in output. After all, real GDP is a very abstract concept, whereas the security of one's job, and the jobs of relatives and friends, has a far bigger personal impact than a percentage-point wiggle one way or the other in real output.

Measuring Unemployment Trends   The most common measure of the national employment situation is the **unemployment rate**, which is the percentage of the labor force that is unemployed at a given time. It is worth looking closely at some terms and methods that underlie this deceptively simple statistic.

The US Bureau of Labor Statistics, in conjunction with the Bureau of the Census, obtains the data used in calculating unemployment from a monthly sample of about fifty thousand randomly selected households. Field agents go to those households and ask a series of questions about the job status of each member of the household: Did anyone work last week? Did anyone look for work? How long has the person been looking for work? How did the person go about looking?

Respondents' answers to these questions determine their employment status. A person is officially **employed** if he or she works at least one hour per week for pay or at least fifteen hours per week as an unpaid worker in a family business. A person who is not currently employed but is actively looking for work is officially **unemployed**. The employed plus the unemployed—that is, those who are either working or looking for work—constitute the **labor force**.

If people are neither employed nor actively looking for work, they do not count as members of the labor force. People out of the labor force include many people who could work but choose not to for one reason or another. For example, they may be full-time students or retired. The most commonly reported measure of the labor force, known as the civilian labor force, also excludes members of the armed forces.

Because some people are always entering the labor force or moving between jobs, the unemployment rate never falls to zero. There is no consensus about exactly what unemployment rate constitutes "full employment." Many economists consider the **natural rate of unemployment**—the rate of unemployment associated with the natural or potential level of GDP—to be a useful benchmark. Others use a benchmark based on a relationship between unemployment and inflation. After a point, as the unemployment rate falls, the rate of inflation begins to accelerate. They define the **non-accelerating inflation rate of unemployment (NAIRU)** as the rate of unemployment below which the rate of inflation begins to rise. Estimates of the natural rate of unemployment or NAIRU have varied over time as social, economic, and demographic conditions have changed. As of 2015, the Federal Reserve Board of Governors estimated the NAIRU to be 5.2 percent.

Figure 4–6 shows the unemployment rate for the United States since 1960. The chart includes a shaded band to represent a range of views about what constitutes low to moderate unemployment. During the 1950s and 1960s, unemployment stayed within this range most of the time. In the 1970s and early 1980s, the unemployment rate took a turn for the worse. It jumped to 8.3 percent in 1975 and fell into the moderate range in only two of the next twelve years. The period from the early 1990s to the mid-2000s marked another extended period of low to moderate unemployment. During the Great Recession, unemployment rose to a peak monthly rate of 10 percent in October 2009 and did not return to the moderate range until 2015.

Unemployment rate

The percentage of the labor force that is unemployed

Employed

A person who is working at least one hour a week for pay or at least fifteen hours per week as an unpaid worker in a family business

Unemployed

A person who is not employed but is actively looking for work

Labor force

The sum of all individuals who are employed and all individuals who are unemployed

Natural rate of unemployment

The rate of unemployment that prevails when real output is at its natural level

Non-accelerating inflation rate of unemployment (NAIRU)

The rate of unemployment below which inflation begins to rise

FIGURE 4–6

US Civilian Unemployment Rate

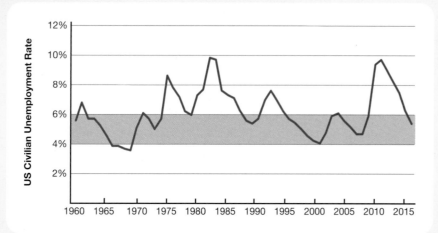

There is no one level of unemployment that is best for the economy. Some unemployment is always present as people change jobs or as they enter the labor force in a normally functioning economy. This figure highlights a range of 4 to 6 percent unemployment that many people consider "low to moderate." Until 1975, unemployment stayed within that range, for the most part. The mid-1970s and early 1980s saw much higher rates. During the 1990s and early 2000s, unemployment returned to the low-to-moderate range. It rose sharply again during the Great Recession, but by 2015, it returned to the moderate range.

Source: Bureau of Labor Statistics.

Gray Areas in the Measurement of Unemployment   There are many gray areas in the measurement of unemployment. People have criticized the official data for both understating and overstating the "true" number of unemployed adults. One way to understand these gray areas better is to compare the official definition of unemployment with two commonsense definitions—namely, "not working" and "can't find a job."

The official definitions of employment and unemployment differ greatly from the simple definitions of "working" and "not working." On the one hand, many people who work are not officially employed. By far the largest such group consists of people who work full-time at housekeeping and childcare. People in those occupations count as employed if they work for pay, but much of such work is done without pay. Also, children under age sixteen do not count either as employed or as part of the labor force, even if they work for pay.

On the other hand, not everyone who does not work counts as unemployed. In addition to those who are not looking for work, and therefore are not in the labor force, people who have jobs but are absent from them because of illness, bad weather, or labor disputes are nonetheless counted as employed. Finally, there are many people who count as employed because they work part-time, but who would prefer full-time work if they could find it. At the peak of the Great Recession, more than 6 percent of people in the labor force fell into the involuntary part-time category—more than double the pre-recession average.

The second commonsense definition of unemployment, "can't find a job," also only loosely fits the official definition. In some ways, the official definition overstates the number of people who cannot find jobs. Some people who count as unemployed are on layoffs from jobs to which they expect to be recalled or have found jobs that they expect to start within thirty days. Other people who count as unemployed could easily find a job of some kind but prefer to take their time and find just the kind of job they want. (People who are not the sole income earners in their households, for example, may be in a position to look longer and be more selective than people in households with no other income.) Finally, there is some doubt as to whether the description "can't find a job" fits people who could have stayed on at their last job but quit to look for a better one.

In other ways, however, the official definition of unemployment understates the number of people who cannot find jobs. For example, it does not include **discouraged workers**—people who are not looking for work because they believe no suitable jobs are available. The Bureau of Labor Statistics officially counts as a discouraged worker anyone who has looked for work within the past year but is no longer actively looking. As of 2015, there were also about four million people (a number equal to about 2.5 percent of the labor force) who said they wanted a job but were not counted as discouraged workers because they had not looked for work for more than a year.

Because the unemployment rate is an imperfect measure of the state of the labor market, the US Bureau of Labor Statistics publishes several alternative measures of labor underutilization. The best known is a measure known as U-6, often called "broad unemployment," which includes discouraged workers and involuntary part-time workers along with those who are officially unemployed. In May 2007, when the official unemployment rate hit a cyclical low of 4.4 percent, U-6 was 8.2 percent. In October 2009, when the official rate reached its high for the Great Recession of 10.0 percent, U-6 reached 17.4 percent.

People who have jobs but are absent from them because of labor disputes are counted as employed. (Shutterstock)

The Payroll Job Indicator

The unemployment rate is not the only measure of the state of the labor market. Quite aside from the problems of definition just discussed, the unemployment rate may give a misleading picture of what is happening in the labor market because it is sensitive both to changes in its numerator (the number of unemployed) and its denominator (the size of the labor force). During the early stages of recovery from a recession, the labor force often grows at the same time that the number of employed people grows, and the unemployment rate remains unchanged or even increases. This happens because news of possible new jobs draws discouraged workers back into the labor force, but the new workers do not immediately find work. Once a recovery is underway, the size of the labor force stabilizes, and the unemployment rate may fall even though just a few new jobs appear.

Discouraged worker

A person who would work if a suitable job were available but has given up looking for such a job

Because month-to-month changes in the unemployment rate do not give a complete picture, news reports of short-term labor market developments often focus on the number of new payroll jobs created in a given month. Government statisticians base the monthly figure for change in payroll jobs on a survey of employers that is entirely separate from the household survey they use to calculate the unemployment rate. The sample size of the employer survey is larger, and some people consider it more reliable. However, it, too, has its limitations. It is often subject to significant revisions. Also, unlike the unemployment rate, it does not include farm workers and the self-employed. As a result, the monthly change in payroll jobs and the monthly unemployment rate sometimes give contradictory indications of the state of the labor market.

Frictional, Structural, and Cyclical Unemployment

One final way to look at the state of the labor market is to ask how long people remain unemployed. During times of prosperity, many of the unemployed are out of work only briefly. For example Figure 4–7 shows that, as of the fourth quarter of 2006, when the job market was strong, 38 percent of unemployed workers were only out of a job for five weeks or less. By the second quarter of 2010, the job market had weakened significantly, and just 19 percent of unemployed workers were out for five weeks or less between jobs.

The term **frictional unemployment** refers to short-term, largely voluntary unemployment spells needed to match jobs and workers. It represents people who quit old jobs to look for new ones, people who take a week or so to move or go on vacation before starting a newly found job, and people who enter occupations, such as construction work, in which temporary layoffs are frequent but year-round earnings are good. Economists view a certain level of frictional unemployment as necessary in a labor market in which information is incomplete and the costs of job search are often high.

In contrast to frictional unemployment, the term **structural unemployment** is applied to people who spend long periods out of work, often with little prospect of finding adequate jobs. Figure 4–7 shows that, as of late 2006, just 16 percent of unemployed workers were out of a job for half a year or more. By mid-2010, that percentage had risen to 45 percent—far higher than at any other time since World War II. Some workers who experience prolonged joblessness once held good jobs but lost them because the shifting structure of the economy has made their skills obsolete. This category of workers also includes people with few skills and without the work experience needed to find steady work. Workers without high-school education are particularly vulnerable to structural unemployment, and structural unemployment rates are higher for some minorities than for the population as a whole.

As Figure 4–7 shows, both frictional and structural unemployment are present in good years as well as bad ones. Frictional plus structural unemployment constitutes the natural rate of unemployment, but unemployment is not always at its natural level.

In some years, a vigorous economic expansion makes jobs so easy to find that the duration of unemployment falls below normal, reducing the number of unemployed below the number of unemployed for frictional and structural reasons. Even many of the hard-core, structurally unemployed find jobs. In other years, business contractions cause unemployment to rise above its natural rate. At such times, even workers who have worked a long time for their present employer and who have excellent skills may find themselves temporarily out of work. The average duration of unemployment rises above normal frictional plus structural levels. Economists use the term **cyclical unemployment** to mean the difference between the actual unemployment rate in a particular month and the natural rate. When the economy slows down, cyclical unemployment adds to frictional and structural unemployment. At the peak of an expansionary period, cyclical unemployment is negative.

Frictional unemployment

The portion of unemployment that reflects the short periods of unemployment needed for matching jobs with job seekers

Structural unemployment

The portion of unemployment that reflects long periods out of work by people whose skills do not match those required for available jobs

Cyclical unemployment

The difference between the actual rate of unemployment at a given point in the business cycle and the natural rate of unemployment

FIGURE 4–7

US Unemployment by Duration

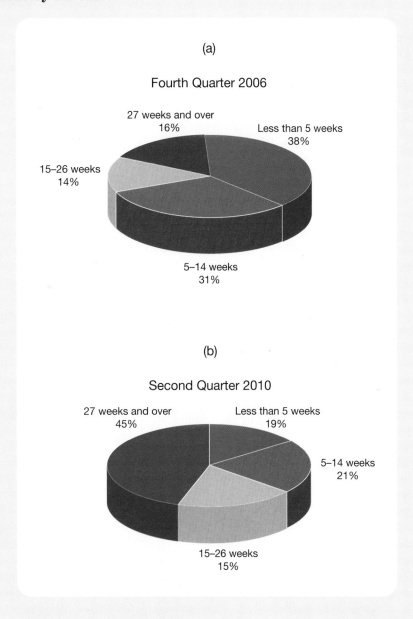

(a)

Fourth Quarter 2006

27 weeks and over
16%

Less than 5 weeks
38%

15–26 weeks
14%

5–14 weeks
31%

(b)

Second Quarter 2010

27 weeks and over
45%

Less than 5 weeks
19%

5–14 weeks
21%

15–26 weeks
15%

As this chart shows, there is considerable variation in the length of time people are unemployed. In 2006, when the job market was strong, short-term frictional unemployment predominated. During a deep recession, as in 2010, structural unemployment rises.

Source: Economic Report of the President, 2011, Table B-44.

4.3 Price Stability

Up to this point, our discussion has focused on real variables—real output and the level of employment. Changes in the prices of goods and services are also important, however. **Inflation**, which means a sustained increase in the average level of prices of all goods and services, is a potential disruptive force in the economic life of nations and individuals. **Price stability**—a situation in which the rate of inflation is low enough so that it is not a significant factor in business and individual decision making—is another of the major goals of macroeconomic policy.

Figure 4–8 shows inflation trends in the US economy and around the world. Before the 1970s, US inflation was low. In fact, for the entire century from the Civil War to the mid-1960s, the US peacetime inflation rate averaged only about 2 percent per year. Beginning in the 1970s, however, inflation rose and became highly variable. The struggle against inflation was a dominant theme in economic policy from the mid-1970s through the 1980s. By the late 1980s, inflation again came under control and has remained low since.

Figure 4–8, Part (b), shows that the decline of inflation since the 1980s was part of a worldwide phenomenon. In the 1980s and 1990s, inflation in emerging and developing economies was much more rapid than in advanced economies. Since that time, inflation has slowed to moderate levels in both groups of countries.

4.3a Short-Run Costs of Inflation

Some of the year-to-year variation of inflation in Figure 4–8 is attributable to the business cycle. As the cycle approaches its peak, inflation tends to accelerate. During recessions, inflation slows again. As inflation rises and falls over the business cycle, its costs affect people unevenly.

Most people receive the bulk of their income in the form of wages and salaries. Wage and salary earners often feel that they suffer from inflation. They compare what their paychecks can buy each month at ever-higher prices with what they would be able to buy with the same paychecks if prices remained stable. However, measured over a period of several years, nominal wages and salaries tend to adjust to inflation. Real wage and salary earnings in the United States rose during the inflationary 1970s and 1980s and also during the low-inflation 1960s and 1990s. People who receive income in the form of Social Security, other government **transfer payments**, and some private pensions receive automatic adjustments that compensate for changes in consumer prices that protect them from inflation. Such automatic adjustments go by the general name of **indexation**.

Most people receive the bulk of their income in the form of wages and salaries. Wage and salary earners often feel that they suffer from inflation. They compare what their paychecks can buy each month at ever-higher prices with what they would be able to buy with the same paychecks if prices remained stable. However, measured over a period of several years, nominal wages and salaries tend to adjust to inflation. Real wage and salary earnings in the United States rose during the inflationary 1970s and 1980s and also during the low-inflation 1960s and 1990s. People who receive income in the form of Social Security, other government transfer payments, and some private pensions, receive automatic adjustments that compensate for changes in consumer prices that protect them from inflation. Such automatic adjustments go by the general name of indexation.

Inflation

A sustained increase in the average level of prices of all goods and services

Price stability

A rate of inflation that is low enough not to be a significant factor in business and individual decision making

Transfer payments

Payments to individuals that are not made in return for work they currently perform

Indexation

A policy of automatically adjusting a value or payment in proportion to changes in the average price level

FIGURE 4–8

Inflation in the United States and Around the World

US Consumer Price Inflation
(Percent per Year)
(a)

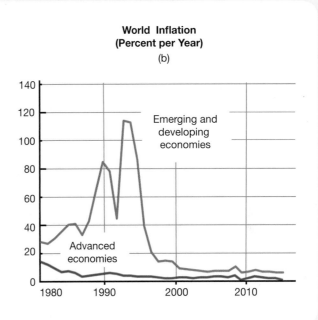

World Inflation
(Percent per Year)
(b)

Part (a) of this figure shows the trend of inflation in the United States since 1960. The 1970s and early 1980s were years of high and variable inflation; but by the late 1980s, inflation came under control and has remained low since. Part (b) shows that, since the 1980s, inflation has slowed—not just in the United States, but around the world, first in advanced economies and later in emerging market and developing economies.

Sources: Part (a), Bureau of Labor Statistics; Part (b): International Monetary Fund, World Economic Outlook Database, April 2015.

Inflation also affects the income of creditors, who receive interest from mortgage loans, corporate bonds, and the like, and that of debtors, who pay interest. The traditional view is that inflation injures creditors and aids debtors. Suppose, for example, that I borrow $100 from you today, promising to repay the $100 of principal plus $5 interest, or $105 in all, at the end of a year. If there is no inflation during the year, I get the use of the funds for the year, and you get $5 of real income in the form of the interest on the loan. Suppose, however, that during the year the price level goes up by 10 percent. In that case, I get the use of the funds for the year, and what is more, I pay you back in depreciated dollars. The $105 I give you at the end of the year will buy only about as much then as $95 will buy today. Your real income is negative because the real value of $105 a year from now is less than the real value today of the $100 that I borrow. I, the debtor, benefit from inflation; you, the creditor, are hurt.

However, the traditional view of the effects of inflation is incomplete because it does not distinguish between unexpected and expected inflation. The example just given implicitly assumes that neither you nor I (the lender and borrower, respectively) expected any inflation at the time of the loan. Suppose, instead, that we both had expected a 10 percent increase in the price level over the life of the loan. In that case, you would not have lent me the $100 in return for a promise to repay just $105 at the end of the year. Instead, you would have insisted on a repayment of $115—the $100 principal, plus $10 to compensate you for the decline in purchasing power of the principal, plus $5 of real interest income. I, in turn, would have agreed to those terms, knowing that the $115 payment under conditions of 10 percent inflation would be no more burdensome than the $105 payment I would have agreed to if I had expected no inflation.

This example shows that we need to distinguish between two interest concepts: the **nominal interest rate**, which is the interest rate expressed in the ordinary way, in current dollars, and the **real interest rate**, which is the nominal rate minus the rate of inflation. In the example, a 15 percent nominal interest rate, given a 10 percent rate of inflation, corresponds to a 5 percent real interest rate.

The distinction between nominal and real interest rates helps us to understand the impact of expected and unexpected inflation on debtors and creditors. Expected inflation, it turns out, is neutral between debtors and creditors because the parties will adjust the nominal interest rate to take the expected inflation into account. If they would agree to a 5 percent nominal interest rate given no expected inflation, they would agree to a 15 percent nominal rate given 10 percent expected inflation, a 20 percent nominal rate given 15 percent expected inflation, and so on. All of these adjusted rates correspond to a 5 percent real rate. Unexpected inflation is not neutral, however. Unexpected inflation harms creditors and benefits debtors. If you lend me $100 at a 5 percent nominal rate of interest, and the price level unexpectedly rises by 10 percent over the year before I repay the loan, the real rate of interest that you receive is –5 percent.

4.3b Long-Run Costs of Inflation

In the short run, unexpected inflation helps some people, while it hurts others. In the long run, however, inflation—whether expected or unexpected—has other costs that harm the economy as a whole without producing offsetting benefits.

One problem arises from the way inflation upsets economic calculations. When the rate of inflation is high and variable, as it was in the United States in the 1970s and early 1980s, business planning becomes difficult. The outcomes of investment projects that require firms to incur costs now in the hope of making profits later come to depend less on manufacturing and marketing skills than on the ups and downs of wages, interest rates, and the prices of key raw materials. As the investment environment becomes riskier, firms may avoid projects with long-term payoffs and gamble instead on strategies that promise short-term financial gains. Similarly, households, facing more uncertainty about future price trends, may reduce their long-term saving in favor of increased current consumption. These effects are hard to measure, but many economists think that they are substantial.

Other costs arise from the effort to rid the economy of inflation that is underway. The experiences of many countries suggest that bringing inflation under control has a cost in terms of higher unemployment and lower real output. For example, the slowdown in inflation in the United States in the early 1980s coincided with back-to-back recessions during which the unemployment rate reached a peak of more than 10 percent.

Nominal interest rate

The interest rate expressed in the usual way: in terms of current dollars, without adjustment for inflation

Real interest rate

The nominal interest rate minus the rate of inflation

4.3c Deflation

Sometimes a country experiences a period in which the price level falls for a sustained period. The term for such an episode is **deflation**. Superficially, one might think that if inflation is bad, deflation must be good. That turns out not to be the case. Deflation can be as harmful to the economy, or even more so, than inflation. For example, from 1929 to 1933, at the beginning of the Great Depression, the price level in the United States fell by more than 25 percent. Real output fell by a third during this period, and the unemployment rate rose to a record high of 25 percent. More recently, Japan has experienced deflation on and off since the early 1990s. Although the rate of deflation has usually been about 1 percent per year or less, it has contributed to a sharp slowdown in Japan's once booming economy. At first, people referred to the period starting in the 1990s as Japan's "lost decade," but now they are beginning to worry that the shift to slow or no growth may last indefinitely.

Because both inflation, if rapid, and deflation, even if moderate, are harmful to the economy, policymakers in most countries aim for a low, but positive, inflation rate. When we speak of price stability as a goal of macroeconomic policy, then, we do not mean a measured rate of inflation of zero. Instead, policymakers in most countries aim to hold the rate of inflation at a rate of something like 2 percent on average over a time horizon of a few years. In later chapters, we will look in detail at strategies for steering the economy between the dangers of excessive inflation and deflation.

Deflation

An episode during which the price level falls for a sustained period

Summary

1. What trend has economic growth followed in the United States?

The most common measure of economic growth is the rate of growth of *gross domestic product (GDP)*, a measure of the value of the economy's total output of goods and services. Economists often express GDP in real terms to avoid distortions caused by inflation. Real gross domestic product in the United States has grown at an average rate of about 2–3 percent since 1950, although that growth has not been steady. Economic growth makes possible higher living standards, jobs for those who want them, and more leisure for those who want it. Some people criticize growth as damaging to the environment. We need to consider composition of real domestic product, as well as its rate of growth, in order to properly assess environmental damage.

2. What is the business cycle?

Over time, the economy undergoes a pattern of irregular but repeated expansion and contraction of aggregate economic activity that we call the *business cycle*. The point at which output reaches a maximum is the peak of the cycle. It is followed by a contraction, a trough, an expansion, and a new peak. A contraction lasting six months or more is a recession. Over the course of the business cycle, the economy sometimes rises above its *natural level of real output*, resulting in a positive *output gap*; other times it falls below the natural level, resulting in a negative output gap.

3. What is unemployment, and why is it important for economic policy?

A person who works at least one hour a week for pay or fifteen hours per week as an unpaid worker in a family business counts as *employed*. A person who is not currently employed but is actively looking for work is *unemployed*. The *unemployment rate* is the percentage of the *labor force* that is not employed. We refer to unemployment as *frictional, structural*, or *cyclical*, depending on its cause. The natural rate of unemployment is the sum of structural plus frictional unemployment.

4. What is inflation, and what impact does it have on the economy?

Inflation is a sustained increase in the average level of prices of all goods and services. *Price stability* is a situation in which the rate of inflation is low enough so that it is not a significant factor in business and individual decision making. In measuring economic quantities, we must distinguish between real values, or values adjusted for inflation, and *nominal* values, or values expressed in the ordinary way, in current dollars. Applying these concepts to interest rates, we can say that the *real interest rate* is equal to the *nominal interest rate* minus the rate of inflation. Inflation disrupts the economy in two ways. First, it harms or benefits individuals according to their source of income; second, it disrupts economic calculation, thereby discouraging saving and investment. In addition, the effort to stop inflation once it has begun often entails substantial costs. *Deflation* means a sustained period during which the price level falls. Deflation is also harmful to the economy.

KEY TERMS

PROBLEMS AND TOPICS FOR DISCUSSION

1. **Your personal labor force status**   What is your current labor force status? Are you a member of the labor force? Are you employed? Unemployed? Explain the basis for your answers. When was the last time your labor force status changed? Do you expect it to change soon? Give details.

2. **Employment hardship**   Some people have suggested replacing the unemployment rate with an "employment hardship index" that tries to measure the percentage of people who suffer hardship because of their labor force status. What kinds of people who are not now counted as unemployed might fit into this category? What kinds of people who are now counted as unemployed would not suffer hardship? Discuss. Do you think the government's broad unemployment measure, U-6, is an adequate expression of unemployment hardship?

3. **Real and nominal interest rates**   Check with your local bank to find out what interest rates currently apply to (a) one-year savings certificates and (b) three-year automobile loans. Compare these nominal interest rates with the current rate of inflation as measured by the most recently announced rate of change in the consumer price index. (You can get this statistic from the website of the Bureau of Labor Statistics, www.bls.gov.) If the current rate of inflation were to continue unchanged, what real rate of interest would you earn on the savings certificate? What real rate of interest would you pay on the loan?

4. **Economic growth and the environment**   The pace of economic growth varies from one area of the United States to another. Some regions are growing rapidly, with people moving in, much new construction, rising incomes, and so on. Other areas are stagnant or declining, with little new construction and people moving away. Which type of area do you live in? Can you identify any environmental problems in your area that seem to be the result of economic growth? Can you identify any environmental problems that stem from economic decline? What policies could you suggest that would permit growth in your area to take place with less environmental disruption?

5. **The current state of the business cycle**   The government publishes unemployment and inflation data monthly (www.bls.gov) and data on economic growth on a quarterly basis (www.bea.gov). What changes have there been? What is happening to the employment rate? Are the employment and unemployment rates moving in the same direction or in opposite directions? What is the current rate of inflation? Is it increasing, decreasing, or staying the same? Judging from available data, in which phase of the business cycle does the economy appear to be now? Use the data you find to update relevant figures in this chapter.

CASE *for* DISCUSSION

Unemployment and Politics

What did the elections of Presidents Truman, Johnson, Nixon, and Clinton have in common? Those of Presidents Kennedy, Reagan, and Obama? The answer, for the first four, is that they all held the presidency for their parties in election years when the unemployment rate was falling. The other three achieved a change of party in years when the unemployment rate was stagnant or rising.

The election of 1992, in which incumbent President George H. W. Bush faced challenger Bill Clinton, provides a particularly interesting example. In the spring of that year, the economy was just beginning its recovery from a recession, although there had not yet been an official announcement of its end. But although the economy was growing, it was doing so at a rate of only about 2 percent per year. That was well below the average rate of growth of 4.6 percent per year for the six post–World War II elections in which the incumbent party retained power. In June, employers slashed 117,000 jobs from their payrolls, and the unemployment rate hit an eight-year high. The jobs data made every news broadcast, and the news was bad.

What about good news that comes just before the election? History suggests that such news can be too little, too late. Economists who have studied the economics–politics link in detail, like Ray Fair of Yale, say that last-minute improvements are not enough. The economy's performance during the spring and summer is more important in an election year.

As it turns out, the economic numbers did improve just before the 1992 election. Unemployment fell, and an early estimate of the rate of economic growth in the third quarter, announced just before the election, turned out to be 2.7 percent—higher than forecasters had anticipated. Three weeks after the election, there was an upward revision to 3.9 percent; but the third-quarter improvement was indeed too little, too late. Challenger Clinton sailed through the election by a wide margin.

The election of 2012 again conformed to the pattern. The job market was not in excellent shape, but it was improving. Over the year preceding the election, the unemployment rate fell by a full percentage point, from 8.9 percent to 7.9 percent, and employers added 1.7 million payroll jobs. GDP growth averaged 2.6 percent. The steady, although gradual, recovery from the Great Recession was enough to secure reelection for Barack Obama, the incumbent.

Questions

1. If the economy was growing at a rate of 2 percent or better in mid-1992, how is it possible that the unemployment rate was rising?

2. The unemployment rate rose by only 2.7 percentage points from its low of 5.1 percent in March 1989 to its peak in June 1992. A loss of 2.7 percent of voters would not have been nearly enough to defeat the incumbent, President George H. W. Bush. However, his actual vote total fell far more than that. This implies that a rise in unemployment affects the voting behavior not just of those who are actually unemployed but also of many more people. Why do you think this is the case?

3. By the time you read this, the 2016 presidential election may be over. If so, track the unemployment rate and GDP growth rate for the year preceding the election. Did the pattern of no change in presidential party when unemployment was low or falling continue?

From Ed Dolan's Econ Blog

Ed Dolan's econ blog offers several slideshows and posts related to the material in this chapter. Here are some items of special interest: Whatever happened to the misery index? In the 1970s, economist Arthur Okun proposed a "misery index" that was the sum of inflation and unemployment. This slideshow shows how Okun's index, and some modern variants, has evolved over the years since then. You can find it at http://bvtlab.com/JPa64 or by scanning the QR code.

Why fear deflation? As high inflation has become less common, many countries, especially Japan and the core economies of the European Union, have begun to worry more about the opposite problem: deflation. This slideshow explains just what deflation is and why it is a source of concern. You can find it at http://bvtlab.com/Ad9D7 or by scanning the QR code.

The answer to "What should we do about growth?" may be "Nothing." Many economists and politicians have proposed programs for stimulating the rate of growth of GDP. This post explores the contrarian view that growth of GDP for its own sake may not be a sensible goal for economic policy, after all. You can find it at http://bvtlab.com/9d7w4 or by scanning the QR code.

SPECIAL INTEREST

Endnotes

1. Chapter 6 will give a more formal definition of GDP and explain the methods used to measure it.

2. For details, see Congressional Budget Office, "Trends in the Distribution of Household Income, 1979–2007," October 2011 (http://bvtlab.com/8rj96). Chapter 14 in the companion volume, *Introduction to Microeconomics,* explores the issues of poverty and equality in the United States and around the world in greater detail.

3. 2015 Social Progress Index. For more information, visit http://bvtlab.com/8qe78.

4. All three measures of the US labor market situation can be obtained from the Employment Situation Summary released monthly by the Bureau of Labor Statistics, available online at www.bls.gov.

CHAPTER 5

THE CIRCULAR FLOW OF INCOME AND EXPENDITURE

AFTER READING THIS CHAPTER,
you will understand the following:

1. How incomes and expenditures link households and firms
2. How to divide expenditure into consumption, investment, government purchases, and net exports
3. The relationships between injections and leakages in the circular flow
4. Why some investments are planned and others are unplanned
5. How to apply the concept of equilibrium to the circular flow of income and expenditure
6. What the multiplier effect is and how it affects the business cycle

BEFORE READING THIS CHAPTER,
make sure you know the following concepts:

Gross domestic product (GDP)

Opportunity cost

Equilibrium

Inventories

Real and nominal values

The business cycle

CHAPTER
Outline

The previous chapter looked at economic growth from a long-term perspective. It analyzed the sources of growth in terms of labor inputs, increases in capital per worker, and improvements in technology and organization. Discussions of changes in GDP in the short run typically take a different perspective. When the government announces new quarterly data for GDP growth, news reports usually focus not on the sources of growth but on the division of growth among sectors of the economy.

For example, in the second quarter of 2015, the US economy was growing more strongly than those of most other wealthy countries. Real GDP for the United States grew at an annual rate of 3.7 percent. More than half of that, or 2.1 percentage points, came from the growth of household consumption. Business investment in structures, equipment, software, and inventories contributed another 0.9 percentage points. Exports, which had been healthy throughout the recovery, added 0.7 percentage points to growth; and growth of government (all at the state and local level) added another 0.5 percent. Together, that adds up to 4.2 percent. The difference between the growth of those four sectors and that of the total economy is explained by the fact that not all of the goods and services produced by consumers, firms, and government were made in the United States. Some were imported. Imports grew enough in the quarter to subtract 0.5 percentage points from total growth; after adding the contributions to growth of consumption, investment, government purchases, and exports, and then subtracting that of imports, the total came to 3.7 percent.

This chapter explores the sector-by-sector approach to GDP in detail. It begins by introducing the **circular flow of income and product**, which shows the key linkages among major sectors of the economy. The second part of the chapter uses the circular flow to explain what it means for the macroeconomy to be in equilibrium, and what happens when it is not.

5.1 The Circular Flow

Figure 5–1 shows the circular flow for a highly simplified economy that consists of just two sectors: business firms and households.[1] Arrows show flows of payments between the sectors. Simple though it is, this version of the circular flow illustrates some key principles.

5.1a Gross Domestic Product, Domestic Income, and Consumption

Circular flow of income and product

The flow of goods and services between households and firms, balanced by the flow of payments made in exchange for goods and services

Gross domestic income (domestic income)

The total income of all types—including wages, rents, interest payments, and profits—that is paid in return for factors of production used in producing domestic product

The first principle we learn from the circular flow is that gross domestic product, which measures the total value of goods and services produced in the economy, is equal to total income earned by households. The bulk of this income consists of wages and salaries. Firms also pay some of it out—to households from which they borrow, buy, or lease—as interest, rents, and other payments on capital and natural resources. Whatever firms have left over, after they have paid all wages and other costs of production, is profit. Profit is a source of income to the households that own the firms as small business proprietors, partners, or corporate shareholders.

The sum of income received in the form of wages, rents, interest, and profit by all households is **gross domestic income** or, for short, simply **domestic income**. Because the circular flow is a closed system, domestic income and domestic product must be exactly equal. Everything that firms receive for selling the output they produce flows through to households, either as elements of costs (wages, interest, rents) or as profit (what is left over when cost is subtracted from the value of output).[2] Any part of profits that a firm retains for future investment counts as being "earned" by the firm's owners, even though they do not receive it as a cash payment.

FIGURE 5–1

The Basic Circular Flow of Income and Expenditure

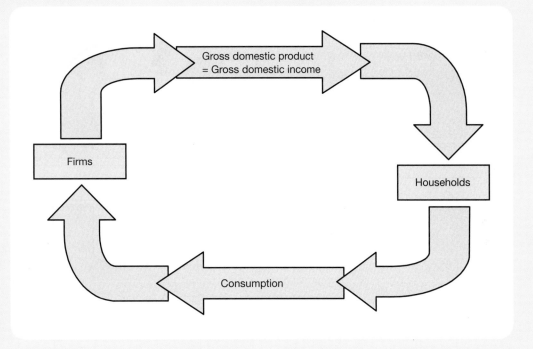

This figure shows flows of income and expenditures for the simplest possible economy. Production, carried out by firms, generates incomes for households in the form of wages, interest, rents, and profits. Households, in turn, immediately spend all of their income on consumption.

In Figure 5–1, which shows the simplest imaginable economy, the only thing households can do with their income is to spend it immediately to buy goods and services from the firms that pay them their incomes. The corresponding arrow, **consumption**, includes all purchases of goods and services for immediate use.

5.1b Leakages and Injections in a Closed Economy

We call the economy shown in Figure 5–1 a **closed economy** because it has no connection with the rest of the world. Even in a closed economy, however, the circular flow is not really so watertight as the one in that diagram. Figure 5–2 shows a more complete form of closed economy that adds two more sectors. The first is government, which combines all units of government at the federal, state, and local levels. The other new sector includes financial institutions of all types—including banks, stock and bond markets, mutual funds, insurance companies, and others.

In this expanded version of the circular flow, it is no longer necessary for households to spend all of their income immediately on consumption. Instead, part of household income "leaks out" of the basic circular flow. Figure 5–2 shows two types of **leakages**.

Consumption

All purchases of goods and services by households for immediate use

Closed economy

An economy that has no links to the rest of the world

Leakages

The saving, net tax, and import components of circular flow

FIGURE 5–2

Leakages and Injections in a Simple Closed Economy

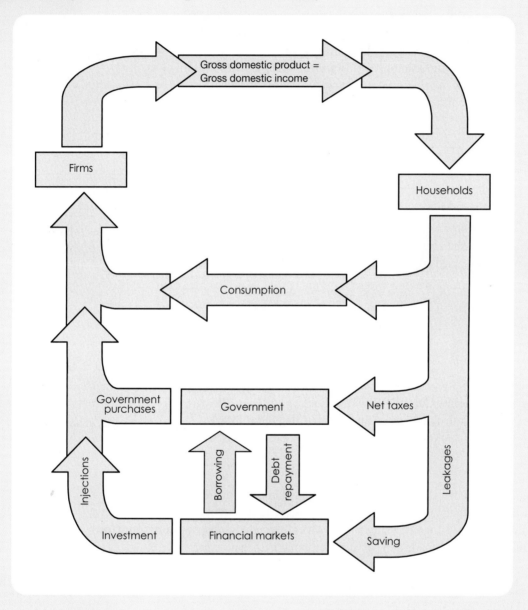

Households do not spend all of their income on consumption. Part of it "leaks out" of the basic circular flow of income and consumption through payments of taxes and through saving. Two "injections" of expenditure into the basic circular flow—government purchases and investment—offset these leakages. Total leakages $(T + S)$ must equal total injections $(G + I)$ for this simple closed economy.

Net taxes are the first leakage. These consist of **tax revenues** that households pay to the government minus **transfer payments** received by households. Transfer payments mean government payments—like pensions, retirement benefits, disability payments, temporary aid to needy families, and so on—that do not represent income from services that the households currently provide. In everyday life, we tend to think of retirement benefits and disability payments as other forms of income, so we might expect them to appear as part of the domestic income component of the circular flow. For reasons that will become clear in the following chapters, however, economists prefer to think of them more as a sort of "tax rebate" that partially offsets the revenue received by government from households in the form of income taxes, sales taxes, property taxes, and so on.

The second leakage shown in Figure 5–2 is **saving**, which is the part of domestic income that households do not use to purchase consumer goods or pay taxes. This economic definition of saving differs a little from the everyday idea of saving, which many people think of as money placed in a bank account or mutual fund. Saving, in the economic sense, also includes repayment of debt and payments that build equity in a home. Also, corporations sometimes retain part of their profit for reinvestment in their operations. From the point of view of the circular flow, we can consider such retained earnings to be first "earned" by the households who own the firms and then "saved" by those households.

To match the leakages, Figure 5–2 also shows two **injections**. Injections are types of expenditure on goods and services that have any origin other than the household consumption that forms part of the basic circular flow in Figure 5–1.

The first injection consists of purchases of goods and services by government at all levels. These include all purchases of goods of all kinds, ranging from printer ink to aircraft carriers, plus services purchased from contractors and the wages paid to all government employees. Economists traditionally call these **government purchases**, which is the term we will use in this book. Government statisticians use the longer term "government consumption expenditures and gross investment" in the official national accounts.

Government purchases do not include transfer payments like Social Security, disability payments, or unemployment compensation. As we explained earlier, we subtract those items, which are not payments for currently performed services, from tax revenue to get the leakage "net taxes." **Government expenditures** means the sum of government purchases and transfer payments.

The second injection is **investment**. Investment, as economists understand it, consists of two components. The first, **fixed investment**, means purchases of newly produced capital goods—machinery, office equipment, software, farm equipment, newly built structures like office buildings and rental housing, and so on. The second component, **inventory investment**, means changes in stocks of finished goods ready for sale, stocks of raw materials, and stocks of partially completed goods in process of production. Inventory investment has a negative value if stocks of goods decrease in a given period.

It is important not to confuse the term *investment* in this macroeconomic sense with *financial investment*, which means purchases of corporate stocks, bonds, and other securities. We do not include financial investment in GDP because it does not represent new production. Instead, financial investment represents changes in ownership of assets that already exist. When we use the term investment without a modifier, it should be clear from context whether we mean *economic* or *financial investment*.

Net taxes
Tax revenue minus transfer payments

Tax revenue
The total value of all taxes that the government collects

Transfer payments
Payments by government to individuals for pensions, unemployment compensation, and other payments that do not represent income from services that the recipients currently provide

Saving
The part of income that households do not use to buy goods and services or to pay taxes

Injections
The government purchase, investment, and net export components of the circular flow

Government purchases
Purchases of goods by all levels of government plus purchases of services from contractors and wages of government employees (The term "government consumption expenditures and gross investment" is used in the official national income accounts.)

Government expenditures
Government purchases of goods and services plus transfer payments

Investment
The sum of fixed investment and inventory investment

Fixed investment
Purchases of newly produced capital goods

Inventory investment
Changes in stocks of finished goods ready for sale, raw materials, and partially completed goods in process of production

5.1c The Role of the Financial Sector

The flows of saving and investment in Figure 5–2 pass through the financial sector. As an element of the circular flow, the financial sector performs two functions.

First, it acts as an intermediary in transmitting flows of funds from savers to investors. In most cases, savers do not directly purchase capital assets like machine tools or office buildings. Instead, they make bank deposits, which banks use to finance loans to business firms, buy securities like stocks and bonds to fund corporate projects, or in other ways indirectly finance the expenditures on capital goods that go into economic investment.

Second, the financial sector plays a key role in redirecting flows of funds between the private and government sectors of the economy. Without the financial sector, the government would always have to balance its budget, exactly, every year. If that were the case, the amount of funds flowing through the "net taxes" arrow would have to be exactly equal to the flow through the "government purchases" arrow. With the help of the financial sector, the government does not have to keep its budget in balance at all times.

If government purchases exceed net taxes, the government has a budget deficit. To cover the deficit, the government must borrow from the private financial sector. In most cases, it does so by selling bonds to private investors through financial markets. The resulting flow of government borrowing appears in Figure 5–2 as an arrow running from the financial sector to the government.

Instead, the government sometimes collects more in net taxes than it spends on purchases of goods and services. In that case, the budget is in surplus. The surplus funds go to repay government debt, a process that we show with an arrow from the government sector to the private financial sector. In practice, since there are many units of government—federal, state, and local—some of them may have budget deficits at any given time. Likewise, others may have budget surpluses. So funds are usually flowing in both ways at once between the financial and government sectors.

Before moving on, it is worth pointing out one more feature of the circular flow. In a closed economy like that of Figure 5–2, which has no links to the rest of the world, the sum of saving plus net taxes must equal the sum of investment plus government purchases, even though the individual leakage and injection items do not have to balance.

The financial sector of the circular flow of income and expenditures plays a key role in redirecting flows of funds between the private and government sectors of the economy. (Shutterstock)

The equality of leakage and investments has important implications for economic policy. If the government runs a large deficit and borrows from financial markets, less saving will remain to meet the private sector's investment needs. That raises interest rates and causes growth to slow for the whole economy. On the other hand, if the government has a budget surplus, additional funds flowing into financial markets can help keep interest rates low and stimulate private investment.

The link between the government budget and private investment does not mean that it is always a mistake for the government to run a deficit. In later chapters, we will discuss circumstances when it can prudently do so. However, we can see even from the simple circular flow that the way the government manages its budget has important implications for the health of the economy as a whole.

5.1d The Open Economy

We do not live in a closed economy. Our economy has many links, both real and financial, with the rest of the world. Figure 5–3 adds those links to represent the circular flow for an **open economy**.

The first link we add to the circular flow for an open economy is another leakage, **imports**. In everyday life, we are used to thinking of imports as goods flowing into the economy, so it might seem surprising to see imports represented as a leakage, not an injection. However, there is a simple explanation. Remember, the circular flow represents flows of money, not flows of physical objects. A more descriptive term for the leakage we call "imports" would be "payments for imports of goods and services." That would more clearly show that the leakage is the part of household income that is devoted to buying goods and services produced in the rest of the world rather than in the domestic economy.[3]

Figure 5–3 also adds a new injection, **exports**, to match the import leakage. Again, we could more fully describe this item as "payments from the rest of the world for goods and services exported from the domestic economy." It would then be apparent why "exports" takes the form of an arrow pointed toward the domestic economy, not away from it.

The final detail to notice in Figure 5–3 is a pair of arrows linking the rest of the world to domestic financial markets. Just as government purchases do not always exactly equal net taxes, resulting in a government surplus or deficit, imports do not always exactly equal imports, resulting in a surplus or deficit of payments with the rest of the world. In the context of the circular flow, we call this external surplus or deficit **net exports**, which means exports of goods and services minus imports. In other contexts, net exports sometimes go by the name of *trade surplus* (or *trade deficit*, if imports exceed exports).[4]

If imports exceed exports, funds from the sale of exports will be enough to pay for only part of the imports. The balance comes from **financial inflows** from the rest of the world, which appear in the diagram as an arrow running from the rest of the world into domestic financial markets. The most common forms of financial inflows are borrowing from foreign banks or other lenders and sales of domestic securities like stocks or bonds to foreign investors. *Capital inflow* is another term for financial inflow.

On the other hand, if exports exceed imports, buyers in the rest of the world do not earn enough from selling us the goods we import to pay for everything we export. In that case, there must be **financial outflows** sufficient enough to make up the balance. The most common forms of financial outflows are lending by domestic banks and other financial institutions to foreign borrowers and purchases of foreign securities like stocks or bonds by domestic investors.

A country can have financial inflows from some trading partners and financial outflows to others at the same time; so, both arrows can be in action. From the point of view of the economy as a whole, there will be a net financial outflow whenever net exports are positive and a net financial inflow whenever net exports are negative.

5.1e The Balance of Leakages and Injections in an Open Economy

As was the case with a closed economy, individual pairs of leakages and injections do not have to be equal, but total leakages must equal total injections. In equation form,

$$S + T + Im = I + G + Ex$$

where S stands for saving, T for net taxes, Im for imports, I for investment, G for government purchases, and Ex for exports. It is not possible to explore every possible

Open economy

An economy that has links to the outside world in the form of imports, exports, and financial transactions

Imports

A leakage from the circular flow consisting of payments for goods and services purchased from the rest of the world

Exports

An injection into the circular flow consisting of payments received for goods and services sold to the rest of the world

Net exports

Payments received for exports minus payments made for imports

Financial inflows

Purchases of domestic assets by foreign buyers and borrowing from foreign lenders; also often called *capital inflows*

Financial outflows

Purchases of foreign assets by domestic residents or loans by domestic lenders to foreign borrowers; also often called *capital outflows*

FIGURE 5–3

Circular Flow in an Open Economy

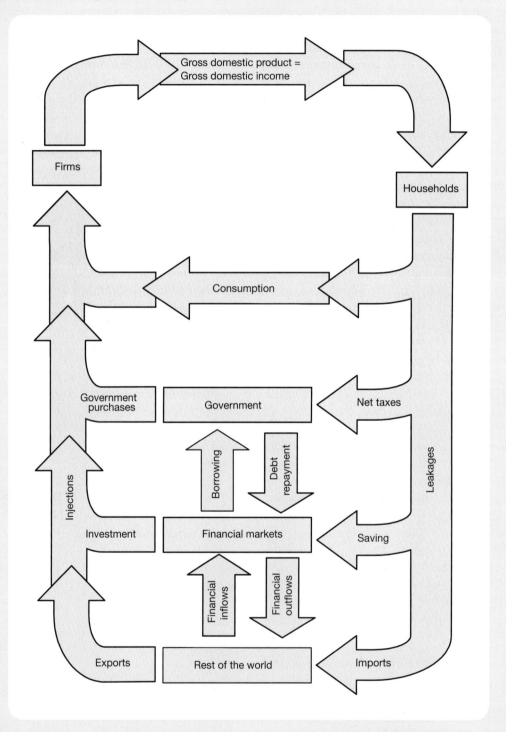

This version of the circular flow represents an open economy that has links to the rest of the world through imports (a leakage) and exports (an injection). Financial inflows from the rest of the world finance any excess of imports over exports. If exports exceed imports, there will be a financial outflow.

way that leakages and injections can balance, but some important variants are worth mentioning.

One possibility is that a country can use a net financial inflow to finance a greater level of domestic investment than would be possible by relying on domestic saving alone. For example, during much of the nineteenth century, the United States had a persistent trade deficit with Europe and, at the same time, a steady financial inflow that made possible the construction of canals, railroads, and other industrial infrastructure that underpinned the country's rapidly developing economy. Today, emerging market economies like Brazil and China often find themselves in a similar position. For such economies, financial inflows are a sign of a strong economy that acts as a magnet for investors from around the world.

In the recent past, the z has borrowed from abroad to finance a government budget deficit.
(Shutterstock)

Another possibility is that a country can use borrowing from abroad not to finance domestic investment but rather to finance a government budget deficit. In terms of the circular flow diagram, such a country would see funds flowing along the arrow from the rest of the world to financial markets, and from there directly along to the government through sale of government bonds to foreign buyers. We sometimes say that a country in such a position suffers from the "twin deficit" syndrome. The United States has been in this position, with both government budget deficits and trade deficits, for much of the recent past.

5.2 THE DETERMINANTS OF PLANNED EXPENDITURE

We turn now from concepts and definitions of GDP and its components to the task of explaining how and why these variables change over time. To do that, we need to look at the choices made by consumers, business managers, and other decision makers. This section provides an overview. An appendix supplements the overview with an optional formal model of planned expenditures.

5.2a The Components of GDP

Our starting point is the circular flow of income and product shown in Figure 5–3. This time our focus is on the total flow of expenditures on goods and services. Those expenditures consist of consumption (by far the largest component) plus purchases of goods and services by government, purchases of investment goods, and expenditures on exported goods and services. Together they equal gross domestic product, which, in turn, equals gross domestic income.

In moving from the circular flow diagram to our macroeconomic model, we need to be careful about one detail. The consumption arrow in the diagram represents consumption expenditures on domestically produced goods. We represent the consumption of imported goods by a separate arrow representing the "imports" leakage. In practice, as we will see in the next chapter, government statisticians do not measure consumption in that way. Instead, the number that they give us in the official national income accounts includes consumption of both domestic and imported consumer goods. The same applies to purchases of imported investment goods by business firms and imported goods used by government. Without adjustment, then, the sum of consumption, investment, government purchases, and exports would overstate expenditures on domestically produced goods and services and, hence, would overstate domestic GDP.

BVT*Lab*

Flashcards are available for this chapter at www.BVTLab.com.

To get an accurate measure of GDP, then, we need to subtract total imports from total measured expenditures. That gives us the following equation, which will serve as the starting point for our model. The Q in the equation stands for the total quantity of output—that is, GDP; the final component, $Ex - Im$, represents net exports:

$$Q = C + I + G + (Ex - Im)$$

5.2b Planned Versus Unplanned Expenditures

Earlier in the chapter, we showed that we could break down investment into *fixed investment* and *inventory investment*. Our next step is to divide inventory investment, in turn, into planned and unplanned components. We say that inventory investment is **planned** if the level of inventories is increased (or reduced) on purpose as part of a firm's business plan. For example, a retail store might increase inventories in response to growth in the number of customers it serves or the number of branch stores it constructs. We call inventory investment **unplanned** if goods accumulate contrary to a firm's business plan. That happens whenever demand is less than expected, so that a firm is unable to sell some of the goods it planned to sell. If demand is greater than expected, so that inventories unexpectedly decrease (or increase at a rate less than scheduled in the business plan), there is negative unplanned inventory investment (disinvestment).

Economists consider all fixed investment to be planned. Total **planned investment**, then, means fixed investment plus planned inventory investment. All other types of expenditure—consumption, government purchases, and net exports—are also considered planned. For that reason, we use the term **planned expenditure** to mean the sum of consumption, government purchases, net exports, and planned investment. In equation form, it is as follows:

$$E_p = C + I_p + G + (Ex - Im)$$

where E_p stands for planned expenditure and I_p for planned investment.

We can explain the level of planned expenditure as a whole by looking at the choices that lie behind each of its components.

5.2c Consumption Expenditure

Choices that consumers make have a more powerful effect on the economy than those of any other group. Consumer expenditure accounts for about two-thirds of GDP in the United States. In some countries, it is a little more; in others, a little less; but almost everywhere, consumption is the largest single component of expenditure. What determines the amount of consumer spending?

Among the first economists to pose that question was John Maynard Keynes (*Who Said It? Who Did It? 5.1*). In his pathbreaking book *The General Theory of Employment, Interest, and Money*, he put it this way:

> The fundamental psychological law, upon which we are entitled to depend with great confidence ... is that men are disposed, as a rule and on the average, to increase their consumption as their income increases, but not by as much as the increase in their income.[5]

He called the amount of additional consumption resulting from a $1 increase in income the **marginal propensity to consume**. For example, if your marginal propensity to consume is 0.75, you will tend to increase your spending by $750 if your income goes up by $1,000.

Planned inventory investment

Changes in the level of inventory made on purpose, as part of a firm's business plan

Unplanned inventory investment

Changes in the level of inventory that arise from a difference between planned and actual sales

Planned investment

The sum of fixed investment and planned inventory investment

Planned expenditure

The sum of consumption, government purchases, net exports, and planned investment

Marginal propensity to consume

The proportion of each added dollar of real disposable income that households devote to consumption

Keynes's "psychological law" regarding consumption needs a few qualifications to state it exactly. First, in place of "income," we really should say **disposable income**, or the amount of income left after taxes. If a person in one state earns $40,000 and pays $5,000 in taxes, while a person in another state earns $50,000 and pays taxes of $15,000, both would have the same disposable income of $35,000. Other things being equal, we would expect them to spend the same amount on consumption.

Second, we need to state the relationship between consumption and disposable income in real terms. If both prices and nominal disposable income rise in exact proportion, there is no change in real income; so we would expect no change in real consumption expenditure, other things being equal.

Third, the marginal propensity to consume—which is the amount of each added dollar of income devoted to consumption—is not equal to the ratio of total consumption to total income. That is because there is a minimum level of consumption that people would like to maintain even if their income were zero. Keynes called that minimum "autonomous consumption." Intuitively, you can think of the case of a college student who has no income but maintains a minimum level of consumption by borrowing against future income, or an unemployed person who has no income but maintains a minimum level of consumption by drawing on past saving. The appendix to this chapter states the relationship between consumption spending and income in mathematical terms, taking into account both autonomous consumption and the marginal propensity to consume.

Disposable income

Income minus taxes

Who Said It? Who Did It? **5.1**

John Maynard Keynes: The General Theory

(Associated Press)

John Maynard Keynes was born into economics. His father, John Neville Keynes, was a lecturer in economics and logic at Cambridge University. John Maynard Keynes began his own studies at Cambridge in mathematics and philosophy. However, his abilities so impressed Alfred Marshall that the distinguished teacher urged him to concentrate on economics. In 1908, after Keynes had finished his studies and done a brief stint in the civil service, Marshall offered him a lectureship in economics at Cambridge; Keynes accepted.

In 1936, Keynes published *The General Theory of Employment, Interest, and Money,* a book that many still see as the foundation of macroeconomics. Although not his first book, it established his reputation as the outstanding economist of his generation. Its major features are a bold theory based on broad macroeconomic aggregates and a strong argument for activist and interventionist policies.

Keynes was interested in more than economics. He was an honored member not only of Britain's academic upper class, but also of the nation's highest financial, political, diplomatic, administrative, and even artistic circles. He had close ties to the colorful "Bloomsbury set" of London's literary world. He was a friend of Virginia Woolf, E. M. Forster, and Lytton Strachey. He was a dazzling success at whatever he turned his hand to, from mountain climbing to financial speculation. As a speculator, he made a huge fortune for himself; and as bursar of King's College, he built an endowment of ₤30,000 into one of over ₤380,000.

(Continues)

(Who Said It? Who Did It? 5.1 Continued)

Keynes wrote in *The General Theory:*

The ideas of economists and political philosophers, both when they are right and when they are wrong, are more powerful than is commonly understood. Indeed little else rules the world. Practical men, who believe themselves to be quite exempt from any intellectual influences, are usually the slaves of some defunct economist. Madmen in authority, who hear voices in the air, are distilling their frenzy from some academic scribbler of a few years back. … There are not many who are influenced by new theories after they are twenty-five or thirty years of age, so that the ideas which civil servants and politicians and even agitators apply to current events are not likely to be the newest.

Was Keynes issuing a warning here? Whether or not he had any such thing in mind, his words are ironic because he himself has become one of those economists whose ideas remain influential long after they were first articulated.

Although income is the principal factor that determines consumption spending, certain other factors could also have an effect.

- *Changes in net taxes (either taxes paid or transfer payments received)*   These act by changing the amount of disposable income associated with a given total income.

- *Changes in consumer wealth—that is, the accumulated value of assets a person owns*   For example, a home is the biggest asset for many households. In a period when housing prices rise more rapidly than income, as happened in the United States in the early 2000s, consumer spending rises more than expected from changes in income alone.

- *Interest rates*   If interest rates fall, people can borrow more cheaply and may buy more goods and services on credit. Also, the amount they have to pay in interest on credit cards, mortgages, and other debt decreases, leaving more to buy consumer goods.

- *Consumer confidence*   In periods when consumers feel secure about their jobs and expect their incomes to rise in line with general prosperity, they tend to spend more for any given level of income. In times of pessimism and insecurity, people tend to be cautious and increase their saving as protection against the expected rainy day.

5.2d Planned Investment

The second component of planned expenditure is planned investment. It depends on two principal factors.

First, planned investment depends on interest rates (more specifically, on real interest rates—that is, interest rates adjusted for inflation, as explained in Chapter 4). For example, suppose you run a construction business and you are thinking about improving the productivity of your workers by buying a new backhoe that costs $50,000. Your banker is willing to lend you the money, but you will have to pay 6 percent per year interest, equivalent to $250 per month on the loan of $50,000. If the bank charged 12 percent interest, your monthly interest payments would rise to $500 and you would be less likely to buy the new machine. If the interest rate were just 3 percent, monthly interest payments would be only $125 and you would be more likely to make the investment.

Although it is not so obvious, interest rates also play a role in investment decisions for a company that plans to finance investment from its own retained profits. Suppose your construction company had put aside $100,000 in cash from profits earned the previous year. Then you would not have to borrow from the bank to buy the backhoe. However, using half of your cash reserves to buy the backhoe still has an opportunity cost. For example, if the rate of interest on government bonds is 6 percent, your company could earn $250 per month by using that $50,000 from your cash reserves to buy bonds instead of buying the backhoe.[6] If the interest rate were 12 percent per year, your monthly income from the bonds would be $500—a greater opportunity cost—and you would be more tempted to buy the bonds instead of the backhoe.

Interest rates influence investment decisions by consumers as well as businesses. Residential construction accounts for about a third of all private fixed investment in the United States. For example, low interest rates contributed to the US housing boom of the early 2000s.

Interest rates are not the only factor influencing investment decisions. Business confidence is also important. By this, we mean the whole complex of expectations and hopes on which firms make their plans for the future. If you expect a boom in the housing market in your area, your construction company is more likely than otherwise to buy that backhoe. If you expect doom and gloom ahead, you'll play it safe by buying the government bonds. Keynes referred to business confidence using the colorful term "animal spirits." In doing so, he wanted to emphasize the fact that business confidence can change quickly for reasons that are hard for economists to measure exactly. A lack of confidence is a major reason housing investment in the United States remained low, despite low interest rates, even after the economy as a whole began to recover from recession.

On a global scale, the decision of how much to invest in a given country depends on the country's investment climate, as well as interest rates. Among the conditions that make up a country's investment climate are its tax laws, the amount of "red tape" the country's bureaucracy generates, the likelihood that criminal gangs or corrupt officials will siphon off profits, and the stability of macroeconomic conditions. In countries where the investment climate is good, domestic firms are willing to put profits into expansion of their operations, and international firms are willing to bring in new capital and know-how. In countries where the investment climate is bad, domestic firms send their profits abroad for safekeeping rather than investing them at home, and global business stays away.

5.2e Government Purchases and Net Exports

In most simple macroeconomic models, including the one outlined in the appendix to this chapter, government purchases are **exogenous**. That means they are determined by politics or other considerations that lie outside the model rather than by any variables that are included in the model. Transfer payments and tax revenues, on the other hand, are **endogenous**, in that they depend on the level of real GDP, a variable that is part of the model. During the expansion phase of the business cycle, tax revenues rise and transfer payments, especially for unemployment benefits, fall. During a recession, tax collections fall and transfer payments rise.

The variable *net exports* is endogenous because it depends on real GDP. As real GDP increases, both consumers and businesses spend some of their increased income on imported goods. For that reason, net exports tend to fall, and a country's trade deficit tends to widen during the expansion phase of the business cycle.

The exchange rate of a country's currency also affects imports and exports. For example, during most of the early 2000s, the US dollar gradually weakened relative to the currencies of its main trading partners. As the dollar weakened, it became easier for

Exogenous

Any variable that is determined by noneconomic considerations, or by economic considerations that lie outside the scope of a given model

Endogenous

Any variable that is determined by other variables included in an economic model

US firms to sell their exports, and, at the same time, imports became more expensive for US buyers. Exchange rates, in turn, depend on many factors, including changes in real GDP, inflation, and interest rates. We will return to the complex interaction between net exports and other economic variables in later chapters.

5.3 EQUILIBRIUM IN THE CIRCULAR FLOW

Chapter 2 introduced the concept of market equilibrium. The market for any single good—say, chicken—is in equilibrium when the amount buyers plan to purchase equals the amount that producers supply for sale. When the market for chicken is in equilibrium, there will be no tendency for accumulation or decrease of inventories, and no immediate pressure for market participants to change their plans.

We can extend the idea of equilibrium as a situation where there is no unplanned inventory change to the circular flow of income and expenditure. When total planned expenditures (consumption plus planned investment plus government purchases plus net exports) equal GDP, total planned purchases will equal total production, and there will be no unplanned inventory change for the economy as a whole. As a result, there will be no pressure from unplanned inventory change to cause changes in production plans. Anything that increases or decreases total planned expenditures will disrupt the equilibrium. Let's see how this process works out as the economy expands and contracts over the business cycle.

When the amount of chicken that buyers plan to purchase equals the amount producers supply for sale, the market is in equilibrium. (Shutterstock)

5.3a Changes in Planned Expenditure

Suppose that the circular flow is initially in equilibrium with total planned expenditure exactly equal to GDP. Since firms are producing goods at just the rate they are selling them, the level of inventories remains constant from one month to the next. Now suppose that something happens to disturb this equilibrium. For example, suppose that development of new, energy-efficient technologies causes an upturn in investment as firms replace obsolete, energy-wasting equipment.

As equipment makers increase their output of goods to satisfy the increased investment demand, they will take on more workers. The wage component of national income will increase. Profits of equipment makers are also likely to increase, further adding to the expansion of national income.

From our earlier discussion, we know that when incomes rise, households will increase their consumption expenditure. So far, there has been no change in the output of consumer goods; so as consumption expenditure begins to increase, the first effect will be an unplanned decrease in inventories. Only then, when makers of consumer goods see inventories falling, will they modify their production plans to meet the new demand. As they do so, they, too, will need to hire new workers, and incomes will rise further.

In this way, the original economic stimulus—which began in the industrial equipment sector—spreads through the economy. GDP and domestic income continue to rise, but not without limit. Because (according to the principle of the marginal propensity to consume) people spend only a part of any increase in income on consumer goods, each round of the cycle of "more production, more income, more spending" is smaller than the previous one. Before long, GDP reaches a new equilibrium where production and planned expenditure balance, and there are no further unplanned changes in inventories.

Recall that the whole process began with an assumed increase in planned investment. By the time the economy reaches a new equilibrium, the total change in GDP will be greater than the original increase in planned investment because it will also include production of additional consumer goods. The principle that a given initial change in planned expenditure changes equilibrium GDP by a greater amount is known as the **multiplier effect**. The appendix to this chapter explains the multiplier effect in more detail.

The same process operates in reverse when there is a decrease in some category of planned expenditure. For example, suppose a crisis in the Mexican economy reduces US exports to that country. The first effect will be that US makers of export goods will find inventories rising because Mexican importers are not buying as much as they had planned before the crisis. To bring inventories in line with reduced sales, US makers of export goods cut their output. The makers of export goods lay off workers or put them on shorter hours, and their incomes fall. As a result, those workers cut back on consumption, following the principle of the marginal propensity to consume. When that happens, makers of consumer goods also find that their inventories unexpectedly increase. They, too, cut back on output, and incomes of their workers also fall.

As the process continues, GDP and domestic income decrease. They do not decrease without limit, however. Before long, the economy reaches a new equilibrium. When it does so, real GDP will have decreased by a greater amount than the original change in exports—an example of the multiplier effect operating in reverse.

5.3b The Multiplier Effect and the Business Cycle

The multiplier effect was one of the key ideas in Keynes's *General Theory*. Coming at the height of the Great Depression, economists immediately seized on this key idea as an explanation for the business cycle.

In its simplest form, the Keynesian explanation of the Great Depression went something like this: During the 1920s, the US economy entered a boom due to the multiplier effect of huge investment expenditures—especially expansion of automobile production and road building. Then, in 1929, came the Black Friday stock market crash. The crash destroyed business confidence, and investment fell. This time the multiplier effect operated in reverse to produce the Great Depression.

At the same time that the multiplier effect seemed to explain the Great Depression, it also seemed to suggest a cure. What if the government increased its purchases of goods and services by enough to offset the drop in private investment? Wouldn't that send equilibrium GDP back to its original level? This reasoning gave rise to various attempts to spend the country back to prosperity—for example, by hiring thousands of unemployed workers for service in national parks. The nation did not fully recover from the Great Depression until the start of World War II brought on a further surge in government purchases.

Modern macroeconomics makes a place for the multiplier effect and recognizes that there is an element of truth in the simple Keynesian view of the business cycle. However, the simple multiplier theory is seriously incomplete. One shortcoming concerns changes in the price level over the business cycle. When producers respond to an unexpected decrease in inventories, do they increase real output without changing prices, do they raise prices to take advantage of unexpectedly strong demand, or do they do a little of both? Another problem is that the simple multiplier theory does not consider capacity constraints related to labor inputs, capital, and technology. Does real output respond in the same way to a change in planned expenditure when the economy is operating above its natural level of real output as it does when the economy is operating below it? Still another limitation is that the theory pays too little attention to the role of money and the financial sector. Later chapters will deal with all of these issues in order to give a more complete picture.

Multiplier effect

The tendency of a given exogenous change in planned expenditure to increase equilibrium GDP by a greater amount

Summary

1. How do incomes and expenditures link households and firms?

In order to produce goods and services, firms pay wages and salaries to obtain labor inputs, interest to obtain capital, and rents and royalties to obtain natural resources. If sales exceed costs, firms earn profits. The sum of wages, salaries, interest, rents, royalties, and profits constitutes domestic income.

2. What are the relationships between injections and leakages in the circular flow?

Saving, net taxes (tax revenues minus transfer payments), and imports are leakages from the circular flow. Investment, government purchases, and exports are injections. The total of leakages must always equal the total of injections, but the individual pairs (saving and investment, net taxes and government purchases, imports and exports) do not need to balance. Flows of funds through the financial sector compensate for any imbalance in the individual pairs.

3. How can we divide expenditure into consumption, investment, government purchases, and net exports?

The largest part of domestic income goes to buy consumer goods and services. Some is also spent on newly produced capital goods or adding to inventories (investment), to pay for goods and services purchased by government, or to buy imported goods. Foreign buyers of a country's exports also make expenditures. The term *net exports* means exports minus imports.

4. Why is some investment planned and other unplanned?

Planned investment means fixed investment (purchases of newly produced capital goods) plus planned inventory investment (changes in inventory made on purpose as part of a business plan). In addition, inventories may change unexpectedly in ways not called for by firms' business plans. We call these changes unplanned inventory investment.

5. How can we apply the concept of equilibrium to the circular flow of income and expenditure?

The circular flow of income and product is in equilibrium when total planned expenditure equals GDP. If planned expenditure exceeds GDP, so that firms are selling more goods than they are producing, there will be unplanned decreases in inventories. In reaction, firms will increase output, and GDP will tend to rise. If total planned expenditure falls short of GDP, there will be unplanned increases in inventories. In response, firms will tend to decrease their output, and GDP will fall.

6. What is the multiplier effect, and how does it affect the business cycle?

According to the multiplier effect, a given change in one type of expenditure (say, planned investment) will produce a larger change in equilibrium GDP. The multiplier effect helps explain how relatively small disturbances in expenditure can cause relatively larger changes in GDP over the course of the business cycle.

KEY TERMS

PROBLEMS AND TOPICS FOR DISCUSSION

1.   **Your personal expenditures**   What was your income last month (or last year) from all current resources, including wages and salaries plus any interest earned or other investment income? Do not count money that you received as transfer payments, such as government benefits, gifts from family, scholarship grants, and so on. How much was your saving? Did you add to your savings or draw down on past savings? How much did you spend on consumer goods or services? Of your spending, approximately how much do you think you spent on imported goods or on services purchased during foreign travel? Identify where the answer to each of these questions appears in the circular flow diagram, Figure 5–3.

2.   **Planned versus unplanned inventory changes**   Suppose your school bookstore manager learns from the admissions office that enrollment of students will rise by 10 percent next year. What planned inventory investments would the bookstore manager make? Suppose that a storm delays the departure of one hundred students from another university who have visited your campus for a hockey game. While waiting for their buses to leave, they decide to browse your school bookstore and buy some items that catch their eye. How would that affect the store's inventories?

3.   **Unplanned inventory change and disequilibrium**   Suppose that you read in the news that inventories in retail stores fell last month, to the surprise of analysts. Would you interpret that as a sign of equilibrium or disequilibrium in the circular flow? Which do you think would be more likely in the coming months, an increase or a decrease in GDP? Why?

4.   **Adjustment to change in planned expenditure**   Starting from a state of equilibrium, trace the effects of each of the following. What happens to inventories? How do firms react? What happens to incomes? To consumption expenditure? To GDP?

   a.   Business managers, anticipating future profit opportunities in consumer electronics, increase orders for production equipment in order to prepare for the expected increase in demand.

   b.   The federal government reduces income tax rates.

   c.   Good harvests in Africa reduce the demand for exports of US farm products.

CASE for DISCUSSION

Rebalancing the Chinese Economy

The rapid growth of the Chinese economy has been the biggest economic story of the twenty-first century; but, as the chart shows, that growth has been slowing. International Monetary Fund data suggest that the rate of expansion of Chinese GDP will fall below 7 percent per year by 2015, far below the average rate since 2000. Outside observers and Chinese officials alike say it will not be able to achieve even that rate unless it can rebalance its economy.

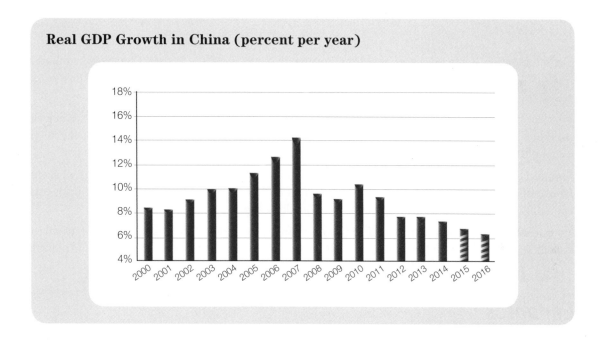

Real GDP Growth in China (percent per year)

The structure of the Chinese economy in recent years has been dramatically different from that of the United States and most other advanced economies. Household consumption accounts for some 68 percent of US GDP, but only about 35 percent in China. Instead, the largest share of China's GDP consists of investment, as much as 45 percent in some years, compared with about 18 percent in the United States. The share of net exports is also dramatically different. During the fastest years of China's growth, net exports averaged around 8 percent of GDP, compared with net imports of about 3 percent in the United States. To round out the picture, government purchases make up only about 12 percent of GDP in China, compared with a little over 17 percent in the US economy. (Government purchases do not reflect the full weight of the Chinese government in the economy, since they do not include the activities of state-owned industries.)

As time has passed, it has become evident that China's investment-led growth model is running out of steam. One sign is falling capacity use in basic industries like steel and cement, where new plants have been built faster than demand for their products has grown. Housing construction has also run ahead of demand, with the result that many new apartment buildings—some say whole cities—stand empty.

(Continues)

(Case for Discussion Continued)

If investment slows, can consumption take its place? Theoretically, yes; but the government cannot just order people to consume more. Chinese families are fanatical savers. Chinese families consider it normal to save a third of their disposable income, compared to an average of about 5 percent in the United States. In part, the reasons for high saving are cultural. In part, also, they are a by-product of a weak social safety net; because government benefits are not as generous as in many Western countries, Chinese families feel they must put ample money aside for health-care needs, education, and retirement.

Meanwhile, the whole world is watching nervously to see whether China will manage its rebalancing smoothly. Already, the slowdown in Chinese growth is undercutting the economies of raw material exporters like Brazil and Australia. In the United States, makers of Buicks, Boeings, and iPhones are worried, too. China is already the world's largest economy by many measures. What happens there is sure to affect everyone.

Source: International Monetary Fund, World Economic Outlook Database, April 2015.

Questions

1. Turn to Figure 5–3. Suppose you were to redraw the figure for both the US and Chinese economies so that the relative size of the arrows was proportional to their share in GDP. Which arrows would be most strongly affected?

2. Why does slowing growth of the Chinese economy spell trouble for raw materials exporters like Brazil and Australia? Which elements of the circular flow in those countries would you expect to change as the direct effect of the slowdown of the Chinese economy? Which might change as an indirect effect?

3. Suppose that total investment in China decreases, but consumers continue their high rate of saving. What kinds of policy changes might the Chinese government try in order to keep the economy from contracting, even if investment were to fall while consumption did not grow?

Bonus question (based on the appendix to this chapter)   Based on information in the case, what could you conclude about the strength of the multiplier effect in the Chinese economy? Explain your reasoning.

Endnotes

1. Economists use the term *households* to refer to families who live together and make economic decisions together about issues of work and spending, as well as to individuals living alone who make such decisions independently.

2. We will add some minor qualifications to this statement in the next chapter.

3. Figure 5–3 is incomplete in that it shows only imports of consumer goods purchased by households. In practice, business firms purchase some imported capital goods as part of their investment spending, and the government also purchases some imported goods and services. We could, in principle, draw in additional small arrows to represent flows of payments for imported capital goods and government purchases, but doing so would make the diagram too complex to read easily.

4. The term *trade deficit*, as it is popularly used, does not always correspond exactly to our term *net exports*. The next chapter will discuss concepts related to imports, exports, and the balance of payments in more detail.

5. John Maynard Keynes, *The General Theory of Employment, Interest, and Money* (New York: Harcourt, Brace and World, 1936), 96.

6. To understand this example, it is important to remember that buying the backhoe is a purchase of newly produced capital goods—that is, part of the fixed investment component of planned expenditure. Buying the government bond is a financial investment—a purchase of the right to receive future payments from the government. The bonds are not newly produced capital goods and do not count as part of GDP.

Appendix to Chapter 5

The Planned Expenditure Model

The Elements of Planned Expenditure

This appendix presents a simple graphical and mathematical model of the factors that determine the equilibrium level of planned expenditure and GDP. Our starting point is the planned expenditure equation given in the chapter:

$$E_p = C + I_p + G + (Ex - Im)$$

Our next step is to look, one by one, at the main components of planned expenditure. We distinguish between two types of expenditures: those that are a function of the level of income, and those that are not. We call the former income-dependent components of planned expenditure, and the latter, autonomous components.

Consumption

The level of consumption, other things being equal, depends on the level of disposable income—that is, on the level of gross domestic income minus net taxes. In equation form:

$$C = \alpha + \beta(Q - T)$$

Economists call this equation the consumption function. In it, α represents *autonomous consumption* (that is, the part of consumption that does not depend on the level of income); β the marginal propensity to consume; and Q, the level of real GDP—which, as we know, is equal to the level of domestic income.

Many kinds of taxes (for example, income and profits taxes) are income dependent. Other taxes, which we call autonomous net taxes, do not depend on the level of income (for example, taxes based on the value of real estate). Taking both kinds of taxes into account, we can represent the level of net taxes, T, by the following equation:

$$T = t_0 + t_1 \times Q$$

where t_0 represents autonomous net taxes and t_1 represents the share of each added dollar of real GDP that goes to net taxes. We call the variable t_1 the *marginal tax rate*.

If we substitute the tax equation into the consumption function, we can restate the latter in terms of GDP rather than in terms of disposable income:

$$C = a + bQ$$

The parameter a, which is equal to $\alpha - \beta t_0$, is the level of autonomous consumption corresponding to zero real GDP. We will call the parameter b, which is equal to $\beta(1 - t_1)$, the marginal propensity to consume from GDP in order to distinguish it from β, which is the marginal propensity to consume from disposable income.

Investment

The main factors that determine planned investment are real interest rates, which determine the cost of financing purchases of inventories and capital goods, and business confidence. (As explained in Chapter 4, the real interest rate is the nominal interest rate minus the rate of inflation.) Using r to represent the real interest rate, we can state the level of planned investment as

$$I_p = i_0 - (i_1 \times r)$$

where i_0 stands for business confidence and i_1 represents the sensitivity of planned investment to the real interest rate. Because it is not a function of the level of GDP, planned investment is a type of autonomous expenditure.

Government Purchases and Net Exports

In simple macroeconomic models, government purchases are exogenous—that is, not determined by variables included in the model. Because government purchases are not a function of GDP, they, too, are a form of autonomous expenditure.

Net exports are an endogenous variable that depends in part on exchange rates and in part on the level of GDP. As mentioned earlier in the chapter, when GDP rises, consumers and businesses tend to spend more on imports. That affects the value of the parameter b, the marginal propensity to consume from GDP. In an economy open to international trade, this variable refers to the consumption of domestically produced consumer goods. As a result, the value of b in an open economy is somewhat less than it would be in a closed economy—that is, in one with no international trade. Export demand is not dependent on domestic GDP; so it is a type of autonomous expenditure.

Putting consumption, planned investment, and government purchases together, the following equation gives level of planned expenditure

$$E_p = A + bQ$$

where A stands for autonomous expenditure—that is, the total of autonomous consumption, planned investment, government purchases, and the autonomous component of net exports; and the parameter b is the marginal propensity to consume from GDP. The value of A must be greater than zero, and the value of b, between zero and one.

The Equilibrium Level of Real Output

Figure 5A–1 shows the planned expenditure schedule, $E_p = A + bQ$, for an economy where the value of autonomous expenditure, A, is 200 and that of the marginal propensity to consume, b, is 0.5. Equilibrium in the circular flow requires that planned expenditure be equal to real output, a condition that holds anywhere along the line $E_p = Q$. Only one value for Q satisfies both conditions—the value for which the two curves intersect. In this case, that occurs at a level of real output of 400.

For any level of real output greater than the equilibrium level, planned expenditure is less than real output. That means that consumers, investors, government, and exporters are planning to buy a smaller volume of goods and services than is being produced. Goods that firms produce but do not sell do not vanish into thin air. Instead, they accumulate in inventory, even though that was not part of the producers' original business plans. We can see, then, that whenever real output is greater than the equilibrium level, there must be unplanned inventory accumulation. For example, in Figure 5A–1, unplanned inventory investment is equal to 100 when real output is 600 (as shown by the arrow). Businesses tend to react to unplanned inventory accumulation by reducing output. When they do so, real GDP will move downward toward its equilibrium level.

Similarly, when real output is below its equilibrium level, total planned expenditure will exceed production. If firms are selling more goods than they produce, there will be an unplanned depletion of inventories. To correct the unplanned depletion of inventories, businesses will tend to increase their level of output, and real GDP will move upward toward its equilibrium level.

FIGURE 5A–1

Equilibrium of Planned Expenditure and Real Output in the Circular Flow

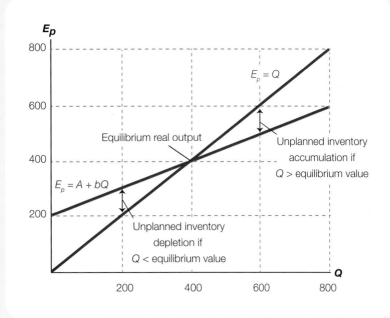

We can express the same equilibrium condition in algebraic terms by substituting the planned expenditure equation, $E_p = A + bQ$, into the equilibrium condition $E_p = Q$. The result is an equation for the equilibrium level of GDP:

$$Q = A \times \frac{1}{1-b}$$

The Multiplier Effect

The term $1/(1 - b)$ is known as the expenditure multiplier because a $1 increase in autonomous expenditure will cause equilibrium real GDP to increase by $1 times the multiplier. For example, in Figure 5A–1, autonomous expenditure is 200, and the marginal propensity to consume from GDP is 0.5; so equilibrium GDP is 400. The value of the expenditure multiplier is two, so a $1 increase in autonomous consumption would produce a $2 increase in the equilibrium level of real GDP.

A change for any reason in any component of autonomous expenditure can cause a change in the equilibrium level of real output. As an example, Figure 5A–2 considers the effect of a change in planned investment resulting from a change in the real interest rate. In that figure, an increase in the interest rate, r, from r_0 to a higher value of r_1 reduces the planned investment component of autonomous expenditure by 80 units. Graphically, we show this as a downward shift of the planned expenditure schedule to a position where the vertical intercept is 120 rather than 200. Through the operation of the multiplier effect, the equilibrium value of real output is reduced from 400 to 240.

The value of two given for the expenditure multiplier in our example is arbitrary. In practice, the value of the expenditure multiplier for a given economy depends on several considerations. Other things being equal:

- The greater the marginal propensity to consume (from disposable income), the greater the multiplier.

- The greater the marginal tax rate, the lower the expenditure multiplier. (The reason for this is that, when the marginal tax rate is high, a given change in GDP will cause a smaller change in disposable income.)

- The greater the share of consumption devoted to imported goods, the less the expenditure multiplier. (As a result, we expect the multiplier effect to be stronger for large, relatively closed economies where most consumer goods are domestic than for small, open economies where more consumer goods are imports.)

FIGURE 5A–2

Effect of an Increase in Interest Rates

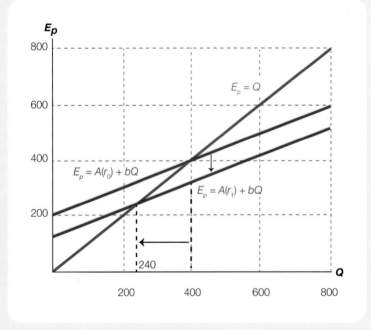

CHAPTER 6

MEASURING ECONOMIC ACTIVITY

AFTER READING THIS CHAPTER,
you will understand the following:

1. How the government measures gross domestic product
2. How domestic income differs from gross domestic product
3. The major types of international transactions
4. How the government measures inflation
5. The limitations of official economic statistics

BEFORE READING THIS CHAPTER,
make sure you know the following concepts:

Real and nominal values

Indexation

Transfer payments

Domestic income and product

CHAPTER
Outline

Measurement matters. Every day, new data on GDP, prices, and trade deficits reach our laptops, smartphones, and tablets. People act on them, instantly, throughout the world. An upward revision of the estimate for real output can send stock markets higher. News that a country's trade deficit has increased can send its exchange rate plunging. News that inflation remains unchanged at a time when traders expect it to increase can affect interest rates, bond prices, and the prices of commodities like gold and oil. Just having instant access to the numbers, however, is not enough. To use the latest data intelligently, you must know what they mean and where they come from. That means knowing not only the meaning of terms and concepts but also how they are measured.

Together, we call the official government data on aggregate economic activity the **national income accounts**. The economists and statisticians whose job it is to make these measurements for the US economy are one of the best such teams in the world. Yet, as this chapter will show, they have a hard job. They must deal with technical problems posed by sampling errors and survey methods. They encounter conceptual problems when real-world data sources do not match the theoretical categories of economic models. They constantly encounter trade-offs between accuracy and timeliness. This chapter addresses all of these issues and more.

6.1 The National Income Accounts in Nominal Terms

We begin with an examination of the national income accounts in nominal terms—that is, in terms of the prices at which sales of goods and services actually take place. Nominal measures do not tell the whole story because they do not include adjustments for inflation. They do provide a starting point, however. Government statisticians first collect the data in nominal form. Only after they have assembled a set of nominal accounts can they begin the process of adjusting for price changes.

6.1a Gross Domestic Product

The most widely publicized number in the national income accounts is gross domestic product. Chapter 4 gave a preliminary definition of **gross domestic product (GDP)** as a measure of the value of total output of goods and services produced within a country. We can now add a more technical definition: GDP is the value at current market prices (that is, the nominal value) of all final goods and services produced annually in a given country.

The term **final goods and services** is a key part of the definition of gross domestic product. GDP attempts to measure the sum of the economic contributions of each firm and industry without missing anything or counting anything twice. To do this accurately, it is important to count only goods sold to *final users*—parties that will use them for domestic consumption, government purchases, investment, or export. **Intermediate goods**—those that firms buy for use as inputs in producing other goods or services—do not constitute part of GDP.

Table 6.1 shows why counting both final and intermediate goods would overstate total production. The table traces the process of producing a kitchen table that has a retail price of $100. The final stage of production takes place in a furniture factory, but the factory does not do $100 worth of work. Instead, it produces the table by taking $40 worth of lumber and adding $60 worth of labor of factory workers. The $40 worth of lumber is an intermediate good; the $60 contribution made by the manufacturer is the **value added** to the product at its final stage. (In practice, the firm would also use other

Sidebar (margin glossary)

National income accounts

A set of official government statistics on aggregate economic activity

Gross domestic product (GDP)

(1) A measure of the value of total output of goods and services produced within a country; (2) The value at current market prices of all final goods and services produced annually in a given country

Final goods and services

Goods and services sold to or ready for sale to parties that will use them for consumption, investment, government purchases, or exports

Intermediate goods

Goods and services that firms buy for use as inputs in producing other goods and services

Value added

The dollar value of an industry's sales less the value of intermediate goods purchased for use in production

intermediate goods, such as paint and fuel for heating the plant, and other factors of production, like capital in the form of woodworking equipment. To simplify the example we assume that lumber and labor are the only inputs.)

Table 6.1 Value Added and the Use of Final Products in GDP

Final stage—manufacturing:			
Value of one table	$100		
Less value of lumber	−40		
Equals value added in manufacturing	60	————————	$60
Next-to-final stage—sawmill:			
Value of lumber	$40		
Less value of logs	−15		
Equals value added at sawmill	25	————————	$25
Second-to-final stage—forest products:			
Value of logs	$15		
Less value of fuel, equipment, etc.	−5		
Equals value added in timber farming	10	————————	$10
All previous stages:			
Value added in fuel, equipment, etc.	$5	————————	$5
Total value added			**$100**

This table shows why GDP must include only the value of final goods and services if it is to measure total production without double counting. We divide the value of sales at each stage of production into the value each firm adds at its own stage of production and the value of intermediate goods it buys. The selling price of the final product (a $100 kitchen table, in this case) equals the sum of the values added at all stages of production.

The second section of Table 6.1 shows the next-to-last stage of production: making the lumber. The sawmill buys $15 worth of logs, adds $25 worth of labor and capital, and produces lumber worth $40. The value added at the sawmill stage is thus $25.

Going still further back, we come to the stage at which the forest products company cuts the logs that are the source of the lumber. Inputs at that stage include $5 worth of fuel and purchased equipment, plus value added of $10 that represents factors of production used in tending the trees and harvesting the logs. That is an additional $10 of value added.

We could trace the process of making the table back to still earlier stages of production. The last section of the exhibit sums up the value added at all stages of production prior to timber farming—the fuel and equipment suppliers, their own suppliers, and so on. If we went back far enough, we could attribute every penny to the value added to the final product somewhere in the chain of production.

Now compare the first and last lines of the table. The value of the final goods turns out to be exactly equal to the sum of the values added at each stage of production. This is why we count only final goods as part of GDP. Adding together the $100 value of the finished kitchen table, the $40 value of the lumber, the $15 value of the timber, and so on would far overstate the true rate of productive activity (the true total value added) in the economy.

6.1b Measuring the Economy by the Expenditure Approach

In principle, we could measure GDP by adding together the value of each good or service sold and adjusting for the cost of inputs to get the value added at each stage of production, as in Table 6.1. However, that is not the principal approach that government statisticians use. Instead, they use what we call the *expenditure approach,* which makes use of the equality of domestic product and total expenditure. It is easier to gather data on the total amount that households, investors, governments, and buyers of exports spend on final goods than it is to stand at factory gates and count goods as they roll off production lines. Table 6.2 shows how it works, using 2015 data for the US economy.

Table 6.2 **Nominal Gross Domestic Product by Type of Expenditure, 2015 (Dollars in Billions)**

Personal consumption expenditure		$12,228.4
Durable goods	$1,326.4	
Nondurable goods	2,651.8	
Services	8,250.2	
Plus gross private domestic investment		3,025.5
Fixed investment	2,897.9	
Change in private inventories	127.5	
Plus government consumption expenditures and gross investment		3,179.2
Federal	1,220.7	
State and local	1,958.4	
Plus net exports of goods and services		−519.3
Exports	2,280.0	
Less imports	−2,799.3	
Equals gross domestic product (GDP)		$17,913.7
Less allowance for consumption of fixed capital		−2,804.4
Equals net domestic product (NDP)		$15,109.3

This table shows the procedure for estimating gross domestic product using the expenditure approach. This approach involves adding together the values of expenditures on newly produced final goods and services made by all economic units to get a measure of aggregate economic activity. Net domestic product is equal to gross domestic product minus the value of expenditures on replacement of worn-out or obsolete capital equipment.

Source: Bureau of Economic Analysis, News Release: Gross Domestic Product, Sept. 25, 2015.

The first line of Table 6.2 gives total household consumption of both domestically produced and imported goods and services. The national income accounts divide consumption into three categories: durable goods like cars and appliances, nondurable goods like food and clothing, and services like medical care and banking. All three components of consumption contain some items that do not pass through markets on their way to consumers. One such item is an estimate of the quantity of food that farm families produce and consume themselves. Another is an estimate of the rental value of owner-occupied homes. However, the national income accounts omit many nonmarket goods and services—for example, unpaid childcare and housework.

The item *gross private domestic investment* is the sum of all purchases of newly produced capital goods (fixed investment) plus changes in business inventories (inventory investment). The fixed investment component includes both business fixed investment—all new equipment and structures bought by firms—and the value of newly constructed residential housing. In effect, the national income accounts treat a family that owns a home like a small firm. When the family buys the home, the accounts treat the purchase as an investment. They then treat the firm's "product"—the rental value of its shelter services—as part of annual consumption.

The gross private domestic investment item does not include investment in structures, software, and equipment by federal, state, and local governments, which accounts for about 25 percent of the total of all investment for the economy. From the point of view of short-run business cycle theory, it makes sense to treat government and private investment differently since the motives for the investment are different. However, from the point of long-term growth theory, government investment, like private investment, adds to a country's stock of capital and increases future natural real GDP.

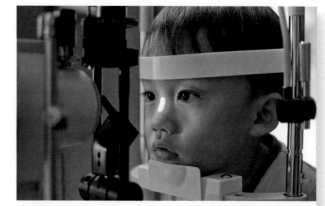

Medical care is included in the services section of the national income accounts. (Shutterstock)

As mentioned in Chapter 5, the item that economists call "government purchases" goes by the name "government consumption expenditures and gross investment" in the official national income accounts. Whether consumption-like or investment-like, government purchases enter into the national income accounts at cost. Accountants make no attempt to measure the value added by government because, in most cases, the goods and services it provides have no prices. Instead, governments pay for things like primary and secondary education, police protection, and national defense with revenue from taxes and provide them to the public without charge. The government's contribution to GDP also does not include transfer payments like Social Security benefits or unemployment compensation. Those are omitted because they are not purchases of newly produced final goods and services.

Net exports—exports minus imports—are the last item in the GDP accounts. In calculating GDP, we must subtract imports from exports to avoid double counting. That is, because some of the goods that consumers, firms, and governments buy come from outside the domestic economy. For example, a consumer might buy a Japanese television set, an insurance company might buy Korean computers for use in its offices, and a city government might buy a Swedish police car. As a result, the figures for consumption, investment, and government purchases would overstate the final use of domestically produced goods and services. Adding total consumption, total investment, total government purchases, and exports less imports yields the same sum we would get by adding domestic consumption of domestically produced goods, domestic purchases of domestically produced capital goods, domestic government purchases of domestically produced goods, and total exports.

What makes gross domestic product "gross"? It is the fact that gross private domestic investment measures total additions to the nation's capital stock without adjusting for losses through wear and tear or obsolescence. For example, gross private domestic investment includes the value of each year's production of new homes and factories without subtracting the value of old homes and factories that are torn down.

Gross private domestic investment minus an allowance for depreciation and obsolescence yields net private domestic investment, which is a measure of the actual net addition to the nation's capital stock each year. Only net investment adds to the capital stock, thereby helping to expand the economy's natural real output over time. The part of gross investment that covers depreciation and obsolescence only keeps the capital stock from shrinking.

Although depreciation and obsolescence are hard to measure accurately, national income accountants use an approximate measure called the *allowance for consumption of fixed capital*. Gross domestic product minus this allowance equals *net domestic product* (NDP).

6.1c Measuring the Economy by the Income Approach

In addition to GDP, measured using the expenditure approach, the national accounts report a measure of national income based on what economists call the *income approach*. The income approach measures wages, rents, interest, and profits as they flow into the household sector. Table 6.3 summarizes this approach.

The first element of national income is *compensation of employees*, which consists of wages and salaries plus certain supplements. Employer contributions to social insurance (Social Security and Medicare) are the most important supplement. By law, employees pay only half of social insurance taxes; employers must pay the other half. However, because both halves contribute to employees' retirement benefits, the national income accounts include both halves as part of employee compensation. Other supplements include employer-paid health insurance and employer contributions to 401(k) and other private pension plans.

Rental income of persons consists of all income in the form of rent and royalties received by property owners. Net interest includes interest income received by households, less the interest they pay as consumers.

Corporate profits include all income earned by the shareholders of corporations. Firms pay part of that income to shareholders in the form of dividends. Another part of corporate profits goes to pay taxes. Firms hold back a third part, undistributed corporate profit, for reinvestment. Because reinvestment of profits adds to shareholder wealth, we count it, too, as a part of household income. The accounts also adjust corporate profits for changes in the value of inventories and for consumption of fixed capital (depreciation).

Corporate profits account for only about 60 percent of all business income. The rest appears on the next line in Table 6.3, *proprietors' income*. This item lumps together all forms of income earned by self-employed professionals and owners of unincorporated business.

Table 6.3 Nominal Domestic Income, 2015 (Dollars in Billions)

Compensation of employees		$9,549.2
Wages and salaries	$7,730.2	
Supplements	1,819.0	
Plus rental income of persons		654.1
Plus net interest		506.6
Plus corporate profits		2,083.0
Plus proprietors' income		1,377.0
Plus indirect business taxes, business transfers, etc.		1,284.5
Equals national income		15,454.4
Less receipts of factor income from rest of world		−845.3
Plus payments of factor income to rest of world		614.7
Equals domestic income		$15,223.8

This table shows the measurement of national and domestic income according to the income approach, which adds together all forms of income earned by a country's residents. US national income includes some income received in return for factors of production used abroad and excludes payments to foreign residents for the use of factors owned by them but located in the United States. Domestic income is the sum of all income that results from production that takes place on the territory of a country. To derive domestic income from national income, we first subtract factor income received by this country's residents from the rest of the world and then add factor income paid to residents of the rest of the world in return for their activities in this country.

Source: Bureau of Economic Analysis.

The final item, *indirect business taxes and business transfers*, is a catchall category that includes items that are expenses to firms but unlike factor payments, do not generate income for individuals. Business property taxes are one such item. Business transfer payments are payments in return for which the firms do not receive services. They include corporate gifts, insurance settlements, and some other small items.

The total of these items is **national income**, the total income received by a country's residents. The term *national* means that this is a measure of income earned by a country's residents, regardless of whether their productive services take place in the home country or another country. For example, corporate profits shown in the table would include the profits earned on capital the Ford Motor Company has invested in a plant in Japan, but they would not include profits earned on capital that Honda Motors has invested in a plant in the United States. In contrast, *domestic* income and product are geographical concepts that measure activity that takes place on the territory of a country, regardless of who owns the factors of production involved. We can obtain a geographical measure of income, **domestic income**, by subtracting factor income received by US residents from the rest of the world and adding factor income paid to foreign residents.[1]

National income

The total income earned by a country's residents, including wages, rents, interest payments, and profits

Domestic income

The total income of all types, including wages, rents, interest payments, and profits, earned by factors of production used in producing domestic product

6.1d Reconciling the Income and Expenditure Approaches

The official accounts measure gross and net domestic product by the expenditure approach, using one set of data, and domestic and national income by the income approach, using a different set of data. No matter how careful the work, there will be some errors and omissions. That means the two sets of figures will not quite fit together. The difference between net domestic product and domestic income is statistical discrepancy. Most of the time this error is very small—well below 1 percent of GDP. Theoretical models, including those in this book, ignore the statistical discrepancy completely. They treat domestic income and domestic product as equal by definition.

US imports totaled 15.4 percent of GDP in 2015.
(Associated Press)

6.2 MEASURING INTERNATIONAL LINKAGES

The item "net exports" in the national income accounts gives a glimpse of the linkage between the domestic economy and the rest of the world. These ties have grown over time. In 1960, US exports amounted to only 6 percent of GDP and imports to less than 5 percent. Today, exports account for about 13 percent of a much larger GDP. Imports have grown even more rapidly and now equal about 15 percent of GDP. In view of the growing importance of the foreign sector, then, it is worth taking a closer look at the international ties of the US economy.

It is not easy to discuss an economy's balance of international payments because thousands of different kinds of international payments take place every day. Payments for exports and imports of goods and services are only part of the story. Equally important are long- and short-term international loans, purchases and sales of securities, and direct investments in foreign businesses. In addition, governments and private individuals make many kinds of transfer payments to residents of other countries, including outright gifts, pension payments, and official foreign aid. Finally, the US Federal Reserve System and foreign central banks engage in many kinds of official transactions. Table 6.4 shows a simplified version of the accounts used to keep track of these international transactions for the United States.

6.2a The Current Account

The first section of the international accounts shown in Table 6.4 is the current account. This section includes imports and exports of goods and services, payments of factor income between countries, and international transfer payments.

Table 6.4 US International Accounts for 2014 (Dollars in Billions)

Current Account			
1.	Balance on goods		−$741.5
2.	Exports of goods	$1,632.6	
3.	Imports of goods	−2,374.1	
4.	Services, net		233.2
5.	Exports of services	710.6	
6.	Imports of services	−477.4	
7.	Net receipts of factor income		238.0
8.	Income receipts from abroad	823.3	
9.	Income payments by the United States	−585.3	
10.	Transfers, net		−119.2
11.	Current account balance (lines 1 + 4 + 7 + 10)		−389.5
Capital and Financial Account			
12.	Net US acquisition of foreign assets. "−" indicates increase in US holdings of foreign assets—that is, a financial outflow)		−792.1
13.	Direct investment	−357.2	
14.	Portfolio investment and other	−438.5	
15.	Change in official reserve assets	3.6	
16.	Net increase in US liabilities to foreign entities ("+" indicates increase in foreign holdings of US assets or increase in US liabilities—that is, a financial inflow)		977.4
17.	Direct investment	131.8	
18.	Portfolio investment	845.6	
19.	Financial derivatives, net transactions		54.3
20.	Capital account transactions, net		0.4
21.	Capital and financial account balance (lines 12 + 16 + 19 + 20)		240.0
22.	Statistical discrepancy		149.5

This table gives details of US international transactions for 2014. The first section shows current account transactions, consisting of imports and exports of goods and services, together with international flows of factor income and transfer payments. The second section shows capital and financial account transactions, consisting of international borrowing and lending, securities transactions, direct investment, and official reserve transactions. If all amounts were complete and accurate, the current account and financial account balances would be equal and opposite in sign. In practice, there is a statistical discrepancy that indicates errors and omissions in measurement.

Source: US Department of Commerce, Bureau of Economic Analysis.

Merchandise balance

The value of a country's exports of goods (merchandise) minus the value of its imports of goods

Imports and exports of goods are the most widely publicized items in the international accounts. During much of the nineteenth century, the United States was a net importer of goods. From 1894 to 1970, it was a net exporter. Since 1970, it has again become a net importer, as shown by the negative balance in Table 6.4. The balance on goods is also known as the **merchandise balance**.

In addition to trade in merchandise, there is a large international trade in services. Travel expenditures, airline passenger fares, and other transportation services account for somewhat more than half of these services. Other services include insurance, royalties, and license fees. The United States is a net exporter of services even though it is a net importer of goods.

Earlier, in drawing the distinction between domestic and national product, we noted that US residents receive substantial flows of factor income (wages, profits, interest, and so on) from production activities that take place abroad. The accounts record those payments as exports; they enter the current account with a positive sign. At the same time, some payments of factor income go to residents of other countries that participate in production activities in the United States. The accounts treat those payments as imports; they enter the current account with a negative sign. The United States typically receives more factor income from abroad than it pays.

The final item on the current account consists of net transfer receipts. This is typically a negative item in the US international accounts because transfers to other countries exceed transfers received from them. This item takes into account both government transfers (for example, foreign aid and Social Security payments to retired workers living abroad) and private transfers (for example, remittances sent to relatives abroad by US residents and private charitable contributions to beneficiaries overseas).

The sum of merchandise trade, services, factor income, and net transfers is the country's **current account balance**. The United States has had a current account deficit every year since 1981. The official term "current account balance" sometimes appears in news reports and other popular discussions, but not everyone is careful in their use of terminology. Sometimes people use the terms "balance of payments" or "balance of trade" when they mean the current account balance. To add to the confusion, people sometimes use the term "balance of trade" to mean the merchandise balance or even the sum of trade in goods and services.

The current account balance is a close relative of the concept "net exports" used in macroeconomic models. For the purposes of this book, we will treat them as being equal—although in practice, for reasons arising from the methodology of national income accounting, the correspondence is not quite exact.

6.2b The Capital and Financial Account

Current account transactions are not the only ones that take place among residents of different countries. International lending and borrowing, and international sales and purchases of assets, also account for an enormous volume of daily transactions. A US company, for example, might obtain a short-term loan from a London bank to finance the purchase of a shipload of beer for import to the United States, which would be recorded as an increase in US liability to foreign creditors. The Brazilian government might sell bonds to Bank of America to help finance a hydroelectric project, which would be recorded as an increase in US holdings of foreign assets. Such transactions appear in the capital and financial account section of Table 6.4.

In this book, we use the shorter term *financial account* to refer to that section of the international accounts. Some writers, instead, use the term *capital account* as shorthand to refer to the entire capital and financial account.

Purchases of US assets by foreign residents and borrowing from foreign financial intermediaries by US firms and individuals create flows of funds into the United States that we call **financial inflows**. (Many writers instead use the term *capital inflows*.) Purchases of foreign assets by US residents or loans by US financial intermediaries to foreigners create flows of funds out of the United States that we call **financial outflows**. (Many writers use the term *capital outflows*.)

Current account balance

The value of a country's exports of goods and services minus the value of its imports of goods and services plus its net transfer receipts from foreign sources

Financial inflows

Purchases of domestic assets by foreign buyers and borrowing from foreign lenders, also often called *capital inflows*

Financial outflows

Purchases of foreign assets by domestic residents or loans by domestic lenders to foreign borrowers, also often called *capital outflows*

Table 6.4 lists several types of capital and financial account transactions. Changes in US private assets include *direct investments* (for example, construction of foreign plants by US firms) and *portfolio investments*—that is, purchases of foreign securities like stocks or bonds. Acquisition of short-term foreign assets like foreign bank balances and foreign currency are also included on this line. Changes in US official reserve assets include foreign currency and other foreign assets acquired by the Federal Reserve System and the US Treasury.

The "capital account," in the narrow sense in which the term is officially used, is a small item that refers to transactions in nonfinancial assets, such as ownership of patents and copyrights, and also includes private and governmental debt forgiveness and defaults on debt. However, keep in mind that some writers use the term *capital account* to refer to the capital and financial account as a whole.

International borrowing and lending appear in the financial section of the US international accounts. (Shutterstock)

6.2c Relationship of the Accounts

There is a close logical relationship between the balance on the capital and financial account and the current account surplus or deficit. Because the United States runs a current account deficit, its earnings from the sales of exports are not enough to pay for all of its imports. It gets the additional funds it needs to finance the excess imports through net financial inflows—that is, through net US borrowing from abroad or net sales of US assets to foreign residents. Any country in this position shows a surplus on the capital and financial account that offsets the current account deficit.

Countries like China that usually have current account surpluses are in the opposite position. They need to find something to do with the extra export earnings not used to buy imports. Their private sectors can use the export earnings to make loans to foreign borrowers or to accumulate foreign assets through direct or portfolio investment, or their governments can use the export earnings to accumulate foreign exchange reserves or to purchase assets for national wealth funds like those of Norway or Saudi Arabia. In either case, countries with current account surpluses have negative balances on their capital and financial accounts.

In principle, the balances of the current and financial accounts should be equal and opposite in sign. If there is a current account surplus of $100 billion (entered with a plus sign in the accounts), there should be a net financial outflow of $100 billion (entered with a minus sign in the accounts). If there is a current account deficit of $500 billion, there should be a net financial inflow of $500 billion. The reason for the symmetry is that the two sections of the accounts, taken together, include all the sources and uses of the funds that change hands in international transactions. Because every dollar used must have a source, when the sources (+) and the uses (−) are added together, the sum should be zero.

In practice, though, government statisticians always miss some items when they tally up imports, exports, and financial flows. As a result, the numbers do not quite add up. The difference between the current and financial account balances is the *statistical discrepancy*. Much of the discrepancy probably reflects unrecorded financial flows—for example, investments made by residents of other countries but never officially reported.

Part of it also reflects incomplete recording of exports. Criminal activities, including drug smuggling (unrecorded current account activity) and money laundering (unrecorded financial account activity), can also contribute to the statistical discrepancy.

6.3 MEASURING REAL INCOME AND THE PRICE LEVEL

From 2009 to 2016, the nominal value of US gross domestic product rose by a little over 25 percent, from $14.4 trillion to about $18.0 trillion. However, that does not mean that the economy produced 25 percent more by way of real goods and services. Part of the increase in nominal GDP—a little less than 10 percentage points, as it turns out—reflected increases in prices. Unless we know how much prices increase from one year to another, we cannot know how much of the change in nominal output was real and how much was the result of inflation. This section discusses two of the most important approaches to measuring changes in the price level.

6.3a Real Gross Domestic Product and the GDP Deflator

Nominal GDP is the answer to the question: What was the value of the country's output of goods and services evaluated using the prices at which sellers actually sold the goods? Real GDP is the answer to a different question: What would the value of the country's goods and services have been if prices had not changed from year to year?

The first step in answering that question would be to choose a year as a basis for comparison—that is, a **base year**. For example, we could ask what the value of the output of the US economy would have been in 2016 if prices in that year were the same as in the base year 2009. That would mean multiplying the number of chocolate bars sold in 2016 by their 2009 price, adding the quantity of gasoline sold in 2016 at its 2009 price, and so on. Following this method, the value of the goods and services produced in 2016 would have been worth approximately $16.5 trillion. That is quite a bit less than the $18.0 trillion nominal GDP for 2016. While nominal GDP increased by 25 percent from 2009 to 2016, real GDP increased by only about 15 percent.

The difference between the current year nominal GDP of $18.0 trillion and the current year real GDP of $16.5 trillion is due to price changes. The ratio of nominal GDP to real GDP gives us a measure of change in the price level that we call the **GDP deflator**. In our example, the ratio of 2016 nominal GDP to 2016 real GDP, calculated using 2009 as the base year, is 18.0/16.5 (or 1.09), indicating an increase in the GDP deflator over the period of about 9 percent.

We can use the base year in one of two ways in stating a measure of average prices, such as the GDP deflator. One way is to let the base-year value equal 1.0. We call a statement of average prices relative to a base-year value of 1.0 a statement of the price level. In our example, the 2016 **price level**, relative to the 2009 base year, is 1.09. The other way is to let the base-year value equal 100. A statement of average prices relative to a base-year value of 100 is a **price index**. In our example, the 2016 price index relative to the 2009 base year was 109. The price level and price index are two different ways of stating the same information. News reports more frequently use the index form. In building economic models, the price level form is more convenient.

Base year

The year used as a basis for comparison when computing real GDP or a price index

GDP deflator

A measure of the average price level of goods and services based on the ratio of nominal GDP to year real GDP, stated relative to the prices of a chosen base year

Price level

A weighted average of the prices of goods and services expressed in relation to a base-year value of 1.0

Price index

A weighted average of the prices of goods and services expressed in relation to a base-year value of 100

The Bureau of Economic Analysis computes official data for GDP using a procedure very similar to that of our simple example. The main difference is that, rather than making the calculation over a period of several years, the BEA uses a "chained" methodology, which means calculating each year's GDP deflator relative to the immediately preceding year. It then restates the chained deflators for each year in terms of a chosen base year that changes only occasionally.

In addition to the economy-wide GDP deflator, it is possible to calculate GDP deflators for individual components of GDP. The deflator for personal consumption expenditures is one example to which we will return shortly.

6.3b The Consumer Price Index

The GDP deflator is the most broadly based price index for the US economy, but "broad" is not always what we want. Instead, what is often of most interest is not the price level for the whole economy but the cost of living, as determined by the prices of goods that consumers typically buy. That requires an index that omits elements of GDP like industrial equipment, office buildings, fighter planes, and fire engines that are not directly relevant to the cost of living.

The most widely used measure of the cost of living is the **consumer price index (CPI)**. In fact, the CPI is not just one index but a whole family of indexes that cover different population groups and regions. The best known is the CPI for all urban consumers. Its official designation is CPI-U, but more often than not people refer to it as just the CPI.

The CPI currently uses the period 1982–1984, rather than a single year, as its base. *Applying Economic Ideas 6.1* explains the method for calculating the CPI.

6.3c Producer Price Indexes

The **producer price indexes (PPIs)** are still another way of measuring price changes. These are price averages for three classes of goods that business firms buy from and sell to one another. The producer price index we encounter most often is that for *finished goods*—investment goods sold to businesses plus other goods that are ready for final use but have not yet reached consumers (for example, wholesale sales of clothing to retail stores). Other producer price indexes cover intermediate goods and crude materials ready for further processing. Because producer price indexes measure prices at early stages in the production process, they can give hints for future trends in consumer prices. Firms also often use them to index payments that they make to one another.

Consumer price index (CPI or CPI-U)

A price index based on the market basket of goods and services for a typical urban household

Producer price index (PPI)

A price index based on a sample of goods and services bought by business firms

Applying Economic Ideas 6.1

How to Calculate a Simple Consumer Price Index

Suppose we want to calculate the change in the cost of living from 2000 to 2016 for a simple economy in which there are only three goods: movies, apples, and shirts. The simplest approach, technically known as a *Laspeyres index,* would proceed according to the following five steps:

Step 1   Choose a base year—2000, in this case.

Step 2   Measure the base-year market basket—that is, the quantities of various goods that consumers bought in the base year. In this example, we see that in 2000, consumers bought tickets to 50 movies, ate 1,000 apples, and purchased 10 shirts.

Step 3   Record the prices of the goods in both the base year (2000) and the current year (2016). We learn that a movie ticket cost $5 in 2000 and $6 in 2016; an apple cost $0.60 in 2000 and $1.20 in 2016; and a shirt cost $15 in 2000 and $20 in 2016.

Step 4   Evaluate the base-year market basket at each year's prices. The table shows that it would have cost $1,000 to buy the full basket in 2000 and $1,700 to buy the same goods and services at the higher prices of 2016.

Step 5   Calculate the CPI itself. To do that, we first take the ratio of the value of the market basket at 2016 prices to its value at base-year prices. Then, to state it as an index, we multiply the ratio by 100.

The bottom line: the CPI for our three-good economy rose from 100 in 2000 to 170 in 2016.

A Consumer Price Index for a Simple Economy

	2000 Quantity	2000 Price	Value of 2000 Quantity at 2000 Price	2016 Price	Value of 2000 Quantity at 2016 Price
Movies	50	$5.00	$250	$6.00	$300
Apples	1,000	0.60	600	1.20	1,200
Shirts	10	15.00	150	20.00	200
Totals			$1,000		$1,700

$$CPI = \frac{\$1,700}{\$1,000} \times 100 = 170.0$$

6.4 How Good Are the National Income Accounts?

The national income accounts of the United States are among the best in the world, but they are far from perfect. In this section, we focus on four possible problem areas: the accuracy and timeliness of the data, the underground sector of the economy, bias in price indexes, and nonmaterial aspects of the standard of living.

6.4a Accuracy Versus Timeliness

As we have emphasized, the measurement of GDP involves an enormous amount of data collection.[2] Both government and private decision makers want the data they use to be timely and accurate; but, in practice, there is a trade-off. It is not feasible to station a monitor at every factory gate and supermarket checkout counter to record real-time data on all production and expenditures. Instead, national income accountants rely on detailed data that they collect at wide intervals and then update with more frequent, but less complete, sampling.

The most detailed data are those in "benchmark" estimates every five years. The benchmarks use an economic census that covers about 95 percent of all expenditures in GDP. Between the benchmarks, statisticians conduct annual surveys for about 150,000 reporting units and monthly surveys for about 35,000 units. The quarterly GDP estimates use a combination of the benchmark, annual, and quarterly surveys. Estimates based on past trends fill in the gaps where complete data are not yet available.

The Bureau of Economic Analysis (BEA) releases its first estimate of GDP for each quarter, called the "advance" estimate, about four weeks after the end of the quarter (for example, near the end of January for the fourth quarter of the preceding year). The advance estimate incorporates actual data for about 45 percent of expenditures, with the rest coming from partial monthly data and trends. A month later, the BEA releases a second estimate, and a month after that, a "final" estimate.

About 85 percent of the final estimate comes from actual data collected in the quarter, with the remaining 15 percent based on trends for data that are still missing. To call it the "final" is a misnomer since the quarterly data are subject to a still more complete annual revision and to further revisions as much as several years later.

Not surprisingly, the advance estimates, which give a first look at activity for a given quarter, are not perfectly accurate. On average, the advance estimate of real GDP is revised up or down by 0.6 percentage points by the time of the "final" quarterly estimate, and on average by a little over one full percentage point by the time all eventual revisions are made. For example, the advance estimate for the second quarter of 2015, released in July 2015, showed real GDP increasing at a 2.3 percent annual rate. The second estimate, released in August 2015, showed growth of 3.7 percent—a larger-than-average revision.

6.4b The Underground Economy

The national income accounts provide a reasonably accurate measure of economic activity in the visible sector of the economy; much production, consumption, and investment escapes official measurement, however. The official accounts try to include some of that when they include estimates of the rental value of owner-occupied housing and the value of food produced and consumed on farms, but those items are only the tip of the iceberg.

Some underground activity is criminal. Economists have estimated that organized crime produces some $150 billion a year in illegal goods and services such as drugs, gambling, and pornography. If those estimates are anywhere near correct, they make organized crime the second-largest industry in the United States after the oil industry.

Even so, organized crime is probably not the largest part of the underground economy. The unreported income of businesses and self-employed people may add as much as $250 billion. That figure includes cash income that goes unreported to escape payment of taxes (for example, a concert pianist failing to report income from occasional piano lessons) and barter transactions that involve no cash at all. (For example, the pianist gets her teeth filled in exchange for giving piano lessons to her dentist's child.)

Even if the US underground economy amounts to as much as 10 percent of officially measured GDP, that proportion is moderate by world standards. Economists estimate that the French underground economy equals one-third of that country's GDP. For Italy, the figure may be as high as 40 percent. In some third-world countries, the official GDP data bear only the haziest relationship to what actually goes on in the economy.

6.4c Biases in Price Indexes

The accuracy of price indexes is the third problem for the national income accounts. The measurement of changes in price levels became a matter of growing concern as inflation increased in the late 1970s, and indexing and automatic cost-of-living adjustments became more widespread. If official price indexes overstate inflation, the adjustments may be too generous.

Specialists have identified two sources of bias that are of particular concern for the consumer price index. One arises from the way consumption patterns react to price changes, and the other from changes over time in the quality of goods and services.

Substitution Bias   The first reason that the consumer price index tends to overstate the true rate of increase in the cost of living is the so-called substitution bias. As we explained in *Applying Economic Ideas 6.1*, the CPI is a weighted average of the prices of goods purchased by urban consumers. The weights for calculating the index are the quantities of goods that made up the consumer market basket in some past year. However, because buying habits change over time, the weights typically are not those of the most recent year under observation.

If changes in buying habits were random, an obsolete set of weights would cause only random errors, not a systematic bias, in the CPI. The bias results from the way changes in relative prices affect demand. When prices change, people tend to buy less of goods that have become more expensive and more of those whose prices have risen less than average or have actually fallen. As a result, the CPI, which uses weights from the past, tends to overstate the increase in the cost of living because it assigns unrealistically large weights to products whose prices have increased.

For example, suppose the price of gasoline rises faster than the average of all consumer prices. If so, consumers buy more fuel-efficient cars, move closer to work, start using public transport, and take other steps to reduce their use of gasoline. That means that, quantitatively speaking, gasoline will have a lower weight in their current market basket than in the base-year market basket. As a result, the CPI will exaggerate the impact of gas prices on the cost of living.

The Bureau of Labor Statistics adjusts the market basket for the CPI every two years to reflect changes in buying patterns. It also makes certain technical adjustments to samples collected in different areas to try to reduce quantity bias. Those adjustments reduce the substitution bias for the official CPI. In a further effort to minimize the substitution bias in the CPI, the Bureau of Labor Statistics now publishes a supplemental "chained" version of the CPI, which it calls C-CPI-U. That new measure has not yet been widely adopted as a basis for indexation, however.

One of the reasons that biases in the consumer price index are so important is that a variant of the CPI is used to index Social Security payments to tens of millions of older Americans. This issue is the subject of *Applying Economic Ideas 6.2*.

Applying Economic Ideas 6.2

How Should We Index Social Security Payments?

Each month, tens of millions of elderly Americans receive payments from the Social Security Administration. For many of them, Social Security is their primary source of income. If Social Security benefits were not protected from inflation, their income security would be fragile.

In recognition of the threat that inflation poses to retirees, the Social Security Administration adjusts payments each year to reflect inflation. Rather than the more widely known CPI-U, which uses a market basket of goods consumed by all urban residents, the SSA uses the index CPI-W, which covers urban wage earners and clerical workers. In practice, the difference between CPI-W and CPI-U is very small.

Not all economists agree that CPI-W is the best basis for indexing Social Security payments. One problem is that the CPI-W is subject to substitution bias. If CPI-W overstates the true rate of increase in the cost of living, Social Security beneficiaries would become gradually better off over time at the expense of working-age people who pay the taxes that support the system.

One suggestion for correcting the situation would be to replace CPI-W with the deflator for personal consumption expenditures (PCE deflator) from the national income and product accounts. Because the PCE is a chained deflator and uses a current-year, rather than a base-year, market basket, it is relatively free of substitution bias. The chart shows that from 1960 to 2015, the cost of living (as measured by CPI-W) increased by 25 percent more than it would have if it had been measured by the PCE deflator.

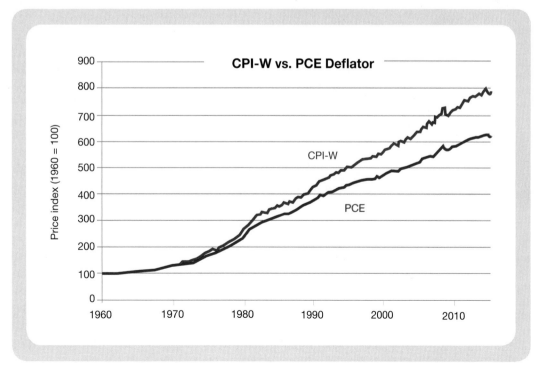

(Continues)

(Applying Economic Ideas 6.2 Continued)

Because use of the PCE deflator would slow the growth of Social Security benefits, it has won favor with some policymakers who are concerned about the effect of rising entitlement spending on the federal budget deficit.

Not everyone agrees that switching Social Security indexation to the PCE deflator would be a good idea. Some advocates for the elderly deny entirely that CPI-W overstates the rate of increase in the cost of living for the elderly. On the contrary, they argue that the cost of living for senior citizens is increasing faster than that for the working-age population. The chief reason, they say, is that the elderly spend more on medical care, which has experienced faster-than-average inflation over the years.

Economists who take this position point to an experimental price index for the elderly called CPI-E. The Bureau of Labor Statistics does not publish CPI-E, but it makes it available for research purposes. Largely because it includes a larger weight for health-care services, CPI-E rises more rapidly than CPI-W (by about a third of a percentage point per year). However, serious methodological problems in measuring prices and quality for medical services have prevented wider use of the CPI-E, so far.

Source: Data for the graph are from the Federal Reserve Bank of St. Louis.

Quality Bias   A second source of bias in the consumer price index is the failure to adjust product prices for changes in quality. It would be highly misleading, for example, to say that a 2016 model car costs three times as much as a 1986 model without considering the fact that the new model requires less routine maintenance, uses less fuel, and is much safer than the old one. In terms of dollars per unit of transportation service, the newer model is clearly less than three times as expensive.

For automobiles, computers, and a few other major goods, the Bureau of Labor Statistics does try to make quality adjustments. To take an extreme case, as recently as the late 1960s, it cost over $1,000 to buy a desk-size electromechanical calculator that would add, subtract, multiply, and divide. Today, it takes far less than $1,000 to buy a laptop or smartphone with many times the power of the 1960s-era computers used to send the Apollo astronauts to the moon. Official price indexes do, at least in part, incorporate those stupendous changes in computer quality; but government statisticians do not have the resources to make detailed studies of all items that enter into GDP.

Taken together, the substitution bias and quality bias are substantial. At one time, they may have added 1.0 to 1.5 percent per year to the rate of inflation as measured by the CPI. Recent changes in methodology have reduced the bias, but it still probably amounts to 0.5 percent to 1.0 percent per year.

Today's basic laptop costs about half of what an electromechanical calculator went for in the 1960s. (Shutterstock)

Perceptual Biases   Although economists argue that substitution and quality biases cause the official CPI to overstate the true cost of living, many people believe the opposite. Public opinion surveys show that, on average, people estimate the rate of consumer price inflation to be 2 percentage points or more higher than officially reported inflation. A significant minority of people think true inflation is 10 percentage points faster than the official rate. Why do so many people perceive rapid inflation, even when economists tell them that the cost of living is stable or rising only very slowly?

One reason is that when many people think of the cost of living, they want to know the changing cost of an unchanged basket of goods of unchanged quality. That question would be answered by a simple Laspeyres index, as explained in *Applying Economic Ideas 6.1*. However, the Bureau of Labor Statistics no longer uses a simple Laspeyres index. Instead, as we have seen, it makes adjustments to reduce the impact of quality and substitution biases.

Economists argue that the CPI, as now calculated, produces a more accurate measure of the changing cost of maintaining a given level of consumer welfare. However, the question, "How much would I have to spend to achieve last year's level of economic welfare?" is a different question from, "How much would I have to spend today to buy exactly the same stuff I bought last year?" To people who think that way, the government's attempt to measure the nebulous concept of economic welfare rather than the more tangible concept of an unchanged basket of goods and services looks like a conspiracy to fudge the numbers.

A second reason that people perceive a higher rate of inflation is a psychological principle called loss aversion. Loss aversion means that people feel more pain from a given loss than the joy they get from an equivalent gain. In simple terms, if you are leaning on the railing of a bridge, and your cell phone falls in the river, the pain you feel is greater than the joy you would feel if a stranger walked up to you unexpectedly and gave you a free cell phone. By the same token, if the price of gasoline goes up by $0.50 a gallon, and at the same time, the price of internet service goes down by enough to make your budget come out even, what you remember at the end of the month is the pain you feel at the gas pump—not the pleasure you get from the lower internet fee.

These and other biases—including the political biases of people who are simply unwilling to believe anything the government tells them—contribute to the tendency of people to perceive a higher rate of inflation than is officially reported.

6.4d Nonmaterial Sources of Welfare

The final problem with GDP is that it measures only material sources of welfare. That is hardly a surprise since that is the only thing it tries to do. Although we often use per capita GDP as a basis for comparing living standards over time and across countries, nonmaterial sources of welfare are important, too.

One key nonmaterial component of the standard of living is the quality of the environment. This not only varies widely from one place to another but has also changed greatly over time. The effects of climate change and toxic wastes are "bads" that, in principle, should reduce GDP just as "goods" add to it. Some economists also recommend adjustment of GDP for depletion of natural resources, such as oil fields and forests, much like adjustments for the capital consumption allowance.

A second nonmaterial source of welfare is the state of human health. By broad measures, especially that of life expectancy, standards of health in the United States appear to be improving. For example, since World War II, the life expectancy of a typical 45-year-old American has increased from 72 years to 77, and a 65-year-old American can now expect to live to the age of 81. This increase clearly improves human welfare, even if many of the added years of life occur after retirement, when people contribute little or nothing to measured GDP.

Education and literacy also contribute to human welfare, independently of income level. The United Nations Development Program publishes an index called the Human Development Index (HDI) that combines information on health, education, and literacy with real GDP. According to the HDI for 2011, Norway, Australia, and the Netherlands had the world's highest standards of living, with the United States in fourth place among the 179 countries studied. Burundi, Niger, and the Democratic Republic of the Congo were at the bottom of the list.

The HDI is hardly the last word in alternative measures of welfare. It contains no environmental component, except to the extent that environmental quality has an impact on health. The HDI also pays no attention to human rights, political freedom, or corruption—all of which are arguably important for human welfare. The Social Progress Index (see Figure 4–3) is one attempt to include all of these elements in a comprehensive measure of wellbeing. The SPI confirms that people do not live by GDP alone. However, especially at low levels of economic development, there is a strong correlation between GDP per capita and other elements of human progress. Although there are many ideas about how to supplement it, there is little chance that anyone will find a replacement for GDP any time soon.

Summary

1. **How does the government measure gross domestic product?**

   The official accounts of the United States feature several domestic product concepts. Gross domestic product (GDP) is the value at current market prices of all final goods and services produced annually in a given country. Gross national product is the product produced by a country's factors of production, regardless of their location. Net domestic product is equal to GDP minus an allowance for consumption of fixed capital that reflects the value of capital goods worn out during the year.

2. **How does domestic income differ from gross domestic product?**

   Domestic income is the sum of wages and supplements, rental income of persons, corporate profits, and proprietors' income earned in a country. In principle, domestic income and gross domestic product should be equal; but in the official accounts, they differ because of the capital consumption allowance, indirect business taxes, and a statistical discrepancy that results from the use of different data sources for income and product measurements.

3. **What are the major types of international transactions?**

   Many types of transactions appear in the nation's international accounts. Exports less imports of goods constitute the merchandise balance. Adding services yields net exports of goods and services. Adding net international transfers (normally a negative number for the United States) yields the most widely publicized measure, the current account balance. In addition, the international accounts record financial inflows and outflows resulting from private financial transactions and official reserve transactions by the Federal Reserve and foreign central banks.

4. **How does the government measure inflation?**

   The GDP deflator is the broadest measure of the price level. It is the ratio of nominal GDP to real GDP in any given year. The consumer price index (CPI) includes only the market basket of goods purchased by a typical urban household. The producer price indexes (PPIs) include goods that business firms typically trade with each other.

5. **What are the limitations of official economic statistics?**

   The national income statistics of the United States are among the best in the world, but they are far from perfect. Problem areas include timeliness of data, the unobserved sector of the economy, price index biases, and nonmaterial aspects of the standard of living.

KEY TERMS

Base year	158	Intermediate goods	148
Consumer price index (CPI or CPI-U)	159	Merchandise balance	155
Current account balance	156	National income	153
Domestic income	153	National income accounts	148
Final goods and services	148	Price index	158
Financial inflows	156	Price level	158
Financial outflows	156	Producer price index (PPI)	159
GDP deflator	158	Value added	148
Gross domestic product (GDP)	148		

PROBLEMS AND TOPICS FOR DISCUSSION

1. **Updating the national income accounts**   The latest data on national income accounts and international transactions for the United States are available from the US Department of Commerce, Bureau of Economic Analysis (http://bea.gov). Current and historical data for individual components, such as real and nominal GDP, investment, exports, and others, are available in both graphical and numerical formats from the FRED database maintained by the Federal Reserve Bank of St. Louis (https://research.stlouisfed.org/). If you plan to continue your study of economics beyond this introductory course, you will definitely want to become a friend of FRED! Use one of these sources to update the tables in this chapter and the charts in Chapter 4 to the most recent year or quarter. If you do not live in the United States, search the internet for similar data for your home country and compare them to the US data given in this chapter.

2. **Inventory in the national income accounts**   Suppose that a firm sells $10,000 worth of shoes that it has held in inventory for several years. What happens to GDP as a result? Which of its components are affected, and how?

3. **International accounts**   Following the pattern in Table 6.4, show how the international accounts might look for a year in which there was a $50 billion surplus on current account, no official reserve transactions, and no statistical discrepancy. What would the capital and financial account balance have to be?

4. **The current account deficit**   "A current account deficit is a very healthy thing. If we can get foreigners to give us real goods and services and talk them into taking pieces of paper in return, why should we want anything different?" Do you agree or disagree with this statement? Discuss.

5. **Real and nominal quantities**   In 1982 to 1984, the base period used for the consumer price index, the average earnings of construction workers were $442.74 per week. By 1989, the earnings of construction workers had reached $506.72 per week, but the consumer price index had risen to 124.0. What were construction workers' real earnings in 1989 stated in 1982–1984 dollars?

CASE *for* DISCUSSION

A Wishbook Journey into a Past Shopper's Fantasyland

The website www.wishbookweb.com archives full-color, page-by-page images of dozens of old mail order catalogs. They provide a vivid picture of how the price and quality of goods have changed over the generations. If you could jump through the screen for a day of shopping in one of these consumer fantasylands of the past, what would you bring home with you? What would you look at, laugh, and leave behind?

Start by jumping back to the Sears Christmas catalog for 1962 and comparing what you find there to items that were available to internet shoppers half a century later, in 2012. How about a turtleneck sweater for $6.94, or a pair of fleece-lined leather gloves for the same price? Classic style, quality materials, and a price that seems quite reasonable today. You'd snap those up for sure.

Need a watch? The men's models on page 164 of the catalog. There's a nice basic Timex for just $14.25. Good deal, huh? Oops! You have to wind it every day and probably set it forward or back a minute or two as well. Ah, there at the bottom of the page is the newest thing—an electric watch. Before you grab it, though, better check out recent offers from the online store at Timex.com. The 1962 model had a price of $43.95; the 2012 model cost just four bucks more, and you can bet it keeps better time. So you won't come back from 1962 with a watch, after all.

How about a TV? Here's the top-of-the line 1962 model on page 200, a twenty-three incher for $189.95. And check this out: "Silicon rectifiers as used in military missiles provide great reliability and long life." Tempted? But … uh … "controls conveniently grouped on the front"? No remote? And color? Ya gotta be kidding! That was 1962!

Before you grab that Sears Silvertone beauty, consider what you could buy in the twenty-first century. By 2012, Amazon was offering a twenty-three-inch flat-screen model. Color? Yep. Remote? Yep. Built-in DVD? Of course, dummy, that was 2012, after all! True, it costs $50 more, at $229; still, I think I'd take the newer one. How about you?

OK, now you're back from your shopping trip. Time to take off those great gloves, slip into your classic turtleneck, and sit down in front of the TV to watch some politician ranting about how much better things were in the good old days before inflation ruined our lives!

Questions

1. How would you adjust the price of the 1962 TV to allow for the difference in quality from the 2012 model? Was it half as good? A tenth as good? Is it something you can even start to put a number on?

2. In 1962, the average hourly wage for US workers was about $2.50. In 2012 it was about $19.00. Use those wage rates to convert all the prices in the story to hours of work. What would you buy from the 1962 Sears catalog if you had to work for the money at 1962 wages but could buy things now being sold by working at today's wages?

3. Spend some time with wishbookweb.com. Check out some buys from the oldest catalogs, which date back to the 1930s. Take a look at a catalog from the 1980s. What would you buy from those catalogs? What would you not buy?

From Ed Dolan's Econ Blog

Ed Dolan's econ blog offers several posts related to the material in this chapter. A good place to start is with the post, "What Does the Consumer Price Index Measure? Inflation or the Cost of Living? What's the Difference?" It can be found by following this link: http://bvtlab.com/9986b, or scanning the QR code. At the end of the post you will find links to a related item discussing perceptual biases that cause overestimation of inflation and another that examines a popular alternative price index.

BLOG POSTS

Endnotes

1. Following the same logic, it is also possible to calculate gross national product (GNP), a measure of goods and services produced by factors of production owned by a country's residents, including factors of production physically located in another country. Until the early 1990s, US accounts emphasized GNP rather than GDP. In practice, the difference between GDP and GNP is small for the United States.

2. The source for much of the material in this section is J. Steven Landefeld, Eugene P. Seskin, and Barbara Fraumeni, "Taking the Pulse of the Economy: Measuring GDP," *Journal of Economic Perspectives* (Spring 2008): 193–216.

PART 3

Banking, Money, and the Financial System

CHAPTER 7

THE BANKING SYSTEM AND ITS REGULATION

AFTER READING THIS CHAPTER,
you will understand the following:

1. What banks are and what their key financial tasks are
2. The main items on a bank's balance sheet
3. The originate-to-hold model of banking
4. The risks of banking
5. The originate-to-distribute model of banking
6. Policies to maintain the safety and stability of the banking system
7. What measures are available to rehabilitate failed banks

BEFORE READING THIS CHAPTER,
make sure you know the following concepts:

The circular flow of income and expenditure

Financial markets

Price level

CHAPTER
Outline

The financial sector lies at the heart of the circular flow of income and product. It gathers savings from households and directs those savings to the investment needed for long-term growth of the economy. At the same time, it redirects the surpluses and deficits of the government, household, and foreign sectors in a way that keeps the circular flow in balance.

This chapter and the following two focus on finance. We begin here with an overview of the banking system. Chapter 8 introduces money and monetary policy. Chapter 9 explores the international financial system and exchange rates.

7.1 THE BANKING SYSTEM

For most of us, the banking system is our first point of contact with the financial system. Very likely, you use the services of your bank without giving much thought to what goes on behind the scenes when you insert your card into an ATM or use your smartphone to make a payment. You may have chosen your bank simply because it has a branch near your home or work, thinking that, in most respects, all banks are alike; yet, in many ways, they are not. Chances are that the architecture and furnishings of your bank are designed to make it look safe and solid, so you may be surprised to learn in this chapter that the banking system can be fragile just when we need it most.

In this book, we use the term **bank**, in a general sense, to refer to all financial institutions that accept deposits and make loans. *Depository institution* is a more technically correct term. The largest and most numerous depository institutions are *commercial banks,* which usually include the word *bank* in their names. Historically, they specialized in business loans and deposits. *Thrift institutions,* which include *savings and loan associations* and *mutual savings banks,* historically specialized in consumer saving deposits and home mortgage lending. *Credit unions* are small financial intermediaries that are cooperatives, serving people who work together, union members, or other groups with shared community ties.

Since the 1980s, the historical distinctions among these four types of institutions have blurred. We will use the simple term *bank* to refer to all of them except when there is a particular reason to single out one type of institution. In fact, at times we will find it difficult to confine our focus to banks even in the broad sense. Increasingly, commercial banks, investment banks, mutual funds, hedge funds, pension funds, and even insurance companies have spread out and overlapped to the point that they share in the core functions of the financial system. The bank-like institutions that do not fall under the full range of regulations that apply to depository institutions constitute the **shadow banking system**.

In addition to privately owned banks and related financial institutions that serve the needs of firms and households, every country also has a **central bank**. A central bank is a government agency that is responsible for regulating the banking system and carrying out monetary policy. In the United States, the central bank is called the **Federal Reserve System** or, for short, simply **the Fed**. The Federal Reserve System consists of twelve regional Federal Reserve Banks plus a Board of Governors located in Washington, DC, that sets monetary policy for the whole system. We will discuss the regulatory functions of the Fed later in this chapter and its role in monetary policy in later chapters.

7.1a The Banking Balance Sheet

We can best understand the operations of a commercial bank by reference to its **balance sheet**. A firm's or household's balance sheet is a financial statement that shows what it owns and what it owes—or, to use more technical language, its *assets, liabilities,* and

---

Bank

A financial institution whose principal business consists of accepting deposits and making loans

Shadow banking system

Investment banks, mutual funds, hedge funds, and other institutions that provide bank-like services but do not fall under the full range of regulations that apply to depository institutions

Central bank

A government agency responsible for carrying out monetary policy and often for regulating a country's banking system

Federal Reserve System (the Fed)

The central bank of the United States, consisting of twelve regional Federal Reserve Banks and a Board of Governors in Washington, DC

Balance sheet

A financial statement showing what a firm or household owns and what it owes

net worth. **Assets**, which appear on the left-hand side of the balance sheet, are all the things that the firm or household owns or to which it holds a legal claim. **Liabilities**, which appear on the right-hand side of the balance sheet, are all the legal claims against the firm by nonowners or against the household by nonmembers. **Net worth**, which also appears on the right-hand side of the balance sheet, is equal to the firm's or household's assets minus its liabilities. In a business firm, net worth represents the owners' claims against the business. *Equity* is another term for net worth. Bankers refer to net worth as *capital.*

The balance sheet gets its name from the fact that the totals of the two sides always balance. That follows from the definition. Since we define net worth as assets minus liabilities, liabilities plus net worth must equal assets. In equation form, this basic rule of accounting reads as follows:

Assets = Liabilities + Net worth

Table 7.1 shows a total balance sheet for US commercial banks. On the assets side of the balance sheet, the first line, cash items, includes deposits that individual banks maintain with the Federal Reserve System, as well as paper currency and coins that banks keep in their own vaults. Paper currency and coins held by banks are known as **vault cash**. The next two items on the asset side of the balance sheet show the bank's main income-earning assets. The largest item is loans made to firms and households. In addition, commercial banks hold a substantial quantity of securities, including private securities and those issued by federal, state, and local governments. The final asset item includes some smaller income-earning items plus the value of the bank's buildings and equipment.

Assets

All the things that the firm or household owns or to which it holds a legal claim

Liabilities

All the legal claims against a firm by non-owners or against a household by nonmembers

Net worth

A firm's or household's assets minus its liabilities, also called *equity* or *capital*

Vault cash

Paper currency and coins held by banks as part of their reserves of liquid assets.

Table 7.1 Total Balance Sheet for US Commercial Banks, September 2015 (billions of dollars)

Assets		Liabilities	
Cash items	$2,809.5	Deposits	$10,915.3
Securities	$3,036.5	Bank borrowing	$1,877.1
Loans	$8,355.1	Other liabilities	$1,122.7
Other assets	$585.4	**Total liabilities**	**$13,915.1**
		Net worth (capital)	$871.4
Total assets	**$14,786.5**	**Total liabilities plus net worth**	**$14,786.5**

This table shows the total balance sheet for all US commercial banks as of September 2015. Assets of banks include cash, securities, and loans. Liabilities include deposits of all kinds and other borrowings. Net worth (capital) equals assets minus liabilities.

Source: Board of Governors of the Federal Reserve System, H.8 Statistical Release Sept. 4, 2015.

Deposits are the largest item on the liabilities side of the bank balance sheet. Banks hold several kinds of deposits. **Transaction deposits** are deposits from which customers can withdraw funds freely by check, debit card, or another form of transfer to make payments to other parties. Transaction deposits sometimes go by other names, as well. In the United States, people often call them *checking deposits* or *demand deposits*. In some countries, they are *current accounts*. Nontransaction deposits include saving deposits, time deposits, certificates of deposit, and others on which banks may impose restrictions on the timing of withdrawals or on the use of funds for making payments. Banks also borrow money from other banks and nonbank institutions and, in relatively small amounts, from the Fed. Because the banks' total liabilities are less than their assets, they have a positive net worth (capital). This sum represents the claim of the banks' owners against the banks' assets.

7.1b The Risks of Banking

While banking can be a very profitable business, it is also risky. Three of the main risks faced by banks arise directly from the nature of the bank balance sheet.

Credit Risk   The first major risk faced by banks is *credit risk*—the possibility that borrowers will not be able to repay their loans on time or in full. Banks list loans on their balance sheet on the assumption that they will receive full payment. If a borrower falls behind or defaults completely, the value of that loan as an asset decreases, possibly all the way to zero. According to the basic equation of accounting, capital is equal to assets minus liabilities, so if the value of a bank's assets falls, while its liabilities (deposits and others) remain the same, its capital will decrease. When a bank's capital falls to zero, it becomes **insolvent**, and it must cease operation.

Banks' first line of defense against credit risk is careful evaluation of the creditworthiness of borrowers before they make a loan. However, banks would not be doing their job if they made loans only to customers who were 100 percent sure to repay. For household loans, there is always some risk that loss of a job, illness, or some other unexpected event will make repayment impossible. For businesses, a downturn in the business cycle, introduction of a superior product by competitors, or rising prices of inputs may make a seemingly sound project turn out to be unprofitable and prevent repayment of the loan used to finance it. Even in good times, then, not every borrower will be able to pay on time and in full.

To guard against insolvency, banks must be sure they have an adequate cushion of capital, so that borrowers' default on one or a few loans does not push their capital too close to the line of insolvency. Table 7.1 shows that, as of September 2015, US commercial banks had capital equal to almost 6 percent of their total assets. That level was adequate, on average, although some individual banks may have been closer to the danger level or even below it. In fact, eighteen banks—all relatively small—failed in 2014 and six more in the first half of 2015. Regulators either shut those banks down or arranged mergers with other, healthier banks.

Market Risk   The second major risk of banking is *market risk*. Market risk means any change in market conditions that changes the value of items on a bank's balance sheet. Either a decrease in the value of assets or an increase in that of liabilities will, in accordance with the equation of exchange, erode capital.

Changes in interest rates are an important example. An unexpected increase in interest rates can lower the market value of bonds or other securities that a bank holds as assets, thereby reducing the bank's capital. An increase in interest rates can also increase the interest a bank must pay on deposits, thereby undermining profitability.

Transaction deposit

A deposit from which customers can withdraw funds freely by check or electronic transfer to make payments to third parties

Insolvency

A state of affairs in which the net worth (capital) of a bank or other business falls to zero

Banks have a number of tactics that they can use to manage market risk. One is to make variable rate loans that automatically adjust to changing market conditions. Another tactic, called *hedging,* uses financial derivatives to provide a sort of insurance against losses due to market risk. None of the available risk-management methods is fool-proof, however. Market risk is thus a second reason banks must be careful to maintain an adequate cushion of capital.

Liquidity Risk The third major risk that banks face is *liquidity risk.* Financial terminology calls an asset **liquid** if it can serve directly as a means of payment and is convertible to cash without loss of nominal value. Currency and bank deposits are examples of liquid assets. The special deposits that commercial banks hold with the Fed are also completely liquid. Bonds and other securities that banks own are not completely liquid because their market price changes from day to day and also because it may be hard to find a buyer for them under distressed market conditions. Loans that banks hold as assets are not fully liquid, either.

Liquidity risk can cause a loss of capital, and eventually threaten insolvency, when circumstances force banks to sell illiquid assets, like bonds or loans, at a price lower than their value as stated on the balance sheet. One kind of circumstance that can cause liquidity problems is a loss of deposits. Depositors have the right to pull funds out of a bank on short notice. If they do so, the bank may have to sell illiquid assets at a loss to meet their obligations. Another possible source of liquidity problems for a bank is the refusal of other banks, or nonbank lenders, to continue supplying the borrowed funds that, in addition to deposits, appear on the balance sheet as liabilities. Still another source of liquidity problems is the possibility that a bank may quickly need to raise funds to make a new loan to a valued customer or meet some other contractual commitment.

As in the case of other risks, banks have several tools they can use to manage liquidity risks. One of the most basic is to hold a certain level of **reserves** in the form of vault cash or deposits with the Fed. The entry "cash items" in Table 7.1 represents banks' liquid reserves. There is an opportunity cost to this line of defense, however, because vault cash and reserve deposits at the Fed pay either no interest at all or low rates relative to other market interest rates.

As an alternative to cash reserves, banks can hold government securities such as Treasury bills, which pay a little more interest than cash and can be sold quickly if the need arises. Still another defense against liquidity risk is to maintain good relations with other banks and nonbank lenders so that the bank can quickly borrow cash when the need arises. None of these defenses against liquidity risk offers full protection, however. If, despite its best defenses, a bank has to sell assets at a cut-rate price, the bank's capital will decrease, and it can fall into insolvency.

Liquidity

An asset's ability to serve directly as a means of payment or be converted to cash without loss of nominal value

Reserves

Cash in bank vaults and banks' deposits with the Federal Reserve System

Traditionally, banks make money by charging interest rates on loans that are higher than those they pay on deposits. (Shutterstock)

7.2 THE EVOLUTION OF THE BANKING SYSTEM

The basic structure of banking balance sheets, with assets dominated by loans and liabilities by deposits, has been the same for centuries. However, the business strategies used to make banking profitable have changed over time. Some of the greatest changes have occurred since the beginning of the century. This section explains those changes and the role that they played in the financial crisis of 2008.

7.2a Traditional Banking: Originate to Hold

Traditionally, the main source of profits for banks was the spread on interest rates between higher interest rates on loans and lower rates on deposits. As part of that business model, it was the general practice to originate loans (banking terminology for lending money to someone) and then to hold those loans to maturity—that is, until borrowers had made all principal and interest payments in full. We call this traditional business model the **originate-to-hold model of banking**.

One reason for the prevalence of the originate-to-hold model in traditional banking was the difficulty of selling individual loans. When a bank first makes a loan, it investigates the creditworthiness of the borrower, including the borrower's reputation, income available for repayment, availability of collateral, and exposure to risk. Over time, the bank learns more about the borrower. Perhaps it finds out that the borrower is even more reliable than first thought, or perhaps unforeseen difficulties make it harder than first thought for the borrower to meet the terms of the loan. Some of that knowledge may take the form of hard facts and numbers that can easily be reduced to computer entries—a procedure known as *automated credit scoring*. Other knowledge may come more from intuition and experience and be harder to quantify. As knowledge accumulates, banks are able to classify loans as being of higher or lower quality.

This situation can create problems when a bank tries to sell a loan to another bank or an outside investor. That was even more true in the past, when more of the relevant information was subjective and less was automated. Suppose that two years ago, your bank made a five-year loan for $100,000 to Ace Co., and now you offer to sell the loan to my bank. I can easily calculate the mathematical value of the three years' worth of interest and principal payments remaining on the loan, but something bothers me. Why is it, I ask myself, that you want to sell *that particular* loan? Maybe you know something about Ace Co. and its ability to make payments that I do not. After all, if Ace were an exceptionally good customer, why would you want to sell its loan? Maybe the reason you are selling the Ace loan is that it is a "lemon"—a loan that looks good on paper but is really at risk of going sour.

To guard against the risk that the Ace loan is a lemon, I must offer you a price that is a substantial discount from what the paperwork indicates the loan's value to be. Anticipating my caution, your bank, as originator, would be reluctant to put any good loans up for sale, knowing that you could only sell them at a deep discount. This "lemons problem" hampered the development of an active secondary market for loans and left banks with little choice but to hold loans to maturity.

7.2b Modern Banking: Originate to Distribute

The early 2000s saw a particularly rapid burst of banking innovation. One of the most significant changes of those years was a move to a new model in which banks are able to sell many kinds of loans soon after they make them and use the cash raised from those sales to make new loans. We call this the **originate-to-distribute model of banking**.

Originate-to-hold model of banking

A model of banking that emphasized making loans and then holding the loans until maturity

Originate-to-distribute model of banking

A model of banking in which banks sell loans soon after they make them and use the proceeds from the sale to make new loans

The originate-to-distribute model brought several potential benefits, for both banks and their customers, but, as we will soon see, it also brought new risks.

One advantage is that, by turning over their money faster, banks can originate more loans. Doing so produces income from fees to supplement their traditional income from the spread between interest rates on loans and rates on deposits. Some of the new income comes from up-front fees charged to borrowers when they first take out loans. Sometimes, after banks sell loans to third parties, they continue to do the work of "servicing" the loans—that is, sending out statements, maintaining tax and insurance escrows, and dealing with delinquent borrowers. They get a separate servicing fee for doing this work, even if some new owner of the loan receives the principal and interest payments. For many banks, fees from loan originations, loan servicing, and other financial services are now more important than interest income.

Another advantage of the originate-to-distribute model is that it gives banks a new tool for managing credit risk. Once a bank sells a loan, the new owner bears the risk of default, which frees the originating bank from the need to maintain capital to guard against the credit risk. From the point of view of the financial system as a whole, originate-to-distribute banking has the potential to move credit risk to parties who are best able to bear it.

A third advantage is that the originate-to-distribute model makes a larger volume of credit available to bank customers. Under the traditional originate-to-hold model, a bank faced limits on its ability to expand its assets because of the need to maintain a cushion of capital to guard against risk. Once a bank's assets increased to the maximum that its available capital could support, the bank was "loaned up" and could only make new loans as borrowers paid off the old ones. Instead, under the originate-to-distribute model, banks can make as many loans as they can find creditworthy borrowers. Because they quickly move the loans off their books, they tie up less capital and total lending expands.

7.2c Securitization

In order for the originate-to-distribute model of banking to become widespread, banks had to find a way to overcome the lemons problem, which had traditionally hampered the sale of loans by the originating bank. The tool they developed to do that was **securitization**. The basic concept of securitization is easy to understand, although refinements and variations can make things very complex.

The first step in securitization is to form a specialized financial intermediary whose job is to act as a go-between to facilitate the sale of the loan to potential investors. The best known of these specialized intermediaries are Fannie Mae and Freddie Mac, which specialize in home mortgage loans. The roots of these organizations go all the way back to the 1930s. We call them **government-sponsored enterprises (GSEs)** because, although they operate like private firms in many ways, the government backs them up and controls them, at least indirectly. In addition to the GSEs, private intermediaries that have the legal form of trusts and the sponsorship of banks or other financial institutions carry out many securitizations.

The second step in securitization is the purchase by the intermediary of a pool of assets. For example, the pool of assets might consist of ten thousand home mortgage loans worth a total of $1,000 million, which the intermediary buys from the banks that have originated them. This pool of loans provides a stream of income to the intermediary in the form of the principal and interest payments that borrowers make on the loans.

The third step in securitization takes place when the intermediary issues securities, backed by the income from the pool of mortgages, and sells them to investors. The simplest way to do this is to issue *pass-through bonds*, which give each bondholder an

Securitization

A process in which a specialized financial intermediary assembles a large pool of loans (or other assets) and uses those loans as a basis for issuing its own securities for sale to investors

Government-sponsored enterprises (GSEs)

Specialized intermediaries that operate like private firms but are backed and controlled by the government and that engage in the business of securitizing home mortgage loans and, sometimes, other loans

equal share in all of the interest and principal payments received from the pool of mortgages. That is only one possibility, however.

Instead of simple pass-through bonds, intermediaries usually issue several different kinds of securities that appeal to the preferences for risk versus return of different kinds of investors. The financial term for each type of security is a *tranche*. Securities in senior tranches give the investors who buy them the first right to receive payments of interest and principal on the pool of mortgages and place them last in line to bear losses from defaults. Investors in junior tranches are first in line to bear losses and last in line to receive income. Obviously, the price of junior tranches has to be low to attract buyers, but some buyers with a high tolerance for risk will take them if the price is low enough. The senior tranches, in contrast, appeal to investors who have low tolerance for risk and who are willing to accept a lower return if the investment is relatively safe.

The fourth step in securitization is to obtain a rating from a nationally recognized statistical rating organization like Standard & Poor's, Moody's Investors Services, or Fitch Ratings. The rating agencies analyze the likely risks and rewards of each tranche of securities, giving them ratings like AAA, B, or C that show them to be of low, medium, or high risk, respectively. Investors who rely on the analysis done by the ratings agencies save costs of hiring their own analysts to do the complex work of judging the risk associated with any given security.

Figure 7–1 gives a schematic representation of the securitization process. The figure is somewhat simplified in that it shows the securities issued by intermediaries as going directly to investors. In practice, the process can be more complicated. Sometimes one intermediary buys tranches of securities issued by another, and then uses them as a basis for further securitizations. Sometimes the "investor" who purchases the securities is itself another kind of intermediary like an insurance company, a mutual fund, or a hedge fund that gets its money from other investors still further down the line.

7.2d New Types of Mortgages

Securitization was one important innovation that allowed rapid expansion of credit markets during the early 2000s, but it was not the only one.

In the late 1990s, a combination of innovations by lenders and pressure from policymakers who wanted to encourage home ownership led to the development of **subprime mortgages**. Subprime mortgages typically had three major features that made it easier for low-income households to get loans. First, they required low down payments, usually less than 10 percent, or sometimes no down payment at all. Second, they had variable interest rates that kept mortgage payments affordably low for the first two or three years of the mortgage, and then increased to higher rates after the owner had had a chance to accumulate some equity. Third, they included prepayment penalties to discourage borrowers from taking advantage of low "teaser" interest rates and then reselling the house before the more profitable "step-up" interest rates came into force.

As long as house prices were rising, subprime mortgages were profitable to both borrowers and lenders. Borrowers were able to buy houses they could not possibly have afforded using a conventional mortgage. By the time the two or three years of low introductory interest rates expired, rising prices would allow them to accumulate equity in their homes. At that point, they could refinance with a conventional mortgage offering better terms or, alternatively, sell the house and buy a better one using a new subprime mortgage. By offering low introductory interest rates, banks lost some potential income in the early years of the mortgage; but they were able to gain this back with prepayment fees, points, and other loan origination fees when owners sold the property or refinanced the mortgage. In the worst case, if the borrower defaulted, rising property values would allow banks to recover the full amount they had loaned through foreclosure.

Subprime mortgage

A mortgage with
features like a low
down payment, variable
interest rate, and
prepayment penalty that
make it attractive to low-
income borrowers

FIGURE 7–1

Schematic Representation of the Securitization Process

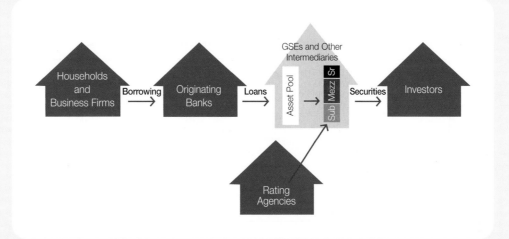

In this simplified version, the securitization process begins when households and firms borrow from originating banks. The banks then sell the loans to an intermediary, which issues securities based on pools of loans or other assets that they buy. The securities are divided in "tranches" of senior (low-risk), mezzanine (medium-risk), and subordinate (high-risk) securities. Each type of security receives a rating from an independent rating agency. Investors buy the securities that best fit their appetite for return versus risk.

It was obvious to everyone that subprime mortgages would be risky if house prices ever began to fall. However, one comforting fact kept this worry in the background: From the time the government first started collecting statistics in 1975 through 2006, there had never been a single year during which the average value of American houses had decreased. It seemed to be a market that could only go up.

Together, subprime lending and securitization transformed the business of banking during the 1990s and early 2000s. They allowed originating banks to sell more than half of all the mortgage loans they made, making it possible to recycle the proceeds from securitization to make more loans.

Banks found that securitization worked so well for mortgages that they extended it to other kinds of loans, including credit card loans, auto loans, and student loans. Figure 7–2 shows the result: an astonishing expansion of household debt that, by 2008, reached 95 percent of GDP. At the same time, with consumer credit so easy to get through mortgages, credit cards, and home equity loans, household saving plunged to less than 3 percent. Truly, it was a golden age of finance.

As long as home prices were rising, subprime mortgages were profitable both to lenders and to home buyers. (Shutterstock)

FIGURE 7–2

Household Debt and Saving in the Golden Age of Finance

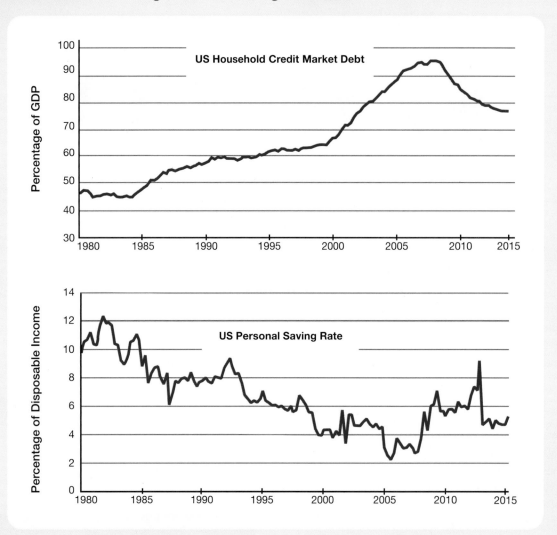

Easy availability of credit and changing social attitudes toward debt and saving led to fundamental changes in the behavior of US consumers during the late 1990s and early 2000s. Household debt—including mortgage debt, credit card debt, and other forms of debt—rose to 95 percent of GDP. With credit so cheap and easy to get, saving almost disappeared. Debt is now lower than it was at its peak, and the saving rate is higher than its lowest level, but debt remains higher and saving lower than in earlier decades.

Source: Federal Reserve Bank of St. Louis.

Unfortunately, the golden age did not last. The originate-to-distribute model of banking turned out to have many weak points. Mortgage companies marketed subprime loans too aggressively, often using exaggerated appraisals, falsified paperwork, and other fraudulent practices. Ratings supplied by independent agencies turned out to be much less reliable than expected. As the process of securitization became more complex, it often ended up transferring financial risk not to those most willing to bear it but to those least able to understand it. The eventual collapse of the housing bubble and the financial structures it supported brought calls for closer regulation of banking—the topic to which we turn next.

7.3 REGULATING THE BANKING SYSTEM

Banks play a vital role in our economy, yet we often take them for granted until they experience problems. Unfortunately, the US banking system has had serious problems several times over the years. A banking panic in 1907 led to the founding of the Federal Reserve. During the 1930s, a wave of bank failures helped plunge the economy into the Great Depression. In the 1980s, there was a wave of failures that began among savings and loan associations and later spread to larger banks. Most recently, beginning in 2007, the banking system of the whole world fell into crisis, with the United States leading the way. This section looks at regulations that aim to reduce the frequency and severity of bank failures. The final section of the chapter will then look at the reasons these regulations failed to prevent the banking crisis that touched off the Great Recession.

7.3a Do Banks Take Excessive Risks?

Earlier in the chapter, we looked at three kinds of risks that are inherent in banking—credit risk, market risk, and liquidity risk. Singly or in combination, these risks can cause a bank to fall into insolvency. The risk of insolvency is not unique to banking, of course. Any business can go broke if things start going wrong. In good times or bad, business failures are common. They can hit a new pizza restaurant with a poorly selected location or a major corporation like the RadioShack, which grew from a one-store hobby shop in 1921 to become one of the nation's largest electronics retailers before falling into bankruptcy in 2015.

The government does not maintain a regulatory system to prevent failures of pizza restaurants or hobby shops. It leaves the task of balancing risk against profit to the companies and their shareholders. The first questions to ask, then, about banking regulation are, Why is there greater reason to fear banking failures? Why might we think that banks and other financial institutions, left to their own devices, will take risks that are excessive from the point of view of public policy?

Spillover Effects   There are two main reasons to think that banks may take excessive risks. The first has to do with the spillover effects of bank failures. If a pizza restaurant or hobby shop fails, most of the loss is borne by its owners (perhaps shared by banks or others who made loans to the firm). Competing restaurants or retailers are likely to gain from the failure since they will divide the business of the failed firm's customers. Things are different when a bank fails.

One problem is that the failure of one bank tends not to strengthen other banks but to weaken them. Rather than dividing the business of the customers of the failed bank, other banks may also lose customers because news of a bank failure makes people distrustful of the banking system as a whole. In the worst case, as happened in the 1930s, there can be a run on the banking system, with people lining up to be the first to withdraw their money before additional failures occur.

Another problem is that the failure of one or several banks can weaken the rest of the economy. When some banks fail and others have to reduce lending because they lose deposits, small businesses cannot get the loans they need to finance inventory or meet payrolls. Farmers cannot get loans to plant crops. Homebuilders cannot get construction loans, and home buyers cannot get mortgages to buy homes if they do get built. The whole economy slows down.

Preventing cascading spillover effects, then, is the first reason to think that banks, without special regulation, might take risks that are excessive from the point of view of the economy as a whole.

Gambling with Other People's Money

The second reason to worry that banks may take excessive risks has to do with the potential for conflicts of interest within a bank—between management and shareholders or between traders and managers, to name just two possibilities. Economists call such conflicts of interest *principal-agent problems* because one party, the agent, fails to fulfill a duty to act in the interest of another party, the principal. In everyday language, we use a simpler expression: gambling with other people's money.

When people gamble with their own money, the most popular games are ones that do not win often but have limited losses when they lose and very large payoffs when they win. Lotteries like Powerball are an example. In contrast, when people gamble with someone else's money, they look for a different pattern of gains and losses. The most attractive strategies are those that win at least a moderate amount most of the time and lose rarely. It does not matter if the losses, when they do occur, are catastrophically large, because the gambler (the agent) keeps the upside winnings and someone else (the principal) is stuck with the downside.

Opportunities to gamble with other people's money can tempt banks to take excessive risks. (Shutterstock)

Opportunities to gamble with other people's money can occur in any complex business organization, but they are especially widespread in the world of finance. One example occurs when a bank establishes a compensation plan for its traders and executives that features large bonuses that depend on the company's quarterly or annual earnings. *Applying Economic Ideas 7.1* gives a numerical example that shows how such plans can create a conflict of interest between bank executives and shareholders.

By law, corporate executives, as agents, have an obligation—a *fiduciary duty*—to choose the strategy that maximizes profit for their principals, the shareholders. If they work under bonus-based compensation plans like the one in the example, they are tempted to gamble with shareholders' money. They pocket their bonus money in good times; and when their luck finally runs out, they keep their accumulated wealth, even if they lose their jobs. Meanwhile, during their years of leadership, they pursue strategies that are excessively risky both from the point of view of their own shareholders and from that of public policy.

Top executives are not the only people in the financial industry who have opportunities to gamble with other people's money. On a smaller scale, department heads, team leaders, and even ordinary traders frequently work under bonus-based compensation schemes that tempt them to take excessive risks at the expense of the companies that employ them. Even shareholders can be in a position of gambling with other people's money to the extent that, in case of insolvency, part of the bank's losses will be borne by bondholders, other creditors, or taxpayers who may have to help clean up the financial mess.

Applying Economic Ideas 7.1

Principal-Agent Problems in the World of Finance

Opportunities to gamble with other people's money, which economists call principal-agent problems, can arise in many business situations, but they are especially common in the world of finance. One reason is the widespread use of executive compensation schemes that emphasize bonuses based on quarterly or annual profits. Often there are no "clawback" provisions to recapture past bonuses if risky strategies result in short-run profits followed later by catastrophic losses.

The table below gives a hypothetical example. It shows the risks and rewards for two different strategies available to an executive who gets a bonus equal to 0.1 percent of the bank's quarterly profit.

If the executive chooses the relatively conservative Strategy A, the bank will make a good profit half the time and a small loss half the time. Averaged over ten good and bad quarters, shareholders earn a solid net profit, and the executive earns a respectable, but not spectacular, bonus.

If the executive chooses the more aggressive Strategy B, the bank earns a larger profit in nine quarters out of ten; and, in those quarters, the executive earns a larger bonus. The problem is that when Strategy B eventually fails, it produces a catastrophic loss for the bank. The shareholders bear all of the loss. With no clawback provision in the compensation scheme, the manager gets to keep bonuses based on past profits.

Under such compensation schemes, risky strategies can generate such high bonuses that executives will be tempted to choose them—even if they know they will lose their jobs when the strategies finally fail.

Payoffs from Two Business Strategies, Assuming Executive Bonus of 0.1% of Company's Net Profit Each Calendar Quarter	
Strategy A	**Strategy B**
• Five quarters of $100 million profit	• Nine quarters of $200 million profit
• Five quarters of $10 million loss	• One quarter of $2,000 million loss
• Ten quarters' net profit for shareholders of $449.5 million	• Ten quarters' net loss for shareholders of $201.8 million
• Ten quarters' total bonus for executive of $500,000	• Ten quarters' total bonus for executive of $1.8 million

7.3b Policies to Ensure Safety and Soundness of Banks

There is nothing new about the idea that banks may be tempted to take excessive risk. Already in the nineteenth century, governments began to introduce measures to restrain excessive risk taking. They added many new regulatory tools during the Great Depression of the 1930s. The resulting system for protecting the safety and soundness of the banking system consists of three main elements: bank supervision and regulation, loans to troubled banks, and deposit insurance.

Supervision and Regulation   Bank examinations are the oldest tool for ensuring the safety and soundness of the banking system. Federal and state officials conduct these examinations to ensure that banks do not make unduly risky loans or investments, that they value their assets honestly, that they maintain adequate levels of capital and liquid reserves, and that they have competent management. Honest book-keeping, prudent lending, and adequate reserves and net worth help banks to survive business downturns without becoming insolvent.

In the United States, several federal agencies—including the Federal Reserve System, the Federal Deposit Insurance Corporation, and the Office of the Comptroller of the Currency (part of the Treasury Department)—share responsibility for supervision and regulation with state agencies. In other countries, bank supervision is sometimes the responsibility of central banks and sometimes of special agencies created for the purpose.

Supervision and regulation do not always ensure sound banking practices. Sometimes examinations fail to spot danger signals. Sometimes fraudulent operators of banks and thrifts conceal information or submit false documents; in other cases, managers are honest, but neither they nor examiners spot serious risks. Sometimes the standards that examiners are responsible for enforcing are themselves too weak. In the wake of the recent financial crisis, governments in many countries conducted thorough reviews of regulatory practices. *Applying Economic Ideas 7.2* looks at two of the most important results of this regulatory review.

Applying Economic Ideas 7.2

New Measures to Improve Bank Regulation

There is a broad consensus that inadequate regulation of banking was one important factor behind the global financial crisis of 2008. In response, policymakers have tightened regulation at both the national and international levels.

Dodd-Frank: The Dodd-Frank Wall Street Reform and Consumer Protection Act is the centerpiece of the regulatory reform effort in the United States. The sponsors of the act were Senator Chris Dodd (CT) and Representative Barney Frank (MA). President Barack Obama signed it into law in July 2010. Its main provisions were as follows:

- It set up a new Financial Stability Oversight Council. The council is supposed to identify and act on systemic risk that affects the whole financial system and may require action by more than one regulatory agency.

- It created a new authority to wind up complex financial firms that are at risk of failure. Under previous law, regulators had the power to liquidate or arrange mergers for individual banks, but not always for complex institutions that crossed international borders or combined banking with securities trading, insurance, and other areas of finance.

- It set up a new agency for consumer financial protection.

- It increased the safety and transparency of markets for financial derivatives (options, swaps, synthetic financial products) by moving them from over-the-counter markets to organized exchanges.

- It limited proprietary trading and ownership of hedge funds by banks, a perceived source of excessive risk taking before the financial crisis.

Will it work? Supporters say yes, it is essential to prevent another financial crisis on the scale of the big meltdown of 2008. Critics, including the executives of many big financial firms, think it will weaken the financial system and limit the availability of credit without really making things safer. Some of the problems are as follows:

- At 2,319 pages, Dodd-Frank is very complex. Complexity invites a search for loopholes and increases the likelihood of unintended consequences.

- Some huge institutions, especially mortgage giants Fannie Mae and Freddie Mac, are not covered.

- The act regulates many specific kinds of risks, but does not curb the overall appetite for risk among financial institutions, nor does it deal effectively with compensation and incentive issues.

President Barack Obama meets with Rep. Barney Frank, Sen. Dick Durban, and Sen. Chris Dodd in the Green Room. (Wikimedia Commons)

Basel III: Not all regulatory problems can be resolved at the national level. If each country regulates banks differently, there is a danger of a "race to the bottom" in which risk-seeking banks will move to the countries that have the weakest regulations.

Recognizing this problem, representatives of the central banks of major countries formed the Basel Committee on Banking Supervision. The committee, which gets its name from the Swiss city of Basel where it meets, helps set uniform standards of bank regulation. Its first set of standards, now known as Basel I, were issued in 1988. They had only limited success and were followed by a more detailed set of standards, Basel II, in 2004. Unfortunately, those standards were not strong enough to prevent the 2008 global crisis.

In 2010, the committee issued a new set of standards, Basel III, that is now the primary international effort to coordinate bank regulations. Basel III has two main parts. One part sets stronger standards for bank capital, not just by raising the required ratio of capital to assets, but also by strengthening the definition of *capital* itself. The other part sets minimum standards for bank liquidity, an area that was poorly regulated under Basel I and II.

It will not really be possible to know how well Basel III national initiatives like Dodd-Frank (and similar undertakings in other countries) will work until the next global financial crisis comes along. Few think that the measures will fully prevent such a crisis, but many hope the damage will be better contained than it was in 2008.

Lender of Last Resort   Bank examinations, introduced more than a century ago, were not by themselves enough to prevent banking panics. One reason was that examinations do not address the periodic failure of interbank loan markets. Normally, banks that are solvent but temporarily short of cash can borrow from other banks. During a crisis, though, banks may all be short of cash at once, or they may not be sure fellow banks will be able to repay the loans. When that happens, the whole banking system can freeze up, exposing banks to a devastating level of liquidity risk.

In 1907, an especially severe panic took place in the United States. In an attempt to prevent a repetition of the crisis, Congress established the Federal Reserve System, which began operation in 1913. Among other duties, the Fed has the power to aid the banking system in times of trouble by acting as a lender of last resort. That means the Fed will make short-term loans to underpin the liquidity of stressed banks. Sometimes it uses the power to help individual banks that are in temporary trouble. Sometimes it serves to help banks through a crisis that originates outside the financial system, as was done following the 9/11 terrorist attacks in 2001. Following the banking crisis of 2008, the Fed lent on an unprecedented scale, not just to commercial banks, but also to other financial institutions.

Deposit Insurance   Even with its power as a lender of last resort, the Fed failed to prevent a major bank panic during the Great Depression. In 1934, in response to that crisis, Congress established the Federal Deposit Insurance Corporation (FDIC). The limit for insurance, last raised in 2008, is now $250,000 per account.

The idea of deposit insurance is to short-circuit runs on banks. Even if a bank fails, depositors need not run to the bank to be first in line to withdraw their funds; the government will pay them or arrange for the transfer of their deposits to a solvent bank. Because insurance keeps runs from spreading, the problems of one or a few banks will not touch off a panic that threatens the whole system. Depository institutions are supposed to bear the cost of deposit insurance through premiums charged by the insurance funds, although sometimes premiums have fallen short of costs and taxpayers have had to make up the difference.

7.4 Rehabilitating Failed Banks

Together, bank examinations, the lender-of-last-resort function, and deposit insurance are supposed to reduce the risk of systemic bank failure; but those measures do not always work. In the fall of 2008, a collapsing housing bubble overwhelmed a fragmented regulatory system and brought on the worst banking crisis in the United States since the Great Depression. In these circumstances, it would hardly have been enough for the government agencies involved to say, "Sorry, we messed up. We'll try not to do it again."

Instead, like the governments of other countries that had experienced systemic banking failure in the past, Congress, the Federal Reserve, the Treasury, and other agencies faced the task of rehabilitating the banking system—that is, its ability to perform its essential functions of facilitating payments, lending, and managing risk.

The centerpiece of the effort was the Treasury's $700 billion Troubled Asset Relief Program (TARP), approved by Congress in October 2008. The Federal Reserve System provided additional billions of dollars of support for banks. This section outlines some of the main decisions and challenges that face any attempt to get a failed banking system back into operation.

Who Should Be Helped?   The first decision that regulators must make is which banks should receive government help. A traditional view is to practice *triage*. This term, borrowed from battlefield medicine, means prioritizing the use of scarce resources in order to help only those who would not survive without aid, without wasting resources on hopeless cases. TARP did not consistently follow the triage principle, however. At least during its first phase, in the fall of 2008, the Treasury provided assistance to many healthy banks as well as to those close to failure. The rationale was that, unless all banks accepted funds, government aid would stigmatize those banks that did receive it. Clients would shun them, and they would fail even faster.

A related issue is whether to help only commercial banks or to extend government aid to all financial institutions whose failure might pose risks for the system as a whole. In this regard, policy during the chaotic fall of 2008 was again uneven. In an early test case, Bear Stearns—a failing investment bank, not a commercial bank—received generous funding that allowed it to find a merger partner. Soon after that, however, the government stood by and allowed the failure of Lehman Brothers, another large investment bank. The failure of Lehman Brothers was such a shock to financial markets that only days later, the government reversed course again and rescued AIG, which was not a bank at all but an insurance company. Of course, judging which institutions really pose

During the 2008 financial crisis, the government provided support not just to banks but also to other financial institutions, including insurance giant AIG. (Associated Press)

"systemic risk" is inherently subjective—but even allowing for that fact, many observers found it hard to see a consistent pattern in these three cases.

Who Should Bear the Losses?

Banks fail when their losses mount to the point that their liabilities exceed their assets. It is rarely possible to recover what has been lost. Instead, someone must decide who should bear the losses.

The traditional view is that the bank's shareholders should stand first in line to absorb the losses. If there are excess losses even after shareholders are fully wiped out, other uninsured parties the bank has done business with—its *counterparties*, to use financial jargon—should be the next to suffer. Ordinary depositors, on the other hand, enjoy protection from deposit insurance. If the deposit insurance funds run out of money (as they did during the US banking crisis of the 1980s), taxpayers have to pick up the tab. Any action by the government to pay losses at the expense of taxpayers is popularly known as a "bailout." The financial press has invented the contrasting term "bail-in" to refer to a situation in which creditors of the bank other than shareholders (that is, bondholders, depositors, providers of short-term credits) are required to cover losses.

Federal authorities did not consistently follow that traditional procedure in the 2008 crisis. Instead, the Treasury and the Fed provided sufficient aid to weak banks to prevent their outright insolvency. Banks' share prices fell sharply, but in most cases they did not fall to zero, and shareholders did not lose everything. The policy of intervening before banks became fully insolvent also had the effect of protecting uninsured bank counterparties (including investment banks, pension funds, hedge funds, and foreign banks) from the losses they would have suffered if regulators had put banks through liquidation.

Regulators justified the policy of bailing out bank shareholders on a "too big to fail" theory—allowing large banks to become fully insolvent was seen as risking a "complete meltdown" of the world financial system. Critics saw the failure to require bail-ins as a way of shifting losses to taxpayers, while some of those who received protection from loss were the very individuals and institutions whose excessive risk taking had caused the crisis in the first place.

What Form Should Aid Take?
The final issue in bank restructuring is what form aid should take when the government offers it. There are two main alternatives.

The first is a *capital injection.* In this approach, the government provides fresh capital to a troubled bank in order to strengthen its balance sheet while other assets and liabilities of the bank stay the same, at least initially. In exchange for the capital injection, the government may require the bank to issue new shares of common stock. In that case, the government becomes a part owner, perhaps even a full owner, of the bank, effectively nationalizing it. Instead, the government may want to avoid political controversy over nationalization of a private company by taking shares of preferred stock, which do not give the government full ownership or control.

The second way to provide aid is through a *carve-out.* This approach begins by identifying the specific bank assets that have suffered the largest losses—for example, tranches of securities backed by low-quality mortgages. People sometimes call these "toxic assets" because, although they might someday turn out to be worth something, no one wants to buy them. In a carve-out, the government acts like a surgeon making an organ transplant. It removes the bad assets from the bank balance sheet and replaces them with good assets—for example, government bonds. If the terms of the exchange are set properly, the exchange of bad assets for good assets raises the bank's net worth, and the bank escapes the threat of insolvency.

During late 2008 and early 2009, the US government tried a mix of both approaches. The Treasury's original plan, presented in October 2008, was to use $700 billion in TARP funds to conduct a massive carve-out. There were immediate protests that doing so would expose US taxpayers to huge losses with no promise of sharing in the gains when the financial system eventually recovered. Treasury Secretary Henry Paulson, the chief architect of TARP, quickly backed down and instead used a large part of the funds for a capital injection in the form of preferred stock.

It is hard to draw a hard-and-fast conclusion as to which method of bank rescue is more likely to be successful. It is possible to find successful examples of each in the experiences of other countries, although capital injections have probably been the more frequent choice and have worked better. On the whole, the capital injections carried out under the TARP program were a success. The banking system was badly shaken, but did not collapse. Furthermore, although the $700 billion authorized for TARP sounded like a shockingly large amount of money, the cost to taxpayers was far smaller since banks eventually repaid essentially all of the injected funds.

Summary

1. What are banks, and what do they do?

Banks are financial institutions that accept deposits and make loans. In addition to private banks, each country also has a central bank, which is a government institution responsible for regulating the banking system and conducting monetary policy. The shadow banking system consists of financial firms that are not subject to the full range of banking regulation but perform bank-like functions.

2. What are the main items on a bank's balance sheet?

A balance sheet is a financial statement that shows the assets, liabilities, and net worth (capital) of a bank or other financial unit. A balance sheet must always conform to the principle that assets are equal to liabilities plus net worth. The principal assets of a bank are cash reserves, securities, and loans. Its principal liabilities are deposits and borrowings.

3. What are the risks of banking?

Credit risk is the risk that borrowers may not repay their loans in full or on time. Market risk is the risk that changes in market conditions (for example, changes in interest rates) will lower the value of assets or increase the burden of liabilities. Liquidity risk is the risk that the bank may have to raise cash by selling illiquid assets below their value as indicated on the bank's books. Banks protect themselves against these risks by holding adequate levels of capital and liquid reserves.

4. What is the originate-to-hold model of banking?

In the traditional originate-to-hold model of banking, banks made loans to customers (that is, "originated" loans) and then held the loans until borrowers paid them in full. Their profit came from the difference between interest on the loan and interest paid on deposits and other liabilities. The reason for holding loans until they matured was partly that it was traditionally difficult to sell loans to another bank because the purchasing bank might fear that any loans offered for sale would be "lemons."

5. What is the originate-to-distribute model of banking?

In the originate-to-distribute model, banks do not hold loans to maturity but instead sell them soon after they originate them. Specialized intermediaries help banks repackage loans for sale to investors in the process of securitization.

6. What policies aim to maintain the safety and security of the banking system?

Because of spillover effects and the temptation to gamble with other people's money, banks may take risks that are excessive from the point of view of the economy as a whole. Several kinds of government policies attempt to contain excessive risk taking. One is a system of supervision and regulation that requires banks to maintain certain standards of safety and soundness. Another is the Federal Reserve's role as a lender of last resort in times of crisis. A third is a system of deposit insurance that discourages bank runs by protecting depositors in case of bank failures.

7. What measures are available to rehabilitate failed banks?

Systemic failure means the failure of so many banks that the financial system can no longer do its job of underpinning the rest of the economy. Following a systemic failure, governments may attempt to rehabilitate the banking system by using capital injections or carve-outs.

KEY TERMS

PROBLEMS AND TOPICS FOR DISCUSSION

1. **Your bank**   Go to the website for the bank where you have an account, and look for information on the bank's assets and liabilities. The information may be contained in the bank's annual report. What are the bank's main assets and liabilities? Is your bank solvent? Are there any reasons to be concerned about its financial conditions? (If you cannot find this information for your own bank, do the same for a major bank like Bank of America.)

2. **The "lemons" problem**   "Loans are just like used cars. If you see an ad in the paper for a used car, you have to wonder, why is the owner selling it? Maybe there is something wrong with the car that is hard to see. As a result, when you approach the seller, you will want to offer a very low price to make up for any hidden defects. Instead, you could buy the used car from a dealer. The dealer offers a warranty on the car to protect its reputation. It is safer to buy from the dealer. In this regard, selling a used car through a dealer rather than directly is just like selling loans through securitization rather than one by one." Do you agree, disagree, or agree in part with this statement? What similarities and differences do you see between securitization and selling used cars?

3. **Your mortgage**   Do you own a home that is financed by a mortgage? If so, how large a down payment did you make? Is the interest rate fixed or variable? If you pay the mortgage off early, are there prepayment penalties? Based on the answers to this question, would you classify your mortgage as prime, subprime, or somewhere in between? (If you do not have a home of your own, base your answers to these questions on an interview with a friend or relative who is a home owner.)

4. **Recent bank failures**   The FDIC maintains a list of recently failed banks online at http://www.fdic.gov/bank. How many banks have failed so far in the year when you are reading this chapter? How many failed in the previous year? Go to this list and download the information for the most recently failed bank. Why did the institution fail? How did federal authorities respond to the failure?

CASE *for* DISCUSSION

Bank Run at Northern Rock: First Domino of the Global Financial Crisis

The United States was not the only country affected by the global financial crisis. In fact, one of the very first large bank failures occurred not in the United States but in the United Kingdom.

The failed bank in question was the Northern Rock Building Society, a large mortgage lender located in northeast England. Northern Rock came into existence in 1965 as the result of a merger of two traditional mutual building societies. After its merger, it became a shareholder-owned corporation and grew rapidly. Its specialty was home loans, many of which required low down payments. In some cases, Northern Rock even made loans that exceeded the value of the property in question.

Like many banks throughout the world, Northern Rock relied on a mixture of deposits and borrowing as a source of funds with which to make loans. Compared with other banks, however, Northern Rock's deposit base was fairly small—just 25 percent of assets. Borrowing, mostly short term, was correspondingly a larger share of its liabilities. The bank's business strategy depended critically on its ability to roll over those short-term loans—that is, to borrow more short-term money on a continual basis as it paid off old borrowing.

Princeton economist Hyun Song Shin has characterized the summer of 2007 as the "Indian summer" of the housing bubble. While defaults and foreclosures had not yet become widespread, signs of strain had become apparent to insiders. The international institutions that supplied short-term credits to Northern Rock and others came under increasing pressure to reduce risky lending. Lenders who had supplied short-term funds to Northern Rock began to refuse to roll over their loans, and the bank almost immediately found itself in serious trouble. By September, Northern Rock had to turn to the Bank of England, the central bank of the UK, for support.

At this point, another factor came into play. The UK, like the United States, has a system of deposit insurance to protect ordinary depositors from loss if a bank fails. However, the British scheme does not operate as smoothly as the American one. Only the first £2,000 of deposits (about $4,000 at the time) were fully guaranteed, with another £33,000 (about $66,000) covered by a 90 percent guarantee. Furthermore, whereas US depositors usually have immediate access to money deposited in failed banks, British depositors can find their money tied up for months before final payout. Knowing of these flaws in the deposit insurance scheme, worried depositors of Northern Rock lined up at bank offices to withdraw funds. Behind the scenes, offshore and postal depositors withdrew an even larger portion of their funds.

Loans from the Bank of England turned out not to be enough to stabilize Northern Rock, however. After months of searching for a private buyer, the British government gave up and fully nationalized Northern Rock. Although larger banks later failed as well, the Northern Rock episode was one of the critical triggers that set off the European phase of the global financial crisis.

Source: Based in part on information provided in Hyun Song Shin, "Reflections on Northern Rock: The Bank Run That Heralded the Global Financial Crisis," *Journal of Economic Perspectives*, Volume 23, Number 1 (Winter 2009), pp. 101–119.

Questions

1. Which of the major risks of banking (credit risk, market risk, and liquidity risk) were involved in the failure of Northern Rock? Explain how each type of risk does or does not apply, based on information in the case.

2. Of the major tools used by governments to ensure the safety and stability of the banking system, which are illustrated by this case? Give specific examples.

3. Why do you think the British government stepped in to save Northern Rock, first using its lender-of-last-resort powers and later nationalizing the bank? Why not just let the bank fail and let the bank's shareholders, depositors, and creditors pick up the pieces?

From Ed Dolan's Econ Blog

Ed Dolan's econ blog offers several slideshows and posts related to the material in this chapter. Here are some items of special interest:

What is Basel III, and why should we regulate bank capital?   This slideshow explains how bank regulators around the world coordinate their policies, with a focus on their efforts to raise bank capital requirements after the 2008 crisis. Follow this link, http://bvtlab.com/7tS7W, or scan the QR code.

More on financial reform and Basel III: Regulating bank liquidity   This post continues the discussion of international bank regulation with a focus on protecting banks from excessive liquidity risk. Follow this link, http://bvtlab.com/X37A7, or scan the QR code

Tutorial on bank failures and bank rescues   This slideshow gives a comprehensive review of restructurings, takeovers, capital injections, carve-outs, and other techniques used to deal with failed banks. Follow this link, http://bvtlab.com/C678Y, or scan the QR code.

Bailouts, bail-ins, haircuts, and all that: Program notes for the Cyprus banking drama   The 2013 Cyprus banking crisis provides a vivid case study in systemic banking failure and resolution techniques. Follow this link, http://bvtlab.com/8tb47, or scan the QR code for more information.

Simplicity versus complexity, Goodhart's law, and the financial regulator's dilemma   This post discusses the problems that financial regulators face as they attempt to devise new regulatory tools like the Dodd-Frank reforms. Follow this link, http://bvtlab.com/6587E, or scan the QR code for more information.

POSTS

CHAPTER 8

MONEY AND CENTRAL BANKING

AFTER READING THIS CHAPTER,
you will understand the following:

1. What money is and how it is measured
2. How banks create money
3. What limits the size of the money stock
4. How the Fed controls interest rates
5. What quantitative easing is and why central banks use it

BEFORE READING THIS CHAPTER,
make sure you know the following concepts:

Balance sheets

Liquidity

Vault cash

Central bank

Federal Reserve System

Bank reserves

The originate-to-hold and originate-to-distribute models of banking

CHAPTER
Outline

veryone knows what money is, right? We see someone driving down the street in a Maserati, and we think, "She must have a lot of money to afford that car!" We see a homeless man sleeping on a heating grate, and we think, "He wouldn't be there if he had enough money for an apartment."

These examples show that the way we think about money every day is very different from the way economists think of it. In the everyday sense, we use "having a lot of money" as a synonym for wealth in general. We think money is important because we can use it to buy a lot of cool stuff, and we can never have too much of it. Economists have a more technical view of money: They see it as one limited class of financial assets among many. They agree that money is important, but not because more of it is always better. In fact, most economists think that too much money can be a bad thing.

We will begin this chapter by providing a formal definition of money and a first look at why money matters for macroeconomics. Next, we explain how the banking system creates money. Finally, we look at how central banks conduct monetary policy.

8.1 What Is Money?

We can best define **money** in terms of what it does. It serves as a means of payment, a store of purchasing power, and a unit of account. Regardless of its name—US dollars, Japanese yen, or gold coins of the Roman Empire—the monies of all countries function in these three ways.

As a means of payment, money makes exchange easier compared to the alternative of barter. Imagine a market in which farmers meet to trade produce of various kinds. Apples will get you peppers, cauliflower will get you beets, and turnips will get you garlic. However, what if you want garlic and have only potatoes? What you need is a universal means of exchange—one that all sellers will accept because they know that others will also accept it, one that is in limited supply so that you know its exchange value will remain constant, and one that people recognize easily so that it is hard to counterfeit. In times past, gold and silver coins served these purposes. In a modern economy, coins and paper currency serve mostly for small transactions. We make larger payments by transferring funds from one bank deposit to another by debit card, electronic transfer, paper check, or other means.

As a store of purchasing power, money makes it possible to arrange economic activities in a convenient manner over time. Income-earning activities and spending decisions need not occur simultaneously. Instead, we can accept money as payment for our work and keep it in the bank or under the mattress until we want to spend it. The US dollar is a good store of purchasing power—so good, in fact, that billions of dollars of US currency are held by citizens of other countries who trust it more than the currencies issued by their own governments.

Money

An asset that serves as a means of payment, a store of purchasing power, and a unit of account

Finally, as a unit of account, money makes it possible to measure and record economic stocks and flows. You can express your own daily spending on food, transportation, and entertainment in terms of money. National income accountants express the whole country's GDP in the same units. Without money as a unit of account, private and public economic planning would be virtually impossible.

8.1a Money as a Liquid Asset

Anything of value can serve as a store of purchasing power if we can sell it and use the proceeds to buy something else. Money, however, has two important traits that no other asset has to the same extent. One is that we can use money itself as a means of payment without first having to exchange it for something else. A house, a corporate bond, or a steel mill may have great value, but we can rarely use such assets to buy anything without first exchanging them for an equivalent amount of money. The other trait is that money can neither gain nor lose in nominal value. That is true by definition because "nominal value" simply means the amount of money something is worth. Where a house, a bond, or a steel mill may be worth more or fewer dollars next year than this year, the nominal value of a dollar is always a dollar—no more and no less. (Of course, as we already know, the real value of money changes when there is inflation or deflation; but that is an issue to which we will return in later chapters.)

As we learned in the previous chapter, if we can use an asset as a means of payment or readily convert it to one, and if it carries no risk of gain or loss in nominal value, we say it is liquid. No other asset is as liquid as money. In fact, if we compare the definitions of money and liquidity, we see that any perfectly liquid asset is, by definition, a form of money.

8.1b Measuring the Stock of Money

For purposes of economic theory and policy, we need to know not only what money is but also how we can measure it. A narrow approach views money as consisting of just two types of assets: currency and transaction deposits. **Currency** means coins and paper money. Transaction deposits, as explained in the preceding chapter, are deposits from which we can withdraw funds or make payments by electronic transfer, debit card, check, or other means without advance notice. Economists refer to this narrow concept of money as **M1**. Table 8.1 shows M1 and its components.[1]

Table 8.1   Components of the US Money Stock, September 2015 (billions of dollars, seasonally adjusted)

	Currency	$1,311.3
+	Transactions deposits	$1,737.9
=	**M1**	**$3,049.2**
+	Savings deposits	$8,006.9
+	Small-denomination time deposits	$460.7
+	Retail money market fund shares	$634.5
=	**M2**	**$12,151.3**

This table breaks down the US money supply into its components as of September 2015. It gives two of the most commonly used money supply measures. M1 is the total of currency and transaction deposits; M2 includes M1 plus other highly liquid assets. Currency includes $2.3 billion in traveler's checks.

Source: Board of Governors of the Federal Reserve System, H.6 Statistical Release, September 10, 2015.

Currency
Coins and paper money

M1
A measure of the money supply that includes currency and transaction deposits

M2
A measure of the money supply that includes M1 plus retail money market mutual fund shares, money market deposit accounts, and saving deposits

The narrow approach to the money stock, M1, focuses on the function of money as a means of payment because firms and households use currency and transaction deposits for almost all the payments they make. If we focus instead on the function of money as a store of value, we need a broader definition, known as **M2**, that includes several other liquid assets.

Savings deposits are the first of the additional items in M2. Customers can withdraw funds from savings deposits at any time at a bank branch, at ATMs, or by online banking; but they have limited, if any, checking privileges. Time deposits differ from savings deposits in that the account holder agrees in advance to leave funds on deposit for a specified period of time—say, three months or five years. They pay higher interest rates than either transaction deposits or savings deposits, but there may be a small penalty if depositors withdraw funds before the agreed period is up. M2 includes only small time deposits of the type commonly held by consumers. It does not include large time deposits held by business firms.

Currency, like other forms of money, serves as a liquid store of purchasing power. (Shutterstock)

M2 also includes shares in money market mutual funds. A *money market mutual fund* is a financial intermediary that sells shares to the public and uses the proceeds to buy short-term, fixed-interest securities such as Treasury bills or high-quality, short-term corporate debt. The fund passes almost all the interest earned on those securities through to its shareholders, after charging a small fee for management services. Shareholders can redeem their shares in a number of ways—by debit card, by electronic transfer to a merchant, by checks, or by transfer to another fund. Because money market funds invest only in very safe short-term assets, a money market mutual fund is able to promise its shareholders a fixed nominal value of $1 per share, although the interest paid on the shares varies with market rates. For all practical purposes, money market mutual fund balances are almost as liquid as transaction deposits in banks. As in the case of time deposits, M2 includes only retail money market funds of the type held by consumers. It excludes large, institutional money market mutual fund shares.

8.1c A Balance-Sheet View of Money

Money, in the form of currency and bank deposits, appears on three important balance sheets, as shown in Figure 8–1. The first balance sheet is that of the Federal Reserve System, the central bank of the United States.[2] The second balance sheet shows the total assets, liabilities, and capital (net worth) of all the country's commercial banks and thrift institutions. The third balance sheet includes the total assets, liabilities, and net worth of everyone else in the economy, including all households and all business firms except banks. (As Table 8.1 showed, some 95 percent of M2 consists of paper currency issued by the Federal Reserve System and deposits at commercial banks and thrift institutions. Other forms of money—traveler's checks and money market mutual fund shares—are small enough that we can leave them out of the picture altogether in this chapter.)

FIGURE 8–1

Balance Sheets

Federal Reserve System

Government securities	Monetary base
Other net assets	*includes*
	Currency
	Reserve deposits

Commercial Banks and Thrifts

Reserves	Bank deposits
includes	Other liabilities
Reserve deposits (at Fed)	Capital (net worth)
Currency (vault cash)	
Loans	
Other assets	

Households and Firms

Currency	Bank loans
Bank deposits	Other liabilities
Other assets	Net worth

Money, consisting of currency and bank deposits, appears on three balance sheets. Currency in the hands of the public is an asset of households and nonbank firms and a liability of the Fed. Currency held as vault cash by banks is not counted as part of the money stock. The remainder of the money stock consists of bank deposits, which are an asset of households and firms and a liability of banks.

We can begin by looking at where currency appears on these three balance sheets. As we saw in the previous chapter, currency is a liability of the Federal Reserve System; it appears on the right-hand side of the Fed's balance sheet. Commercial banks and thrifts keep currency on hand for their tellers to hand out over the counter and to fill their ATM machines. The currency held by banks—called *vault cash*—counts as part of the bank's reserves. Because vault cash is an asset, it appears on the left-hand side of the banks' balance sheet. The rest of the currency issued by the Fed appears as an asset on the balance sheets of households and firms, who use it as a means of payment and a store of value. Only that currency—called *currency in circulation*—is included in the official measures of the money stock. Vault cash does not count as part of the money stock.

The second component of the money stock consists of funds on deposit at the nation's commercial banks and thrift institutions. These are assets of households and firms and liabilities of banks. Firms and households use them as a means of payment and a store of value.

One last item links the balance sheet of commercial banks and thrifts with that of the Fed. This item consists of reserves that banks deposit with the Fed in somewhat the same way that businesses and households keep money on deposit in commercial banks. Banks use these reserve deposits, together with vault cash, to help customers meet their payment needs and as a means of managing liquidity risk. The total reserves of the banking system thus consist of reserve deposits at the Fed plus currency held as vault cash.

By convention, the Fed's balance sheet shows only its monetary liabilities—currency and the reserve deposits of commercial banks and thrifts—on the right-hand side. To construct this version of the Fed's balance sheet, we move nonmonetary liabilities and net worth, which would normally appear on the right-hand side, to the left-hand side, with the sign reversed, and include them in the item "Other net assets." Economists call the sum of currency and reserve deposits the **monetary base**. Notice that the monetary base includes both currency in circulation, which appears on the balance sheet of households and firms, and vault cash, shown on the commercial bank balance sheet.

8.2 HOW BANKS CREATE MONEY

Where does money come from?[3] There is no mystery about the creation of the part of the money stock that consists of currency. The government prints paper money and mints coins, which it then distributes through the banking system whenever banks ask for it. However, the bulk of the money stock, which consists of bank deposits, does not come directly from the government. Instead, it comes from commercial banks, mostly in the process of making loans. A simple example will show how a bank creates new money by making a loan.

8.2a Creating Money with a Loan

Suppose that I am a banker and you are one of my customers. You have found a nice new car at a local dealer and have agreed on a price of $25,000. Before you sign the purchase contract for the car, you look on your smartphone to check the balance in your account at my bank. You find that you have $10,000 on deposit—more than enough for a down payment but not enough to buy the car for cash.

Promising the car dealer that you will return soon, you come to my bank and apply for a loan of $20,000. I check your credit history and approve the loan. You sign a promissory note, agreeing to repay the $20,000 with interest over a three-year period. I give you the $20,000 by crediting that amount to your account. The next morning, you go online and check your account balance once again. Sure enough, you now have $30,000—the $10,000 you started with plus the $20,000 loan proceeds that my bank credited to your account. You go back to the dealer, write a check for $25,000, and drive off in your new car. You have $5,000 left over to pay for groceries and rent for the rest of the month. Later in the day, the dealership deposits the check in its account at whatever bank it does business with—maybe my bank, but more likely another one.

Figure 8–2 shows how these transactions affect the three key players in the monetary system: the Fed, the banking system, and the rest of the private sector, consisting of firms and households. Unlike Figure 8–1, this one does not show complete balance sheets for the three key players. Instead, the figure shows **T-accounts**, which are simplified versions of the balance sheets that show only the items that change as a result of a given set of transactions.

Monetary base

The sum of currency and reserve deposits, the monetary liabilities of the central bank

T-account

A simplified version of a balance sheet that shows only items that change as a result of a given set of transactions

FIGURE 8–2

T-Accounts for Bank Loans

Federal Reserve System	
No changes	No changes

Commercial Banks and Thrifts			
Reserves	No changes	Bank deposits +20,000	
Loans	+20,000		

Households and Firms		
Bank deposits +20,000	Bank loans +20,000	

This diagram shows the effects of a bank loan on the money stock. Instead of complete balance sheets, it uses T-accounts, which show only items that change as the result of the loan. The loan causes an increase in bank assets and consumer liabilities; at the same time, it produces an increase in bank deposits, which are consumer assets and bank liabilities

First, look at the T-account for the banking system. When you signed the promissory note for the loan, my bank gained a new asset worth $20,000, which appears as an entry of +20,000 under loans. At the same time, when I credited the $20,000 of loan proceeds to your account, my bank gained a new liability, which appears as an entry of +20,000 under deposits. Later, when you bought the car, the deposit moved from my bank to the bank where the car dealer maintains an account. That transaction does not appear on this T-account, which shows only the total balance sheet for all banks. Just moving funds from an account at one bank to an account at another does not affect total bank assets or liabilities.

Next, look at the T-account for firms and households. The increase in deposits when my bank credited your account with the proceeds of the loan appears on the asset side of the T-account as an entry of +20,000. Your obligation to repay the loan according to the terms of the promissory note appears on the liability side as an entry of +20,000. Later, you used the $20,000 to pay for the car, but that part of the transaction does not show up here because this is the total balance sheet for all firms and households. Just moving the funds from your account to that of the car dealer does not affect the totals.

There are no changes in the balance sheet of the Fed while all of this goes on.

Finally, look at the three T-accounts together to see what has happened to the money stock. The Fed has issued no new currency, so that part of the money stock is unchanged. However, the total amount of deposits in the economy has increased by $20,000. That is a net addition to the money stock. The lesson we can learn from the example is this: Whenever a bank makes a loan, the immediate effect is to increase the money stock by the amount of the loan.

8.2b Other Ways to Create and Destroy Money

Making a loan is the most common way for banks to create money, but not the only way. Banks can also create money by buying assets from the public. As we saw in the previous chapter, in addition to reserve deposits and loans, banks also hold securities, such as government bonds, as assets. The bonds pay interest at a lower rate than loans, but they have less credit risk and are more liquid than loans.

Suppose, for example, that my bank buys $1 million worth of government bonds from a securities dealer. If the dealer has an account at my bank, the payment is made by crediting $1 million to the dealer's account. If the dealer's account is at another bank, my bank transfers the funds to the dealer's bank, which credits the amount to the dealer's account. Either way, the result is to increase securities holdings of the banking system by $1 million and increase by $1 million the total deposits held by nonbank firms (the dealer, in this case).

Figure 8–3 shows the T-accounts for these transactions. The section for banks looks much the same as in Figure 8–2, except now the new asset acquired by the banking system is securities, rather than loans. The section for firms and households, instead of showing an increase in deposit assets and an increase in loan liabilities, shows an increase in deposit assets and a decrease in securities assets.

For completeness, we should note that the transactions illustrated in both Figures 8–2 and 8–3 can work in reverse. For example, suppose a consumer pays off a $20,000 bank loan using funds on deposit in that bank or another one. The T-accounts for that transaction would look exactly like Figure 8–2, except the signs would be reversed. Total deposits and total outstanding loans would both decrease by $20,000. The money stock would decrease by that amount.

FIGURE 8–3

T-Accounts for a Securities Purchase by a Bank

Federal Reserve System	
No changes	No changes

Commercial Banks and Thrifts			
Reserves	No changes	Bank deposits	+1,000,000
Securities	+1,000,000		

Households and Firms		
Bank deposits	+1,000,000	No changes
Securities	−1,000,000	

This diagram shows the effects of a bank purchase of $1 million in government bonds from a private securities dealer. The purchase causes an increase in bank assets and deposits. Deposits of private firms increase, while their holdings of securities decrease.

Similarly, if a bank sold $1 million in government bonds to a private dealer, the T-accounts would look just like Figure 8–3 but with the signs reversed. Banks' security holdings and deposits would decrease. The dealer's account would show a decrease in deposits and an increase in securities. Again, the money stock would decrease.

8.2c Limits to Banks' Ability to Create Money

But wait a minute, you say. I know bankers are rich, but this looks too easy! If banks can create money whenever they want, what keeps them from creating *unlimited* amounts of money? Why don't bankers create enough money to buy up everyone and everything there is?

These are good questions, and they deserve careful answers. Although banks do create money when they make loans or buy other assets, they can't create unlimited amounts of money. They face several constraints on their powers of money creation. Let's look at three of the most important constraints.

The Reserves Constraint The first constraint arises from the need for banks to hold reserves of liquid assets in the form of currency or reserve deposits at the central bank. In part, they need reserves because, at any time, their customers can demand currency in exchange for deposits, either over the counter at a bank branch or from an ATM machine. Also, they need to hold reserves on deposits with the central bank in order to clear payments that their depositors make to other banks. For example, suppose I have authorized my cable TV provider to withdraw $100 a month from my checking account to pay my cable bill. It is unlikely that the cable company holds its accounts at the same bank that I do. To carry out the payment, my bank asks the Fed to deduct $100 from its reserve account and credit the same amount to the reserve account of the cable company's bank. That bank then credits the same amount to the cable company's account. When the whole transaction is completed, my bank ends up with $100 less in its reserve account at the Fed and $100 less in my deposit account. The cable company's bank ends up with $100 more in its reserve account at the Fed and $100 more on deposit in the account of the cable company.

The larger the bank, the more reserves it will need to meet its transaction requirements. We can refer to the bank's minimum acceptable level of reserves, stated as a percentage of deposits, as its **target reserve ratio**. The target reserve ratio depends on two considerations. First, the bank uses its own business judgment to set the target reserve ratio, taking into account interest rates, liquidity risks, and other factors. Second, the Fed (and the central banks of many other countries) sets minimum **required reserve ratios** for certain kinds of deposits. In practice, in modern banking systems, required reserve ratios are almost always lower than the target ratios that banks set for themselves. The central banks of some countries, including the United Kingdom, Canada, and New Zealand, do not set reserve requirements at all, and the Fed no longer sets them for the saving and time deposits that make up the majority of all deposits.

Under certain conditions, the availability of reserves can be the decisive constraint that determines the amount of money banks can create. Imagine a banking system in which (1) deposits are the only form of money, (2) the central bank's required reserve ratio is higher than what banks would voluntarily hold on their own, and (3) the central bank limits the total amount of reserves that it provides to the banking system. In that case, if R is the required reserve ratio, then the maximum amount of money banks can create is equal to $1/R$ times the total quantity of reserves that the central bank supplies to the banking system. In such a system, the ratio $1/R$ is known as the **money multiplier**. The appendix to this chapter explains the money multiplier in more detail.

Target reserve ratio
The minimum acceptable quantity of bank reserves, stated as a percentage of deposits

Required reserve ratio
The minimum level of reserves that the central bank requires a commercial bank to hold, stated as a percentage of deposits

Money multiplier
The maximum amount of money that the banking system can create, stated as a multiple of reserves

In practice, though, for the United States and other advanced economies, reserves do not impose a binding constraint on the ability of individual banks to create money or on the ability of the banking system as a whole to do so. If any one bank wants to make a loan but finds itself low on reserves, it can simply borrow reserves from some other bank that has more than it needs. If the banking system as a whole falls below its target level of reserves, any individual bank can borrow additional reserves from the central bank. Furthermore, as the final section of this chapter explains, the central bank can, and often does, increase the supply of reserves even when banks do not actively seek to borrow them. In practice, then, central banks do not impose a strict limit on the quantity of reserves nor does the required reserve ratio represent a binding constraint on lending.

The Demand Constraint

The demand for loans is a more important constraint on banks' ability to create money. As explained in the previous chapter, banks earn profits by making loans at interest rates that are higher than the rates they pay on deposits and other liabilities (the originate-to-hold model) or by making loans that they can profitably securitize (the originate-to-distribute model). Regardless of the model banks follow, loan opportunities are not unlimited.

A bank that wants to expand its lending can do so, but the tactics it would employ to do so would incur opportunity costs. One tactic would be to offer lower interest rates on its loans. Another would be to keep interest rates the same but approve loan applications with higher credit risk. If the bank follows the originate-to-hold model, it will have to fund the loans by taking on additional liabilities to match the increase in loans on its balance sheet—another major expense. If it follows the originate-to-distribute model, it must find buyers for its new loans, something that will become harder if it has lowered its loan rates or its credit standards.

What is true for any one bank is true for the economy as a whole. Under any given demand conditions, there is a point beyond which the banking system cannot expand total loans without lowering lending rates or credit standards to levels that are no longer profitable.

The Capital Constraint

One other constraint is sometimes important. When an individual bank, or the banking system as a whole, expands both its assets and its liabilities by making loans, its **capital ratio**—that is, the ratio of its total capital to its total assets—will decrease. That is a simple consequence of the accounting equation, which states that capital is equal to assets minus liabilities. If a bank's capital ratio gets too low, it faces trouble.

Two factors set the lower limit to the amount of capital a bank needs. First, the lower a bank's capital ratio, the greater its risk of insolvency if credit risks, market risks, or liquidity risks cause the value of its assets to decrease. Second, as explained in the previous chapter, regulators, who are concerned that banks might take excessive risks, impose minimum capital requirements. Often, the minimum capital ratio imposed by regulators is higher than what banks are willing to hold voluntarily. If a bank's capital is already at or below the minimum acceptable ratio, the bank cannot make new loans, even if it has adequate reserves and attractive lending opportunities.

In good times, individual banks, and the banking system as a whole, can gradually increase capital by retaining profits rather than paying them out to shareholders as dividends. Banks can also raise new capital by selling common stock or issuing certain special types of liabilities that count as capital for regulatory purposes. As a result, under normal conditions, loan demand, rather than capital, is the most important constraint on bank lending.

Capital ratio

The ratio of a bank's
capital (net worth) to its
total assets

However, in the period after a banking crisis like that of 2008, things change. Because of loan losses and losses on trading operations, many banks are likely to find themselves at or below the regulatory minimum capital ratio. Some banks may barely be solvent. At the same time, profits are likely to be low or negative in the post-crisis period, making it difficult to rebuild capital through retained earnings. Raising new capital from investors may also be prohibitively expensive, if not impossible.

Under such conditions, capital can become the key constraint on lending. Far from expanding their loan books, banks may be forced to reduce total loans outstanding by not replacing those that borrowers pay off. The reluctance of banks to lend makes life difficult for nonfinancial businesses and slows the recovery of the economy as a whole.

8.3 CENTRAL BANKING AND THE INSTRUMENTS OF MONETARY POLICY

As we learned in Chapter 7, the Fed, like the central banks of many countries, has a major role in ensuring safety and stability. Now we turn to an even more important function of central banks—the monetary policies by which central banks control the money stock and interest rates. These provide the single most important means by which governments can influence short-run macroeconomic variables like unemployment, inflation, and real output.

8.3a Why Monetary Policy Matters

Why is monetary policy so important? Many economists answer that question with the help of the **equation of exchange**: $MV = PQ$. The variable M stands for the money stock (usually measured by M2), P for the price level, and Q for real GDP. V stands for **velocity** or, more fully, the **income velocity of money**.

Formally, we define velocity as the ratio of nominal GDP to the money stock. More intuitively, we can think of it as the rate at which money circulates through the economy—that is, the average number of times people spend each dollar of the money stock each year to purchase final goods and services. For example, if a country had a money stock of $200 billion and a nominal GDP of $1,000 billion, velocity would be five, indicating that each dollar of the money stock changed hands about five times a year for purchases of final goods and services.

The equation of exchange shows that any change in the money stock must affect the price level, real output, velocity, or some combination of those variables. That, in turn, suggests that monetary policy allows the government to influence key macroeconomic variables. However, it is important to emphasize that the equation of exchange is only an accounting relationship that is true by definition. We cannot fully understand the way monetary policy affects the economy without considering interest rates—a variable that does not appear in the equation of exchange. With that in mind, let's look at the way central banks use interest rates in their conduct of monetary policy.

8.3b Three Key Interest Rates

Three interest rates have particular importance for monetary policy as conducted by the Fed and the central banks of many other major countries.

The first is the rate that the central bank charges banks for reserves that it loans to commercial banks. The Fed calls this the **discount rate**; it goes by other names in some other banking systems. Following rules that it revised in 2003, the Fed offers overnight loans to healthy banks without administrative restrictions. However, troubled banks,

Equation of exchange

An equation that shows the relationship among the money stock (M), the income velocity of money (V), the price level (P), and real domestic product (Q); written as $MV = PQ$

Velocity (income velocity of money)

The ratio of nominal GDP to the money stock; a measure of the average number of times that people use each dollar of the money stock each year to purchase final goods and services

Discount rate

The interest rate charged by the Fed on loans of reserves to banks

including those whose capital ratio has fallen below the minimum permitted level, may face closer supervision in their use of discount borrowing.

The second key interest rate is the rate the Fed pays to banks for the reserves they keep on deposit. Paying interest on reserves is a relatively new practice for the Fed; before 2008, banks earned no interest on reserve deposits. From 2009 through 2015, the Fed held this rate steady at 0.25 percent. The practice is too new to be certain about how often the Fed will adjust the deposit rate in the future.

The third key interest rate is the one that banks pay when they borrow and lend reserves among themselves. As mentioned earlier, when individual banks see profitable lending opportunities, they do not need to wait passively for new reserves to arrive via deposits or repayments of previous loans. Instead, they can borrow the reserves they need from another bank that has a temporary excess. The market in which US banks make short-term loans of reserves to other banks is the **federal funds market**. A more general term is the *interbank loan market*. All countries have interbank loan markets, although the local names differ. The interest rate charged on such loans is the **federal funds rate**. Transactions in this market total billions of dollars per day. Most federal funds loans are made on an overnight basis, but some are made for longer terms.

The federal funds rate is especially important because it affects the cost to banks of making loans. When the rate is high, banks that need more reserves because their loans and deposits are growing find it more expensive to obtain them. The higher cost of reserves gives them an incentive either to raise interest rates on loans or tighten their standards for credit risk. In either case, the result is a reduced availability of credit throughout the economy. Similarly, a decrease in the federal funds rate signals easier credit conditions for everyone from home owners to giant corporations.

8.3c How the Fed Controls Interest Rates

The interest rates that are central to monetary policy fall into two groups: those that are under the central bank's direct administrative control and those that are determined by supply and demand conditions in financial markets. The discount rate and the interest rate paid on reserve deposits are in the administrative category, while the federal funds rate is determined by the market for interbank loans. We will begin by describing the way these rates are determined in normal times. Special conditions since the 2008 financial crisis have led to some departures from normal procedures, to which we will return shortly.

In normal times, the first step is to set the administrative rates. The discount rate, or the rate at which banks can borrow reserves, is set higher than the rate the Fed pays on reserve deposits. That puts bank in a situation vis-à-vis the Fed similar to that which consumers face when their retail banks charge rates on auto loans or mortgages that are higher than those they pay on deposits.

Federal funds market

A market in which banks lend reserves to one another for periods as short as twenty-four hours

We can think of the discount rate and the deposit rate as forming a sort of corridor for the federal funds rate. The discount rate is the ceiling of the corridor. If banks can borrow reserves from the Fed at the discount rate, they would not normally pay more than that to borrow from other banks in the interbank market. Similarly, if banks can earn a certain rate by depositing reserves with the Fed, they will not normally lend reserves to other banks for less than the deposit rate.

Federal funds rate

The interest rate on overnight loans of reserves from one bank to another

The federal funds rate moves up and down within the corridor in response to changes in supply and demand conditions. However, the Fed is able to exercise a powerful influence over those supply and demand conditions by buying and selling government securities, including bills (short term), notes (medium term), and bonds (long term) that the Treasury issues to finance the federal government's budget deficit.

FIGURE 8–4

Immediate Impact of an Open Market Purchase

Federal Reserve System

Government securities	+1,000,000	Reserve deposits	+1,000,000

Commercial Banks and Thrifts

Reserve deposits	+1,000,000	Bank deposits	+1,000,000

Households and Firms

Bank deposits	+1,000,000		
Government securities	−1,000,000		

This figure shows the T-account effects of a $1,000,000 open market purchase of securities by the Fed. The immediate result is an increase in commercial bank reserves, bank deposits, and the money stock.

When the Fed buys securities, it does not buy notes, bills, and bonds newly issued by the Treasury. Instead, it buys and sells previously issued securities through securities dealers that operate in public financial markets. Because the Fed operates in public markets that are open to traders of many kinds, rather than dealing directly with the Treasury, we call the Fed's purchases and sales of government securities **open market operations**.

The Effects of Open Market Operations   Figure 8–4 shows the immediate impact of an open market purchase of $1,000,000 of securities by the Fed. The purchase appears on the Fed's T-account as a $1,000,000 increase in assets. The dealer who sells the securities is part of the "households and firms" sector, so the asset side of that T-account shows a decrease of government securities. The Fed pays the dealer by issuing a payment order to the commercial bank where the dealer maintains a deposit. Completion of the payment order causes an increase of $1,000,000 in the dealer's deposit, as shown by an entry on the left-hand side of the households and firms T-account and a corresponding entry on the right-hand side of the banking sector's T-account. At the same time, the bank's reserve deposit account at the Fed increases by $1,000,000. The increase in reserve deposits appears on the left-hand side of the banking sector's T-account and the right-hand side of the Fed's T-account. Looking at Figure 8–4 as a whole, we see that the immediate impact of the open market operation is an increase of $1,000,000 in bank reserves, bank deposits, and the money stock.

The increase in the supply of reserves, in turn, affects the federal funds rate. Other things being equal, the greater quantity of reserves makes it harder for banks that want to lend reserves to find borrowers who are short on reserves and easier for banks that want to borrow to find lenders who have excess reserves; so the federal funds rate tends to fall. As it does, it becomes less expensive for banks to make loans to households or to their business customers. Credit conditions become easier throughout the economy. If there is adequate loan demand from creditworthy customers, and if banks are not short

Open market operation

A purchase or sale of government securities by a central bank

on capital, a decrease in the federal funds rate will tend to increase the total amount of bank lending. As a by-product of the greater lending, the money supply can expand by more than the initial amount of the open market operation.

This example assumes that the Fed makes an outright purchase of securities from a dealer. In that case, the effect on the monetary base and the money stock will be permanent. Instead of buying securities outright, the Fed often buys them subject to a repurchase agreement. Under a repurchase agreement, the Fed agrees to sell the securities back to the dealer for an agreed-upon price at some specific date in the future, often as soon as the next day. The effects of an open market purchase subject to a repurchase agreement are only temporary because the change in the monetary base lasts only until the repurchase is completed. The Fed routinely uses repurchase agreements to make small, day-to-day adjustments to monetary policy.

When the Fed sells securities, rather than buying them, the entire process we have just described operates in reverse. When the Fed sells securities, the securities dealers who buy them pay by drawing on their accounts at commercial banks. Deposits, bank reserves, and the money stock all fall. We could show the immediate impact on reserves and the monetary base using a set of T-accounts identical to Figure 8–4, but reversing all the plus and minus signs. The reduced supply of reserves would cause the federal funds rate to rise. As a result, credit conditions will become tighter throughout the economy.

The Federal Funds Target   The use of open market operations to affect the supply of reserves allows the Fed to set and maintain a target for the federal funds rate. Under normal conditions, the target rate is set somewhere within the corridor determined by the discount rate and the rate paid on reserve deposits. For example, the Fed might set the discount rate at 2 percent and the deposit rate at 1 percent. It could then set a federal funds rate target somewhere in between—say, at 1.5 percent. If stronger market demand for interbank loans of reserves began to push the federal funds rate above the target, the Fed could use open market purchases of securities to increase total reserves and nudge the rate back down toward the target. If weakening demand began to push the federal funds rate down, the Fed could use open market sales to reduce total reserves and nudge the rate back up again.

In principle, the Fed could move the federal funds rate target up or down within the corridor without changing its upper and lower limits. In practice, however, the Fed (and other central banks that use a similar approach) adjusts the discount and deposit rates at the same time it changes the federal funds target, at least if any large or lasting change is made in the target.

In normal times, the federal funds rate target is by far the most influential indicator of the stance of the Fed's monetary policy. It is set by a committee called the **Federal Open Market Committee (FOMC)**. The FOMC, which meets eight times a year, includes the chair of the Federal Reserve System, its other board members, and (on a rotating basis) the heads of five of the regional Federal Reserve Banks. Changes in the federal funds rate target—or even discussion of possible changes in the target—are headline news in the financial press around the world.

Federal Open Market Committee (FOMC)

A committee within the Federal Reserve System that makes key decisions on monetary policy, including the target level of the federal funds rate

Changes in Required Reserve Ratios   In principle, a central bank could use changes in required reserve ratios, rather than open market operations, to raise or lower interest rates. An increase in the quantity of reserves that banks were required to hold per dollar of deposits would leave fewer reserves available for interbank lending. That would tighten market conditions and push the interbank lending rate up. Decreasing required reserve ratios would ease market conditions and push interest rates down.

In the past, the Fed did occasionally use changes in required reserve ratios as an instrument of monetary policy. However, it has not done so since 1992, and most observers think it is unlikely to resume the practice. The same is true for the central banks of other advanced economies. It is worth noting, however, that the central banks of some emerging market countries—China is an example—do continue to use this policy instrument.

Purchases and Sales of Foreign Reserves

In addition to conducting open market operations with US government securities, the Fed, working together with the Treasury, has the power to buy and sell assets denominated in foreign currencies—for example, bonds issued by the governments of Germany (denominated in euros) or Japan (denominated in yen). It does not buy such securities directly from the foreign governments in question but, instead, from private securities dealers, much in the same way that it makes open market purchases of domestic securities. The monetary effects of purchases or sales of foreign assets are essentially the same as for the kind of domestic open market purchases we examined in Figure 8–4.

The Fed, working with the Treasury, has the power to buy and sell assets denominated in foreign currency. (Shutterstock)

In addition to their effects on the money stock, purchases and sales of foreign assets also tend to affect the exchange rates between currencies. For example, if the Fed were to buy German bonds denominated in euros, the exchange rate of the euro would tend to strengthen relative to the dollar. If the Fed sold euro-denominated bonds, the dollar would tend to strengthen.

In recent decades, the Fed has not used this instrument of monetary policy, although there have been times in the past when it did so. However, purchases and sales of foreign assets are a very important instrument of monetary policy for the central banks of many countries. We will return to central bank purchases and sales of foreign assets and their effects on exchange rates in the following chapter.

8.3d Quantitative Easing and Monetary Policy in Abnormal Times

The previous section described the monetary policy we would expect the Fed, or the central bank of another advanced economy, to use under normal conditions. However, conditions following the global financial crisis of 2008 were anything but normal in the United States, the European Union, Japan, and elsewhere. In many ways, they have not fully returned to normal as of this writing. Our discussion would be seriously incomplete if we did not briefly explain some special features of recent monetary policy.

Changes in the Federal Funds Market

Normally, monetary policy focuses on setting nominal interest rates; but most kinds of nominal interest rates cannot fall below zero, and some rates reach an effective floor even before they get to zero. As market rates fell in 2008 and after, the Fed's interest rate policy changed in some significant ways from the "corridor" procedure described above.

First, even though important market interest rates, such as the yield on three-month Treasury bills, fell close to zero, the Fed hesitated to lower its entire family of policy rates to such low levels. Among other concerns, it was afraid that setting its policy target at or close to zero would disrupt the operation of money market mutual funds, which play an important role in meeting the liquidity needs of many nonfinancial businesses. The result was a configuration of interest rates that included a discount rate of 0.75 percent, a deposit rate of 0.25 percent, and a target rate for the federal funds rate stated as a range of zero to 0.25 percent, rather than as a single number. That configuration remained in place for several years.

Second, the nature of the federal funds market itself changed. The traditional function of the federal funds market has been to facilitate borrowing and lending of reserves among banks. However, in practice, certain other institutions have also been allowed to participate. The most important of those are the so-called government-sponsored enterprises (GSEs)—such as the Federal National Mortgage Association, or Fannie Mae, and the Federal Home Loan Mortgage Corporation, or Freddie Mac.

However, even though the GSEs can hold reserves at the Fed and can buy and sell them through the federal funds market, they, unlike banks, are not eligible to earn interest on their reserves. As a result, they, unlike banks, are willing to lend reserves at a rate below the deposit rate. In practice, that has led to a situation in which GSEs, not banks, are the most active participants in the federal funds market, and the effective federal funds rate has fallen below the lower bound of the corridor formed by the discount rate and the deposit rate. That abnormal relationship among the three key policy rates is not expected to continue indefinitely, but at the time of writing, no one is sure how soon things will return to normal.

Quantitative Easing

Central banks have traditionally eased monetary policy by cutting interest rates. Does that mean that when interest rates approach zero, as they have in recent years, central banks entirely lose their power to stimulate the economy through monetary policy? The answer from the Fed and several other major central banks is, "Not necessarily."

Instead, these central banks, beginning with the Bank of Japan, have experimented with a monetary policy strategy known as **quantitative easing (QE)**. Quantitative easing means the use of open market operations to increase the quantity of reserves in the banking system, even after short-term interest rates have reached their lowest possible levels. Part of the idea is that, even if banks that receive new reserves do not make more loans, they will try to exchange some of the new reserves for longer-term securities, driving down long-term interest rates and encouraging investment. Some economists also maintain that QE shows a determination on the part of the central bank to do everything possible to stimulate the economy, and that such a signal of determination will, by itself, encourage investment.

As the crisis deepened in the fall of 2008, the Fed began to employ quantitative easing on a large scale. The program featured purchases of vast quantities of mortgage-backed securities in addition to the Treasury securities traditionally used in open market operations. The program continued on and off over the next five years. As Figure 8–5 shows, the result was a vast increase in the reserve holdings of US banks.

The effectiveness of quantitative easing remains a matter of controversy. The US economy continued to contract for nearly a year after QE began; and, even after that, the recovery was initially slow. Obviously, QE did not lead to an increase in bank lending that was remotely proportional to the increase in reserves.

Quantitative easing (QE)

A monetary policy strategy that uses open market operations to increase reserves of the banking system even after interest rates have fallen to or near zero

Still, the Fed itself, the International Monetary Fund, and many independent economists think that without QE, the recession would have been even deeper and the recovery even slower. QE has its critics, though. Some think it had little effect on the economy as a whole and may have contributed to uncertainty in financial markets. Some initially feared that QE would lead to inflation—and a few still do, despite the fact that inflation remains low some seven years after the program began. We will return to quantitative easing and its effects in later chapters.

FIGURE 8–5

Reserve Balances of US Banks

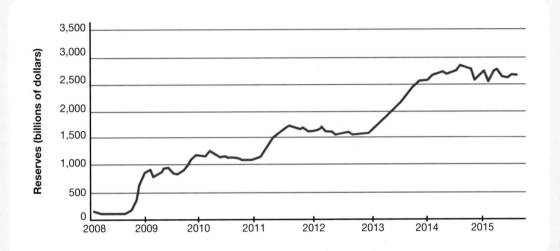

The Fed began its program of quantitative easing in November 2008 with massive purchases of mortgage-backed securities. It continued the program on and off for the next five years. The result, as shown in this chart, was a massive increase in the reserves of US banks.

Source: Federal Reserve Bank of St. Louis, St. Louis adjusted reserves.

Summary

1. What is money, and how is it measured?

Money is an asset that serves as a means of payment, a store of purchasing power, and a unit of account. A narrow measure of the money stock, M1, includes *currency* (coins and paper money) plus *transaction deposits* (deposits from which customers can make payments directly). A broader and more widely used measure, M2, includes the components of M1 plus *money market mutual fund shares, savings deposits, small-denomination time deposits,* and certain other liquid assets.

2. How do banks create money?

Banks create money, in the form of deposits, by making loans. When a bank makes a loan, it records the loan as an asset on its balance sheet and credits the proceeds to the borrower's account, an action that increases the bank's liabilities. The borrower's balance sheet shows the increase in deposits as an asset and the loan as an increase in liabilities. The increase in total bank deposits adds to the money stock.

3. What limits the size of the money stock?

Banks need to hold adequate reserves to clear payments and as part of their strategy for managing liquidity risk. Also, some central banks impose minimum required reserve ratios on some deposits. However, under normal circumstances, availability of reserves is not a binding constraint on bank lending because, in most countries, central banks stand ready to supply additional reserves as needed. Often the most important constraint on lending is the demand for loans. In judging the adequacy of loan demand, banks must take into account the interest borrowers are willing to pay, the credit risks of lending, and the cost of liabilities (if banks intend to hold the loans) or opportunities for securitization (if they intend to sell them). Finally, banks cannot make loans unless they have adequate capital. Following a crisis, the availability of capital may be the key constraint that limits lending.

4. How does the Fed control interest rates?

The first step in controlling interest rates is for the Fed to set the discount rate on reserves loaned to banks and the interest rate paid on reserve deposits of banks. Next (in normal times), the Fed sets a target for the federal funds rate that is between the discount rate and the rate paid on reserves. Although the federal funds rate is a market rate, determined by supply and demand, the Fed can hold the rate to the target level by using open market operations to adjust the quantity of reserves it supplies to the banking system.

5. What is quantitative easing, and when do central banks use it?

Quantitative easing means the use of large-scale open market purchases to provide monetary stimulus when interest rates have fallen close to zero. The Fed and the central banks of some other countries employed quantitative easing following the financial crisis of 2008.

KEY TERMS

PROBLEMS AND TOPICS FOR DISCUSSION

1. **Barter on the internet**   For most purposes, money lowers the cost of making transactions compared with barter—the direct exchange of one good or service for another. However, barter has not disappeared; in fact, in the internet age, it is even flourishing. Visit some barter websites such as u-exchange.com or paperbackswap.com. How do these sites facilitate bartering? Why might someone prefer to use these barter services rather than buying and selling items for money?

2. **Current monetary data**   Every Thursday the Federal Reserve reports certain key data on money and the banking system. These reports are available from the Board of Governors of the Federal Reserve System H.6 *Statistical Release*. Obtain the most recent H.6 release online at federalreserve.gov/releases/ and answer the following questions:

    a. What items are included in M2 that are not included in M1? What was the total of such items in the most recent month? Which of these money measures grew most quickly in the most recent month?

    b. Demand and other transaction deposits at these banks account for about what percentage of M1? What percentage of M1 consists of currency and traveler's checks?

3. **Repayment of a loan**   Suppose that you have a checking account with a $5,000 balance and an outstanding loan with a remaining balance of $1,000. You have more than that amount in your checking account, so you write a check to the bank to pay off the loan in full. Using the T-accounts of Figure 8–2 as an example, show what happens to total bank reserves, total loans, total deposits, and the total money stock as a result of your loan repayment. Does it make any difference whether your checking account and your loan are with different banks or the same bank?

4. **The reserve constraint**   Suppose you are a bank manager. Your bank has a required reserve ratio of 10 percent on demand deposits; initially, you have $10 million in loans on your balance sheet and exactly $1 million in demand deposits. A customer comes in with a request for a loan of $500,000. What will happen to your reserve ratio if you make the loan and then the borrower immediately uses the proceeds to make a payment to another bank? How could you bring your ratio of reserves to deposits back to the required ratio?

5. **The capital constraint**   This time imagine that your bank has total assets of $100 million, total liabilities of $95 million, and a minimum required capital ratio of 5 percent. Suppose you make $500,000 in new loans and fund them by issuing a $500,000 certificate of deposit. What happens to your capital ratio? How could you restore your capital ratio to the required level?

CASE *for* DISCUSSION

Monetary Chaos in Post-Soviet Russia

The Soviet Union came to an abrupt end in December 1991 with little advance planning for monetary policy or financial affairs. What followed in the Russian Federation—the largest of the fifteen countries formed from the remains of the Soviet Union—was a period of monetary chaos.

Although the Soviet Union no longer existed, its currency, the Soviet ruble, continued as the official monetary unit of the new Russian Federation. The Russian government used Soviet rubles to pay its workers and accepted them in payment of taxes.

The ruble, however, did not retain its popularity with the population at large. The main reason was the outbreak of rapid inflation, which exceeded 2,000 percent per year in 1992. No one wanted to hold rubles, which lost value daily. They would rather hold foreign currency—mainly, US dollars. In Soviet times, it had been illegal to own foreign currency. In those days, black market operators traded rubles for dollars in dark alleys and under bridges. Now the market came out in the open. Entrepreneurs set up thousands of exchange kiosks, seemingly on every corner in Moscow and other cities.

At that time, most people still received their salaries weekly in paper currency. As soon as they got their pay envelopes, they ran to the nearest exchange kiosk and swapped the rubles for dollars. Soon ordinary stores began to accept dollars in payment. It was easier to post prices for meat or T-shirts in dollars than in rubles, because the dollar prices stayed about the same, whereas inflation caused the ruble prices to rise constantly.

The government didn't mind if people held their savings in dollars, but they were not pleased when stores started posting prices in the US currency. Soon a new law made it illegal to post prices in dollars. Clever shopkeepers were not deterred. They started posting prices in something they called "artificial units" (AUs). Everyone knew that one AU was equal to one dollar, but the ruse was enough to get around the new law.

Eventually, inflation slowed, and the government got around to printing new Russian rubles to replace the old Soviet ones. They even chopped off three zeros to make accounting easier, so that one new Russian ruble was worth a thousand old Soviet rubles. Today, Russia has a normal monetary system, but people who lived through the breakup of the Soviet Union still remember those months of monetary chaos.

Questions

1. What was the official unit of account immediately after the breakup of the Soviet Union? The unofficial unit of account?

2. During the period of monetary chaos, what means of payment were in use in Russia? What purposes did each means of payment serve?

3. What was the preferred store of value during the period of monetary chaos? Why?

4. Was the "AU" a form of money? A unit of account? A store of value? A means of payment?

From Ed Dolan's Econ Blog

For further details on topics discussed in this chapter, check out the following items from Ed Dolan's econ blog:

Quantitative Easing and the Fed   This slideshow provides a detailed discussion of the technicalities of quantitative easing, its use by the Fed from 2008 to 2014, and an overview of the controversy regarding whether the policy sped the recovery. You can find it at http://bvtlab.com/2C986 or by scanning the QR code.

Whatever Happened to the Money Multiplier?   There have been periods in US economic history when the money multiplier looked like a reliable constant that could be used as a guidepost for the conduct of economic policy. However, since 2008, the money multiplier has entered a period of unprecedented instability. For a post with all the details and charts, follow this URL http://bvtlab.com/68287 or scan the QR code.

SLIDESHOWS

Endnotes

1. It is important to be careful when making international comparisons because different countries measure money somewhat differently. For example, the US M2 measure is close, but not identical, to a measure that the European Central Bank calls M3.

2. To construct this version of the Fed's balance sheet, we move nonmonetary liabilities and net worth, which would normally appear on the right-hand side, to the left-hand side, with the sign reversed, and include them in the item "Other net assets."

3. This section relies, in part, on Michael McLeay, Amar Radia, and Ryland Thomas, "Money Creation in the Modern Economy," *Bank of England Quarterly Bulletin*, 2014 Q1.

Appendix to Chapter 8

More on the Money Multiplier and Equation of Exchange— An Alternative View of Monetary Policy

This appendix presents an alternative model of monetary policy in which the money multiplier and the equation of exchange play a more prominent role. It depicts an economy in which banks are constrained in their lending by the availability of reserves, in which the Fed uses the size of the monetary base as its principal operating target and in which the money multiplier and velocity are at least approximately constant over time. We offer this model as an aid to understanding how the various parts of the monetary system fit together rather than as a realistic description of the structure of the economy or the way the Fed actually conducts policy.

The Money Multiplier in an Economy with Currency

As explained in the body of the chapter, in a simplified banking system where deposits are the only form of money and where the availability of reserves is the principle constraint on lending, there would be a simple relationship between the total amount of deposit money and total reserves:

$$\text{Total deposits} = \text{Total reserves} \times \frac{1}{\text{Reserve ratio}}$$

We call the term "1/Reserve ratio" the deposit multiplier. For example, if the required reserve ratio were 10 percent, and if the Fed supplied \$1 billion in total reserves to the economy, the maximum total amount of deposits that banks could create would be \$10 billion. If the Fed supplied an additional \$100 million in reserves, total deposits would increase to \$11 billion as banks used the additional reserves as a basis for new loans. (We are assuming that both loan demand and capital are sufficient to make it worthwhile for banks to expand loans to the limit set by the required reserve ratio.) However, the simple deposit multiplier leaves out an important aspect of the monetary system—currency. An example will show why.

Suppose that you want to borrow \$2,000 from my bank to go on vacation. You sign the papers for a loan, and my bank credits \$2,000 to your account. As soon as you verify that the funds are on deposit in your account, you go to the nearest ATM and withdraw \$1,000 in currency to take with you on your trip. You will use it for small purchases for which you pay cash, and you leave the rest on deposit to cover parts of your vacation that you plan to pay for by debit card.

The T-accounts in Figure 8A–1 show the combined effects of this set of transactions. As in the example given in Figure 8–2 in the body of the chapter, the loan appears as an increase in bank assets and an increase in household liabilities. Also, as before, the loan produces an equal increase in the money stock, this time consisting of \$1,000 of additional deposits and \$1,000 of currency in circulation. The big difference between Figure 8A–1 and Figure 8–2 lies in what happens to bank reserves. When you withdraw \$1,000 from the bank's ATM, the vault cash portion of the banking system's reserves decreases by \$1,000, in contrast to the earlier example where the loan left total bank reserves unchanged.

FIGURE 8A–1

Balance Sheets

Federal Reserve System

No changes	No changes

Commercial Banks and Thrifts

Reserves (vault cash) –1,000	Bank deposits +1,000
Loans +2,000	

Households and Firms

Bank deposits +1,000	Bank loans +2,000
Currency +1,000	

This figure shows the T-account effects of a loan when the borrower withdraws part of the loan proceeds as cash. The end result is an increase in the money stock (bank deposits plus currency in circulation) and a decrease in total bank reserves.

For an economy where deposits were the only form of money, we were able to state the money stock as a multiple of bank reserves. We can do something similar for an economy that includes currency, except that now reserves are a variable, not a constant, so they no longer make a suitable reference point. Instead, the best reference point for the size of the money stock is the monetary base—the sum of bank reserve deposits and currency issued by the Federal Reserve. Although total bank reserves change when currency moves from banks into the hands of the public, the monetary base does not. The monetary base includes all currency, regardless of whether it appears on the balance sheets of banks, households, or firms.

In equation form, we can state the relationship between the money stock (currency in circulation plus bank deposits) and the monetary base (total currency plus bank reserve deposits at the central bank) as follows:

$$\text{Money stock} = \text{Monetary base} \times \frac{1 + \text{Cur}}{\text{Res} + \text{Cur}}$$

In this equation, we use RES to stand for the minimum reserve ratio that banks are required to maintain. CUR stands for the amount of currency that the public chooses to hold per dollar of bank deposits. The expression (1 + CUR)/(RES + CUR) on the right-hand side of the equation is the expanded money multiplier. The expanded money multiplier gives the total quantity of money that the banking system can create for each dollar of the monetary base, given the assumptions of our model.[1]

For example, suppose that banks must hold $1 in reserves for each $10 in deposits, so that the variable RES equals 0.1. Suppose also that the public decides to hold $2 in currency for each $10 in deposits, so that the variable CUR equals 0.2. In that case, the expanded money multiplier will be (1 + 0.2)/(0.1 + 0.2) = 1.2/0.3 = 4. The system can create a maximum of $4 of money for each $1 of the monetary base.

Monetary Policy in a Reserve-Constrained Economy

The body of the chapter explains how, in normal times, the Fed's principle operating target is the interest rate on federal funds. It uses open market operations to hold the rate at or close to its target as market conditions change. In the abnormal conditions following the 2008 crisis, when the federal funds rate approached zero, the Fed used open market purchases to implement quantitative easing. Availability of reserves is not a constraint on bank lending under either the normal or abnormal versions of these policy procedures.

However, the Fed could, theoretically, set a quantitative operating target for some monetary aggregate, rather than an interest rate target. Total reserves of the banking system would be one possibility, but not necessarily the best. In a system with currency, it would make more sense to target the monetary base, which includes all currency (whether held by the public or held by banks as reserves) plus balances held by commercial banks in their reserve accounts at the Fed.

---

[1]   We can derive the formula for the expanded money multiplier as follows:

Eq1   TR = DEP × RES (TR is total reserves held by banks including reserve deposits and vault cash, DEP is total deposits held by firms and households in commercial banks, and RES is the target reserve ratio. This equation is an equilibrium condition for banks, indicating that reserves are at their target level.)

Eq2   CC = DEP × CUR (CC is currency in circulation, and CUR is the public's desired ratio of currency to deposits. This is an equilibrium condition for public distribution of money holdings between currency and deposits.)

Eq3   B = CC + TR (B is the monetary base, which can be stated either as reserve deposits plus total currency or as total reserves plus currency in circulation.)

Eq4   M = CC + DEP (Definition of money stock.)

Substitute Eq2 into Eq4 to get
Eq5   M = DEP × CUR + DEP

Simplify this to get
Eq5a   M = (1 + CUR) × DEP

Substitute Eq1 into Eq3 to get
Eq6   B = CC + DEP × RES

Substitute Eq2 into Eq6 to get
Eq7   B = DEP × CUR + DEP × RES

Solve this for DEP to get
Eq7a   DEP = B/(CUR + RES)

Substitute Eq7a into Eq5a to get
Eq8   M = (1 + CUR) × [B/(CUR + RES)]

Restate this to get
Eq8a   M = [(1 + CUR)/(RES + CUR)] × B

The term in brackets [ ] is the expanded money multiplier.

In a banking system that was constrained by reserves and had a stable money multiplier, a monetary base target would give the Fed effective control over the total money stock. If the Fed wanted to stimulate the economy, it would conduct open market purchases, causing the money stock to expand. If it wanted to tighten policy, it would contract the money stock by means of open market sales. For example, if the money multiplier were 4, an open market purchase of $100 million would dependably produce an increase of $400 million in the money stock.

A side effect of such a policy would be greater short-term variability of interest rates. If the Fed held the monetary base constant in the face of increasing demand for money and credit, interest rates would rise. If it held the base constant when demand weakened, interest rates would fall. Such a situation contrasts with one under which the Fed uses open market operations to hold the interest rate constant and allows the monetary base to rise and fall in response to changes in demand.

If we further assume that velocity is constant, or at least reasonably stable, control over the money stock would allow the Fed to control nominal GDP. That is evident from the equation of exchange, $MV = PQ$, in which nominal GDP is represented by the PQ term on the right-hand side. It could speed or slow the growth of nominal GDP at will by appropriate adjustments of the money stock.

Even under those conditions, however, the Fed could not fully control inflation and growth of real output. It could cause nominal output to grow, but it could not be sure that doing so would not cause undesired increase in the price level instead of higher real GDP. The same is true, of course, when the Fed applies monetary stimulus in the form of lower interest rates. The linkage to a change in nominal GDP is not as direct as it is under the assumptions of this appendix, but the outcome will still be some combination of inflation and real growth that the Fed cannot fully control. Chapter 10 will introduce a model that shows how any given change in nominal GDP is divided between change in P and change in Q.

The Money Multiplier and Velocity in Recent US Experience

In closing, we can compare the key assumptions of the model presented in this appendix with the actual operation of the US economy in recent years. We have already noted that US banks are not, in practice, constrained in their lending by the availability of reserves and that the Fed uses the federal funds rate, not the level of reserves or the monetary base, as its principal operating target. That leaves the question of whether or not the expanded money multiplier and velocity are, in practice, at least approximately constant.

As it turns out, they are not. Figure 8A–2 shows that both the expanded money multiplier and velocity have varied considerably over the past half century. In the years since the 2008 financial crisis, they have departed even farther from stability.

As Part (a) shows, the money multiplier grew steadily in the period from 1960 to 1985, nearly doubling over that period before falling again in the later 1980s. The rise and fall of inflation, as well as changes in banking institutions and regulations during the 1980s, contributed to the variability of the multiplier. In the late 1990s and early 2000s, the multiplier experienced a period of unusual stability; but that period ended abruptly as interest rates approached zero and the Fed engaged in quantitative easing after the 2008 financial crisis.

FIGURE 8A-2

The Money Multiplier and Velocity in the US Economy, 1960–2015

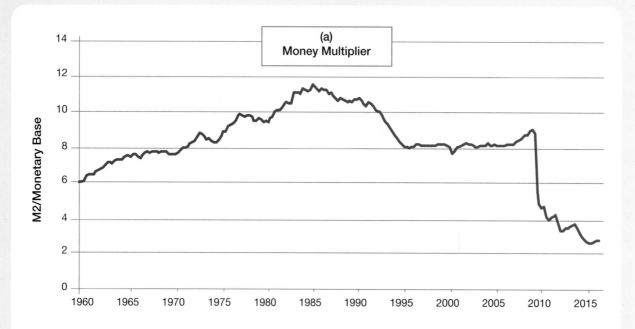

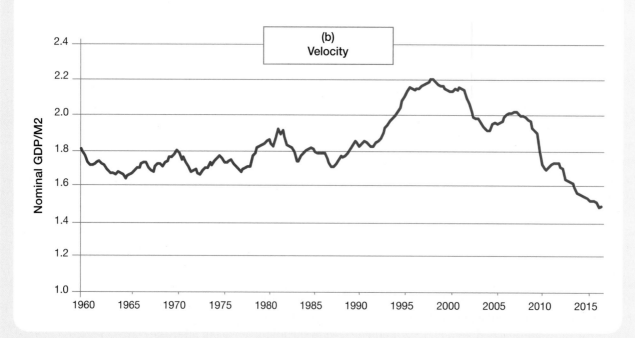

Part (a) of this figure shows the expanded money multiplier for the US economy since 1960, measured by the ratio of M2 to the monetary base. Part (b) shows velocity, measured by the ratio of nominal GDP to M2. Neither variable has been stable over time. Both fell to new lows following the financial crisis of 2008.

Part (b) shows velocity over the same period. From 1960 to 1990, the velocity of M2 varied within a fairly narrow range. In the 1990s, nominal GDP grew much faster than the money stock, as indicated by a rise in velocity. Velocity had already fallen back part way to its earlier range, even before the financial crisis. During the period of quantitative easing that followed the crisis, the money stock grew much more rapidly than nominal GDP, and velocity fell to a new low.

It is possible that as interest rates gradually rise above zero, the money multiplier and velocity will move back toward their historical averages. Even if they do, however, it seems unlikely that the Fed will choose to treat them as constants in conducting monetary policy.

CHAPTER 9

MONEY, EXCHANGE RATES, AND CURRENCY AREAS

AFTER READING THIS CHAPTER,
you will understand the following:

1. How supply and demand determine exchange rates
2. The distinctions between real and nominal exchange rates
3. How central banks can influence nominal exchange rates
4. The exchange rate policies of the Chinese central bank
5. The benefits of the euro currency area and the problems it faces

BEFORE READING THIS CHAPTER,
make sure you know the following concepts:

Planned expenditure

Current account balance

Financial inflows and outflows

Real and nominal values

Open market purchases

CHAPTER
Outline

At one time, economics textbooks left the subject of exchange rates and international monetary policy to a chapter at the end of the book, where everyone could skip it if time ran out at the end of the semester. That approach will not work in today's global economy. Whether we tune in to a presidential campaign debate on television or look at the headlines on our favorite internet news site, we can hardly escape international monetary issues. Is China manipulating its currency at the expense of US jobs? Is the euro area about to fall apart? Is a strengthening dollar about to undercut American exports? This chapter will focus on these issues and more.

We begin with a quick introduction to the factors that determine the value of one country's currency relative to those of its trading partners. Next, we look at how the concepts of real and nominal values apply to exchange rates. We then conclude with two extended case studies: one focusing on China's economic relations with the United States and the other on the challenges faced by the euro area, a great experiment that seems to be in trouble.

9.1 UNDERSTANDING EXCHANGE RATES

In Chapter 8, we briefly noted that central banks, in addition to setting interest rates and buying government securities, also have the ability to buy and sell foreign currencies. The Federal Reserve, acting as the central bank for the United States, has made little or no use of these powers in recent decades. However, foreign currency operations are vital to the way the central banks of many other countries operate. Because those policies affect their country's currencies relative to the dollar, they affect the US economy, too. This section briefly outlines how monetary policy works in countries that actively manage their exchange rates and explains why some countries adopt such strategies.

9.1a The Structure of the Foreign-Exchange Market

As a traveler, you may have had occasion to exchange US dollars for Canadian dollars, Mexican pesos, or the currency of some other country. Such trading in paper currencies is a small corner of the largest set of markets in the world—the **foreign-exchange markets**—in which trillions of dollars are traded each day. Such trading reflects the fact that many, if not most, international transactions in goods, services, or financial assets require the exchange of one currency for another.

Large trades in foreign-exchange markets, like large domestic financial transactions, use transfers of funds among deposits in commercial banks rather than paper currency. The large banks at the center of these transactions are known as trading banks. They have their headquarters in New York, London, and other financial centers, and networks of branches throughout the world. They accept deposits not only in the currencies of their home countries but also in many other currencies.

Suppose that a supermarket chain in the United States needs to buy pesos that it will use to purchase a shipment of asparagus from a grower in Mexico. The supermarket will ask the commercial bank at which it maintains its accounts to take funds from its dollar-denominated account and make an increase of equal value in a peso-denominated account in Mexico. It can then use the peso account to pay the Mexican supplier. Similarly, if a Mexican pension fund wants to buy US Treasury bills, it can exchange a deposit denominated in pesos for an equivalent deposit denominated in dollars and use those dollars to buy the Treasury bills. The banks charge a fee of a small fraction of 1 percent for these transactions, proportionately far less than the fee you would pay for currency exchange as a tourist visiting Mexico.

Foreign-exchange markets

Markets in which the currencies of different countries are traded for one another

9.1b Supply and Demand in the Foreign-Exchange Market

What determines the number of pesos that a customer gets in exchange for dollars? Why, on a given day, is the exchange rate ten pesos per dollar rather than eight or twelve? The rate depends on supply and demand, as shown in Figure 9–1.

The supply curve for dollars in Figure 9–1 reflects the activities of everyone who offers dollars in exchange for pesos. They include importers, like the US supermarket chain mentioned earlier, and tourists who travel to Mexico. They also include US residents who want to invest in Mexico by buying Mexican securities or making direct investments in Mexican resorts, factories, or other projects. Remittances that Mexicans working in

FIGURE 9–1

The Foreign-Exchange Market for Dollars and Mexican Pesos

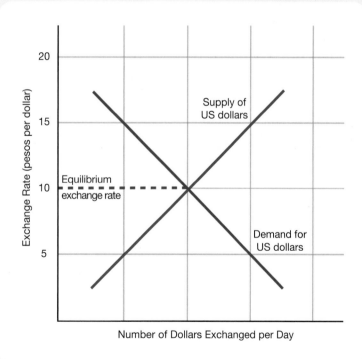

This diagram represents the foreign-exchange market in which people exchange US dollars for Mexican pesos. We express the exchange rate as the number of pesos needed to purchase one dollar. The supply curve of dollars reflects, in part, the activities of US importers of Mexican goods and services, who sell dollars to obtain the pesos they need in order to buy Mexican asparagus, cars assembled in Mexico, and so on. It also reflects the activities of US investors who need pesos in order to buy Mexican stocks, bonds, or other assets. The demand curve for dollars reflects the activities of Mexican buyers of exports from the United States. They use pesos to buy the dollars they need to buy Boeing aircraft, American corn, and other goods. The demand curve also includes the effects of financial inflows into the United States. For example, a Mexican pension fund that wants to buy US government bonds first needs to exchange pesos for dollars to use in purchasing the bonds.

the United States send home to their families are a further important supply of dollars in this market.

The demand curve for dollars reflects the activities of everyone who comes to the foreign-exchange market with pesos that they want to exchange for dollars. They include Mexican importers of US consumer goods, Mexicans making trips north of the border, Mexican firms buying production equipment or other capital goods from the United States, and Mexican investors buying US assets.

9.1c Changes in Exchange Rates

Foreign exchange rates—the prices of one currency in terms of another—change constantly as supply and demand conditions change. You can find up-to-the-minute exchange rates for any pair of currencies that exist. For example, the website xe.com reports that, at the moment I am writing this, 1.0 US dollar is worth 16.9 Mexican pesos. It also reports—just in case my business dealings might require such a trade—that ₽1.00 (Russian ruble) is worth ¥1.80 (Japanese yen). Notice that we can quote any exchange rate in two ways—for example, as 16.9 pesos per dollar or as 0.059 dollars per peso.

George Soros is a renowned currency trader. In 1992, he was dubbed "the man who broke the bank of England." When the United Kingdom withdrew from the European Exchange Rate Mechanism, devaluing the pound, Soros earned an estimated $1.1 billion. (Wikimedia Commons)

As supply and demand conditions change, exchange rates also change. If a currency becomes more valuable, we say that it **appreciates**. For example, in 2010, one US dollar would buy about twelve Mexican pesos. Five years later, one dollar would buy almost seventeen pesos. The dollar appreciated relative to the peso over that period. If a currency loses value, we say it **depreciates**. For example, in August 2012, $1.00 (US dollar) would buy €0.82 (euros). By the end of the year, it would buy just €0.76. The dollar depreciated relative to the euro over that period.

Notice that an appreciation of one currency always means depreciation of another. For example, a movement of the exchange rate from twelve pesos per dollar to seventeen pesos per dollar is an appreciation of the dollar and, at the same time, a depreciation of the peso. When we draw the supply and demand diagram with "pesos per dollar" on the vertical axis, as in Figure 9–1, a movement in the upward direction is an appreciation of the dollar but a depreciation of the peso. Because the geometrical direction of a movement of the exchange rate depends on how we label the vertical axis, it can be confusing to use the words *up* or *down* to describe exchange rate movements. It is better always to say "the peso appreciates" or "the dollar depreciates" than to say "the peso goes up" or "the dollar goes down." (Alternatively, we can say "the peso strengthens" or "the dollar weakens.")

A number of factors can cause a currency to appreciate or depreciate. We will give just two of many possible examples, again based on the market for US dollars and Mexican pesos.

As one example, suppose that there is an outbreak of a dangerous strain of flu in Mexico. Worried about the disease, many American tourists cancel their vacations to Mexico, which in turn reduces the number of dollars supplied by US tourists in exchange

Appreciate

An increase in value of one country's currency relative to the currency of another country

Depreciate

A decrease in value of one country's currency relative to the currency of another country

for pesos. The supply curve for dollars shifts sharply to the left, as shown in Part (a) of Figure 9–2. The shift of the supply curve changes the equilibrium exchange rate from ten pesos per dollar to fifteen pesos per dollar—an appreciation of the dollar and a depreciation of the peso.

Our second example shows how changes in financial flows can affect exchange rates. Suppose interest rates increase in the United States, while interest rates remain unchanged in Mexico. US bonds and other assets would become relatively more attractive to Mexican investors, so net financial outflows from Mexico to the United States would increase. The result would be an increase in demand for dollars and an appreciation of the dollar (depreciation of the peso), as shown in Part (b) of Figure 9–2.

FIGURE 9–2

Changes in the Peso-Dollar Exchange Rate

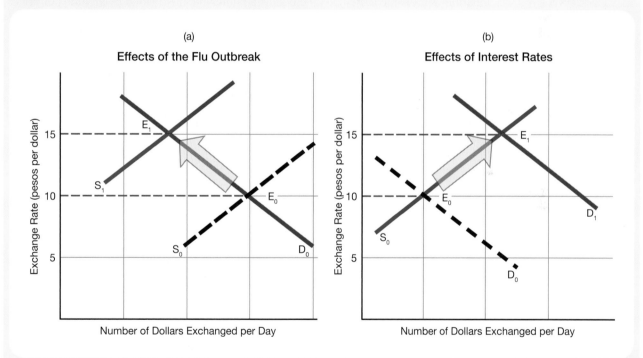

Part (a) shows the effects on the peso-dollar exchange rate of an outbreak of flu in Mexico. A decrease in US vacation travel to Mexico shifts the supply curve of dollars to the left. As it does so, the exchange rate moves from ten pesos per dollar to fifteen pesos per dollar—an appreciation of the dollar and a depreciation of the peso. Part (b) shows the effects of an increase in US interest rates. The increase in interest rates increases the quantity of dollars demanded by Mexican investors wishing to purchase US bonds. The demand curve shifts to the right. As it does so, there is again an appreciation of the dollar and a depreciation of the peso.

These are only a few of the many events that can cause exchange rates to change. Generally, anything that increases a country's demand for imports will tend to cause its currency to depreciate. The causes could be healthy, like higher consumer incomes or greater demand by businesses for imported raw materials, or unhealthy, like a failure of domestic industry to offer goods and services of a quality that satisfies domestic consumers. Anything that increases demand for a country's exports tends to cause its currency to appreciate. Examples could include changes in fashion, stronger growth of foreign trading partners, or technical changes that increase demand for some specialized export such as rare earth metals. Many different factors can cause changes in financial flows as well, including improvements in a country's investment climate, greater political stability or instability, changes in interest rates or asset prices, and more.

9.1d Nominal and Real Exchange Rates

In many areas of macroeconomics, we make a distinction between nominal and real values of key variables. Nominal values reflect prices the parties actually pay at the time a transaction takes place. We transform them to real values by adjusting for the effects of inflation. For example, real income equals nominal income divided by an index of prices. To take another example, the real interest rate equals the nominal interest rate minus the rate of inflation.

The exchange rates we have looked at so far are nominal rates—the rates at which banks carry out exchanges of one currency for another to serve the needs of traders and travelers. Like other nominal values, we can adjust nominal exchange rates to reflect inflation, but the process is a little more complex because we have to adjust for the rates of inflation in both the domestic and foreign economies. The simplest way to make the adjustment is like this:

Let H = nominal exchange rate expressed as units of domestic currency
per unit of foreign currency[1]

h = real exchange rate

Pd = domestic price level

Pf = foreign price level

$$\text{then: } h = H\left(\frac{Pf}{Pd}\right)$$

This formula gives the real exchange rate in the same units as the original nominal exchange rate—for example, pesos per dollar if we are talking about the United States and Mexico. In practice, people more often state real exchange rates in the form of an index rather than in terms of currency units. To do so, we first choose some convenient year—say 2000—and assign a value of 100 to the real exchange rate for that year. After doing that, we state the real exchange rate index for any other year by giving its value relative to the base year, just as we do with the price indexes we discussed in Chapter 6.[2]

The nominal and real exchange rates we have looked at so far are so-called bilateral exchange rates because they show the value of the domestic currency relative to one foreign currency. The dollar (or any other currency) always has many bilateral exchange rates: pesos per dollar, euros per dollar, Eritrean nakfa per dollar, and so on. A country's bilateral exchange rate may appreciate against one currency, while at the same time it depreciates against another.

Often it is useful to have a single number that gives an indication of the overall value of a country's currency. One indicator that does so is the **real effective exchange rate (REER)**. The REER is a weighted average of bilateral exchange rates, using as weights the shares of each currency in a given country's imports and exports. The REER is an index with a base year value of 100; an increase in the index indicates an appreciation of the country's currency.

The real exchange rate is useful in part because of its close relationship to the popular notion of "competitiveness." As a country's real exchange rate appreciates, its exporters and producers of goods that compete with imports find it harder to meet international competition. At the same time, consumers and firms that use imported inputs enjoy the benefits of relatively cheap imports. When a country's real exchange rate depreciates, exporters and producers of import-competing goods rejoice, while consumers of imports weep.

9.1e Purchasing Power Parity

To round out the discussion, we will introduce one more concept that is useful in discussing exchange rates: **purchasing power parity (PPP)**. Purchasing power parity means a situation in which goods cost the same in one country as in another when prices are compared using the market exchange rate. For example, we would say that purchasing power parity existed for beer between the Czech Republic and the United States if a bottle of Pilsner Urquell® cost 25 Kč (Czech koruna) in Prague and $1 in New York, and the market exchange rate was 25 Kč per dollar. If those were the prices but the exchange rate were 50 Kč per dollar, a New Yorker visiting Prague would find beer to be a bargain; if the exchange rate were 12 Kč per dollar, the New York visitor would find beer to be more costly than at home.

Instead of calculating purchasing power parity for just one good at a time, economists more often calculate it as an index based on a whole market basket of goods purchased by a typical consumer. In practice, market exchange rates are not always equal to purchasing power parity. Part of the reason is that the tendency toward purchasing power parity holds much more strongly for goods that are widely traded on world markets than for services and goods that are traded only locally. As a rule, market exchange rates tend to be below purchasing power parity for poor countries and above them for wealthy countries. The reason, in part, is that services tend to be much less expensive in poor countries. *Applying Economic Ideas 9.1* shows that using purchasing power parity rather than market exchange rates gives a very different picture of the relative sizes of countries' economies and, hence, of their relative living standards.

Real effective exchange rate (REER)

A weighted average of the exchange rate of a country's currency relative to those of all trading partners

Purchasing power parity (PPP)

A situation in which goods cost the same in one country as in another when prices are compared using the market exchange rate

If purchasing power parity always held, traded goods like televisions would cost the same everywhere when prices were converted at market exchange rates. (Shutterstock)

Applying Economic Ideas 9.1

Purchasing Power Parity and International Economic Comparisons

Because market exchange rates do not consistently reflect purchasing power parity, they can be a misleading basis for international comparisons of the relative sizes of the world's economies and of their standards of living. For a rich country like Switzerland, GDP per capita measured at market exchange rates tends to overstate the size of the economy and the standard of living. For such countries, the ratio of GDP measured at the market exchange rate to GDP measured at PPP is greater than one. For a poor country like India, GDP per capita at market rates understates the size of the economy and the standard of living; the ratio of GDP at market exchange rates to GDP at PPP is less than one.

Even when stated in terms of purchasing power parity, GDP per capita may give a misleading impression of the relative quality of life in different countries because it does not directly consider issues like public health, environmental quality, or personal security. The PPP data in this table use the US dollar as the reference point for market exchange rates; so the market to PPP ratio for the United States is, by definition, 1.0.

Country	Population (millions)	GDP at PPP (billions of USD)	GDP at Market Exchange Rate (billions of USD)	Per Capita GDP at PPP (USD)	Per Capita GDP at Market Exchange Rate (USD)	Market/ PPP Ratio
India	1,207.0	$4,469.0	$1,843.0	$3,703.0	$1,527.0	0.41
Ghana	24.0	$74.0	$38.0	$3,083.0	$1,583.0	0.51
Haiti	10.0	$12.0	$7.3	$1,240.0	$730.0	0.59
China	1,348.0	$11,316.0	$6,988.0	$8,395.0	$5,184.0	0.62
USA	312.0	$15,064.0	$15,064.0	$48,282.0	$48,282.0	1.00
France	63.0	$2,216.0	$2,808.0	$35,175.0	$44,571.0	1.27
Japan	128.0	$4,395.0	$5,855.0	$34,336.0	$45,742.0	1.33
Switzerland	7.8	$340.0	$665.0	$43,590.0	$85,256.0	1.96

Source: World Bank, World Development Indicators Database, September 2011.

9.2 CENTRAL BANKS AND THE FOREIGN-EXCHANGE MARKET

In Chapter 8, we made brief note of the fact that central banks participate in foreign-exchange markets, as well as in domestic securities markets. Their purchases of assets denominated in foreign currencies affect monetary conditions in much the same way as do domestic open market purchases. Purchases of foreign assets are an instrument of expansionary policy; they increase bank reserves and tend to cause interest rates to fall. Sales of foreign assets are an instrument of contractionary policy.

In addition to affecting domestic monetary conditions, central bank purchases and sales of foreign assets also affect exchange rates. An example will show how these effects come about. Figure 9–3 shows how Mexico's central bank, the Bank of Mexico,

could intervene to maintain an exchange rate of 10.0 pesos per dollar, if it wanted to do so. (The Bank of Mexico does not currently maintain a fixed exchange rate relative to the dollar, but it has done so at times in the past.) Suppose that, originally, the supply and demand curves are in the positions S_0 and D_0. Then suppose that fast growth of GDP in Mexico increases demand for imports from the United States and shifts the demand curve for dollars rightward to D_1.

If the Bank of Mexico does nothing, the peso will depreciate to a rate of 12.5 pesos per dollar, shown by a movement from point E_0 to point E_1. In order to hold the exchange rate at 10.0 pesos per dollar, the Bank of Mexico can sell dollars from its foreign exchange reserves. The sales of dollars, added to the dollars already offered for sale by private parties, would shift the supply curve rightward to S_1. Instead of moving to E_1, the market would move to E_2, and the exchange rate would remain at its target level.

Headquarters of Banco de México, Mexico's central bank. (Shutterstock)

On another occasion, the Bank of Mexico might want to offset a different combination of market forces that would tend to cause an unwanted appreciation of the peso. To do so, it would buy dollars to add to its foreign reserves. All the effects described above would then operate in reverse.

9.2a Why Maintain a Fixed Exchange Rate?

The preceding example explains how a central bank can intervene in foreign exchange markets to maintain an exchange rate at some level stronger or weaker than what would otherwise be the market equilibrium. What we have not yet explained is why policymakers might want to do so. There are two principal reasons.

The first reason is that exchange rates affect patterns of trade. When a country's exchange rate appreciates, its residents find it less expensive to buy goods made in other countries, and imports increase. That benefits buyers of imported consumer goods and firms that use imported inputs. At the same time, an appreciation of the currency harms exporters and firms that compete with imported consumer goods and inputs. A depreciation of the exchange rate has opposite effects.

FIGURE 9–3

Effects of Central Bank Intervention on the Peso-Dollar Exchange Rate

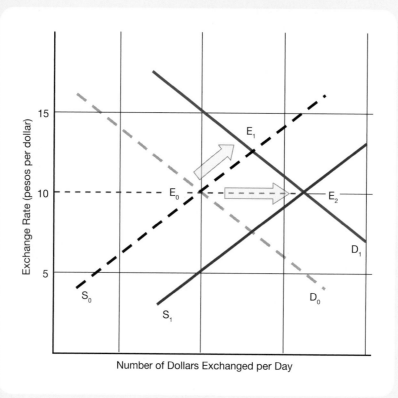

Number of Dollars Exchanged per Day

Suppose that fast growth of the Mexican economy increases the demand for imports from the United States, shifting the demand curve for dollars from D_0 to D_1. By itself, that would cause the peso to depreciate from 10.0 pesos per dollar to 12.5 pesos per dollar (a movement from E_0 to E_1). If the Bank of Mexico wanted to hold the exchange rate at 10.0 pesos per dollar, it could sell dollars from its reserves of foreign currency. Doing so would shift the supply curve to the right from S_0 to S_1. The market would end up in a new equilibrium at E_2, where the exchange rate stays at its target value.

Because exchange rates affect patterns of trade, uncertainty about them increases the risks for importers, exporters, and international investors. Firms engaged in international trade can take measures to reduce their exposure to exchange rate risks, but doing so is costly. Also, exchange rate uncertainty has a political cost. Every change in the exchange rate produces winners and losers. The losers from exchange rate changes are likely to express anger at the government and demand compensation, while the winners are likely to quietly count their gains without offering to share them. In short, the economic and political costs of exchange rate uncertainty are one factor that makes an exchange rate target attractive.

The second reason to use an exchange rate target as a basis for economic policy is to help control inflation. In the late twentieth century, many countries around the world—Argentina, Brazil, Israel, Russia, and Bulgaria, to name just a few—had periods of extreme inflation. As we will explain in detail in Chapter 14, one policy that has been found effective in bringing inflation under control is to set a fixed exchange rate link to a stronger, more stable currency like the dollar or the euro. The expectation of a stable exchange rate acts as an anchor to promote domestic price stability.

For one of these reasons, or both, the central banks of many countries actively manage their exchange rates. Some central banks, like those of China and Russia, manage exchange rates in a way that reduces short-term fluctuations without keeping to a specific target for a long period or eliminating all day-to-day exchange rate movements. Others—for example, Hong Kong and Bulgaria—maintain exchange rates that are precisely fixed relative to the dollar or euro. Not even the smallest day-to-day variations are allowed.

Still other countries go even further in their efforts to eliminate exchange rate movements. They abandon their own currencies altogether and opt, instead, to use a common currency shared with one or more of their trading partners. We call such an arrangement a **currency union**. The final two sections of this chapter will present two important case studies of the way countries manage their exchange rates: China, which has a managed but not a fixed exchange rate, and Europe's currency union, the euro area.

BVT *Lab*

Improve your test scores. Practice quizzes are available at **www.BVTLab.com**.

9.3 IS THE CHINESE YUAN UNDERVALUED?

China's remarkable economic growth has been due, in part, to its success in export markets. Many factors have helped China become the world's biggest exporter. An abundant supply of relatively inexpensive labor, a high savings rate that fuels investment in factories and infrastructure, and a business-friendly environment—each has played a role. Another part of the story has been the export-friendly policies pursued by the People's Bank of China (PBoC), China's central bank.

The PBoC's policy has alternated between maintaining a fixed exchange rate and allowing carefully managed appreciation of the Chinese currency, the yuan (also known, officially, as the renminbi). The PBoC held the exchange rate fixed relative to the US dollar up to 2005. From 2005 to 2008, it allowed the yuan to appreciate gradually. In 2008, it once again fixed the exchange rate, out of fear that further appreciation would slow exports and make it harder for China to survive the gathering global financial crisis.

The US government strongly protested the return to a fixed rate. It argued that an artificially weak yuan was giving Chinese goods an unfair competitive advantage in world markets. In June 2010, the PBoC again began letting the yuan appreciate gradually. However, the PBoC did not allow the yuan to float freely to its market equilibrium value. Instead, it continued to manage the exchange rate in a way that controlled the rate of appreciation. The yuan appreciated only about 10 percent over the next two years. Alleged undervaluation of the yuan remained a political issue, with many US critics blaming the slow recovery of the US job market on Chinese currency manipulation.

However, economists were quick to point out that the bilateral yuan-dollar exchange rate does not tell the whole story. The real effective exchange rate of the yuan gives a more complete picture of the situation. As explained above, the REER adjusts each currency to take international differences in inflation into account and averages exchange rates against the currencies of all of a country's trading partners.

As Figure 9–4 shows, the yuan's REER has appreciated much more strongly than the nominal bilateral rate against the dollar. Part of the reason has to do with inflation. Over the period shown, Chinese inflation has averaged about 1 percent per year higher than the US rate and about 2 percent higher than inflation in the EU, which is China's largest trading partner. Since early 2014, the gap between the two exchange rate measures has widened, in part, because the dollar has appreciated strongly against the euro.

Currency union

Two or more countries that share a common currency

By 2014, the Chinese economy had begun to slow down. Growth of real GDP, which had exceeded 10 percent per year during the early 2000s, had fallen below 8 percent. The country's current account surplus had fallen to half the level reached before the 2008 crisis (see Chapter 5, Case for Discussion). The yuan stopped appreciating against the dollar and even depreciated in the first months of 2014.

The depreciation of the yuan against the dollar came at an unwelcome moment for China. True, other things being equal, a depreciation would help China's exports; but the country's leaders now had another goal. They wanted to persuade the International Monetary Fund (IMF) to admit the yuan to the elite status of a "reserve currency," along with the US dollar, the euro, the British pound, and the Japanese yen. Stabilizing the exchange rate became a priority—even if that meant reversing course and intervening in foreign exchange markets to prevent depreciation.

The PBoC is not very transparent about its policy, but outsiders can get a good idea of what is going on by watching what happens to Chinese reserves of foreign currency. Currency reserves rose steadily from about $500 million in 2005 to almost $4 trillion in early 2014. The increase was the result of persistent central bank intervention to prevent or slow the pace of appreciation. However, beginning in mid-2014, reserves began to drop rapidly. By the late summer of 2015, they were nearly half a trillion dollars below the level they had been just a year earlier. Clearly, the PBoC had switched from a policy of buying foreign assets to prevent an appreciation of the yuan to one of selling foreign assets to prevent a depreciation.

FIGURE 9–4

Exchange Rate of the Chinese Yuan Relative to the US Dollar

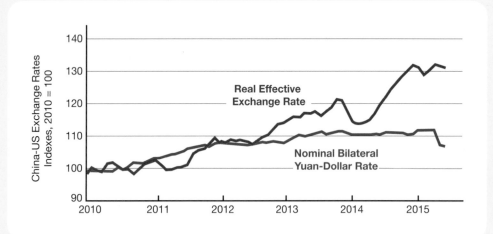

Until 2005, the People's Bank of China (PBoC) held the exchange rate of the Chinese yuan at a fixed value relative to the US dollar. From 2005 to 2008, it allowed the yuan to appreciate gradually. During the global financial crisis that began in 2008, it returned to a fixed exchange rate policy. Starting in mid-2010, it once again allowed gradual appreciation. Over the period shown, the yuan has appreciated much more strongly as measured by the real effective exchange rate rather than by the nominal yuan-dollar rate.

In August 2015, the PBoC surprised financial markets by allowing the yuan to depreciate sharply. Some US politicians accused the Chinese government of artificially devaluing the yuan to boost exports, but most economists interpreted the depreciation differently. Rather than actively weakening the yuan, they thought it looked like the PBoC was reducing its efforts to prop up the currency.

Unless the Chinese government decides to allow the yuan to float freely, something that seems unlikely at the time of writing, currency policy will no doubt continue to be a source of friction in US-China relations. However, it does appear as though the Chinese government is no longer pursuing a consistent policy of undervaluation.

The exchange rates of the Chinese yuan relative to the US dollar and the euro have been a source of considerable controversy. (Shutterstock)

9.4 EUROPE'S STRUGGLING CURRENCY UNION

For our second case study in exchange rate policy, we turn from China to Europe. Ever since the end of World War II, European leaders have worked toward closer economic and political integration. One of the first steps was the formation, in 1951, of the European Coal and Steel Community. At first comprising just four countries, it grew into the European Economic Community and eventually, in 1993, into the European Union (EU), which now has twenty-eight member countries.

January 1, 2002, saw the launch of the most ambitious effort of all toward European economic integration. After several years of careful preparation, a unified currency—the euro—entered circulation in eleven EU countries and replaced familiar historical currencies like the franc, the mark, and the peseta. Nineteen EU countries now use the euro, as well as several small states that are not EU members, including Montenegro, Kosovo, and the Vatican. Other EU countries, except for the United Kingdom and Denmark, are formally obligated to adopt the euro eventually, though some, like Sweden, have made it clear that they are in no hurry to do so.

This section addresses a seemingly simple question: Is a single currency for Europe a good idea? The answer, it turns out, is far less simple than the question.

9.4a The Case for a Currency Union

The euro area is by far the largest currency area in the world today, but there are a few other examples of countries that share currencies. For example, Ecuador and Panama use the US dollar, while Swaziland and Lesotho use the South African rand.

In some ways, the United States is a currency union among its fifty states, all of which use the dollar. That was not always the case. During the Civil War, the Union and the Confederacy used separate currencies. California, although a member of the Union, stayed with a gold standard when the government in Washington, DC, began issuing a new paper currency, nicknamed the "greenback," to pay for the war. Throughout the nineteenth century, private banks printed their own paper banknotes. Although they all had the name "dollar," they did not always exchange at a one-to-one rate. The United States did not achieve a fully unified currency until the Federal Reserve System came into existence in 1913.

The principle advantage of a currency union is that it makes trade, travel, and financial relations among countries much simpler. Imagine the hassles that would exist if New York and New Jersey used separate currencies. Every time you crossed the

George Washington Bridge, you would either have to stop to change currencies or carry currencies of both states with you. If a grocery store in New York bought apples from New Jersey, it would face the risk that a depreciation of the New York dollar would turn a profitable contract with its supplier into a losing one. If you were a New York financial adviser who bought New Jersey securities for your clients' 401(k) plans, you would constantly face the risk of unpredictable gains or losses from exchange rate changes.

Similarly, trade, travel, and finance in Europe became less costly and less risky as soon as the euro came into circulation. Combined with rules that allow travel among most EU countries without stopping for border checks, the euro succeeded in creating a highly integrated economic space covering much of the continent.

9.4b The Downside of a Shared Currency

Like everything in economics, a common currency has its opportunity costs. The main opportunity cost for a country that joins a currency area is that its central bank loses independent control over monetary policy. In the euro area, the European Central Bank (ECB) makes monetary policy decisions. The ECB is a democratic institution; each member country gets a say in its operations, but no one country has control over its monetary policy. Each member country retains its own central bank, but the national central banks have no independent power to fix interest rates or otherwise change monetary conditions. Much like the twelve regional member banks of the Federal Reserve System, the national central banks within the euro area largely serve administrative functions in carrying out ECB policy.

Headquarters of the European Central Bank, which is responsible for monetary policy in the euro area (Shutterstock)

Central control over monetary policy would work fine if the economies of all euro areas moved harmoniously together. The ECB could offset a threat of inflation that affected all countries by tightening monetary policy. It could counteract high unemployment that hit all members at once by cutting interest rates. However, when an economic shock hits just one or a few members, all euro members must live with whatever policy the ECB sets for all. National central banks cannot act independently to help their countries.

What is more, if an individual member of a currency union experiences an unfavorable economic shock, it cannot use a change in its exchange rate to ease adjustment. The exchange rate of the euro as a whole can change relative to the US dollar or Chinese yuan, but there can be no change in the exchange rate of France relative to Germany or of Greece relative to Italy. That can cause serious problems. For example:

- If a country experiences inflation, its exports become less competitive, and imports tend to increase. The resulting decrease in planned expenditures puts a drag on the economy, causing unemployment to rise. If the country has an independent currency, its nominal exchange rate will tend to depreciate, which will help maintain competitiveness and employment. If the country is part of a currency area, adjustment is more difficult.

- Financial inflows often benefit a country, but excessive financial inflows can cause overheating. If the country has an independent currency, financial inflows will tend to cause its currency to appreciate. That, in turn, will slow the country's exports of goods and services and encourage imports, which will ease adjustment to the increased financial flows. In a country with a common currency, the exchange rate will not change. That increases the risk that excessive financial inflows could cause a disruptive housing bubble or some other form of instability.

- Productivity growth can vary among countries for many reasons. If a country finds its productivity growing less rapidly than that of its trading partners, its goods will lose competitiveness on international markets, and a trade deficit develops. If the country has an independent currency, its exchange rate will depreciate to restore competitiveness. A country with a shared currency cannot count on exchange rate movements to offset differences in productivity growth.

9.4c When Do the Advantages Outweigh the Disadvantages?

We see, then, that a common currency has both advantages and disadvantages. The advantage is that a common currency reduces the costs and risks of international trade and finance, thereby promoting greater economic integration. The disadvantage is that a common currency makes it more difficult for a country to adjust to shocks that do not affect all countries the same way. Under what conditions do the advantages outweigh the disadvantages, or vice versa? Economists point to four conditions as being favorable or unfavorable to a common currency.

Patterns of Trade   If a group of countries trade mostly with one another, the case for a common currency is stronger because the reduction in costs and risks of trade will be greater. That is true for the states of the United States when thought of as members of a currency union. It is also true of the members of the EU, most of which carry on 60 to 70 percent of their external trade with other EU members. In this regard, conditions in the EU are favorable to operation of a currency area.

Structural Similarities   If a group of countries share a similar economic structure, so that external shocks affect them similarly, they are more suited to form a currency union. As we have seen, changes in central bank policies and exchange rates can help a currency area adjust to economic shocks that affect all members the same way. On the other hand, a currency area makes it more difficult for an individual member country to adjust to shocks that affect it differently from other members.

One important aspect of structure is the pattern of a country's imports and exports. If some member countries export mainly manufactured goods, others mainly raw materials, and still others mainly services (like tourism), there is a greater risk that economic shocks will affect countries differently. In that case, the currency area will function less smoothly.

Several other structural characteristics of economies also matter. Are productivity trends similar among members of the currency union? Savings rates? Financial systems? Currency unions work better when the answers to such questions are "yes."

Flexibility of Labor Markets   When a country with an independent currency runs into difficulties, it can restore competitiveness and growth, in part, through depreciation of its currency. That is not possible for a member of a currency union. Because such a country cannot adjust through changes in its exchange rate, other markets must bear the burden of adjustment. Labor markets are especially important. If labor markets are flexible, unemployed workers from one part of a currency union may be able to find jobs in other regions where conditions are better. Also, a country with flexible labor markets may be able to restore lost competitiveness through decreases in nominal wage rates, even if it cannot do so through depreciation of its currency. Labor markets in the United States are among the most flexible in the world, with regard to both geographical mobility and wage rates, which makes it easier for all fifty states to share the dollar as their currency. The relative inflexibility of European labor markets is an unfavorable factor for the smooth operation of the euro area.

Fiscal Policy   Fiscal policy means government policy regarding spending, taxes, and government debt. We will explore fiscal policy in detail in Chapters 12 and 13, but we need to say a few words here since the right kind of fiscal policy is important for the smooth operation of a currency union. Two aspects of fiscal policy are of particular importance.

First, each government within the currency union needs to control its tax and spending policy in a way that avoids excessive buildup of government debt. The reason is that a debt crisis in one member of a currency union threatens the stability of the whole. A default, or threat of default, by one member can drive up borrowing costs for everyone who shares the same currency. That, in turn, can lead to pressures for solvent members of the currency union to bail out irresponsible members.

Second, a currency union works more smoothly when there is a large central budget that can redistribute public funds from parts of the area that are doing well to those that are experiencing economic problems. For example, a central budget that is responsible for pensions, unemployment benefits, or medical costs can provide support for regional governments when they experience temporary economic downturns.

The fiscal relationship between the federal and state governments in the United States is more suited to smooth operation of a currency union than that between the central institutions of the EU and its member countries. The US federal government accounts for about 60 percent of all government spending in the country, whereas the central budget of the EU accounts for only about 2 percent. At the same time, budget discipline is stronger in the United States at the state level than it is at the federal level. Most state governments, unlike the national government, are required to keep their budgets in balance or close to it. Fiscal discipline is much weaker among the member countries of the euro area. In principle, member countries are subject to limits on their government debts and deficits, but those limits have proved impossible to enforce.

9.4d The Ongoing Crisis of the Euro Area

When we take all of the above factors together, the countries of the euro area are not as well suited for smooth operation of a currency union as the states of the United States. The first years after introduction of the euro were a period of relative prosperity during which it was possible to keep structural weaknesses in the background. The global financial crisis brought underlying problems into the open, however, leaving the euro area divided among relatively strong and relatively weak members.

One important source of the crisis has been persistent divergence in competitiveness among euro area members. **Unit labor costs** are one commonly used indicator of competitiveness. Unit labor costs are a measure of nominal wages adjusted for labor productivity. If a country's nominal wages rise faster than labor productivity, the cost of producing a unit of output increases. Other things being equal, that undermines the competitiveness of its exports and makes it more difficult for domestic producers to compete with imports. If, instead, nominal wages fall (or rise more slowly than labor productivity), the cost of producing each unit of output decreases. Other things being equal, that improves competitiveness.

Unit labor cost

A measure of nominal wage rates adjusted for labor productivity

When exchange rates are flexible, depreciation of a country's currency can offset a rise in unit labor costs, restoring competitiveness. When exchange rates are fixed, as within the euro area, changes in relative unit labor costs are harder to deal with.

As Figure 9–5 shows, from 2001 to 2008 (the early years of the euro), unit labor costs in Germany, the largest economy in the euro area, did not change significantly. However, over the same period, unit labor costs in Greece, Ireland, Italy, Portugal, and Spain increased by double-digit amounts. Those increases were driven, in part, by slower productivity growth than in Germany and, in part, by faster inflation. The loss of competitiveness left these countries vulnerable when the global financial crisis hit in 2008.

After the crisis, the weaker euro area economies came under intense pressure from Germany and central EU authorities to reverse their earlier loss of competitiveness through structural reforms of labor markets and other institutions. As the chart shows, these measures were partly successful insofar as unit labor costs have fallen, or grown less rapidly than in Germany, in all of the affected countries. However, the decreases or slowing increases of unit labor costs came largely from cuts in nominal wages and only partially from growth of labor productivity. In fact, in Greece and Italy, labor productivity actually decreased from 2008 to 2014.

EU budget rules compounded the economic pain suffered by the weakest euro area economies. Under those rules, member countries are not supposed to have government budget deficits higher than 3 percent of GDP or total government debt higher than 60 percent of GDP. In the years leading up to the crisis, Greece and Portugal were

FIGURE 9–5

Diverging Competitiveness in the Euro Area

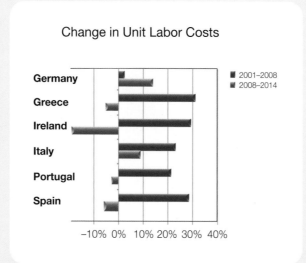

This chart shows the divergence of competitiveness, as measured by unit labor costs, among members of the euro area. Relatively rapid growth of unit labor costs in Greece, Ireland, Italy, Portugal, and Spain in the early years of the euro was due in part to slow growth of labor productivity and in part to higher rates of inflation. With a single currency, countries that lost competitiveness were not able to restore it through depreciation of their currencies. Instead, under pressure from EU authorities, these countries implemented painful austerity and structural reforms that have only partially reversed earlier losses of competitiveness.

Source for data: Eurostat.

in violation of both rules. Italy had a relatively small budget deficit, but due to earlier borrowing, it had a total debt of over 100 percent of GDP. The budgets of Spain and Ireland looked relatively healthy going into the crisis, but their deficits soared and debt grew rapidly as recession spread through the euro area.

As a result, all of these countries found it necessary to raise taxes and cut spending at the same time they were coping with the recession and implementing structural reforms. This budgetary austerity made the social and economic pain of adjustment to the crisis even greater than it would have otherwise been.

By 2015, the worst of the recession appeared to be over in much of the EU. Real GDP in the euro area, as a whole, was back to approximately the level it had been in 2008. (By comparison, US real GDP was 9 percent higher in 2015 than in 2008.) However, real GDP remained below the 2008 level in Greece, Italy, Spain, and Portugal. In Greece, the cumulative decrease in real GDP from 2008 was a stunning 25 percent. Not surprisingly, an economic collapse of that magnitude led to profound political turmoil. Despite a series of controversial measures taken by EU authorities to prevent complete economic collapse, it is not yet certain that Greece will remain within the euro area. All things considered, it is hard to see the world's most ambitious experiment in establishing a common currency as a resounding success.

Members of a currency union like the euro cannot use exchange rate changes to ease adjustment to economic difficulties.
(Shutterstock)

Summary

1. **How do supply and demand determine exchange rates?**

    Supply and demand determine the exchange rate of one currency relative to another. The market where Mexican pesos trade for US dollars is an example. The supply curve of dollars in that market reflects the activities of US importers, who sell dollars to obtain the pesos they need in order to buy Mexican goods and services, and the activities of US investors, who need pesos in order to buy Mexican stocks, bonds, or other assets. The demand curve for dollars reflects the activities of Mexican buyers of exports from the United States and Mexican investors in dollar-denominated assets. An increase in the value of the peso relative to the dollar is an appreciation of the peso. A decrease in the value of the peso is a depreciation.

2. **What is the distinction between nominal and real exchange rates?**

    Nominal exchange rates are expressed in terms of the actual number of currency units needed to buy another currency. Real exchange rates are adjusted for the effects of inflation. If we let H stand for the nominal exchange rate expressed as units of domestic currency per unit of foreign currency, h for the real exchange rate, Pd for the domestic price level, and Pf for the foreign price level, then we can express the real exchange rate using the formula $h = H(Pf/Pd)$. We express the real exchange rate using an index with a value of 100 for a chosen base year.

3. **How do central banks influence exchange rates?**

    Central banks can influence exchange rates by buying and selling assets denominated in a foreign currency. A purchase of foreign assets, other things being equal, will tend to cause the value of a country's currency to depreciate. A sale of foreign assets will tend to cause the country's exchange rate to appreciate. Some central banks commit themselves to holding their currency at an exact target value. Others intervene frequently to resist undesired appreciation or depreciation without trying to maintain a fixed rate. Still other central banks, including the US Federal Reserve, do not intervene at all in foreign exchange markets.

4. **What has been the exchange rate policy of the Chinese central bank?**

    China's central bank, the People's Bank of China, frequently intervenes in foreign exchange markets. For many years, the PBoC either held the value of the yuan (also known as the renminbi) fixed relative to the dollar or allowed it to appreciate, but not as rapidly as market forces alone would have done. Since 2014, intervention has been more symmetrical, sometimes aimed at resisting appreciation and sometimes at resisting depreciation.

5. **What are the benefits of the euro currency area, and what are the problems it faces?**

    The euro, which first came into general circulation in 2002, is now the currency of nineteen members of the European Union. The purpose of the common currency area is to improve economic integration and lower the costs and risks of trade and international finance. However, the euro area has faced a number of problems in recent years. Its member countries do not share the degree of structural similarity needed for smooth operation of a currency area. Also, some countries have experienced problems with fiscal discipline, and some have needed emergency assistance from their more stable partners.

KEY TERMS

Appreciate	230	Purchasing power parity (PPP)	233
Currency union	237	Real effective exchange rate (REER)	233
Depreciate	230	Unit labor cost	242
Foreign-exchange markets	228		

PROBLEMS AND TOPICS FOR DISCUSSION

1.   **Exchange rates on the web**   Numerous websites give up-to-the-minute quotes of foreign exchange rates. These exercises will familiarize you with some of them.

   a.   Go to the website xe.com. What is the current nominal exchange rate of the dollar relative to the euro? Quote the rate both in euros per dollar and dollars per euro.

   b.   Visit the website oanda.com and find the currency tool that provides historical exchange rates (http://www.oanda.com/currency/historical-rates/). How has the exchange rate of the dollar moved relative to the euro over the past year?

   c.   The Bank for International Settlements maintains a database of real effective exchange rate indexes (http://www.bis.org/statistics/eer/index.htm). Download the database and look up the real effective exchange rate of the US dollar. Has the dollar appreciated or depreciated in real terms over the past year?

2.   **Canada-US exchange rate**   Draw a diagram showing supply and demand in the market where US dollars (USD) are exchanged for Canadian dollars (CAD). Put CAD per USD on the vertical axis. The supply curve represents the quantity of USD offered in exchange for CAD. The demand curve represents the quantity of USD that people want to buy in exchange for CAD. Suppose that initially the two dollars are "at par"—that is, the exchange rate is 1 USD = 1 CAD. Next, suppose that a fall in world oil prices decreases the demand for Canadian oil exports. Will that shift the supply curve, the demand curve, or both in your diagram? Will the CAD appreciate or depreciate? Will the USD appreciate or depreciate? Bonus question: Find a chart of the CAD/USD exchange rate for recent years (http://www.oanda.com/currency/historical-rates/). Did the exchange rate behave as expected when global oil prices fell in the second half of 2014?

3.   **Real and nominal exchange rates**   Explain whether each of the following will cause the Russian ruble to appreciate or depreciate in real terms relative to the US dollar.

   a.   The rate of inflation is the same in the two countries; at the same time, an increase in the world price of oil, Russia's major export, causes the ruble to appreciate in nominal terms.

   b.   There is no change in the nominal exchange rate; at the same time, the rate of inflation in Russia is greater than the rate of inflation in the United States.

PROBLEMS AND TOPICS FOR DISCUSSION

4. **China's exchange rate**   Using the sources listed in Question 1, or other sources, find the current bilateral nominal exchange rate of the yuan relative to the US dollar. Has the yuan appreciated or depreciated relative to the dollar since Figure 9–4 was drawn? What has happened to the real effective exchange rate of the yuan? Look for recent news items commenting on the yuan-dollar exchange rate. Do US commentators continue to complain that the yuan is undervalued? Explain your answer.

5. **Euro area developments**   Use your internet research skills to find a list of countries that are currently members of the euro area. Have any members left the euro, or joined it, since this chapter was written (in late 2015)? In particular, has Greece remained a member of the euro area? How has the exchange rate of the euro changed since late 2015(bilateral relative to the dollar and REER)?

CASE *for* DISCUSSION

Argentina's Failed Currency Board

One of the most ambitious currency experiments of the late twentieth century was Argentina's attempt to link its currency, the peso, to the US dollar. Starting in 1991, the Argentine government declared that the peso, henceforth, would be worth exactly one US dollar, no more and no less. Argentines called the arrangement the "convertibility plan." The technical name for the type of permanently fixed exchange rate the country chose is a *currency board*.

The principle objective of the currency board was to put an end, once and for all, to the repeated episodes of inflation that had plagued the Argentine economy for decades. At the time the currency board was implemented, Argentine inflation was over 2,000 percent per year. The first results of the plan were very promising. Inflation came down rapidly. Within two years, the rate of inflation had almost completely disappeared, and the Argentine economy grew rapidly.

However, not everything went according to plan. One problem was that the United States, to which Argentina linked its currency, accounted for only about 8 percent of Argentina's foreign trade. Other Latin American countries, and especially neighboring Brazil, were much more important. Although the convertibility plan held the nominal exchange rate relative to the dollar constant, it did not stabilize the real effective exchange rate of the peso. In 1999, Brazil underwent an economic crisis and devalued its currency. That had the indirect effect of causing Argentina's real effective exchange rate to appreciate.

As the peso appreciated in real terms, Argentina developed a large trade deficit. Financial outflows also developed as Argentines came to believe their money would be safer if invested abroad. To hold the nominal exchange rate at the promised one-to-one ratio with the dollar, the Argentine central bank repeatedly had to sell dollars from its reserves. Doing so caused a decrease in the domestic monetary base. A drop in the number of pesos in circulation pulled the Argentine economy into a deep recession. Unemployment rose. Argentine labor markets, among the least flexible in the region, were unable to adjust through wage decreases.

It did not help that Argentina also had problems with fiscal discipline. The central government retained reasonable, although not perfect, control of its budget; but Argentina, like the United States, is a federal system with much spending taking place at the provincial level. Provincial governments, many of which were in the hands of opposition parties, ran large deficits.

Eventually, the whole experiment fell apart. At the end of 2001, a combination of high unemployment and political unrest forced the Argentine government to abandon the currency board. The central bank allowed the peso to float freely in response to supply and demand. It promptly depreciated to a rate of about three pesos per dollar.

Interestingly, though, the story had a happy ending: Once the link to the dollar was broken, the Argentine economy entered a period of rapid growth. In fact, over the next ten years, Argentina grew more rapidly than any country in Latin America.

Questions

1. Why would establishing a fixed exchange rate to the US dollar help Argentina bring its extremely high rate of inflation under control?

2. Suppose that during the effective period of the currency board, an increase in demand for the peso created pressure for the peso to appreciate. Would the Argentine central bank need to respond to that pressure by buying dollar-denominated assets to add to its foreign currency reserves or by selling dollar-denominated assets? Explain.

3. Following its 1999 crisis, Brazil allowed the value of its own currency, the real, to depreciate sharply relative to the dollar. Brazil accounted for 30 percent of Argentina's foreign trade at the time. If the peso had not been linked to the dollar, which of the following would have been to Argentina's advantage—to let the peso depreciate relative to the dollar along with the real, to hold it constant relative to the dollar, or to move in the opposite direction from the real and appreciate relative to the dollar? Why?

4. The last section of this chapter gives a list of factors that make a country more or less suited to having a fixed exchange rate or shared currency. Which of these factors, if any, favored a rigid link between the Argentine peso and the US dollar?

5. Do you think it is only coincidence that Argentina's economy began to grow rapidly after the peso depreciated sharply relative to the dollar? Or would the depreciation cause the Argentine economy to expand? Explain in terms of the multiplier effect, as discussed in Chapter 5.

6. What is the value of the Argentine peso today? Has it been appreciating, depreciating, or stable in recent months? Summarize the current state of the Argentine economy according to internet news sources. (Hint: A good place to start your search for data on recent economic developments in Argentina, or any other country, is the website Trading Economics, http://bvtlab.com/83B8V.)

From Ed Dolan's Econ Blog

Ed Dolan's Econ Blog offers several slideshows and posts related to the material in this chapter. Here are some items of special interest:

Real and Nominal Exchange Rates: A Tutorial   This slideshow provides additional detail on real and nominal exchange rates. You can find it at http://bvtlab.com/9X4A7 or by scanning the QR code.

The Breakup of the Ruble Area (1991–1993): Lessons for the Euro   After the Soviet Union was dissolved in 1991, the fifteen former Soviet Republics continued, for a time, to use the ruble as their common currency. However, this attempt to form a currency area quickly fell apart. This slideshow tells the story of the breakup of the ruble area and its lessons for the euro. You can find it at http://bvtlab.com/7e6XK or by scanning the QR code.

What Lies Behind the Plunge of the Ruble?   During the second half of 2014, the Russian ruble lost half of its value. This post from Ed Dolan's Econ Blog tracks the plunge of the ruble in both real and nominal terms and explains the connection of the ruble's exchange rate to global oil prices. Follow this link http://bvtlab.com/7va49, or scan the QR code.

POSTS

Endnotes

1. If the nominal exchange rate is originally expressed in terms of units of foreign currency per unit of domestic currency, then the ratio of price indexes in the formula must be inverted:

$$h = H\left(\frac{Pd}{Pf}\right)$$

2. If we let O denote values in the base year and t denote values in year t, then the formula for computing the real exchange rate index in year t is:

$$h_t = 100\left(\frac{H_t}{H_0}\right)\left(\frac{Pf_t}{Pd_t}\right)$$

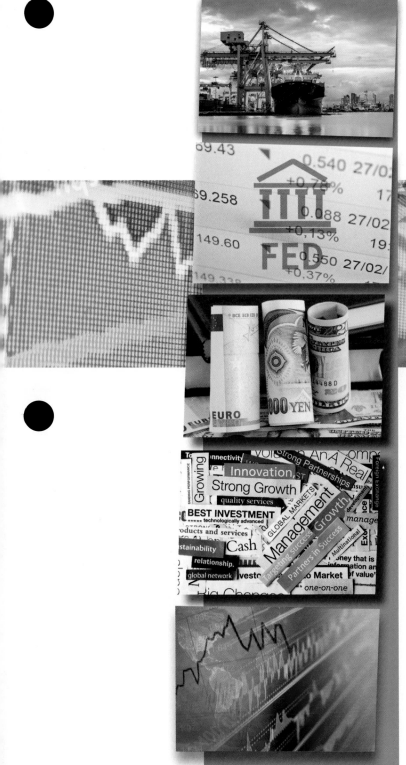

PART 4

Macroeconomic Policy

CHAPTER 10

PRICES AND REAL OUTPUT
IN THE SHORT RUN

AFTER READING THIS CHAPTER,
you will understand the following:

1. The conditions that determine the slope of the aggregate demand curve
2. The sources of shifts in the aggregate demand curve
3. The conditions that determine the slopes of short- and long-run aggregate supply curves
4. The sources of shifts in the aggregate supply curve
5. How prices, real output, and unemployment behave as the economy responds to a change in aggregate demand

BEFORE READING THIS CHAPTER,
make sure you know the following concepts:

Supply and demand

Real and nominal values

Natural level of real output

Money

Planned expenditure

The multiplier effect

Final goods

Price level

Output gap

CHAPTER
Outline

In Chapter 4, where we first introduced the search for prosperity and stability, we saw that two great sets of questions dominate macroeconomics. One set of questions is posed by Adam Smith's book *The Wealth of Nations*: Why are some countries rich and others poor? What are the sources of economic growth in the long run? What can government do to create a favorable context for long-term growth? The other set of questions are those addressed in John Maynard Keynes's book *The General Theory of Employment, Interest, and Money*: Why does the economy not grow steadily in the short run? Why does it sometimes drop below its long-run trend of growth and fall into recession? What causes inflation? What, if anything, can government do to tame the business cycle?

Chapter 4 introduced the key distinction between nominal and real output. Next, Chapter 5 introduced the concept of an equilibrium level of nominal GDP within the circular flow of income and product. We saw how a change in any one element of the circular flow—consumption, investment, government purchases, or net exports—brings about a change in equilibrium nominal GDP via the multiplier effect. This chapter will take the next step by introducing a model that shows how any change in nominal GDP is divided between change in real output and change in the price level. We will then be ready to examine public policy related to inflation, real output growth, and unemployment in the final four chapters of the book.

10.1 THE AGGREGATE DEMAND CURVE

Our first step will be to develop a new type of supply and demand model. We call it the aggregate supply and demand model because it shows supply and demand relationships, not for individual goods but for the economy as a whole. **Aggregate demand** means total real planned expenditure. **Aggregate supply** means total real output of final goods and services and is a synonym for *real GDP*.

10.1a Aggregate and Market Demand Curves

Figure 10–1 shows a typical **aggregate demand curve**. In some ways, it resembles the microeconomic demand curves for individual markets, like chicken, that we introduced in Chapter 2. Both kinds of curves represent inverse relationships between price and quantity variables. Both summarize the market choices made by many individual buyers. Both show a price variable on the vertical axis. Both the market and aggregate demand curves interact with other curves representing supply to determine equilibrium conditions.

However, there are some key differences between the aggregate demand curve and market demand curves. Two of those differences concern the "other things being equal" conditions that lie behind the curves:

- The market demand curve for a single good such as chicken shows the price of chicken on the vertical axis. Market demand curves assume that the prices of all other goods remain constant as the price of the good varies. Instead, the vertical axis of the aggregate demand curve shows a price index, that is, a measure of the average prices of goods and services that go into GDP, as discussed in Chapter 6. The prices of individual goods need not all change by the same amount when the average changes

- Market demand curves assume that consumers' incomes remain constant at all points along the curve. That assumption does not hold for the aggregate demand curve. As explained in Chapter 5, because of the closed nature of the circular flow of income and expenditure, any change in real output necessarily causes a change in real income.

Aggregate demand

Total real planned expenditure

Aggregate supply

Total real output of final goods and services (real GDP)

Aggregate demand curve

A graph showing the relationship between aggregate demand and the aggregate price level

FIGURE 10–1

The Aggregate Demand Curve

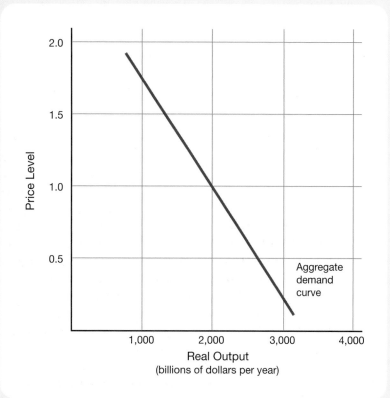

The aggregate demand curve shows the relationship between total real planned expenditure on final goods and the average price level of final goods. The curve has a negative slope because each of the major components of real aggregate demand—consumption, planned investment, government purchases, and net exports—varies inversely with the price level of final goods.

Instead of holding the prices of other goods and incomes constant at all points, the aggregate demand curve assumes a different set of "other things being equal" conditions. We will discuss each of them in detail as the chapter goes along. Here is a quick preview of the main items that the model assumes to be constant for all points along a given aggregate demand curve:

- Expectations that affect planned expenditure—for example, consumer confidence and business confidence

- Policy-related variables, including taxes and government spending and monetary policy

- Economic conditions in the rest of the world, including real output and interest rates in other countries and exchange rates of various currencies against one another

It is important to keep these points in mind as we discuss the slope of the aggregate demand curve. It is tempting to reason that the aggregate demand curve must have a negative slope simply because the individual demand curves for all the goods that enter into aggregate demand have negative slopes. However, because the two kinds of demand curves involve different "other things being equal" assumptions, that reasoning is not valid. Understanding the slope of the aggregate demand curve requires a different approach.

10.1b The Slope of the Aggregate Demand Curve

The best approach to understanding the slope of the aggregate demand curve is to break down aggregate demand into its principal components: consumption, planned investment, government purchases, and net exports. We can understand why the aggregate demand curve as a whole has a negative slope by looking at how changes in the price level affect decisions regarding the real levels of each of these components.

Consumption   First, consider how an increase in the average price level affects the real demand for consumer goods. When the price level rises, firms' revenues from sales of a given quantity of goods and services rise by the same proportion. Firms pass part of those revenues along to households in the form of wages, salaries, and other factor payments. Any increase in profits raises the incomes of business owners and corporate shareholders. The net effect is that an increase in the price level tends to raise consumers' nominal incomes.

However, even if nominal consumer incomes keep up with the increase in the price level, inflation can still affect consumers' real wealth. In particular, as the price level increases, the real purchasing power of the nominal money balances that they hold in cash or in bank accounts falls. For example, $100 in twenty-dollar bills might be enough to buy yourself a week's worth of groceries today; but if you hold onto those five twenties for a few years while the average price level rises 15 percent, the same money will buy only enough groceries to last about six days. Because of the falling real value of nominal money balances, consumers become less wealthy in terms of real purchasing power when the price level rises. They will correspondingly tend to buy less real output than they would have if the price level had not risen.

Similar reasoning would apply to a period of falling prices. As a decreasing price level increased the purchasing power of each dollar of money balances, real wealth would rise. That would stimulate real consumption spending, which is the largest component of real aggregate demand. Because of the way changes in the price level affect real wealth, real consumption expenditure varies inversely with the price level. That is the first reason for the negative slope of the aggregate demand curve.

Investment   Changes in the price level may also affect real planned investment. The reason is that a change in the price level, other things being equal, will change interest rates; and, as we know, interest rates are a key determinant of planned investment. As rising prices increase the nominal incomes of consumers and the revenues of firms, both firms and households are likely to increase their borrowing from the banking system. Other things being equal, rising loan demand would push up interest rates. As rates rose, businesses and households would revise their plans. Firms would tighten up their cash management practices and cut back or postpone long-term investment projects. Households would find it more difficult to buy homes, and construction activity would fall. The net effect on interest rates of increased loan demand depends on the specific rules that the central bank follows in setting monetary policy—a topic we will examine in detail in the following chapter. Provisionally, however, we will assume a tendency for the financial effects of an increased price level to decrease planned investment.

Government Purchases   The effect of a change in the price level on real government purchases is a little harder to analyze because it is not the same for all budget items or for all levels of government. Governments make many purchase decisions in real terms. For example, Congress might decide to authorize the Pentagon to buy one hundred jet fighters. If the price per plane goes up, Congress may add more dollars to the defense department budget to purchase the authorized number of fighters.

If Congress decides to authorize the purchase of one hundred jet fighters and the price per plane goes up, more dollars will need to be added to the defense department budget to complete the purchase. (Shutterstock)

However, legislatures do not always automatically increase spending authorizations to match price increases. At the federal level, Congress periodically imposes nominal limits on spending and borrowing. Even though the limits are not permanent, raising them can be politically difficult in the short run. State and local governments also make some spending decisions in nominal terms. For example, the Virginia Department of Transportation may have a budget of $50 million for road improvements. If the price of asphalt goes up, the department, constrained by its $50 million budget, will be unable to pave as many miles of roads as it had planned. Perhaps it will be able to persuade the legislature to increase its budget next year; but, in the meantime, the price increase results in less real spending.

Generalizing from this example, we conclude that, to the extent that budgets are set in nominal terms, government purchases will tend to fall in real terms as the price level rises—at least in the short run. Over a longer period, inflation raises tax revenues, which allows governments to maintain a given level of real purchases; so this component of planned expenditure is less sensitive to changes in the price level.

Net Exports   As explained in the preceding chapter, prices can increase in one country while they remain the same in others. Suppose, for example, that the United States experiences higher prices while prices in Japan stay the same. With a given nominal exchange rate between the dollar and the Japanese yen, US goods will become more expensive for Japanese buyers and Japanese goods will become relatively cheaper for US buyers. As US buyers switch from domestic goods to imports and US exports become harder to sell abroad, the real net export component of aggregate demand falls.

The tendency of real net exports to decrease when a country's price level rises, other things being equal, is another reason for the negative slope of the aggregate demand curve. Over a longer period, nominal exchange rates tend to adjust to reflect differences in national rates of inflation, so this effect is less important.

10.1c Shifts in the Aggregate Demand Curve

As in the case of individual demand curves, a change in market conditions other than the price level will cause the aggregate demand curve to shift to the left or right. However, because of differences in the "other things being equal" assumptions underlying the two kinds of demand curves, the sources of the shifts are different. Three of the most important sources of shifts in aggregate demand curves are changes in expectations, changes in government policy, and changes in the world economy.

Changes in Expectations   Expectations are one of the conditions we hold constant when drawing an aggregate demand curve. Chapter 5 emphasized the importance of consumer and investor confidence as determinants of planned expenditure. If consumers become more optimistic about the future, they may increase their real planned expenditures at any given price level. Similarly, an increase in firms' optimism about future profit opportunities may increase real planned investment at any given price level. In either case, the aggregate demand curve shifts to the right, as illustrated by the shift from AD_1 to AD_2 in Figure 10–2. A swing toward pessimistic expectations by consumers or firms would shift the aggregate demand curve to the left.

Changes in Government Policy

Fiscal policy

Policy that is concerned with government purchases, taxes, and transfer payments

Changes in government policy can also affect aggregate demand. That is true both of **fiscal policy**, meaning policy related to government spending and taxes, and monetary policy.

First, consider an increase in government purchases. Because government purchases are a component of planned expenditure, an increase shifts the aggregate demand curve to the right. Similarly, a decrease in government purchases shifts it to the left. As Chapter 5

FIGURE 10–2

Shifts in the Aggregate Demand Curve

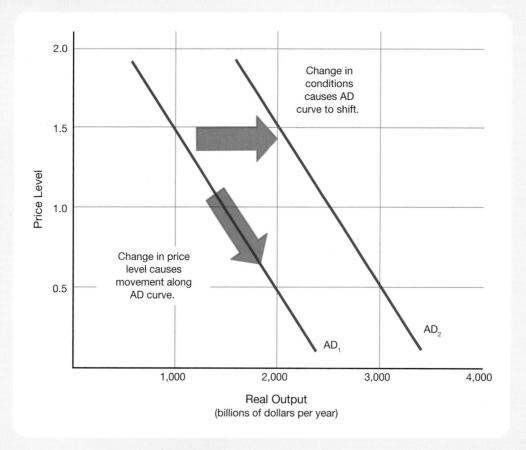

Other things being equal, a change in the price level causes a movement along a given aggregate demand curve. A change in economic conditions other than the price level can cause the quantity of real planned expenditure associated with a given price level to change. In that case, the aggregate demand curve will shift, as this diagram shows. Among the sources of shifts are changes in consumer or business expectations; changes in policies regarding government purchases, taxes, or money; and changes in the world economy.

explained, the multiplier effect operates to increase the impact of a change in government purchases on aggregate demand. For example, suppose the government of the state of Montana hires one hundred previously unemployed people as maintenance workers for state parks at a total cost of $250,000 per month. When these workers receive their paychecks, they spend much of their new income on consumer goods, in accordance with the marginal propensity to consume, thereby further adding to planned expenditure. The added expenditures stimulate hiring by consumer goods producers, continuing the multiplier process. In the end, the total addition to planned expenditure is likely to be greater than the initial $250,000 addition to government purchases.

Decreases in net taxes also cause aggregate demand to increase. A reduction in tax rates gives consumers more disposable income for any given total income. They use some of the extra income to buy consumer goods, adding to planned expenditure. The same is true if a reduction in net taxes takes the form of an increase in transfer payments. For example, an increase in unemployment benefits adds to demand by allowing people who are out of work to maintain a basic level of consumption expenditure.

Changes in monetary policy are another way that the government can increase or decrease aggregate demand. As we saw in Chapter 8, the central bank can make monetary policy more expansionary by lowering interest rates to ease credit market conditions. That, in turn, will lead to increased planned investment in business equipment and housing. Similarly, if the central bank tightens monetary policy by raising interest rates, investment will tend to decrease. Also keep in mind that, as Chapter 9 explained, the central banks of some countries (but not, in recent years, the United States) influence aggregate demand through policies that affect exchange rates and net exports.

Both fiscal and monetary policies play important roles in short-run stabilization of the economy. Chapter 11 will provide more detail on monetary policy, and Chapters 12 and 13 will discuss fiscal policy.

Growth in one country stimulates aggregate demand in its trading partners by increasing demand for their exports. (Shutterstock)

Changes in the World Economy   Events in foreign countries have impacts on aggregate demand in the United States via the net exports component of planned expenditure. For example, suppose that the rate of real economic growth increases in a major US trading partner—say, Canada. When that happens, Canadian firms and consumers will tend to buy more imported goods, thereby boosting the real net exports component of US planned expenditure and shifting the aggregate demand curve to the right. Also, depending on what happens to exchange rates, changes in price levels in foreign countries may affect US net exports by changing the relative prices of imported and exported goods.

10.2 THE AGGREGATE SUPPLY CURVE

We turn now to the supply side of our aggregate supply and demand model. An **aggregate supply curve** shows the quantity of real domestic product supplied by the economy at various price levels. Together, the aggregate supply and demand curves determine the economy's equilibrium real output and price level.

10.2a The Importance of Input Prices

As we did for the aggregate demand curve, we must pay careful attention to the "other things being equal" assumptions that underlie the aggregate supply curve. In Chapter 2, where we dealt with individual goods like chicken and chocolate, we assumed that **input prices** remained unchanged as firms moved along the supply curve. By input prices, we mean the

Aggregate supply curve

A graph showing the relationship between real output (real domestic product) and the average price level of final goods

Input prices

A measure of the average prices of labor, raw materials, and other inputs that firms use to produce goods and services

average price level for labor, raw materials, and other inputs that firms use to produce goods and services. For example, the input prices for an automaker would include the wages of production workers, the price of steel, and rates paid for electric power, along with prices of many other inputs.

Although it is reasonable to assume that input prices for an individual firm remain unchanged as prices and output vary along its own individual supply curve, the assumption makes less sense for aggregate supply. It is not so obviously true that input prices will remain unchanged when *all* firms in the economy vary prices and outputs. There are two reasons for this.

Input prices for an automaker include wages, the price of steel, and rates paid for electric power, among many others. (Shutterstock)

The first reason is that some firms' outputs are other firms' inputs. When an electric utility increases its rates, that increases the cost of electricity not only for homeowners who consume electricity as a final good but also for an automaker that uses electricity as an intermediate good. At the same time, the electric utility buys cars and trucks for its own corporate fleet. An increase in output prices by the automaker is thus an increase in input prices for the electric utility. It follows that an increase in the average price level of all goods in the economy, reflected in a move along the economy's aggregate supply curve, must sooner or later affect input prices as well.

The second reason a change in the average price level for final goods affects input prices has to do with the impact on wages of changes in the cost of living. Suppose there is a 10 percent increase in the average price of all final goods, including all consumer goods. If workers' nominal wages remain unchanged, they will experience a decrease in their standard of living. Some workers—individually or collectively through union action—will react by demanding raises from their bosses to make up for the higher cost of living. If their employers are getting higher prices for the goods they produce, they may well be willing to grant the wages. Other workers will react to the decrease in living standards by looking for better jobs. If some employers resist demands for wage increases while others grant them, workers will move from lower-paying to higher-paying jobs. In one way or another, then, it is reasonable to expect that, for the economy as a whole, an increase in output prices will cause upward pressure on the wage component of input prices.

For these reasons, the simple "other things being equal" assumption that input prices are independent of output prices will not work for the aggregate supply curve. That leaves us with another question: How rapidly and completely will input prices adjust when there are changes in aggregate demand and supply? The answer depends on the amount of time allowed for the economy to adjust to changed conditions.

10.2b Long-Run and Short-Run Aggregate Supply Curves

First, let's take a long-run perspective. The long run, in this case, means a period long enough for all markets in the economy to adjust fully to changes in conditions of aggregate supply and demand. Given enough time to adjust, it is reasonable for firms to expect input prices to adjust fully in proportion to any change in output prices. For example, suppose there is a 10 percent across-the-board increase in the prices of final goods, as measured by the GDP deflator. If you are, say, a chicken farmer, you expect the price you get for a broiler to go up by 10 percent; and you expect the prices of feed, fuel to heat your buildings, and the wages of your employees to increase by 10 percent, as well.

When a firm's input and output prices change immediately and in proportion, its profit per unit of output, adjusted for inflation, will not change at all. As a result, it has no incentive to either increase or decrease output. If all firms in the economy behave the same way, there will be no change in real GDP as the economy moves along its aggregate supply curve. Consequently, the long-run aggregate supply curve will be a vertical line, like the one in Figure 10–3 Part (a). The intercept of the long-run aggregate supply curve with the horizontal axis coincides with the economy's natural level of real output.

Next, consider a short-run perspective. Even if we can expect input prices to move proportionately to output prices in the long run, that does not mean they do so immediately. In the short run, it is reasonable for firms to expect some, if not all, input prices to adjust only gradually when aggregate demand increases. In that case, there will be a chance for firms to take advantage of strong demand to improve profits by raising prices or increasing output during the interval, while costs have not increased fully in proportion to revenues.

If we assume that, in the short run, some firms respond to an increase in aggregate demand by increasing output, others by increasing prices, and others by doing a little

FIGURE 10–3

Aggregate Supply Curves

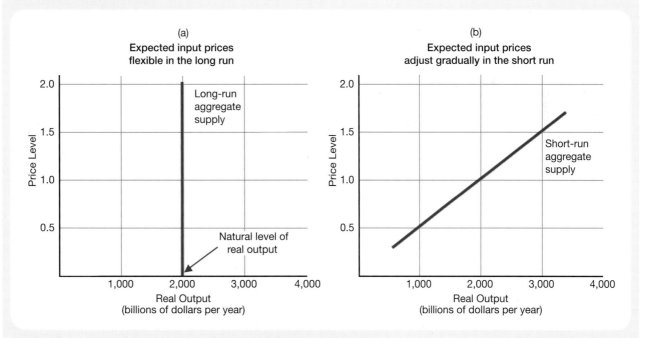

An aggregate supply curve shows the relationship between the level of final-goods prices and the level of real output (real domestic product). The slope of the aggregate supply curve depends on the way input prices change when the prices of final goods change. In the long run, it is reasonable to expect input prices to change in proportion to changes in the prices of final goods. The long-run aggregate supply curve, therefore, is a vertical line at the economy's natural level of real output, as in Part (a) of this figure. In the short run, it is reasonable to expect input prices to adjust more slowly than the prices of final goods. Thus, the short-run aggregate supply curve has a positive slope, as in Part (b).

of both, the economy's average price level and total output will both increase. As a result, the short-run aggregate supply curve will have a positive slope, like the one in Figure 10–3 Part (b).

There are several reasons input prices do not adjust fully to changes in aggregate demand in the short run.

1. *Long-term contracts*   Long-term contracts determine the prices of some inputs in advance. Union labor contracts are one example. Some firms may also rent buildings, buy fuel, or hire transportation services under long-term contracts. When the price level of final goods rises, the prices of these inputs cannot rise until it is time to renegotiate the contracts.

2. *Inventories*   Inventories tend to have a cushioning effect on input prices. For example, suppose that a bakery experiences an increase in demand for its bread. At first, it may gladly bake and sell more bread, using up its inventories of flour in the process. If prices have been increasing throughout the economy, the bakery may have to pay more for the next batch of flour it orders. That change in input prices will cause it to revise its output and pricing plans—but, by then, a certain amount of time will have passed. Economists have sometimes argued that rational managers should adjust output prices immediately to reflect the expected replacement cost of inputs that they take from inventory; but, in practice, many firms do not do so.

3. *Incomplete knowledge*   Firms may mistakenly interpret broad changes in demand as local changes affecting only their own market. For example, a bakery might mistakenly think that an increased nationwide demand for bread is limited to the city it serves. It would not expect a local increase in bread demand to have a perceptible effect on the price of flour, which is determined in a national market. Only later will the bakery find out that the increase in demand for its bread is part of a broad increase in aggregate demand, so that it does, after all, affect the price of flour.

4. *Cost of changing prices*   When input prices change by small amounts, some firms may find it too costly to make immediate changes in the prices of the goods they produce. For example, suppose the owner of an independent pizza restaurant visits the market one morning and finds that the price of onions has increased from $0.20 per pound to $0.25 per pound. That will increase the cost of producing one of her specialty onion pizzas by $0.01. Should she reprint her menu to show a price of $2.96 for an onion pizza instead of the previous $2.95? Probably not. The cost of printing the menu is greater than the gain from fine-tuning the product price to reflect the small change in input prices. It would take a larger and more persistent change in input prices to trigger a change in the price of pizza as stated on the menu. Many firms other than restaurants experience costs of changing prices and do not change them immediately in response to small or transitory changes in input prices. Although this phenomenon is not unique to the restaurant business, economists use the term *menu costs* to refer to the costs of changing prices regardless of the product involved. *Applying Economic Ideas 10.1* reports a specific example of menu costs in action.

Applying Economic Ideas 10.1

Menu Costs and the Introduction of the Euro

In January 2002, twelve European countries made a historic policy change. Hoping to encourage further integration of their economies, they abandoned their long-established national currencies—the French franc, the German mark, the Spanish peseta, and others—in favor of a brand new currency: the euro.

Preparation for introduction of the euro had begun several years earlier. Long before paper euro notes came into circulation, the euro was already in use as an electronic unit of account in banking and financial markets. Economists had made precise calculations of how many euros each historical currency would be worth. For example, the German mark came into circulation at a rate of 1.95583 marks per euro, rather than rounding off to a more convenient 2:1 ratio.

One of the main aims of the planning was to avoid any unpleasant jump in inflation when the euro came into circulation. The European Commission, which planned the change, was rightly worried that any such burst of price increases would undermine public confidence in the new currency.

By and large, the careful planning paid off. On average, prices in the twelve euro area countries increased by just twelve-hundredths of 1 percent in January 2002—a barely measurable amount. But in one sector, there was a big surprise. Restaurant prices increased by 15 percent, on average, for the twelve countries. In Germany, the increase was 28 percent. Consumers were angry, and the European Commission went on the defensive. What went wrong?

According to a study by economists Bart Hobijn, Federico Ravenna, and Andrea Tambalotti, the sudden jump in restaurant prices was largely due to menu costs. In their view, menu costs interacted with the introduction of the euro in two ways.

First, introduction of the euro affected the timing of menu revisions. Without the euro, each month a few restaurants would have decided that cost increases had accumulated to the point at which it was worth printing new menus. The increases would have been staggered over time, so that the average increase in restaurant prices would have been gradual, in line with the general rate of inflation for all goods and services. However, introduction of the euro meant that all restaurants knew they would have to print new menus for January 2002. Restaurants that might normally have raised their prices in, say, September 2001 would think, "Why bother—? Wait until January." Restaurants that might normally have waited until June 2002 to revise prices would decide to do so early, since they had to print new menus denominated in euros whether they raised prices or not. As a result, a higher than normal percentage of restaurants raised prices at the moment the new currency was introduced.

The other mechanism acting on menu costs has to do with the time horizon taken into account by restaurants when they print new menus. Normally, when setting prices, they would take into account cost increases that they expect to occur for many months ahead. However, restaurants that printed new menus in the last months before the end of 2001 would have had a shorter time horizon. They would have taken into account only cost increases up to January 2002, because they would have known they would have to print new menus again at that time. For that reason, part of the price increases normally expected in 2001 shifted forward to 2002.

Using a mathematical model that incorporates the ideas of timing and horizon effects, the authors compared the behavior of restaurant prices in the twelve countries that adopted the euro with those in other European countries, like the UK and Sweden, that did not do so. Their conclusion: menu costs explain most, if not all, of the unusual jump in restaurant prices.

Source: Bart Hobijn, Federico Ravenna, and Andrea Tambalotti, "Menu Costs at Work: Restaurant Prices and the Introduction of the Euro," *Federal Reserve Bank of New York Staff Report* No. 195, October 2004.

Just how short is the short run in which prices do not adjust fully, and how gradual is the gradual adjustment of prices in the long run? There is no simple answer. In reality, the rate at which input prices adjust will depend on a variety of circumstances and will vary from one input to another. In what follows, we will make a simplifying assumption: When prices of final goods change, we will assume, for the case of discussion, that firms expect the prices of all inputs to remain unchanged for one year. We assume that input prices then move up or down all at once in proportion to the change in the prices of final goods in the previous year. This stepwise adjustment of input prices is, of course, only a convenient approximation of the more complex adjustment process that takes place in the real world, where some prices adjust easily and others are very sticky.

10.2c Shifts in the Short-Run Aggregate Supply Curve

The distinctions between input and output prices and between long-run and short-run adjustments provide a basis for understanding shifts in the aggregate supply curves. We begin with shifts in the short-run curve.

When the economy is in long-run equilibrium at its natural level of real output, markets for individual goods, services, and factors of production are also in equilibrium. In that situation, the prices of final goods and services that firms sell and the prices of the inputs they use must be related in certain consistent ways:

1. In equilibrium, the prices of final goods must be at levels that will bring in enough revenue for firms to cover the costs of all inputs and to earn a normal profit.

2. In equilibrium, the prices of labor inputs must be at a level that balances supply and demand in labor markets. Given the cost of living as determined by the prices of consumer goods, wages and salaries must be high enough to make it worthwhile for workers to acquire the skills they need for each kind of job and to show up for work each day. Also, in equilibrium, unemployment must be at its natural rate, which corresponds to the natural level of real output.

Suppose that we choose as a base year, call it year 1, in which the economy is in long-run equilibrium. In that year, the relationship between the prices of inputs and those of final goods will be as just described. We can assign a value of 1.0 to both the average level of input prices and the average level of prices of final goods for that year. We can then measure changes relative to those base year levels.

Point A in Figure 10–4 represents the situation in such a base year. Real output is equal to its natural level, which is also its long-run equilibrium level. Thus, point A is on the long-run aggregate supply curve, which is a vertical line at the natural level of real output. The short-run aggregate supply curve for year 1, AS, passes through point A. It shows the way firms will react to changes in aggregate demand during the interval before they expect any change in the prevailing level of input prices, 1.0.

Over a longer period, however, firms will expect input prices to adjust in response to an increase in demand. Suppose, for example, that over time, the average price level of final goods rises to 2.0, and input prices have time to adjust fully; they too rise to an average level of 2.0. Point B in Figure 10–4 shows such a situation. At point B, input prices and the prices of final goods will once again be in an equilibrium relationship. Firms will be selling their outputs for twice as much, enabling them to pay for their inputs, which also cost twice as much. Workers will be earning double the nominal wages and salaries they earned previously, which is just enough to allow them to maintain their original standard of living, given the doubled price of consumer goods.

Given this new equilibrium situation, we can draw a new short-run aggregate supply curve, AS$_2$, through point B. This new aggregate supply curve shows how firms will react to changes in aggregate demand if they expect input prices to remain at the new level of 2.0 for the short run. The short-run aggregate supply has shifted upward because there has been an increase in the level of input prices that firms expect to prevail when they make short-run production plans.

To summarize:

1. The short-run aggregate supply curve intersects the long-run aggregate supply curve at a height corresponding to the level of input prices that firms expect to prevail in the short run. The expected level of input prices is the key "other things being equal" assumption underlying the short-run aggregate supply curve.

2. Over a longer period, a change in the expected level of input prices will cause the short-run aggregate supply curve to shift upward or downward to a new intersection with the long-run aggregate supply curve.

FIGURE 10–4

A Shift in the Short-Run Aggregate Supply Curve

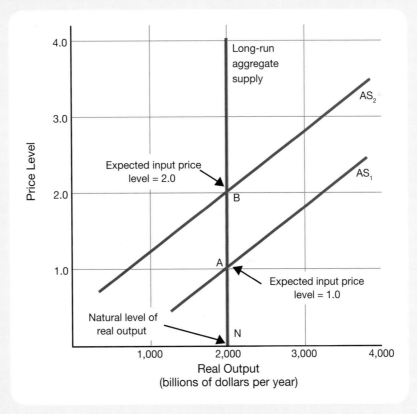

The short-run aggregate supply curve intersects the long-run aggregate supply curve at the expected level of input prices. Here, the short-run aggregate supply curve AS$_1$, which intersects the long-run aggregate supply curve at point A, assumes an expected input price level of 1.0. If the expected level of input prices later increases to 2.0, the aggregate supply curve will shift upward to the position AS$_2$.

10.2d Shifts in the Long-Run Aggregate Supply Curve

The key "other things being equal" assumption that underlies the long-run aggregate supply curve and determines its position is the economy's natural level of real output—the level of real output that the economy can produce with given technology and productive resources when unemployment is at its natural rate. As we first saw in Chapter 4, over time the economy can expand its production potential through development of new technologies, growth of the labor force, investment in new capital, and development of new natural resources. As Chapter 4 showed, long-run growth of that kind corresponds to an outward expansion of the economy's production possibility frontier. Using the model presented in this chapter, we could represent the same kind of expansion by a rightward shift in the long-run aggregate supply curve.

The remainder of this chapter and the next three will focus on the short run. During that part of the discussion, we will assume that the position of the economy's long-run aggregate supply curve remains fixed.

10.3 THE INTERACTION OF AGGREGATE SUPPLY AND DEMAND IN THE SHORT RUN

Now that we have reviewed the conditions that determine the slopes of the aggregate supply and demand curves and shifts in those curves, we can put the curves together to form a complete model of short-run changes in prices and real output. We apply the model to several issues of theory and policy in the following chapters. Right now, we will illustrate the model's basic principles by showing how the economy responds to an increase in aggregate demand, beginning from a position of long-run equilibrium.

10.3a Characteristics of Short- and Long-Run Equilibrium

The story begins at point E_0 in Figure 10–5, where the economy is in a position of both short- and long-run equilibrium. Whenever the economy is in long-run equilibrium, three curves intersect at a common point: the aggregate demand curve (AD_0), the short-run aggregate supply curve (AS_0), and the long-run aggregate supply curve. The significance of each of the intersections is as follows:

1. Expected input prices and prices of final goods are in their long-run equilibrium relationship at the intersection of the short-run aggregate supply curve AS_0 with the long-run aggregate supply curve. *The height of the intersection of the long- and short-run aggregate supply curves indicates the expected level of input prices.*

2. The intersection of AS_0 with AD_0 indicates the level of final-goods prices and real domestic product for which aggregate supply equals aggregate demand, given the expected level of input prices used in drawing AS_0. *The intersection of the short-run aggregate supply curve with the aggregate demand curve is always the economy's point of short-run equilibrium.*

3. The intersection of AD_0 with the long-run aggregate supply curve indicates the price level at which total real planned expenditures are equal to the economy's

natural level of real output. *The economy can be in long-run equilibrium only at a point where the aggregate demand curve intersects the long-run aggregate supply curve.*

4.   The intersection of all three curves at E_0 indicates a price level and real domestic product level that meet both the short-run and the long-run equilibrium conditions.

These four characteristics of short- and long-run equilibrium are the keys to understanding the aggregate supply and demand model. Along with an understanding of the sources of shifts in each of the curves, they provide a set of basic working rules that we can apply to solve any problem that falls within the scope of the model.

FIGURE 10–5

Short-Run and Long-Run Equilibrium

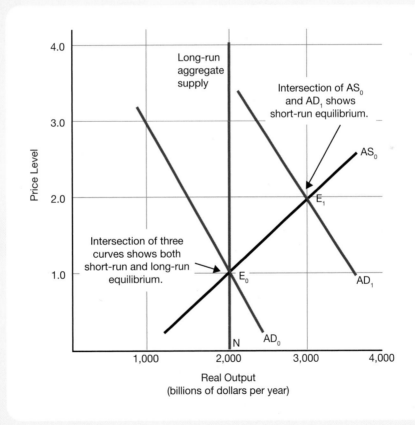

The economy is in short-run equilibrium at the point where the aggregate demand curve intersects the short-run aggregate supply curve. It can be in long-run equilibrium only at a point where the aggregate demand curve intersects the long-run aggregate supply curve. In this diagram, point E_0 is a point of both long- and short-run equilibrium, given the aggregate demand curve AD_0. If the aggregate demand curve shifts to the position AD_1, the short-run equilibrium point moves to E_1, where there is a positive output gap. E_1 is not a point of long-run equilibrium because it is not on the long-run aggregate supply curve.

10.3b Short-Run Effects of an Increase in Aggregate Demand

Now suppose that, beginning from point E_0 in Figure 10–5, something causes an increase in total real planned expenditure so that the aggregate demand curve shifts to the right from AD_0 to AD_1. For the moment, it does not matter just what causes the shift. It could be a change in government policy, a spontaneous increase in real consumption spending, an increase in real planned investment resulting from greater business confidence, a boom in demand for US exports, or some combination of these factors.

Whatever the cause, the immediate effect of the increase in planned expenditure will be an unplanned decrease in inventories. Seeing that they are selling their output faster than they can produce it, firms will alter their plans accordingly. As explained earlier, they will not expect input prices to change immediately. As a result, they will react to the increase in demand in the short run partly by increasing output and partly by raising prices. The figure shows these reactions as a movement up and to the right along the short-run aggregate supply curve AS_0. Real output increases and the unemployment rate falls. Using a term introduced in Chapter 4, we can say that a *positive output gap* develops as real GDP rises above its natural level.

When the economy reaches point E_1, where AS_0 and AD_1 intersect, planned expenditure and real output will be back in balance and the unplanned inventory depletion will cease. That is a new position of short-run equilibrium for the economy. It will apply as long as the aggregate demand and short-run aggregate supply curves remain in the positions shown.

10.3c Transition to a New Long-Run Equilibrium

The point at which curves AS_0 and AD_1 intersect is a point of short-run equilibrium for the economy, but not long-run equilibrium. Whenever there is a positive output gap, the price level of final goods will be greater than the expected level of input prices. For example, at point E_1, expected input prices are still at level 1.0, as indicated by the intersection of AS_0 with the long-run aggregate supply curve. Prices of final goods, however, have risen to a level of 2.0. The economy cannot stay in that situation indefinitely. Over time, input prices will gradually adjust to the change that has taken place in final-goods prices.

Figure 10–6 shows what happens as this adjustment takes place. Suppose that after a certain period (one year, in our simplified version), input prices increase to a level of 2.0, catching up with the increase in prices of final goods that took place as the economy moved from E_0 to E_1. The new level of input prices will become the basis for business expectations in the subsequent year. Graphically, the increase in the expected level of input prices appears as an upward shift in the short-run aggregate supply curve, from AS_0 to AS_1. AS_1 now intersects the long-run aggregate supply curve at the new expected level of input prices, 2.0.

Assuming that no further change takes place in planned expenditures, the aggregate demand curve will remain at AD_1. Given an unchanged level of aggregate demand, firms will react to the new, higher expected level of input prices by raising their prices and reducing their output. As they do so, the economy will move along the aggregate demand curve from E_1 to E_2, where AS_1 and AD_1 intersect. Because the output gap is decreasing, the unemployment rate begins to rise.

However, like E_1, E_2 is not a point of long-run equilibrium. In the process of moving to E_2, the prices of final goods have increased again, reaching a level of about 2.7. They are again out of balance with the expected level of input prices, which is now 2.0. Whenever the price level of final goods is above the expected level of input prices, input prices will

FIGURE 10–6

Short-Run and Long-Run Adjustment to an Increase in Aggregate Demand

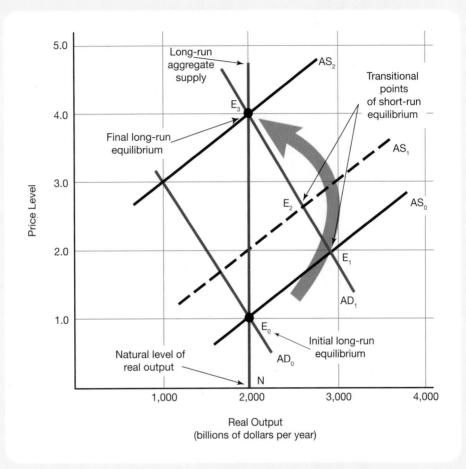

Beginning from an initial long-run equilibrium at E_0, a shift in the aggregate demand curve to AD_1 will cause the economy to move to a new short-run equilibrium at E_1. As it does so, real output will rise above its natural level, the price level of final goods will rise, a positive output gap will develop, and unemployment will fall below its natural rate. After a time, the expected level of input prices will begin to move upward in response to the increase that has taken place in the prices of final goods. As that happens, the short-run aggregate supply curve will shift upward, and the economy will move up and to the left along AD_1. Eventually it will reach a new equilibrium at E_3. As the economy moves from E_1 to E_3, the price level of final goods will continue to rise, the output gap will decrease until real output returns to its natural level, and unemployment will rise back to its natural rate.

tend to increase. Input prices thus will continue their gradual upward adjustment. As they do so, the short-run aggregate supply curve will continue to shift upward.

We could show additional intermediate positions as the aggregate supply curve shifts upward along the aggregate demand curve; instead, to make a long story short, we will jump ahead to the point at which it has shifted all the way up to the position AS_2. When it reaches that position, its intersection with the aggregate demand curve AD_1 is at point E_3. That is also where AD_1 intersects the long-run aggregate supply curve. At E_3, all three curves again intersect at a common point. The economy is once again in both short-run and long-run equilibrium. The gradual process through which expected input prices catch up to the prices of final goods is complete. Both input prices and output prices have reached the level of 4.0 and are in a consistent relationship to one another. Real output is back to its natural level, the output gap is zero, and unemployment is back to its natural rate. If there is no further shift in aggregate demand, the economy can remain at E_3 indefinitely.

10.3d Effects of a Decrease in Aggregate Demand

After a time, events may cause aggregate demand to change again. Beginning from the long-run equilibrium point E_3, let's see what will happen if the aggregate demand curve shifts all the way back to its initial position, AD_0. Again, it does not matter for the moment whether the decrease in demand takes the form of a decrease in consumption, planned investment, government purchases, or net exports. Nor does it matter whether the change originates with a change in government policy or with a change in the choices made by households, firms, or buyers of exports.

Figure 10–7 shows how firms will react to the leftward shift of the aggregate demand curve. Firms will notice a reduction in planned expenditure through an unplanned increase in their inventories. At first, they may not know whether the decrease in demand is local or is occurring throughout the economy. In any event, some will react by cutting output, some by reducing their prices, and many by doing some of both. The economy will move down and to the left along the aggregate supply curve AS_2 to a short-run equilibrium at E_4. There, the price level will have fallen to 3.0, and real output to $1,000 billion. Unemployment will also have increased, and a negative output gap will have developed. The economy will enter a recession.

As in the case of an increase in aggregate demand, point E_4 is not a possible long-run equilibrium, because final-goods prices are out of line with the expected level of input prices. The negative output gap will soon begin to exert a downward pull on the expected and actual levels of input prices. Firms that produce intermediate goods, such as energy and semifinished products, will find that demand for those goods is weak and will react by cutting prices (although perhaps only when long-term contracts are up for renewal). Unemployed workers will accept lower nominal wages in order to find some work. Even workers who have kept their jobs may be willing to accept lower nominal wages when their contracts come up for renewal if they realize that lower final-goods prices mean that it costs less to maintain a given standard of living.

In response to the drop in input prices, and the expectation that they will fall still more, the aggregate supply curve shifts downward. AS_3 is an intermediate position corresponding to an expected input price level of 3.0. However, E_5, at the intersection of AD_0 and AS_3, is still not a long-run equilibrium because the level of final-goods prices there is less than 3.0. The economy will not reestablish a long-run equilibrium until it moves all the way back to its natural level of real output at E_0 and the negative output gap has disappeared. During the transition from E_4 to E_0, output will be increasing and unemployment decreasing, even while the price level of final goods continues to fall.

FIGURE 10–7

Short-Run and Long-Run Adjustment to a Decrease in Aggregate Demand

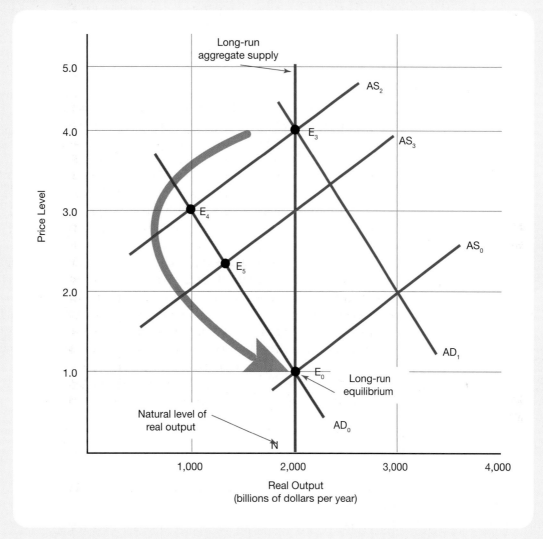

This figure begins from point E_3, the end point of the sequence of events illustrated in Figure 10–6. From this point, we assume that aggregate demand shifts back to the position AD_0. At first, firms respond to falling demand and unexpected inventory accumulation by cutting back output and reducing prices. As the economy moves to a short-run equilibrium at E_4, the unemployment rate rises and final-goods prices fall. When expected input prices also begin to fall, the aggregate supply curve begins to shift downward. As it does so, the economy moves along AD_0, through the intermediate point E_5, and on down to E_0. If there is no further change in aggregate demand, the economy will remain in equilibrium at that point.

10.3e Aggregate Supply, Demand, and the Business Cycle

If we look at the entire sequence of events shown in Figures 10–6 and 10–7, we can see that the economy has traced out something that looks very much like the business cycles that we discussed in Chapter 4:

1. Beginning from the natural level of real output, the economy expands. A positive output gap develops as domestic product rises above its natural level, unemployment falls below its natural rate, and the price level begins to rise.

2. After a time, the economy reaches a peak of real output—the point farthest to the right in the aggregate supply and demand diagram. From there, real output, although still above its natural level, begins to decrease and unemployment begins to increase as the economy enters a recession.

3. If aggregate demand shifts to the left again after real output returns to its natural level, the economy will continue to contract. It will pass through the natural level of real output and a negative output gap will develop. As the recession continues, unemployment will rise above its natural rate and the price level will begin to decrease.

4. Eventually real output reaches a minimum—the trough of the recession, the point farthest to the left in the diagram. From there, output will begin to move back toward its natural level. During this recovery phase, unemployment again decreases. In principle, the economy could come to rest at the natural level of real output. If aggregate demand increases once more, however, the economy will experience a new expansion and the cycle will begin again.

This is not yet a complete theory of the business cycle, but it is a step forward compared to the simple Keynesian multiplier model. We can now see clearly how changes in nominal planned expenditure are divided between changes in real output and changes in the price level, both in the short run and the long run. We will build further on the model in the next three chapters.

Summary

1. What are the conditions that determine the slope of the aggregate demand curve?

The *aggregate demand curve* shows the relationship between real planned expenditure on final goods and the average price level of final goods. The curve has a negative slope because each of the components of real aggregate demand—consumption, planned investment, government purchases, and net exports—varies inversely with the price level.

2. What are some sources of shifts in the aggregate demand curve?

Movements along the aggregate demand curve are associated with changes in the price level of final goods. Changes in other conditions can cause shifts in the curve. Among the sources of shifts are changes in consumer or business expectations, policy regarding government purchases, taxes, monetary policy, and the world economy. Because of the *multiplier effect*, an initial $1 change in any of the components will cause the curve to shift to the right or left by more than $1.

3. What are the conditions that determine the slopes of the short- and long-run aggregate supply curves?

An *aggregate supply curve* shows the relationship between the quantity of real output supplied (that is, real domestic product) and the average price level of final goods. The slope of the curve depends on what we assume about the way firms expect changes in the prices of final goods to affect input prices. In the long run, it is reasonable to expect input prices to adjust proportionately to changes in the prices of final goods. In that case, firms have no incentive to increase or decrease output so the long-run aggregate supply curve is a vertical line drawn at the economy's natural level of real output. In the short run, actual and expected input prices adjust only gradually to changes in the prices of final goods. Thus, in the short run, firms find it worthwhile to increase both output and prices in response to an increase in demand.

4. What are the sources of shifts in the aggregate supply curves?

At the intersection of the long- and short-run aggregate supply curves, the price level of final goods and the expected level of input prices are equal. An increase (or decrease) in the expected level of input prices thus will cause the short-run aggregate supply curve to shift up (or down) along the long-run aggregate supply curve. The location of the long-run aggregate supply curve is determined by the natural level of real output. An increase in natural real output resulting from improved technology or greater availability of productive resources will cause a rightward shift in the long-run aggregate supply curve.

5. How do prices, real output, and unemployment behave as the economy responds to a change in aggregate demand?

Beginning from a state of long-run equilibrium, an increase in real aggregate demand will, in the short run, cause the economy to move up and to the right along its short-run aggregate supply curve. As it does so, the prices of final goods will rise, a positive output gap will develop as real output rises above its natural level, and unemployment will fall below its natural rate. After a time, the expected level of input prices will begin to rise as a result of the increases that have taken place in the prices of final goods. As that happens, the economy will move up and to the left along the aggregate demand curve, assuming no further shift in that curve. The price level of final goods will continue to rise, real output will fall back toward its natural level, and unemployment will rise back toward its natural rate. If, after the economy reaches its new equilibrium, aggregate demand shifts to the left, a negative output gap will develop as real output drops below its natural level, and unemployment will rise above its natural rate. The level of final-goods prices will fall below the expected level of input prices. Soon, the expected level of input prices, too, will begin to fall. If there is no further change in aggregate demand, the economy will return to equilibrium at the natural level of real output.

KEY TERMS

PROBLEMS AND TOPICS FOR DISCUSSION

1. **Elasticity of aggregate demand**   Turn to the aggregate demand curve AD_2 in Figure 10–2. Along that curve, as the price level rises from 0.5 to 1.5, the quantity of real output demanded declines from $3,000 billion to $2,000 billion. What happens to the aggregate quantity demanded in nominal terms over this interval? Using the formula for price elasticity of demand (the ratio of the percentage change in the quantity of a good demanded to a given percentage change in its price), what is the elasticity of aggregate demand over this interval?

2. **The multiplier effect**   Suppose that a newly released popular hit by a US rock group causes fans in Asia to order $50,000 worth of American-made T-shirts featuring the band's picture. Other things being equal, would this tend to increase planned expenditure in the United States by exactly, more than, or less than $50,000? Would it shift the aggregate demand curve to the right, the left, or not at all? Explain in detail.

3. **Long- and short-run aggregate supply curves**   Draw a set of axes like those in Figure 10–4, but do not draw the supply curves shown there. Instead, draw a long-run aggregate supply curve based on the assumption that the natural level of real output is $3,000 billion. What is the slope of the curve? At what point does it intersect the horizontal axis? Next, draw a short-run aggregate supply curve based on the assumption that the expected level of input prices is 1.5. Where does this short-run aggregate supply curve intersect the long-run aggregate supply curve that you drew?

4. **Final-goods prices and expected input prices**   Given an aggregate demand curve and a short-run aggregate supply curve, how can you determine the short-run equilibrium price level of final goods? Given a long-run aggregate supply curve and a short-run aggregate supply curve, how can you determine the expected level of input prices? Turn to Figure 10–6. Give the short-run equilibrium price level of final goods and the expected level of input prices for each of the points E_0, E_1, E_2, and E_3.

PROBLEMS AND TOPICS FOR DISCUSSION

5.   **Long- and short-run equilibriums**   Draw a set of axes identical to those in Figure 10–6. Draw a long-run aggregate supply curve based on the assumption that the natural level of real output is $2,500 billion. Draw a short-run aggregate supply curve that passes through the points (2,500, 1.0) and (3,500, 2.0). Label it AS_1. What is the expected level of input prices indicated by this supply curve? Draw an aggregate demand curve that passes through the points (2,000, 2.0) and (2,500, 1.0). Label it AD_1. Given these three curves, where is the economy's point of short-run equilibrium? Where is its point of long-run equilibrium? Now draw another aggregate demand curve that passes through the points (2,500, 4.0) and (4,000, 1.0). Label it AD_2. Given AD_2 and the aggregate supply curves on your diagram, where is the economy's point of short-run equilibrium? What is the relationship between the short-run equilibrium price level of final goods and the expected level of input prices? Is there a possible point of long-run equilibrium for the economy, given AD_2 and the long-run aggregate supply curve? If so, explain how the economy can reach that point starting from the short-run equilibrium just described.

CASE *for* DISCUSSION

Hard Times

Times were hard in the United States during the Great Depression. The Depression was a monster business cycle that began in 1929 and did not reach its trough until 1933. The US economy did not get back to its former level of real output until 1939, when World War II was already underway in Europe.

Statistics from the Great Depression are grim. The price level fell by a quarter. Real output fell by a third. The unemployment rate soared to over 20 percent of the labor force. If we count workers employed in emergency government jobs programs as unemployed, the rate would have reached almost 25 percent.

Statistics are not enough to tell the real impact of the Depression on people's lives. Writer Studs Terkel interviewed hundreds of people who lived through the Depression to get their stories for his book *Hard Times*. Ed Paulsen was one of them.

Paulsen's family was from South Dakota. He finished high school in 1930, as the country was sliding toward the trough of the Depression. He went west to pick apples in Washington state and then worked on road gangs. In 1931 he ended up in San Francisco.

"I tried to get a job on the docks," he told Terkel. "I'd get up at five in the morning and head for the waterfront. Outside the Spreckles Sugar Refinery, outside the gates, there would be a thousand men. You know dang well there's only three or four jobs. The guy would come out with two little Pinkerton cops: 'I need two guys for the bull gang.' A thousand men would fight like a pack of Alaskan dogs to get through there. Only four of us would get through."

If you are reading this book, chances are you did not live through the Great Depression. If you have a grandparent who did, talk to them about it. If you do not, watch a movie about the Great Depression. My favorite is *The Grapes of Wrath,* but there are many others. The website Gawker.com has a list of the twenty best movies about the Depression (http://bvtlab.com/787M6). Watching one or more of them will help you understand that a depression is more than just lines on a graph.

Source: Paulson quotes are from Studs Terkel, *Hard Times: An Oral History of the Great Depression* (New York: Pantheon Books, 1970), 29–31.

Questions

1. Economic historians most frequently cite a decrease in planned investment as one of the major causes for the Great Depression of the 1930s. Explain how a decrease in planned investment, other things being equal, would affect planned expenditure and the aggregate demand curve. How would the resulting shift in the aggregate demand curve affect real output and employment?

2. If wages and prices adjusted immediately and fully to changes in demand, what would happen to unemployment when planned investment decreased?

3. What does the story of Ed Paulsen suggest regarding the speed of adjustment of wages and prices to a shift in aggregate demand? What might cause a gradual, rather than a rapid, adjustment?

4. Using data from the charts in Chapter 4, how does the Great Depression of the 1930s compare with the more recent Great Recession in terms of movements in prices, unemployment, and real output? What are the main similarities? What are the main differences?

CHAPTER 11

STRATEGIES AND RULES FOR MONETARY POLICY

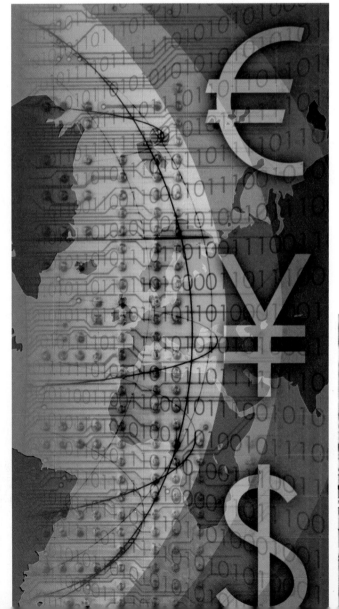

AFTER READING THIS CHAPTER, you will understand the following:

1. Why lags, forecasting errors, and time inconsistency make it difficult to fine-tune the economy
2. The distinctions among policy instruments, operating targets, intermediate targets, and goals
3. How policy rules attempt to overcome the limits of fine-tuning
4. The advantages and disadvantages of various policy rules and targets

BEFORE READING THIS CHAPTER, make sure you know the following concepts:

The aggregate supply and demand model

Monetary policy instruments

Fiscal policy

Money

Planned expenditure

The multiplier effect

Equation of exchange

Velocity

Transmission mechanism

CHAPTER Outline

Stability and prosperity are the twin goals of macroeconomic policy. Achieving stability means taming the business cycle by moderating short-term swings in real output, inflation, and unemployment. Achieving prosperity means promoting productivity and growth of real output over a longer time horizon. There is a close relationship between the two goals: if short-term stabilization policy fails, long-run prosperity will prove elusive.

To achieve stability and prosperity, monetary and fiscal policy must work together. This chapter focuses primarily on strategies and rules for monetary policy, although some of the ideas it presents apply to both areas of policy. Chapters 12 and 13 will undertake a more detailed look at fiscal policy. Chapter 14 will show how policy rules can be used to tame inflation and deflation.

11.1 THE LIMITS OF FINE-TUNING

Countercyclical policy

A pattern of monetary or fiscal policy that applies stimulus when the economy is at risk of falling into recession and restraint when it is in danger of overheating

Fine-tuning

An economic policy strategy that attempts to avoid even small, short-run departures from full employment and price stability

The discussions of domestic and international monetary policy instruments in Chapters 8 and 9, together with the aggregate supply and demand model developed in Chapter 10, provide a framework for our discussion of stabilization policy. They suggest the possibility of **countercyclical monetary** and fiscal policy—a pattern of policy that would moderate the business cycle by applying monetary or fiscal stimulus whenever the economy was in danger of falling into recession and restraint when it was in danger of overheating. As this chapter will make clear, however, the models make countercyclical policy look far too easy—as if policymakers were like engineers in a recording studio, who could just twist a few knobs with labels like "taxes" and "federal funds rate," and presto! Aggregate demand, real output, and the price level would slip into harmony with one another.

As *Applying Economic Ideas 11.1* explains, some economists came to think that countercyclical policy could be perfected. They envisioned a strategy of monetary and fiscal **fine-tuning** that would avoid even small, short-run departures from full employment and price stability. Over the years, however, it has become apparent that between the clean, orderly, world of the models and the real world where policymakers operate, there exist some messy problems that make it frustratingly difficult to fine-tune the economy into a state of harmonious stability.

Applying Economic Ideas 11.1

"It Is Now Within Our Capabilities ..."

The 1960s were an exciting decade for the economics profession. Some people had feared that the United States would sink into renewed depression after World War II; instead, the economy returned to prosperity. Although the 1950s were, on the whole, a good decade for the economy, many people thought the country could do even better.

In the 1960s, Harvard-educated President John F. Kennedy brought some of the country's best and brightest economists to Washington, including some of his former professors. His successor, Lyndon Johnson, kept them there. By 1966, the president's Council of Economic Advisers consisted of three of the most distinguished professionals ever to sit on that body: Gardner Ackley, Otto Eckstein, and Arthur Okun.

Armed with refined versions of theories that John Maynard Keynes had developed in the 1930s and with newly available computers, these policymakers became convinced that it was time to attempt more than just safeguarding the economy from deep depression and runaway inflation. In their 1966 *Economic Report of the President*, they wrote,

> It is now within our capabilities to set more ambitious goals. ... We strive to avoid recurrent recessions, to keep unemployment far below rates of the past decade, to maintain price stability at full employment, ... and indeed to make full prosperity the normal state of the American economy. It is a tribute to our success ... that we now have not only the economic understanding but also the will and determination to use economic policy as an effective tool for progress.

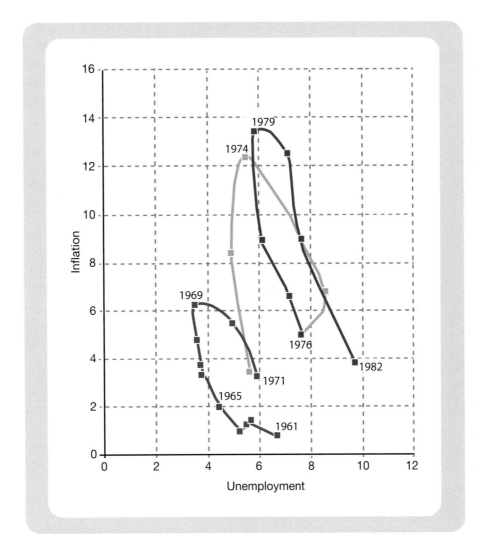

It was a high-water mark of professional self-confidence. Regrettably, the hope that policymakers would be able to fine-tune the economy to recession-free and inflation-free prosperity proved unfounded. As the figure shows, 1965—with its enviable achievements of 4.5 percent unemployment with just 1.9 percent inflation—was the last good year before a long period of serious instability. Between 1965 and 1982, the US economy went through three severe cycles of inflation and unemployment. In each cycle, the highest rates of inflation and unemployment exceeded the cycle before. 1960s-style fine-tuning failed dismally to live up to expectations.

Source of Quotation: Annual Report of the Council of Economic Advisers, 1966. Washington, DC: Government Printing Office, p. 186. Data for figure from Bureau of Labor Statistics.

11.1a The Problem of Lags

The first problem standing in the way of fine-tuning is that of *lags*, a term economists use to refer to unavoidable delays in the execution of monetary or fiscal policy. There are two kinds of these lags. **Inside lags** are delays between the time a problem develops and the time policymakers decide what to do about it. **Outside lags** are delays between the time policymakers reach a decision and the time the resulting policy action affects the economy. Both kinds of lags are a problem for both monetary and fiscal policy.

Inside Lags   Some inside lags arise because of the time required to collect and report economic data. A few kinds of data, like interest rates and exchange rates, are available almost instantly; other important data take longer to gather. Data on inflation, unemployment, consumer confidence, and several other variables come out monthly. The longest lags are for data on GDP and foreign transactions, which are available only quarterly. Furthermore, the first estimates for each quarter, published about four weeks after the close of the quarter, are subject to significant revisions. Final data are not available until nearly three months after the close of the quarter.

Another problem compounds the effect of lags. Random events like weather and measurement errors influence all macroeconomic variables in a way that causes unpredictable ups and downs in monthly or quarterly indicators. That means it is usually not enough to base policy decisions on the single, most recent observation. It may take several monthly or quarterly observations to establish a clear trend on the basis of which policymakers can reach sound decisions.

The long lags in collection of macroeconomic data, especially data on real GDP and its components, mean that policymakers may not be aware of a turning point in the business cycle until long after it has occurred. Consider the example of the mild recession from January to November 2001, which marked the end of the dot-com boom. In May 2001, when the recession was already half over, the latest government data still showed the economy to be expanding, although at a slowing rate. Only after the recession was over did revised data clearly show that the economy had begun to shrink at the end of 2000. Even the Great Recession had an ambiguous beginning. It is now known to have begun in the last quarter of 2007, but the first full quarter of falling GDP was the first quarter of 2008. However, GDP rose slightly in the second quarter of 2008. Just as some people began to think there might be a quick recovery, GDP turned down again and shrank for four more quarters.

In addition to delays in data collection, the time needed to make decisions adds to the inside lag. The Fed makes decisions on interest rates and other instruments at regular meetings of the Federal Open Market Committee, which occur just eight times a year. Before those meetings can take place, the Fed's professional staff spends weeks of work preparing background materials. The Fed has the power to make emergency changes in policy between regular meetings, but it does so only rarely. Decision-making lags for fiscal policy can be even longer since many key fiscal policy decisions require action by Congress. The next two chapters will return to the problem of lags in fiscal policy.

Inside lag

Delay between the time a problem develops and the time policymakers decide what to do about it

Outside lag

Delay between the time policymakers reach a decision and the time the resulting policy action affects the economy

Outside Lags   Even after policymakers reach a decision, their actions do not affect the economy immediately. Consider the use of expansionary monetary policy in the form of lower interest rates, which are supposed to stimulate aggregate demand by reducing the cost of business investment and home mortgages. Firms and households do not react instantly to interest rate changes. It takes time for them to make investment decisions. Even after they make decisions, they must draw up designs, place orders, and obtain permits before projects actually get underway.

The aggregate supply and demand model allows for some of the most important outside lags. Suppose a policy change shifts the aggregate demand curve to the right, as shown in Figure 10–6 of the previous chapter. At first the economy begins to move up and to the right along the short-run aggregate supply curve, with both prices and output rising. After a lag, the short-run aggregate supply curve begins to shift upward. Prices rise even more, but real output begins to move back toward its natural level. The economy does not reach a new long-run equilibrium until it returns to a point where the aggregate demand curve and the short- and long-run aggregate supply curves all intersect at a common point equal to the natural level of real output.

The model makes the sequence of events clear enough, but policymakers need to know more than that. Just how long, according to the calendar, are the abstract intervals of "short run" and "long run" that mark stages in the adjustment process? Econometric studies shed some light on the issue. Studies based on data from both the United States and Europe suggest that the "short run," during which real output increases following a reduction in interest rates (or falls following an increase in rates), lasts for at least one year and sometimes as much as two years. The full effect of an interest rate change on the price level, allowing time for real output to return to its natural level, appears to take three years or longer. By the time the full effects of one policy change work their way through the economy, it is likely that new events will disturb aggregate demand and supply. In reality, the economy is constantly in motion and never reaches a full long-run equilibrium of the kind we show so easily in textbook graphs.

11.1b Forecasting Errors

Lags in data collection and policy effectiveness are serious problems, but they would cause less trouble if we had accurate forecasts. For comparison, suppose you were the captain of a giant oil tanker. As captain, you would also face a problem of lags. If you turned the wheel of your ship or signaled for a change in engine speed, it might take several miles for the ship to steady on its new course. Even so, you would be better off as captain than as an economic policymaker because you would have accurate charts of the waters you were navigating and radar to show obstacles ahead. Based on the charts and radar, you could give orders well in advance, so that the ship changed course long before it went on the rocks. In contrast, the economic policymaker has no good way to see into the future. The economic ship might end up on the rocks before anyone knows what has happened.

Instead of charts and radar, policymakers must rely on economic forecasts. In every country, competing teams of economists—some private and some in government agencies like the Fed and the Office of Management and Budget—publish estimates of key variables for the year ahead. Unfortunately, those forecasts are not as reliable as we would like. According to a study by the International Monetary Fund, one-year forecasts of the rate of real GDP growth for industrialized countries are, on average, wrong by more than a full percentage point (disregarding the sign of the error).[1] For two years ahead, the error is nearly two percentage points. For developing countries, accuracy is worse than this by still another full percentage point.

What is more, forecasts are least accurate at turning points in the business cycle, just when we need them most. Looking at an international sample of seventy-two recessions in the 1990s, the IMF study found only two cases in which forecasters accurately predicted the recession two years in advance. Even more than halfway through the year in which a recession began, only about half of forecasters were predicting that a recession would occur.

Economic forecasts tend to be least accurate at turning points in the business cycle, when we need them most. (Shutterstock)

Several factors combine to reduce the accuracy of forecasts. First, forecasters themselves must cope with the problem of lags in data collection: They must try to see into the future when they are not yet sure what has happened in the recent past. Second, the real-world economy is much more complex than any model—not just more complex than the simplified models of textbooks like this one, but more complex than even the most sophisticated multivariate models of the best professional forecasters. Third, because the structure of the economy is always changing, models that rely on data from past periods may not be reliable for forecasting the future.

Finally, forecasts are subject to bias. Government forecasts may have a bias toward optimism because politicians do not like to hear or deliver bad news. Private-sector forecasters may see a marketing advantage in developing a reputation as being persistently optimistic or persistently gloomy. The private clients of forecasters may reinforce those tendencies when, knowing that forecasts are not accurate, they play it safe by buying forecasts from several sources with differing methodologies and reputations.

11.1c Time Inconsistency

Lags and forecasting errors together make the conduct of economic policy very difficult, but they are not the whole story. We must add one more factor to see the full difficulty of fine-tuning the economy. Economists call that factor **time inconsistency**, by which they mean a tendency of policymakers to take actions that have desirable results in the short run but undesirable long-run results.

Time inconsistency is not unique to economic policymaking. It occurs in many situations of everyday life. Perhaps some readers may have had the experience of accepting a glass of tequila or vodka at a party. The short-run effects of drinking it are pleasant, so down goes another glass, and then another. The next day, the undesirable results come on in full force in the form of a hangover. As another example of time inconsistency, patients with drug-resistant forms of tuberculosis or malaria must take heavy doses of strong medications over a long period in order to achieve a full cure. Often, such patients feel better after just a few weeks; they then stop taking their medicine because of the unpleasant side effects (a desirable short-run choice). However, by stopping the medications before the cure is complete, they become carriers of drug-resistant forms of the disease. In the long run, they endanger their whole community.

Time inconsistency is especially troublesome when policymaking interacts with the cycle of democratic elections. The aggregate supply and demand model shows that expansionary policies like tax cuts initially have desirable results. They shift the aggregate demand curve, and the economy moves up and to the right along its short-run aggregate supply curve. Real output increases, incomes increase, unemployment falls, and there is only mild inflation. This process takes place over a short-run time frame of one to two years.

Time inconsistency

Tendency of policymakers to take actions that have desirable results in the short run, but undesirable long-run results

BVT *Lab*

Flashcards are available for this chapter at **www.BVTLab.com**.

Later, as expectations adjust and the short-run aggregate supply curve begins to shift upward, less desirable consequences occur. Real output falls back toward its natural level, and unemployment rises back toward its natural rate. The rate of inflation increases. That process occurs over a time frame of one or two additional years, perhaps longer.

Taking all of the lags into account, we can see that if expansionary policy comes into effect a year or so before an election, the beneficial effects will be at their strongest just as the election approaches. The harmful effects will come along in due time, but not until the election has passed.

For contractionary policy, the sequence of events works in reverse. Suppose policymakers use an increase in interest rates or taxes to combat overheating of the economy. The immediate effect will be a leftward shift of the aggregate demand curve and a move down and to the left along the short-run aggregate supply curve. During this painful phase, which lasts a year or two years, unemployment rises, real output and incomes fall, and the rate of inflation slows only a little. Later, after expectations adjust, the short-run aggregate supply curve will begin to shift downward. Real output will again rise toward its natural level, and unemployment will fall back toward its natural rate. There will be additional progress toward slowing, or even reversing, previous inflation.

In short, from a political point of view, the period just before an election is not a good time to make a move toward stopping inflation. There will be a temptation to let the economy overheat for a few months longer and begin to apply contractionary medicine only after the election has passed.

11.1d Unintended Consequences

When lags, forecasting errors, and time inconsistency are combined, well-intentioned efforts to fine-tune the economy are in danger of producing two types of unintended consequences.

First, there is a danger that lags and forecasting errors alone will lead policymakers to apply expansionary or contractionary policy too late in the business cycle. Expansionary policies, intended to combat a recession, may not have their full effect until the next upturn of the business cycle has already begun. When they do, they will push the economy past the point of equilibrium and promote inflationary overheating. Similarly, contractionary policies, intended to prevent overexpansion during a boom, may come into effect only after the economy has already begun to slow. They will make the next recession worse than it would have been if policymakers had done nothing. Together, then, lags and forecasting errors create a danger of a **procyclical pattern of policy**—one that applies restraint when the economy is already at risk of recession and that applies stimulus when it is already beginning to overheat.

Second, when we add the problem of time inconsistency to those of lags and forecasting errors, policy may develop a systematic bias toward expansion and inflation. Fiscal and monetary policy would be strongly procyclical during expansions and insufficiently countercyclical during recessions, cutting contractions short before they have fully squeezed out inflation. The motives for such an asymmetrical pattern of policy are largely political. Policymakers want to prolong expansionary policies like tax cuts, spending increases, or interest rate reductions, even at the risk of inflation, in order to keep unemployment low ahead of the next election. For the same reason, they want to delay the application of contractionary policies like tax increases, spending cuts, or interest rate increases.

Procyclical policy

A poorly timed pattern of monetary or fiscal policy that applies restraint when the economy is already at risk of recession and stimulus when it is already beginning to overheat

Is this purely a theoretical danger, or could it actually happen? Look back for a moment to the diagram in *Applying Economic Ideas 11.1*. It shows inflation rates at the cyclical peaks of 1969, 1974, and 1979 that are each higher than the peak rate of the preceding cycle. Similarly, the unemployment rates at the cyclical troughs of 1971, 1976, and 1982 are each higher than those at the preceding trough. Clearly, the experience of the 1960s and 1970s failed to justify hopes that economists had finally acquired both the tools and the political will to implement successful fine-tuning.

11.2 POLICY RULES

Since the 1970s, there has been a widespread shift in the way economists think about stabilization policy.[2] They no longer view fine-tuning with favor. That does not mean economists think monetary and fiscal policy are ineffective. It does not mean that the government should always take a hands-off approach to the business cycle. It does not deny that emergency measures may be helpful in extreme situations. What it does mean is that in a world of lags and forecasting errors, frequent discretionary tinkering with monetary and fiscal policy is more likely to be destabilizing than stabilizing. When we take politics and time inconsistency into account, there is a real risk that monetary and fiscal policy will become procyclical.

In place of fine-tuning, a majority of economists now favor moderately countercyclical stabilization strategies based on preset **policy rules**. Not only should policymakers follow the rules, but they should also announce in advance the way they will respond to unfolding developments in the economy. There is a growing consensus that such rules minimize not only the risk that lags and forecasting errors will lead to overshooting at peaks and troughs of the business cycle but also the unintended consequences of politically motivated time inconsistency. If successful, policy rules will provide a stable framework for planning by private firms and households and promote long-run prosperity. This section focuses primarily on rules for monetary policy. We will look at rules for fiscal policy in Chapter 13.

11.2a Instruments and Targets

As background for our discussion of policy rules, it is useful to distinguish among instruments, targets, and goals of economic policy.

- A **policy instrument** is a variable that is directly under the control of policymakers. For example, open market purchases and the discount rate are policy instruments of the Federal Reserve.

- An **operating target** is a variable that responds immediately, or almost immediately, to the use of a policy instrument. For example, the federal funds rate for interbank lending (an operating target) responds almost immediately to an open market purchase (a policy instrument).

- An **intermediate target** is a variable that responds to the use of a policy instrument or a change in operating target with a significant lag. For example, inflation and real GDP (intermediate targets) respond to changes in interest rates (an operating target), but not immediately.

- A **policy goal** is a long-run objective of economic policy that is important for economic welfare. Stated in their broadest forms, the goals of macroeconomic policy are prosperity and stability.

Policy rules

A set of rules for monetary and fiscal policy that specifies in advance the actions that policymakers will take in response to economic developments

Policy instrument

A variable directly under the control of policymakers

Operating target

A variable that responds immediately to the use of a policy instrument

Intermediate target

A variable that responds to the use of a policy instrument or a change in operating target with a significant lag

Policy goal

A long-run objective of economic policy that is important for economic welfare

We can illustrate the hierarchy of instruments, targets, and goals by returning to our example of the oil tanker. The ship's wheel and engine speed control are the captain's main policy instruments. The ship's speed and course are operating targets that respond immediately, or almost immediately, to use of those instruments. The captain's intermediate target, on a given voyage, is to get the ship to a certain harbor by a certain date. Long-run goals, over a series of voyages, are to establish a reputation for reliability and earn a profit for the company that owns the ship.

Debates over strategies for stabilization policy do not usually focus on the choice of policy instruments or the long-term policy goals of prosperity and stability. More often, they focus on which operating targets to emphasize and the choice of intermediate targets that link changes in operating targets to long-term goals. The remainder of the chapter will look at several alternative policy rules, each having its supporters and critics.

11.2b Monetarism: The Grandparent of Policy Rules

Monetarism
A school of economic thought that emphasized the importance of the quantity of money and advocated the use of stable rules for monetary policy

Even when enthusiasm for macroeconomic fine-tuning was at its peak in the 1960s, there were dissenters. One of the best known was University of Chicago professor Milton Friedman (see *Who Said It? Who Did it? 11.1*). Friedman was the intellectual leader, although by no means the only prominent member, of a school of thought that economists came to call **monetarism**.

Who Said It? Who Did It? **11.1**

Milton Friedman and Monetarism

(Wikimedia Commons)

In October 1976, Milton Friedman received the Nobel Memorial Prize in Economic Sciences, becoming the sixth American to win or share that honor. Few people were surprised. Most people wondered why he had to wait so long. Perhaps it was because Friedman had built his career outside the economics establishment, challenging almost every major doctrine of the profession.

Friedman was born in New York in 1912, the son of immigrant garment workers. He attended Rutgers University, where he came under the influence of Arthur Burns, then a young assistant professor and later chairman of the Federal Reserve Board. From Burns, Friedman learned the importance of empirical work in economics. Statistical testing of all theory and policy prescriptions became a key feature of Friedman's later work. From Rutgers, Friedman went to the University of Chicago for an MA and then east again to Columbia University, where he received his PhD in 1946. He returned to Chicago to teach. There, he and his colleagues of the "Chicago school" of economics posed a major challenge to economists of the "Eastern establishment."

If one could single out a recurrent theme in Friedman's work, it would be his belief that the market economy works—and that it works best when left alone. "The Great Depression," Friedman once wrote,

(Continues)

(Who Said It? Who did It? 11.1 Continued)

"far from being a sign of the inherent instability of the private enterprise system, is a testament to how much harm can be done by mistakes on the part of a few men when they wield vast power over the monetary system of the country."

Friedman strongly favored a hands-off policy by government in almost every area. In his view, the problem was not that government is evil by nature, but that so many policies end up having the opposite of their intended effects. He thought that social reformers who claimed to do nothing but serve the public interest would invariably be led to serve some private interest, even if doing so was not part of their intention. Not just monetary policy but also transportation regulation, public education, agricultural subsidies, and occupational licensing were among the many policy areas in which Friedman believed that the government has done more harm than good and for which a free competitive market would do better.

Source for quotation: Milton Friedman, *Capitalism and Freedom*, Chicago: University of Chicago Press, 1962.

In his most famous work, *A Monetary History of the United States*, co-authored with Anna Schwartz, Friedman argued for a reinterpretation of the causes of the Great Depression. Friedman and Schwartz took issue with the approach that John Maynard Keynes had taken in the 1930s (see *Who Said It? Who Did It? 5.1*). Rather than tracing the causes of the depression to an inherent instability of market economies, they saw mistakes in monetary policy as the principal factor that turned an ordinary cyclical recession into a national disaster. In *Monetary History* and elsewhere, Friedman consistently argued that the correct conduct of monetary policy was the key to economic stability. That emphasis on monetary policy gave the monetarist school its name.

A second element of Friedman's thinking was his argument that neither monetary nor fiscal policy is capable of fine-tuning the economy. Instead, the Federal Reserve should conduct its policy according to a simple rule that would avoid the problems of lags, forecasting errors, and time inconsistency. Specifically, Friedman recommended that the Fed use open market operations to hold growth of the money stock at a target equal to the economy's long-run rate of growth of real GDP. In his view, such a cyclically neutral policy would avoid the procyclical tendencies that inevitably undermine any more active stabilization strategies.

Support for a monetary growth target is a direct outgrowth of the equation of exchange. As explained in Chapter 8, the equation of exchange tells us that the quantity of money times the price level is, by definition, equal to the velocity of circulation of money times the price level. It follows that if M grows steadily at the same rate as Q and V is subject only to minor or predictable variations (as Friedman thought), the price level P would remain approximately constant in the long run. Although random events might cause short-term variations in prices, real output, and employment, Friedman thought that a monetary growth target would inoculate the economy against the risk of runaway inflation or deep, lasting depression.

The Fed never made a commitment to Friedman's rule. Structural reforms in the banking industry during the 1980s increased the variability of velocity and weakened the link between the growth rate of the money stock and the rate of inflation. However, the idea that policy rules were a better basis for stabilization strategy than fine-tuning prevailed. It was just a matter of finding the right rule.

11.2c Inflation Targeting

By the end of the twentieth century, economists and central bankers who argued in favor of policy rules had largely turned away from a money growth target to **inflation targeting**. They use that term to describe any stabilization strategy that focuses on a target range for the rate of inflation.

The basic idea behind inflation targeting, like Friedman's money growth target, can be explained in terms of the equation of exchange, $MV = PQ$. A money growth target achieves long-term price stability only if both velocity (V) and the growth rate of real output (Q) are stable. If either or both are subject to significant, unpredictable changes, even a steady rate of money growth can lead to undesired inflation or deflation. Inflation targeting is supposed to guard against these sources of instability by focusing on the rate of change of the price level itself.

Interest Rates as an Operating Target   Although the concept of inflation targeting is simple, implementing it is not so easy. One major problem is that policymakers cannot use the rate of inflation itself as a short-run operating target. Inflation simply does not respond fast enough to the use of policy instruments. Instead, as our discussion of the aggregate supply and demand model has shown, inflation responds to policy actions only after a lag of months or even years. Policymakers can use the rate of inflation, averaged over a one- or two-year time horizon, as an intermediate target; but in order to implement an inflation targeting strategy, they must also have a suitable operating target over which they can exercise closer control.

Most central banks that pursue inflation targeting in any form use short-term interest rates as their principal operating target. That is true both for central banks, like those of the UK and Australia, that have explicitly adopted inflation targeting and for others, like the Fed and the European Central Bank, that pursue a mixed strategy that includes some elements of inflation targeting. This section illustrates this approach by showing how the Fed might implement a strict inflation targeting strategy if it chose to do so.[3]

As discussed in Chapter 8, the Fed, like most other modern central banks, maintains direct or indirect control over three short-term interest rates, as shown in Figure 11–1. The first two are administrative rates set directly by the central bank: the discount rate (that is, the rate charged on loans of reserves to commercial banks) and the rate paid on reserves that commercial banks keep on deposit with the central bank. The third interest rate is the federal funds rate—that is, the rate on interbank loans of reserves. The discount rate and deposit rate are administratively set, while the federal funds rate depends on supply and demand in the interbank loan market.

Figure 11–1 also shows commercial banks' demand curve for reserves. As explained in Chapter 8, commercial banks hold reserves of liquid assets to meet their customers' needs and minimize liquidity risk, but the amount of reserves they hold depends on the interest rate. Other things being equal, the lower the interest rate, the lower the opportunity cost of holding reserves—so the greater the quantity of reserves demanded. The demand curve becomes horizontal as it approaches the central bank's deposit rate, because if the interbank rate were to fall below the deposit rate, banks could make an effortless, risk-free profit by borrowing reserves from other banks and depositing them with the central bank.[4]

Inflation targeting

A strategy for stabilization policy that focuses on holding the rate of inflation within a target range

FIGURE 11–1

How Interest Rates Work as Operating Targets

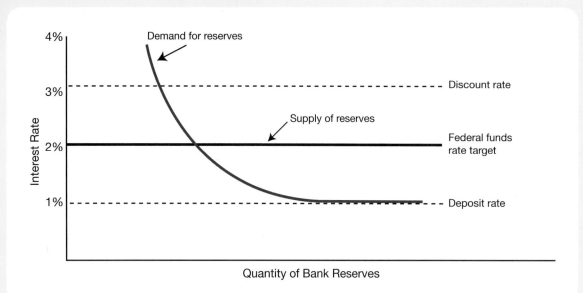

Quantity of Bank Reserves

The Fed's discount rate and deposit rate instruments are under its direct administrative control. The federal funds rate for interbank lending is a market rate set by supply and demand. Commercial bank demand for reserves has a negative slope because lower interest rates mean a lower opportunity cost of holding reserves. To implement an interest rate operating target, the Fed would set a target value for the federal funds rate (2 percent in this example) and set its administrative rates to form a corridor above and below the target. If the demand curve shifted to the right or left, the Fed would use open market purchases or sales to hold the federal funds rate at its target. In effect, then, the supply curve of reserves becomes a horizontal line at the federal funds rate target.

The figure assumes that the Fed selects 2 percent as its target for the federal funds rate. To implement that target, it first sets the discount rate and the deposit rate so that they form a corridor above and below the federal funds rate target. Although the Fed cannot directly control the federal funds rate, it can control it indirectly by using open market operations to adjust the quantity of reserves available to the banking system. If the demand curve shifted to the right, the Fed could use open market purchases to keep the federal funds rate from rising above the 2 percent target. If the demand curve were to shift to left, it could use open market sales to keep the federal funds rate from falling. In effect, until the Fed changed its federal funds rate target, the supply curve of reserves would be a horizontal line at 2 percent, as shown in Figure 11–1.

Setting the Right Operating Target

How would the Fed or another inflation-targeting central bank know where to set the operating target for the interbank lending rate? Why should the federal funds rate target be 2 percent rather than, say, 1 percent or 5 percent?

To set the right operating target, the Fed would have to use a forecasting model to predict how a given interest rate target will affect the rest of the economy. A reduction in interest rates stimulates planned investment and purchases of durable consumer goods. As explained in Chapter 10, the increased planned expenditure shifts the aggregate demand curve to the right. In the short run, real output and the price level both increase. In the long run, the price level increases more and real output returns to its natural level. A forecasting model would be able to estimate the rate of inflation over the next year or two that would result from any given interest rate operating target.

Figure 11–2 shows how the Fed would use forecasting as a bridge between its interest rate operating target and its intermediate inflation target. First, it would set its intermediate target for the inflation rate. Fed officials would know they cannot control inflation precisely, so they would name a target range of inflation—for example, between 2 percent and 4 percent on average over the next two years. Starting from the current price level, P_0, the target range for inflation defines a cone-shaped area of acceptable values for the future price level.

FIGURE 11–2

Implementation of Inflation Targeting

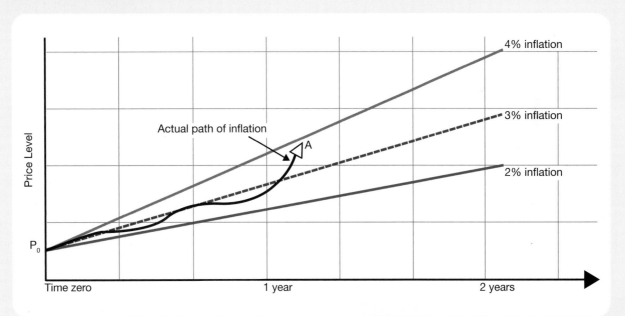

The Fed would implement a policy of inflation targeting as follows. First, it would set upper and lower limits on the acceptable rate of inflation over a one- or two-year time horizon. Here the limits are 2 and 4 percent. They define a cone-shaped area of acceptable values for the price level. Next, the Fed would use a forecasting model to determine an interest rate that would put the expected rate of inflation on a path in the middle of the target cone. As time goes by, unexpected developments might push the actual inflation rate higher or lower than the forecast. If the rate of inflation threatened to move the price level above the acceptable range, as at point A, the Fed would raise its interest rate target until the forecast rate of inflation fell back within the target cone.

Next, the Fed would use its forecasting model to find an operating target for the federal funds rate that appeared likely to result in a rate of inflation near the center of the cone. It would then use open market operations, as shown in Figure 11–1, to maintain the interbank rate at that level.

Now comes the tricky part. As we know from our earlier discussion, forecasting models are far from perfect. Even if policymakers maintain their operating target for the interest rate, unforeseen events are likely to cause the actual path of inflation to swing above or below the center of the target cone, as shown in Figure 11–2. In order to anticipate such developments, the Fed would need to revise its inflation forecasts on a regular basis. If a revised forecast indicated that the price level might cross the limits of the target cone, as it does at point A in the figure, the central bank would have to act. It would raise its operating target for the interbank interest rate and use open market operations to nudge the rate toward the new target. Doing so would restrain the growth of aggregate demand. When the forecasting model indicated that predicted inflation was back in the acceptable range, the Fed would stop tightening policy and would hold interest rates steady until new developments occurred. In the opposite case, if the economy slowed and the rate of inflation started to drop near the bottom of the target cone, the Fed would lower its interest rate operating target in order to stimulate aggregate demand.

11.2d Other Proposed Policy Rules

The monetary policy of the Federal Reserve has, in recent years, resembled inflation targeting in some—but not all—ways. The Fed does place a higher priority on price stability than on any other single intermediate policy target. In 2011, for the first time, it openly announced that it considered "price stability" to mean a rate of inflation close to 2 percent. With this goal in mind, it uses open market instruments to hold the federal funds rate at a chosen target very much as described above.

Even so, the Fed's policy is not true inflation targeting because it pursues other targets as well. The most important of those is the unemployment rate—which, by law, is a goal that the Fed is required to balance with its duty to maintain price stability. The twin targets of full employment and price stability are known as the "dual mandate." Up to now, the Fed has balanced the two parts of its dual mandate somewhat subjectively, but a number of economists have suggested that the subjective approach could be replaced by an explicit rule that took both parts of the mandate into account.

Taylor rule

A rule that adjusts monetary policy according to changes in the rate of inflation and the output gap (or unemployment)

The Taylor Rule   The best known of these rules is the **Taylor rule**, proposed by Stanford University economist John Taylor. Under a Taylor rule, the Fed would tighten policy by adjusting its interest rate operating target upward by a specified amount whenever the rate of inflation increased, and also raising interest rates whenever real output exceeded its natural level—that is, when a positive output gap developed.

Despite its resemblance to what the Fed actually does, explicit implementation of a Taylor rule would encounter practical difficulties. One is the question of how much to adjust interest rates for a given change in inflation or the output gap. If the adjustment were too small, the policy would not be effective in damping the business cycle. If it were too large, policy might overshoot its goals at cyclical peaks and troughs, making things worse rather than better. Taylor's original formulation also encounters the difficulty that data on the output gap are available to policymakers only with a

The Taylor rule was developed by Stanford University economist John Taylor. (Associated Press)

long lag. A variation of the Taylor rule would instead watch the unemployment rate. Unemployment varies inversely with changes in the output gap, but data are available with a much shorter lag.

NGDP Targeting   Another scheme that some economists prefer to the Taylor rule is **NGDP targeting**, which focuses on the rate of growth of nominal GDP—that is, on the right-hand side of the equation of exchange, $MV = PQ$.

Because the level of nominal GDP is equal to the price level, P, times real output, Q, the rate of growth of nominal GDP is the sum of the rate of growth of real GDP and the rate of inflation. The average rate of growth of US real GDP in recent decades has been about 2.5 percent. If we combine this with the Fed's 2.0 percent target rate of inflation, we get 4.5 percent as an appropriate target rate of growth for NGDP, or perhaps 5.0 percent just to make it a round number.

If velocity were constant, then maintaining NGDP growth at a steady 4.5 percent would simply require an equal steady rate of growth of the money stock. In that sense, many economists consider NGDP targeting to be the natural heir of Milton Friedman's monetarism. NGDP targeting is more flexible than simple monetary targeting, however. It takes into account the fact that velocity has proved much more variable in recent years than was foreseen in the 1960s. Under NGDP targeting, an unexpected increase in velocity could be offset by a slowdown in the rate of growth of the money stock, or vice versa.

Among the considerations that favor NGDP targeting is the possibility that inflation targeting, under some conditions, can have harmful unintended consequences. One problem occurs when an event arising outside the control of policymakers causes a burst of inflation. For example, suppose an increase in world oil prices causes upward pressure on the rate of inflation for some oil-importing country. Holding to a strict inflation target would require the central bank to raise interest rates and pursue a strong contractionary policy that could cause a decrease in real output and send the unemployment rate up sharply. If the central bank were, instead, targeting NGDP growth, the oil price shock could be absorbed partly by a higher price level and only partly by a reduction in real output. NGDP targeting, in this sense, is less rigid and more inclusive of multiple policy objectives than is inflation targeting.

NGDP targeting would also give the central bank more flexibility when the economy enters a deep recession. In that case, the rate of inflation may fall to zero, or even below. Under those circumstances, if the central bank did no more than aim for an inflation target of 2.0 percent, it could be years before real GDP recovered to its potential level. Instead, a central bank that set a 4.5 percent target for NGDP growth would be willing to tolerate a more aggressive expansionary policy. Doing so might, in the short run, allow inflation to rise well above 2.0 percent; but once real GDP returned to its long-run potential growth of 2.5 percent, inflation would slow again. We will return to these and other NGDP targeting scenarios in Chapter 14, where we will discuss inflation and deflation in more detail.

Overall, there is no simple answer to which monetary policy strategy is best for any given country. The choice of an inflation target, an NGDP target, or some mixed target involves both economic and political considerations. Nonetheless, over the past couple of decades, economists have more and more come around to the view that transparent policy rule, based on preset targets of some kind, does a better job of promoting stability and prosperity than the kind of ad hoc fine-tuning that many countries attempted in the past.

NGDP targeting

A policy under which the central bank adopts the rate of growth of nominal GDP as its principal intermediate target

Summary

1. Why do lags, forecasting errors, and time inconsistency make it difficult to fine-tune the economy?

Simple textbook models make it look as if it would be easy to *fine-tune* the economy to achieve a perfect countercyclical policy. In practice, three problems make fine-tuning difficult. *Lags* create delays between the time problems develop and the time policies take effect. *Forecasting* errors make it difficult for policymakers to overcome the problem of lags by acting before a turning point in the business cycle approaches. *Time inconsistency* is a tendency for policymakers to take actions that are beneficial in the short run but make problems worse in the long run.

2. What are the distinctions among policy instruments, operating targets, intermediate targets, and policy goals?

Policy instruments are variables that are under direct control of policymakers. *Operating targets* are variables that respond immediately, or almost immediately, to changes in policy instruments. *Intermediate targets* are variables that respond to changes in operating targets with a significant lag. *Policy goals,* like prosperity and stability, contribute directly to people's long-run economic welfare.

3. How do policymakers attempt to overcome the limits of fine-tuning?

If policymakers follow transparent, preset policy rules, there is less chance that lags and forecasting errors will lead to a procyclical policy that features overshooting at the top and bottom of the business cycle. Also, preset rules reduce the risk that time inconsistency will lead to politically motivated destabilizing actions.

4. What are the advantages and disadvantages of various policy targets?

The school of monetarism, which emerged in the 1960s, advocated using the money stock as the Fed's chief policy target. Under inflation targeting, the central bank uses its policy instruments to hold the forecast rate of inflation within a target range over a one- to two-year time horizon. Under a Taylor rule, the central bank would watch developments both of inflation and of real output or unemployment. NGDP targeting makes nominal GDP (real output times the price level) the target for monetary policy. All such policy rules face a trade-off between simplicity and flexibility.

KEY TERMS

PROBLEMS AND TOPICS FOR DISCUSSION

1. **Terms of Federal Reserve governors**   The Federal Reserve System operates under a seven-member Board of Governors. The term of a governor is fourteen years, and governors usually cannot serve more than one term (except for an additional partial term to fill a vacancy). Terms are staggered, so that one governor's term expires every other year. Governors can only be removed from office "for cause"—that is, for abuse of their office, not just for policy disagreements. In what way do the long terms and secure tenure of Federal Reserve governors help to overcome the problem of time inconsistency in monetary policy? In practice, Fed governors rarely serve out their full fourteen-year term. Is that a problem? Discuss.

2. **Monetary policy targets in Eudemonia**   Suppose that natural real output in the country of Eudemonia grows at a steady rate of 3 percent per year. In the past, velocity has been approximately constant, and the Eudemonian Central Bank has maintained a target rate of growth of 4 percent per year for the money stock. What would be the resulting rate of inflation? Now suppose that the introduction of internet banking allows people to make transactions online without holding large amounts of currency or bank balances. As internet banking spreads, velocity begins to increase at a rate of 3 percent per year. What will happen to the rate of inflation if money growth is unchanged? How would the central bank react to the change in velocity if it pursued an NGDP target instead of a money stock target?

3. **Core versus headline inflation**   Among central banks that practice inflation targeting, there is a debate over whether to target "headline" inflation or "core" inflation. Headline inflation means the consumer price index for all items. Some central banks favor headline inflation as a target because promising to stabilize a widely publicized inflation measure has maximum psychological impact on public expectations. Core inflation means consumer price inflation with adjustments to remove the most variable prices, like those of food and energy. Some central banks favor core inflation because food and energy prices are set in world markets and are beyond the control of domestic monetary policy. Compare the rates of core and headline inflation for the most recent month and the past year (for the United States, these data can be found on the web at www.bls.gov/cpi).

4. **Inflation targeting in Norway**   The Fed does not pursue a true inflation targeting strategy, but many central banks around the world do. The central bank of Norway is a good example. Visit the bank's website, www.norges-bank.no/en, and type "inflation targeting" in the search box to find several papers about the bank's strategy. Among other things, look for charts that give the bank's forecasts for consumer price inflation (CPI). In what ways do they resemble Figure 11–2 in this chapter? In what ways do they differ? Is the Norwegian central bank currently succeeding in its policy for maintaining price stability in that country?

CASE *for* DISCUSSION

The FOMC Reveals Its Strategy

The main policymaking body of the Federal Reserve is the Federal Open Market Committee (FOMC), which meets eight times per year. After each meeting, the FOMC issues a brief statement explaining its views on the state of the economy and the monetary policy actions it sees as appropriate. Following is a slightly truncated version of the statement for September 17, 2015.

Press Release (September 17, 2015)

Information received since the Federal Open Market Committee met in July suggests that economic activity is expanding at a moderate pace. Household spending and business fixed investment have been increasing moderately, and the housing sector has improved further; however, net exports have been soft. The labor market continued to improve, with solid job gains and declining unemployment. On balance, labor market indicators show that underutilization of labor resources has diminished since early this year. Inflation has continued to run below the Committee's longer-run objective, partly reflecting declines in energy prices and in prices of non-energy imports. Market-based measures of inflation compensation moved lower; survey-based measures of longer-term inflation expectations have remained stable.

Consistent with its statutory mandate, the Committee seeks to foster maximum employment and price stability. Recent global economic and financial developments may restrain economic activity somewhat and are likely to put further downward pressure on inflation in the near term. Nonetheless, the Committee expects that, with appropriate policy accommodation, economic activity will expand at a moderate pace, with labor market indicators continuing to move toward levels the Committee judges consistent with its dual mandate. The Committee continues to see the risks to the outlook for economic activity and the labor market as nearly balanced but is monitoring developments abroad. Inflation is anticipated to remain near its recent low level in the near term, but the Committee expects inflation to rise gradually toward 2 percent over the medium term as the labor market improves further and the transitory effects of declines in energy and import prices dissipate. The Committee continues to monitor inflation developments closely.

To support continued progress toward maximum employment and price stability, the Committee today reaffirmed its view that the current 0 to 1/4 percent target range for the federal funds rate remains appropriate. In determining how long to maintain this target range, the Committee will assess progress— both realized and expected—toward its objectives of maximum employment and 2 percent inflation. This assessment will take into account a wide range of information, including measures of labor market conditions, indicators of inflation pressures and inflation expectations, and readings on financial and international developments. The Committee anticipates that it will be appropriate to raise the target range for the federal funds rate when it has seen some further improvement in the labor market and is reasonably confident that inflation will move back to its 2 percent objective over the medium term.

Questions

1. What does the FOMC mean by its "dual mandate"? What are the target variables about which the Fed expresses the greatest concern in this memo? On the basis of this statement, would you classify the Fed as pursuing an inflation targeting strategy? Why or why not?

2. What is the federal funds rate? Would you classify the federal funds rate as a policy instrument, an operating target, an intermediate target, or a policy goal? Explain.

3. Based on the information in this statement, does it appear that the Fed is attempting to fine-tune the economy—that is, to adjust its policy on a month-to-month basis in response to the latest economic data? What parts of the statement give you a clue as to the Fed's attitude toward fine-tuning?

4. Visit the Fed's website, www.federalreserve.gov. Click on the tab labeled "Monetary Policy" and look for the most recent FOMC statement. After some meetings, the FOMC also holds a press conference and posts the video to its website. Based on the latest FOMC statement, how has the state of the US economy changed since September 2015? Is the Fed still pursuing its policy of a very low (0 to 0.25 percent) target for the federal funds rate?

Endnotes

1. Grace Juhn and Prakesh Lougani, "Further Cross-Country Evidence on the Accuracy of the Private Sector's Output Forecasts," *IMF Staff Papers* Vol. 49, No. 1 (2002).

2. For an excellent account of the evolution of economists' views on policy rules, see Marvin Goodfriend, "How the World Achieved Consensus on Monetary Policy," *Journal of Economic Perspectives* (Fall 2007): 47–68.

3. The appendix to this chapter gives an alternative presentation of interest-rate targeting.

4. The diagram assumes that banks are the dominant participants in the interbank loan market. As explained in Chapter 8, in the special circumstances that followed the financial crisis of 2008, government-sponsored enterprises came to dominate the federal funds market. Because GSEs are not eligible to receive interest on deposits of reserves held at the Fed, they are willing to lend and borrow reserves at rates below the deposit rate. Presumably, this situation is a temporary departure from normal.

Appendix to Chapter 11

Supply and Demand for Money

As we have seen, central banks control interest rates in two ways. First, the discount rate charged on borrowed reserves and the deposit rate for reserves that commercial banks hold on deposit at the central bank are set administratively. Second, central banks control interest rates indirectly by adjusting the monetary base and the quantity of money using open market operations or other instruments. Some central banks use interest rates as their principal operating target, while some use other targets. This chapter has explained the technicalities of an interest rate operating target using a diagram that shows the supply and demand for bank reserves (see Figure 11–1). This appendix takes an alternate approach that explains interest rates in terms of the supply and demand for money itself. The model presented here also provides insight into how monetary policy would be conducted by a central bank that used the money stock, rather than an interest rate, as its principal operating target, as recommended by economists of the monetarist school. Keep in mind, however, that the Fed has never adopted such a policy.

The Money Demand Curve

What do we mean when we speak of the "demand for money"? As used in daily conversation, the term *money* is a synonym for income or wealth; in that case, the answer would be that people seem to have an unlimited demand for money:

> *"I'm studying economics because I want to work on Wall Street and make a lot of money when I graduate," a friend might tell you.*

> *"How much money do you want?" you might ask.*

> *"The more the better!" your friend would say.*

This use of the term *money* is imprecise. When economists discuss the demand for money, they have something different in mind. As we saw in Chapter 8, economists use the term *money* to mean a specific set of liquid assets—the currency, transaction deposits, and other elements that make up M2 or some other specific measure of the money stock. To an economist, the demand for money means how much of those particular assets a person wants to hold at any one time, other things being equal. The "other things" include one's total wealth (that is, the sum of all of one's assets, including less liquid assets like houses, cars, and shares of stock) and also one's income.

The quantity of money demanded, given one's level of income, depends on the opportunity cost of holding money. For an ordinary good like chicken or movie tickets, the measure of opportunity cost is the market price—the amount of money per unit needed to buy it. However, people do not "buy" money in the same sense that they buy other goods. Instead, they obtain money by exchanging other assets for it—for example, by selling securities in exchange for bank deposits. In that case, the "price"—or, more accurately, the opportunity cost—of obtaining money is the rate of interest that they could have earned by holding securities instead of currency or transaction deposits that pay no interest.

In this brief appendix, we will make two simplifications with regard to the opportunity cost of money. First, we will assume that money earns no interest at all. It is true that some forms of money, like savings deposits, do pay a small rate of interest, but we will leave these out of consideration. Second, there are many different kinds of securities that we could exchange for money, each of which would pay a different interest rate and, therefore, imply a different opportunity cost. To keep things simple, we will consider only one nonmonetary asset—namely, a short-term, interest-bearing asset that has zero default risk (for example, Treasury bills).

Figure 11A–1 shows the demand for money in graphical form. The vertical axis shows the interest rate chosen to measure the opportunity cost of money. The horizontal axis shows the quantity of money. We will represent the quantity of money in real terms, so the horizontal axis is labeled M/P, meaning the quantity of money divided by the price level. It would be possible, instead, to place the nominal money stock, M, on the horizontal axis, but the real-money version of the diagram is the one economists most often use.

FIGURE 11A–1

Demand for Money

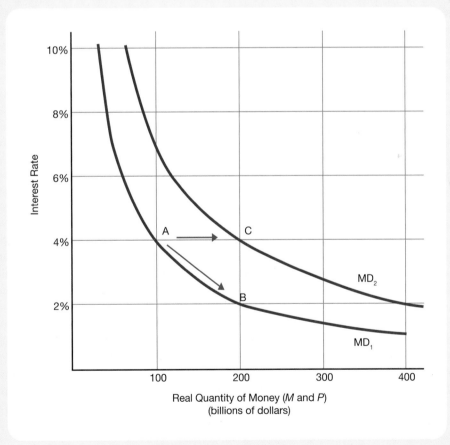

The money demand curve shows the real quantity of money balances that people want to hold at any given interest rate. A change in the interest rate causes a movement along a given money demand curve (for example, from A to B). An increase in real income causes a shift in the money demand curve (for example, from MD$_1$ to MD$_2$).

Along the money demand curve MD$_1$, the real quantity of money demanded increases as the interest rate decreases. For example, at an interest rate of 4 percent, the quantity of money demanded is $100 billion (point A). If the interest rate falls to 2 percent, the quantity demanded increases to $200 billion (point B).

If real domestic income increases, people will want to buy more goods and services. Other things being equal, people will demand more money to carry out the greater volume of transactions. An increase in real domestic income thus shifts the money demand curve to the right. For example, suppose that MD$_1$ corresponds to a domestic income of $1 trillion. If domestic income increases to $2 trillion, the money demand curve will shift rightward to MD$_2$. If the interest rate were to remain at 4 percent as domestic income increased, the quantity of money demand would increase to $200 billion (point C).

To summarize, we see that the demand for real money balances is inversely proportional to the interest rate and directly proportional to real domestic income, other things being equal. A change in the interest rate causes a movement along the money demand curve, and a change in real income causes a shift in the curve.

The Money Supply Curve

The central bank can control the quantity of bank reserves directly using open market operations. In principle, it could also control the supply of money, provided it also used open market operations appropriately to offset changes in the value of the money multiplier. Figure 11A–2 shows how money supply interacts with money demand in an economy where the central bank maintains a specific target value for the money stock.

Starting from point E$_1$, any change in money demand, while money supply remains constant, would change the equilibrium interest rate. For example, suppose that real domestic income increases, shifting the money demand curve to MD$_2$. If the interest rate remained unchanged, people would want more money to carry out the greater volume of transactions associated with their higher income. Firms and households would try to get the money they want by borrowing it from their banks. However, if the central bank held the quantity of reserves unchanged, and if the money multiplier remained constant, the banking system would not have the reserves needed to supply the desired amount of money. As the demand for loans increased with limited reserves available, banks would raise their interest rates. Increasing interest rates, in turn, would cause firms and households to tighten up their cash management practices and find ways to make do with less money per dollar of income. As interest rates rose, the economy would move to a new equilibrium at E$_2$.

Interest rates would also increase if the central bank used open market sales of securities to reduce the real money supply while real income and the price level remained unchanged. For example, suppose the central bank reduces the real money supply from $200 billion to $100 billion. We would show that by a leftward shift in the money supply curve from MS$_1$ to MS$_2$. Banks would suddenly find themselves short on reserves. They would have to reduce their volume of lending by refusing to extend new loans when customers paid off existing loans. Competition among borrowers for the limited volume of loans available would drive up interest rates, and the economy would move from equilibrium at E$_1$ to a new equilibrium at E$_3$.

A third factor that can affect the equilibrium interest rate is a change in the price level. Again we start from equilibrium at E$_1$. Now assume that real income remains constant but the price level increases. The increase in the price level will not shift the demand curve because its position depends on real, not nominal, income. However, if the central bank does not use open market operations or other instruments to increase the nominal quantity of money, the real quantity of money, M/P, will decrease, because P is

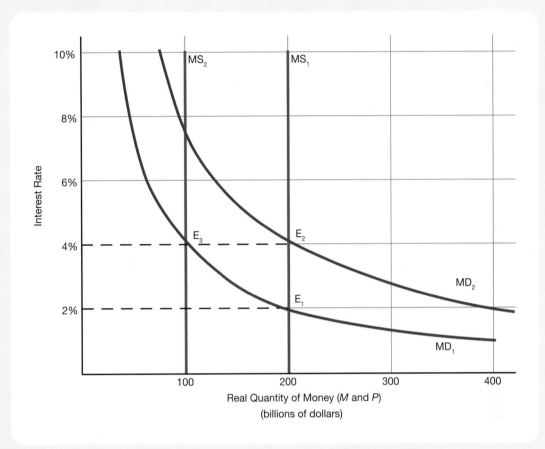

FIGURE 11A–2

How Money Supply Interacts with Money Demand

Suppose, for example, that the central bank uses open market operations to adjust the real money supply to $200 billion. The result is the money supply curve MS_1. If the money demand curve is in the position MD_1, the equilibrium interest rate will be 2 percent, shown by the intersection of MS_1 and MD_1.

increasing while M is constant. If the price level doubled, the real money supply curve would shift from MS_1 to MS_2, and the equilibrium interest rate would rise to 4 percent, as shown by E_3.

We can summarize our findings by saying that any of the following three events will cause the interest rate to increase, other things being equal:

1. An increase in real domestic income while the price level and the real money supply are constant

2. A decrease in the real money supply while the price level and real domestic income are constant

3. An increase in the price level while real domestic income and the nominal money supply are constant

Money Supply Target Versus Interest Rate Target

The diagrams in this appendix provide additional perspective on the use of different targets and policy rules by the central bank. A monetarist policy rule of the kind favored by Milton Friedman would use open market operations to hold the nominal money stock constant in the short run, and allow it to grow at a predetermined rate over the long run. Under such a policy rule, any short-run increase in nominal domestic income—whether in the form of inflation, an increase in real income, or a combination of the two—would cause interest rates to rise. As interest rates rose, credit market conditions would tighten, planned investment would decrease, and the growth of nominal income would go down. Similarly, any decrease in nominal income would cause interest rates to fall. Planned investment would be encouraged, counteracting the slowdown of nominal income. In short, under the monetarist rule, countercyclical changes in interest rates would tend to moderate excessive variations in the growth of nominal income.

A central bank that used an interest rate operating target would operate differently. After setting its interest rate target, it would use open market operations to adjust the position of the money supply curve as needed to hit the target. However, the central bank would have to be careful that the interest rate target was set at the right level. If it maintained too low an interest rate target for too long, it would risk an inflationary spiral. When inflation accelerated, it would have to increase the nominal money stock in order to prevent a rising price level from shifting the real money supply curve to the left and, thereby, increasing interest rates. The increase in the nominal money stock, in turn, would feed further inflation, unless it were offset by a decrease in velocity. To avoid this trap and prevent unwanted inflation, a central bank must supplement an interest rate operating target with inflation targeting, a Taylor rule, an NGDP rule, or some other intermediate target that tells it when and by how much to adjust the short-run interest rate operating target.

CHAPTER 12

FISCAL POLICY AND THE BUSINESS CYCLE

1. The use of taxes and government purchases as tools of stabilization policy
2. The practical problems of implementing fiscal stimulus
3. How the federal budget process works
4. The role of tax expenditures in the federal budget
5. How we can measure the stance of fiscal policy

Disposable income	**Expenditure multiplier**
Government purchases	**Multiplier effect**
Transfer payments	**Output gap**
Net taxes	**Countercyclical and procyclical policy**

CHAPTER
Outline

No area of economic policy is more closely enmeshed in politics than fiscal policy. Politicians must decide not just how much total tax revenue they should collect, but also exactly who should pay those taxes—businesses or consumers, the rich or the middle class, farmers or city dwellers. Similarly, politicians do not just determine total government expenditure. They spend money on specific things—unemployment benefits, health care, military hardware, and bridges to somewhere or to nowhere—each of which has its own political constituency.

This chapter and the next one will attempt to blend economic and political perspectives in a way that allows us to make sense of fiscal policy as a whole. We begin with a short-term perspective, first discussing the use of fiscal policy to control the business cycle and then looking at budget procedures. The next chapter turns to the long term, taking up the important question of whether a country's fiscal deficits and debt are sustainable over time.

12.1 USING FISCAL POLICY TO MODERATE THE BUSINESS CYCLE

In Chapter 11, we saw that a country's central bank can use its influence over aggregate demand to moderate the business cycle. The central bank's principle instruments of countercyclical policy are changes in interest rates and open market operations. Instead, the government can pursue countercyclical fiscal policy using fiscal instruments—changes in tax rates, transfer payments, and government purchases. Those instruments have the potential to affect all the major components of aggregate demand—consumption, investment, net exports, and, of course, government purchases.

12.1a Countercyclical Fiscal Stimulus

Figure 12–1 applies the aggregate supply and demand model to show how fiscal stimulus can combat a recession. Suppose some disturbance to aggregate demand, perhaps

Increased purchases of military hardware are one way to bring about an increase in aggregate demand. (Shutterstock)

a drop in exports, threatens to cause a contraction. In the diagram, the aggregate supply curve AS_1 meets the aggregate demand curve AD_1 at a point like E_1, where real GDP is less than its natural level. There is a negative output gap of $500 billion between the short-run equilibrium value of real GDP ($1,500 billion) and its natural level ($2,000 billion). If policymakers do nothing, unemployment will rise above its natural rate.

As we explained in Chapter 10, if aggregate demand were to remain at this low level, the combined effect of high unemployment and low capacity utilization would put downward pressure on prices. Over time, the aggregate supply curve would shift downward, and the economy would move down and to the right along AD_1. As it did so, real output would eventually return to its natural level. That kind of adjustment, however, occurs only with a substantial lag. Reluctance of firms to lower their prices and the unwillingness of workers to accept lower nominal wages could make the return to full employment via price and wage decreases slow and painful.

Why wait so long? Suppose that policymakers, impatient with the economy's natural speed of adjustment, want to do something immediately. In the context of the simple

textbook model, the solution seems simple. The government can shift the aggregate demand curve rightward to the desired position AD_2 either by increasing government purchases to increase aggregate demand directly or by reducing net taxes to induce additional consumer demand. Later on, if the initial problem (in this case, a decrease in exports) corrects itself, it would be possible to reverse the extra fiscal stimulus. The economy would then remain in full-employment equilibrium at E_2.

12.1b Practical Problems of Fiscal Stimulus

In the real world, the application of fiscal stimulus to close an output gap is more complicated than in the simple model. This section examines some of the most important problems of implementing fiscal policy.

Problems of Timing   The first problem is that of correctly timing the needed fiscal stimulus given the inevitable lags and forecasting errors. Look again at Figure 12–1.

FIGURE 12–1

Using Fiscal Policy to Combat a Recession

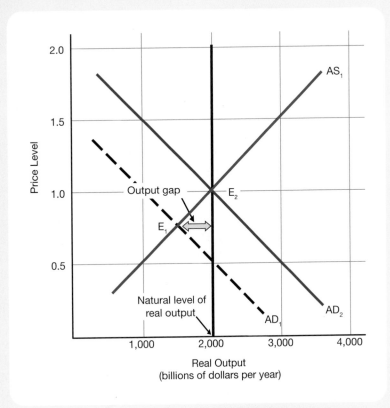

In this figure, there is a negative output gap at point E_1. If nothing is done, a downward shift of the aggregate supply curve will eventually restore output to its natural level. Instead, to reach the natural level of real output at E_2 more quickly, the government could shift the aggregate demand to the right, by either increasing real government purchases or reducing net taxes.

With accurate forecasting, policymakers would be able to prevent the $500 billion output gap from developing in the first place. If applied in time, fiscal or monetary stimulus could keep the aggregate demand curve from shifting to the position AD_1. Real output would then remain at its natural level, and there would be no recession to deal with. In the real world, however, forecasting is imperfect. Policymakers often do not discover problems until they have done much damage.

Even when policymakers recognize that an unforeseen recession has begun, they still may not be able to act immediately. Most fiscal policy actions, whether changes in taxes or in spending, require legislative action. Occasionally Congress acts with commendable swiftness to fight an economic downturn; more often, however, legislators take their time.

Once Congress passes a fiscal stimulus package, there will be more lags before policy instruments begin to work. These lags tend to be longer for fiscal policy than for monetary policy. The Fed can implement instruments like open market operations or discount rate changes immediately after its Open Market Committee takes a vote. Deployment of fiscal policy instruments takes longer. If the chosen instrument is a tax cut, it will be necessary to publish new schedules for withholding or to mail rebate checks, either of which can take weeks or months. If the instrument is a change in government purchases, the lag may be even longer.

Sometimes federal, state, or local governments have "shovel ready" projects—for example, highway repairs—on which work can begin immediately. Often, however, projects require extended planning, design, permitting, bidding, and hiring before work can start, and they can take up to several years to complete.

Even after the government pays out tax rebates and makes purchases, there are still more lags before intermediate targets like output, employment, and the price level respond. As we explained in the previous chapter, those lags add up to at least a year or two. Putting it all together, several years are likely to elapse, in the real world, between the onset of a recession and a return of the economy to its natural level of real output.

Fiscal policy actions in 2008 and 2009 illustrate these lags. According to the Business Cycle Dating Committee of the National Bureau of Economic Research, the US economy entered recession in December 2007; yet the Committee did not officially reach that conclusion until December 2008, a full year later. Meanwhile, there were growing signs that the economy was slowing. Policymakers did not want to wait until all the data were in. Congress acted swiftly to pass the Economic Stimulus Act of 2008, which President George W. Bush signed into law in February of that year. The act authorized some $100 billion in tax rebates to US households, but the government did not mail the rebate checks ($1,200 each for most families) until April and May. The checks brought only a brief pause in the downturn.

The contraction became much more severe in the fall of 2008. The following February, Congress passed a much larger fiscal stimulus package called the American Recovery and Reinvestment Act of 2009 (ARRA). That legislation, which newly inaugurated President Barack Obama quickly signed into law, had a nominal value of $787 billion, nearly eight times larger than the 2008 stimulus package. Like the 2008 act, the ARRA did not go into effect immediately. The first spending from the new package did not begin to flow until the spring of 2009, more than fifteen months after the official start of the recession. The trough of the recession occurred soon after that, in June 2009. Given this timing, it would be more accurate to say that the stimulative effects of the ARRA helped speed the recovery than to say that it hastened the end of the recession.

How Large a Stimulus?
The second problem is determining how large a stimulus to apply. In part, the problem is one of measuring the output gap. The output gap of $500 billion is easy to measure in Figure 12–1, but in reality, policymakers do not have such a tidy diagram. They must make do with data on prices and real GDP that are incomplete; and forecasts, although helpful, are far from fully accurate.

Even with an accurate estimate of the output gap, it can be difficult to know how much new aggregate demand any given fiscal stimulus will produce. In Figure 12–1, the aggregate demand curve would have to shift horizontally by $1 trillion to close the $500 billion output gap, but that does not necessarily mean that government purchases would have to increase by $1 trillion to shift the curve by that amount. As explained in Chapter 5, any increase in government purchases has a *multiplier effect*, which means the new government spending causes additional planned expenditure outside the public sector.[1]

The amount of new government purchases needed to close a given output gap depends on the size of the multiplier. For example, if the multiplier were 2, a $500 billion increase in government purchases would be enough to shift the aggregate demand curve by $1 trillion, taking secondary increases in consumption into account.

The American Recovery and Reinvestment Act of 2009 authorized $787 billion in stimulus spending and tax cuts. (Wikimedia Commons)

Tax cuts also have a multiplier effect, although it tends to be somewhat weaker than the multiplier for government purchases. The reason is that tax cuts are not themselves additions to planned expenditure; instead, they add to the disposable income of households. Tax cuts stimulate planned expenditure only to the extent that households spend part of any new disposable income.

In the simplest case, the amount of new consumption expenditure would equal the amount of the tax cut multiplied by the marginal propensity to consume. However, when tax cuts are temporary, the amount of new spending may be less. People often use part of temporary tax rebates to pay off debt, especially credit card debt. Some estimates suggest that households may have spent as little as 15 to 20 percent of their 2008 tax rebates on new consumption.

Just how large, effectively, is the multiplier for fiscal policy in the US economy? The truth is, economists do not really know. In January 2009, when the ARRA was being prepared, presidential advisers Christina Romer and Jared Bernstein released a paper that estimated that each $100 million in new government purchases would add about $160 million to real GDP, an effective multiplier of 1.6.[2] That estimate formed the basis for the policy proposals of the incoming Obama administration. The multipliers used by Romer and Bernstein are near the high end of recent estimates, however. Other studies suggested that the effective fiscal multiplier might be much less, perhaps as little as 0.5. That would mean that $1 trillion of government purchases would add only about $500 billion to real GDP.

Differences in models and assumptions account for the wide range of estimates for the fiscal policy multiplier. One key set of assumptions concerns monetary policy. A given increase in government spending will have maximum effect if the Fed **accommodates** the fiscal policy by holding interest rates constant. If the Fed does not fully accommodate the fiscal stimulus, interest rates will rise as aggregate demand increases. The increase in interest rates, in turn, will tend to reduce private investment spending, partially offsetting the initial increase in government purchases. The strength of that tendency, which economists call the **crowding out effect**, depends critically on what kind of policy rules the Fed follows. For example, if the Fed pursues an explicit or implicit inflation target, it may need to raise interest rates to counteract the expected impact of fiscal policy on the price level. In that case, the crowding out effect will be strong, and the effective fiscal policy multiplier will be small.

In evaluating the multiplier that would apply to the 2009 fiscal stimulus package, most economists expected the Fed to keep interest rates low in order to minimize any crowding out effect. Accordingly, even relative pessimists found that the multiplier would be

Accommodating monetary policy

A policy in which the central bank holds interest rates constant in response to a fiscal stimulus

Crowding out effect

The tendency of expansionary fiscal policy to raise the interest rate and thereby cause a decrease in real planned investment greater than one in the short run. Over a longer time horizon, those who expected the Fed to raise interest rates more sharply as the economy recovered expected a smaller impact from fiscal stimulus. As it turned out, the Fed did keep interest rates low throughout the recovery, lending retroactive support to those who expected a small crowding out effect.

Another source of difference in multiplier estimates has to do with assumptions about how fiscal policy affects expectations. Some economists argue that, because fiscal stimulus increases the budget deficit in the short run, people will expect Congress to raise taxes in the future to return the budget to balance. Accordingly, consumers will be more cautious in their current spending. Such caution will reduce the effective fiscal multiplier.

In short, economists simply do not know exactly how much fiscal stimulus is needed to close a given output gap. Once again, the real world is much more complicated than the textbook model.

Reversibility and Time Inconsistency
A third problem concerns the reversibility of fiscal stimulus. If fiscal policy is to succeed in moderating the business cycle, it should add to deficient aggregate demand during contractions and then be reversed to restrain excessive demand during the expansion. Policies that are inappropriately timed or not symmetric over contractions and expansions can easily become procyclical. They can cause the economy to overshoot peaks and troughs, making the business cycle more, not less, severe.

The problem of reversibility affects both monetary and fiscal policy, but not equally. The Fed is able to implement its policy instruments quickly through administrative decisions and enjoys at least partial insulation from day-to-day politics. It can reverse a monetary policy more easily. Reversing fiscal policy can be harder. US congressional elections interact with fiscal policy lags to create a serious problem of time inconsistency. With an election never more than two years away, it is always a good time, politically, to cut taxes or increase government spending. It is always a good time to promise to reduce the budget deficit, but never a good time actually to do so.

With an election never more than two years away, it is always a good time to cut taxes and never a good time to raise them. (Wikimedia Commons)

The large tax cuts enacted early in the administration of George W. Bush illustrate the problem of reversibility. Originally, the cuts were justified as needed to speed recovery from the mild recession of 2001. They were subject to "sunset" provisions that would have phased them out in 2009 and 2010, at which time the economy was supposed to be in good shape. Those tax cuts, together with relatively easy monetary policy, did encourage economic expansion over the next several years; but as the date for phaseout approached, Republicans in Congress and the White House argued strongly for making the tax cuts permanent. By 2009, when a new Democratic administration took over, the economy was in recession again. Neither Congress nor the administration was willing to reverse the tax cuts in full. Eventually, the bulk of the Bush tax cuts did become permanent.

The Problem of Priorities
A final problem is that of reconciling short-term fiscal stimulus with longer-term spending priorities. At one time, economists thought that the multiplier was larger than it now appears to be, perhaps even as large as 8 or 10. In that case, it would take only a small fiscal stimulus to get the economy moving, and it would not matter much what kind of spending the government undertook. Economists used to joke about stimulating the economy by hiring one team of workers to bury jars of money and another team to dig them up again. Today, when few economists

think the effective multiplier is even as large as 2, it is clear that closing any given output gap would require a much larger dose of stimulus. When that stimulus comes in the form of added government spending, it is all the more important that it buy something the country really needs. However, that is easier said than done.

For one thing, there are often conflicts between long-term priorities and the short-term goal of getting stimulus money flowing as fast as possible. The fiscal stimulus package passed by Congress in February 2009 is one example. Policymakers wanted to devote a healthy share of the money to infrastructure and construction, but they could find only a few projects that were both worthwhile and shovel-ready. They allocated other parts of the stimulus to some of the administration's long-term priorities—for example, computerization of medical records and other health-care reforms. Spending that part of the stimulus required more preparation and therefore extended over a much longer period.

Politics can also make it hard to reconcile short-term stimulus spending with long-term priorities, especially when Congress has to make spending decisions in a hurry. Consider the legislation that authorized the Troubled Asset Relief Program (TARP) in the fall of 2008. In its original form, the act was purely a financial-sector rescue plan that contained little by way of conventional fiscal stimulus. However, when it first came up for a vote on September 28, Congress narrowly rejected it. Over the next week, lawmakers hastily added $132 billion in "sweeteners," including both new spending and tax breaks. This bill passed Congress in its new form on October 3. Unfortunately, many of the added sweeteners seemed more like political pork than long-term national priorities. For example, the package included tax breaks for rum distillers in the Virgin Islands, makers of adult films, and automobile racetracks.

Fiscal Stimulus as a Weapon of Last Resort   In terms of lags, reversibility, and freedom from short-term political pressures, monetary policy looks more flexible and reliable than fiscal policy. Most economists would agree that in normal times, a responsible central bank, guided by transparent, preset rules, can do a better job of stabilization than the more politicized and unpredictable apparatus of fiscal policy. However, times are not always normal. When inflation is low, aggregate demand is falling, and financial markets are in crisis, monetary policy may lose much of its effectiveness. The Great Recession appears to be a sobering example. By the end of 2008, the Fed had reduced its federal funds rate target effectively to zero, meaning that further interest rate reductions were impossible. As explained in Chapter 8, it next resorted to quantitative easing, but the jury is still out as to the effectiveness of that policy.

In the atmosphere of economic crisis that prevailed in 2008 and 2009, then, many economists and policymakers saw fiscal policy as the weapon of last resort. Accordingly, they applied fiscal stimulus on an unprecedented scale—not just in the United States, but also in many other countries. As *Applying Economic Ideas 12.1* explains, the stimulus had mixed results. It did not, as some had hoped, produce a quick return to normal. On the other hand, many economists argue that the Great Recession would have been even deeper and lasted even longer without it. It is likely that the debate over the effectiveness of the ARRA will never be fully resolved. The dispute itself may make the government less willing to undertake fiscal stimulus when the next recession strikes.

12.1c Automatic Fiscal Policy

The type of fiscal policy discussed so far—changes in the laws regarding government purchases, taxes, and transfer payments that are designed to increase or decrease aggregate demand—is known as **discretionary fiscal policy**. There is also a second aspect of fiscal policy—**automatic fiscal policy**—that concerns the way taxes and government spending respond to changes in income, unemployment, and the price level, even when laws remain unchanged.

Discretionary fiscal policy

Changes in the laws regarding government purchases and net taxes

Automatic fiscal policy

Changes in government purchases or net taxes that are the results of changes in economic conditions, given unchanged tax and spending laws

Applying Economic Ideas 12.1

Did the 2009 Fiscal Stimulus Work?

The effectiveness of the $787 billion American Recovery and Reinvestment Act of 2009 remains a major political and economic controversy. To Republicans, it is the "failed Obama stimulus." To Democrats, it "saved us from a new Great Depression." Here are some of the reasons there is no simple answer that can lay the controversy to rest.

The range of estimates is wide.   One problem is that small changes in methods and assumptions can produce large differences in the estimated effects of the ARRA. Consider, for example, the charts given here, which show year-by-year estimates of the program's effects on real GDP and unemployment. The charts come from a 2012 study by the Congressional Budget Office. For 2010, the year of the ARRA's greatest impact, the ARRA may have added as little as 0.7 percent or as much as 4.1 percent to real GDP. In the same year, it may have reduced the unemployment rate by as little as 0.4 percentage points or as much as 1.8 percentage points.

Keep in mind that those results come from a single study by a group that is required by law to look at the issue from a nonpartisan perspective. Other studies, some of them more politically motivated, have found impacts greater than the CBO's high estimates or no impacts at all.

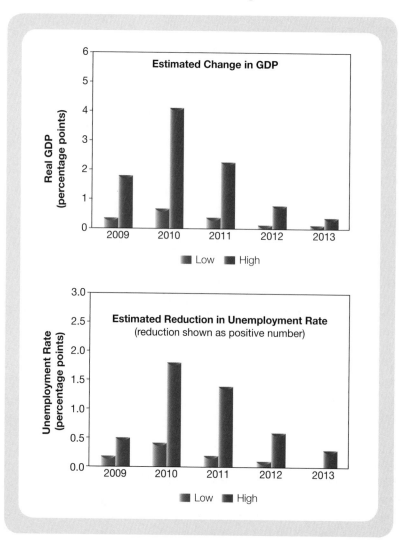

Econometric studies versus modeling. Some studies take an econometric approach; that is, they apply statistical analysis to the data from the years when the ARRA was in force and compare them to prior years. One limit of econometric studies is that the maximum effect of the ARRA lasted just a few quarters. Another is that the previous periods that provide data for comparison contain few recessions, and only mild ones. Other studies use mathematical models to simulate the impact of the ARRA. The problem with those studies is that they are only as good as the assumptions that go into the models—for example, estimates of the size of multipliers. Both approaches produce a wide range of estimates.

Fiscal policy does not occur in a vacuum. If the ARRA were the only thing that affected unemployment and real output in the years in question, its effects would be easier to estimate. However, many other things were going on at the same time. Monetary policy was also at work to stimulate the economy. Exchange rates and foreign demand for US exports had a big impact, as did world oil prices. The crisis damaged the financial system, limiting the availability of credit. It is ultimately impossible to sort out how much of the observed GDP and unemployment trends were due to the ARRA itself.

Sources: The chart is taken from the CBO report, "Estimated Impact of the American Recovery and Reinvestment Act on Employment and Economic Output from October 2011 Through December 2011," February 2012. For a side-by-side comparison of several other economic studies of the ARRA, see Dylan Matthews, "Did the stimulus work? A review of the nine best studies on the subject," *Washington Post,* August 24, 2011.

As the economy moves through the business cycle, changes in real output and employment affect both tax revenues and outlays. An increase in real output increases real revenues from all major tax sources, including income taxes, payroll taxes, taxes on corporate profits, and sales taxes. At the same time, an increase in real output cuts real government outlays for transfer payments. That happens in large part because higher real output means less spending on unemployment benefits. Payments to support low-income families through programs like Medicaid and food stamps also move inversely with real GDP.

Taking all these effects together, as real output and the price level rise and unemployment falls during an expansion, the government budget moves toward surplus. Automatic fiscal policy thus operates to moderate aggregate demand during an expansion. By the same token, when the economy slows down, inflation and the growth rate of real output decrease and unemployment rises. As a result, the budget swings toward deficit during a contraction.

Because automatic fiscal policy operates to offset changes in other elements of planned expenditure, economists call budget components like income taxes and unemployment benefits **automatic stabilizers**. Automatic stabilizers serve to moderate the economy's response to exogenous changes in consumption, private planned investment, and net exports. The strength of automatic stabilizers varies substantially from one country to another. The United States lies somewhere near the middle of the spectrum.

12.1d The Role of State and Local Government Budgets

Up to this point, we have focused entirely on the federal government budget. Doing so significantly understates the total size of the government sector. The federal government accounts for only about 60 percent of all government receipts and expenditures in the United States, with state and local governments making up the rest. In terms of the impact on planned expenditure and aggregate demand, a dollar of state or local government revenue or expenditure is exactly equivalent to a dollar at the federal level.

Automatic stabilizers

Those elements of automatic fiscal policy that move the federal budget toward deficit during an economic contraction and toward surplus during an expansion

When it comes to stabilization policy, however, state and local government budgets are less important than their size would indicate. Most state and local governments, by law, must balance their budgets for current expenditures. They are allowed to borrow only for capital expenditures—that is, long-lived projects like major bridges or public buildings.

The states undertake little discretionary fiscal policy. The sum of the budgets of all units of government below the federal government typically shows a slight surplus. During the depth of the Great Recession, many state and local governments, under severe economic stress, missed their budget targets and ran deficits. However, even in 2009—the worst budget year in recent history—the consolidated deficit of all state and local governments was just 0.6 percent of GDP.

Because their budgets are kept close to balance year in and year out, state and local governments contribute little to automatic fiscal policy. To the extent that they contribute at all, their effect is slightly procyclical. The reason is that when the economy slips into recession, state and local government revenues fall, so they must cut spending in order to keep deficits from exceeding permissible limits. When the economy recovers again, they take advantage of rising revenues to catch up on items they had previously postponed.

The procyclical effect of state and local balanced budget requirements is somewhat offset by grants from the federal budget to state and local governments. These grants average about 15 percent of federal expenditures or about 2 percent of GDP. During recessions, federal grants to support state spending on education, unemployment benefits, Medicaid, and the like increase. Although the increase does not fully offset the need of state and local governments to tighten their belts during a recession, it helps.

12.2 THE BUDGET PROCESS

As we explained in Chapter 11, both monetary and fiscal policy face problems arising from lags, forecasting errors, and time inconsistency. These problems are inherently more serious for fiscal policy than for monetary policy. Just how serious they are depends on the details of budget procedures. This section looks at the federal budget process of the United States and some of its chronic shortcomings.

12.2a The Annual Budget Cycle

Federal fiscal policy is a joint responsibility of the executive and legislative branches of government. Aside from limited emergency funds, the executive branch of government cannot simply spend money whenever the mood strikes. Congress must authorize all taxes and expenditures. Congress, in turn, is constrained by the political influence of the executive branch (and occasionally the threat of presidential veto), by the Constitution, and by budget procedures that it has set for itself.

The Fiscal Year   The US government operates on a **fiscal year** that runs from October through September. For example, the fiscal year 2016 means the period from October 1, 2015, through September 30, 2016. About eighteen months before the beginning of a fiscal year, the budget cycle gets underway.

The process is supposed to follow a step-by-step scenario that starts with preparation of a budget by the executive branch. The Office of Management and Budget (OMB) takes the lead in this process. It receives advice from the Council of Economic Advisers, the Department of the Treasury, and other sources. After the OMB has drawn up an outline of the budget, it sends it to the various departments and agencies. Within the executive branch, a period of bargaining ensues in which the Pentagon argues for more defense spending, the Department of Transportation for more highway funds, and so on.

Fiscal year

The federal government's budgetary year, which in the United States starts on October 1 of the preceding calendar year

During this process, the OMB is supposed to act as a restraining force, keeping macro-economic goals in mind.

By January—nine months before the fiscal year starts—the president must submit the budget to Congress. From that point on, Congress is supposed to assume the lead. Its committees and subcommittees look at the president's proposals for the programs and agencies under their jurisdiction. The Congressional Budget Office (CBO) employs a staff of nonpartisan professionals who advise the committees on economic matters, in somewhat the same way that the OMB advises the president. In the spring, the House and Senate are supposed to pass a first budget resolution that sets forth overall spending targets and revenue goals.

Bargaining among committees—between the House and the Senate, and between Congress and the executive branch—continues throughout the summer. During this period, committees are supposed to prepare specific spending and tax laws called *appropriations bills*, without which no money can actually be spent. The appropriations bills are supposed to follow the guidelines of the budget resolution. The deadline for their passage is the start of the fiscal year on October 1.

Limitations of the Budgetary Process

In practice, many things can—and do—go wrong with the budget process. The first and most basic problem is that tax and spending decisions are made in dozens of committees and subcommittees where interest group pressures, vote trading, and the desire of each member of Congress to help the folks at home are the dominant influences. There is no mechanism to ensure that these decisions are consistent with long-run goals of full employment, price stability, and economic growth.

A second problem is that Congress has not been willing to follow its own rules. It often does not pass the required budget resolutions on time. If it does pass them, it does not treat them as binding. More often than not, the fiscal year starts before passage of all twelve of the required appropriations bills, and sometimes before the passage of any of them. If that happens, the agencies of government must operate on the basis of "continuing resolutions," meaning that they can go on doing whatever they were doing the year before until the resolution expires. For example, in September 2015, Congress passed a resolution that allowed the government to continue operations until December 11 of that year.

Sometimes Congress does not even manage to pass a continuing resolution, in which case the government is limited to performing a narrow range of essential functions. In one such episode, much of the government shut down from October 1 to October 16, 2013, when Congress failed to pass a continuing resolution due to a dispute over health-care policy. Economists estimated that the government shutdown cost some $24 billion, including the value of services of federal employees—who received their pay but did not report to work—and revenues lost to private businesses that lose business when museums and parks close.[3]

Often, to avoid a costly and embarrassing government shutdown, Congress short-circuits the appropriations process by rolling several of the twelve separate appropriations bills into a single "omnibus" spending bill. The omnibus bills rarely receive the kind of careful consideration that is supposed to mark the work on regular appropriations bills. Individual members of Congress often pack them with spending provisions that bypass merit-based evaluation. Recent years have seen attempts to limit these so-called "earmarks," but special-interest items tend to work their way into bills under other names.

Attempts at Budget Reform

Over the years, there have been several attempts to introduce stronger rules to govern the federal budget process. None of them has been fully successful. One of the more ambitious efforts at reform was the PAYGO (pay-as-you-go) system, which existed from 1990 to 2002. Under that system, Congress was not supposed to pass any new spending or tax cuts unless it offset them with spending cuts or revenue increases elsewhere in the budget. If the Office of Management and Budget certified that Congress had violated the rules, the president could enforce **sequestration**, a procedure that requires proportional, across-the-board cuts in discretionary spending to bring the budget back in line with a cap on total spending.

Some observers believe that the PAYGO rules made a significant contribution to the emergence of federal budget surpluses in 1998 through 2001, the first in many years. However, the surpluses themselves created a temptation to weaken budget rules, much as a person might celebrate a two-pound weight loss by eating a pint of ice cream. At first, Congress made technical changes in the "scorecard" for PAYGO, so that some kinds of spending no longer came under its limits. When it became apparent early in the Bush administration that tax cuts, Medicare drug benefits, and Iraq war costs would not fit within the PAYGO rules, both the White House and Congress abandoned the rules. The House of Representatives tried to reestablish pay-as-you-go rules in 2007, but the effort did not last long.

The onset of the Great Recession caused the federal deficit to swell, leading to one of the most contentious periods in budget history. In 2011, in an attempt to set new rules that would simultaneously keep the government running and cut the deficit, Congress revived the mechanism of sequestration. Sequestration did slow the growth of federal spending, but at a cost. It substituted crude, across-the-board cuts to defense and nondefense spending for the evaluation of individual programs on their merits. Furthermore, as noted above, it did not prevent the costly government shutdown of 2013 or several other brushes with budget calamity. In short, as of this writing, the federal budget process remains in complete disarray.

12.2b Spending Not Subject to the Annual Budget Cycle

Not all government spending is subject to the annual appropriations process. More than half of the federal budget consists of so-called mandatory items, the most important of which are **entitlements**, including Social Security and Medicare. Expenditures under these programs follow long-term laws that are not subject to annual review. Congress could control entitlement costs by passing new laws to replace the current ones, but doing so is not part of the normal budgetary process.

As Figure 12–2 shows, entitlements have grown in relative importance, while discretionary spending (including education, courts, defense, highways, and all the rest) now accounts for a smaller share of GDP than in the past. If current law remains unchanged, entitlements will continue to grow as the population ages, and discretionary spending will fall below the low levels reached in the 1990s.

Interest Expenditures   Interest payments on the national debt are another category of expenditure that is not subject to annual review. Once the government has borrowed to finance its deficit, interest on the debt becomes a legal obligation that Congress cannot override. It is very rare for the government of any country to default on principal or interest payments on its debt; the United States has never done so, and most people find it inconceivable that it ever would.

Interest payments were a larger share of GDP in the 1980s, when the debt was large and interest rates were high. They fell in the 1990s as debt decreased as a share of GDP. Although the debt has begun growing again, interest rates have been unusually low in recent years, so interest payments as a share of GDP remain lower than in the past.

Sequestration

A budget procedure that requires proportional, across-the-board spending cuts to meet a cap on total spending

Entitlements

Federal benefit programs such as Social Security and Medicare that are not subject to the annual budget process

FIGURE 12–2

Federal Expenditures by Category as a Share of GDP

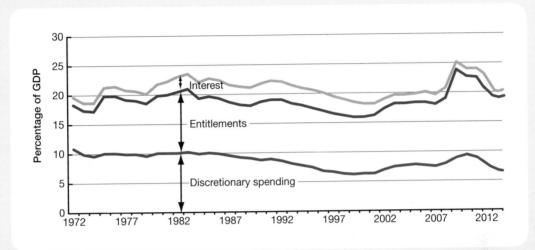

This chart breaks federal spending down into broad categories. Discretionary spending includes all items subject to the annual appropriations process, including education, courts, defense, highways, and all the rest. It has fallen over time as a share of GDP. Entitlement spending consists of benefits that follow long-term laws that are not subject to annual review. Social Security and Medicare are the largest entitlements. Such entitlements have grown more important over time. The third item that escapes annual review is interest on the national debt.

Source: Congressional Budget Office.

12.2c Tax Expenditures

The discussion of budget policy would not be complete without consideration of **tax expenditures**, which are tax deductions or other tax preferences that the government enacts to encourage households or firms to behave in a way that serves some purpose of public policy.

As fiscal policy, tax expenditures are fully equivalent to other kinds of government expenditure. Suppose, for example, that the government wants to encourage people to buy electric cars. One way to do so would be to mail an incentive check of $3,000 to anyone who buys an electric car. It could use tax revenue to pay for the incentive or it could finance it by borrowing. Instead, the government could offer a tax credit of $3,000 to buyers of electric cars. Unless the buyer, for some reason, does not owe any federal taxes, the tax credit is every bit as good an inducement as receiving a check for $3,000 from the Treasury. Just as if it had mailed out rebate checks, the government would have to cover the cost of the tax credit by raising taxes elsewhere or by borrowing.

Altogether, estimated total tax expenditures for 2015 came to about $1.5 trillion. Figure 12–3 lists the ten largest tax expenditures, which together account for more than half of the total.

Tax expenditure

A tax deduction or other tax preference that the government enacts to induce households or firms to behave in a way that serves some purpose of public policy

Although tax expenditures are no different from ordinary cash expenditures in terms of their fiscal impact, they have certain political advantages that make them popular in Washington, DC. For one thing, in a country where many voters view "big government" with suspicion, tax expenditures make government look smaller than it really is. If tax expenditures were included in the total, government expenditures would be about a third larger than now reported.

Another advantage is that tax expenditures allow the government to support activities that might not be politically popular or that it cannot legally support through cash expenditures. For example, the charitable deduction subsidizes the practice of religion, among other activities—something the government could not do using direct expenditures. The deduction for employer-provided health care allows the federal government to minimize the on-budget costs of controversial government health-care programs. Numerous deductions and credits in corporate tax laws attempt to micromanage what companies invest in, where they conduct their business, and what technologies they choose, while allowing the government to claim that it supports free markets.

FIGURE 12–3

Ten Largest Tax Expenditures for 2015 (in millions of dollars)

1	Exclusion of employer contributions for medical insurance premiums and medical care	$200,640
2	Deductibility of mortgage interest on owner-occupied homes	120,240
3	Tax exclusion for 401(k)-type retirement plans	86,740
4	Accelerated depreciation of machinery and equipment	77,350
5	Exclusion of net imputed rental income	66,860
6	Deductibility of nonbusiness state and local taxes other than on owner-occupied homes	60,500
7	Tax exclusion for employer retirement plans	59,840
8	Capital gains (except agriculture, timber, iron ore, and coal)	59,380
9	Deductibility of charitable contributions	47,800
10	Exclusion of interest on public-purpose state and local bonds	46,920

Tax expenditures are tax deductions or other tax preferences that the government enacts to encourage firms or households to behave in a way that serves some purpose of public policy. This table lists the ten largest tax expenditures for 2015. Total tax expenditures that year were almost $1.5 trillion, about one-third of the amount of ordinary cash expenditures.

Source: Tax Policy Center, Tax Facts. http://www.taxpolicycenter.org/taxfacts/displayafact.cfm?Docid=375.

Finally, tax expenditures have the advantage that they are not subject to the annual appropriations process. Once a tax preference makes it into law, it stays there unless Congress repeals it. That is especially advantageous for the beneficiaries of small, narrowly focused tax expenditures that benefit a single company, industry, or region. The lobbyists who get them written into the tax code in the first place can hope that no one will notice them among the thousands of pages of the federal tax code, so that they will live on forever.

Tax expenditures affect short-run fiscal policy in relation to the business cycle, just like other tax and spending measures do. At the same time, they have similar implications for the long-run sustainability of the federal deficit and the growth over time of the national debt. We will take up those issues in the next chapter.

12.3 MEASURING THE STANCE OF FISCAL POLICY

According to the theory and terminology introduced in this chapter, fiscal policy can be either expansionary or contractionary, depending on whether it increases aggregate demand or reduces it. It can be countercyclical if it becomes expansionary when the economy would otherwise contract and contractionary when it would otherwise expand, or it can be procyclical if the timing of expansionary and contractionary policy reinforces the ups and downs of the business cycle rather than offsetting them. These are only general categories, however. How can we measure the stance of fiscal policy in a given country at a given time?

12.3a Three Kinds of Fiscal Balance

The examples given earlier in this chapter show that the instruments of expansionary fiscal policy are tax cuts and spending increases—measures that increase deficits. The corresponding instruments of fiscal restraint are tax increases and spending cuts, which increase deficits. However, considerations other than fiscal policy also influence deficits. To properly measure fiscal policy, we need to strip away these other considerations to measure the fiscal balance in a way that isolates the effects of policy instruments.

The simplest budget measure is the **actual budget balance**—that is, government revenues minus expenditures for a given year. The balance is positive if there is a surplus and negative if there is a deficit. However, the actual balance is not a good indicator of the stance of fiscal policy because it is strongly influenced by automatic stabilizers. As explained earlier, when the economy enters a recession, tax revenues fall and outlays for unemployment insurance and social programs increase, moving the actual balance toward deficit. During an expansion, increases in tax revenues and reductions in outlays move the balance toward or into surplus.

If we remove the effects of automatic stabilizers from the actual balance, we get the **structural balance**. Economist often use the structural balance as an indicator of the stance of fiscal policy because it reflects changes in tax and spending laws, but removes changes in the actual budget that take place automatically as output and unemployment rise and fall over the business cycle. An even better measure of the stance of fiscal policy is the **primary structural balance**, which removes net interest payments from the structural balance. Net interest payments (government payments on the debt minus receipts of interest on loans made by the government) do not depend on current fiscal policy. They depend, in part, on the past tax and spending decisions that determined the size of the outstanding debt. They also depend, in part, on financial market conditions and monetary policy, which determine interest rates. None of these factors is under the direct control of Congress or of state and local governments.

Actual budget balance

Total government revenues minus expenditures for a given period

Structural balance

The balance of the government budget adjusted to remove the effects of automatic stabilizers

Primary structural balance

The structural budget balance adjusted to remove government net interest payments

Figure 12–4 compares the three measures of the balance, shown as a percentage of GDP, for the combined budgets of federal, state, and local governments. Because of automatic stabilizers, when the economy is in recession, as in 2009, the structural balance shows a larger deficit than the actual balance. Near the peak of the business cycle, the structural balance shows a larger deficit (as in 2006) or a smaller surplus (as in 1999). The primary structural balance is always above the structural balance, by an amount that depends on interest rates and the size of the debt. In this chart, the difference between the two measures is largest in the late 1990s, when interest rates were much higher than they are today, despite the fact that the total debt was then smaller. During the Great Recession, the low–interest rate policies pursued by the Federal Reserve kept interest expenses low even though the debt itself grew.

12.3b Procyclical or Anticyclical?

The primary structural budget balance is useful as an indicator of whether the stance of budget policy is anticyclical or procyclical. Policy is anticyclical if it tends to smooth the business cycle. The simplified example at the beginning of the chapter showed how a budget deficit can be used to reduce the severity of a recession, but a deficit during a recession is not a sufficient condition to indicate that policy is anticyclical. It is also true that a surplus at the peak of the business cycle is not necessary for policy to be procyclical. To judge the stance of fiscal policy accurately, we must take three additional factors into account.

FIGURE 12–4

Three Measures of the Government Budget Balance

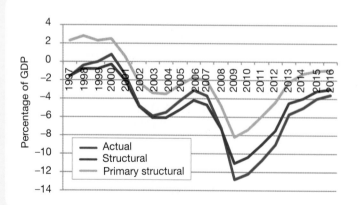

The actual budget balance is the difference between revenues and expenditures in a given year. It is positive if there is a surplus and negative if there is a deficit. The structural balance is adjusted to remove the effect of automatic stabilizers. The primary structural balance removes net interest from the structural balance. The structural balance is above the actual balance during a recession and below it near the peak of the business cycle. The primary structural balance is always above the structural balance.

Data source: OECD, www.oecd.org, 2015.

BVT *Lab*

Visit **www.BVTLab.com** to explore the student resources available for this chapter.

First we need to look not only at the size and sign of the budget balance but also at changes in the balance. The important thing is whether the budget moves toward deficit during a recession or toward surplus during an expansion.

Second, we need to look at the cause of a change in the balance. We cannot speak of changes in the balance as being anticyclical or procyclical unless they are the result of discretionary fiscal policy decisions. Changes that occur as the result of automatic stabilizers do not count, even though, in the long run, changes in tax laws or social insurance programs can affect the strength of automatic stabilizers. Similarly, changes in the government's net interest expenditures cannot be attributed to current fiscal policy. Rather, they are the result of past fiscal policies that have determined the size of the government's accumulated debt and current monetary policies that determine interest rates. That is why we use the primary structural deficit as our key indicator.

Third, we need to look at the timing of changes in the budget balance. Both monetary and fiscal policies act on the economy only with a significant lag. We have seen that using discretionary fiscal policy to move the balance toward deficit during a recession can be anticyclical. However, if expansionary policies are cut off too soon, they may unnecessarily prolong the subsequent recovery, or if they are continued too long, they may overstimulate the economy during the subsequent expansion. Similarly, contractionary policy that is applied too late may not prevent overheating during a boom or may cause a sudden crash rather than a gradual slowdown. In such cases, fiscal policy becomes procyclical.

Economists often disagree, not only about the appropriate fiscal policy at the present time, but also about whether past policies helped to keep the business cycle under control or made it worse. We can look at some controversial episodes with the help of Figure 12–5, which compares the primary structural surplus with an estimate of the output gap.

We can begin by identifying two clear episodes of countercyclical fiscal stimulus. The OECD output gap data used in Figure 12–5 show business cycle peaks in 2000 and 2007.[4] As the chart shows, the primary structural balance moved toward deficit from 2000 to 2002, and again from 2007 to 2009, indicating application of economic stimulus during these periods of recession. The major policy actions in the latter period—namely, the Bush administration's tax rebates in the spring of 2008 and the ARRA early in the Obama administration—were discussed earlier in this chapter. Debate continues as to just how effective they were in mitigating these two cyclical downturns, but most economists would agree that the direction of the policy changes were appropriately countercyclical.

For an example of countercyclical fiscal policy during an expansion, we can turn to the dot-com boom of the 1990s. Only the last years of the boom are shown on the chart, but complete data for that business cycle (starting from 1991) show a steady upward movement of the primary structural balance. The movement first took the form of a decreased deficit. Later, in 1997–2000 (as shown in the chart), the primary structural balance moved into surplus. Other things being equal, that pattern of fiscal policy would have tended to soften the boom and can plausibly be said to have helped to make the 2001 recession an unusually mild one.

The chart also includes two episodes of discretionary fiscal policy that many economists have argued were procyclical. The first occurs during the expansion phase that is marked in this chart by the upward movement of the output gap from 2002 to 2006. In 2003, fiscal policy moved further toward deficit; it stayed level in 2004. Other things being equal, the fiscal stimulus would have added to the housing boom that was then getting underway. From 2004 to 2006, the chart shows a moderate reduction in the primary structural deficit. However, even though the output gap reached as strong a peak as it did in 2000, the primary structural balance never came close to surplus. Critics of fiscal policy in this period maintain that the large tax cuts sponsored by the

FIGURE 12–5

Is Fiscal Policy Anticyclical or Procyclical?

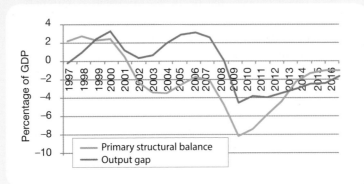

A comparison of the primary structural budget balance with the output gap helps identify anticyclical and procyclical episodes in US fiscal policy. For example, from 2000 to 2002 and again from 2007 to 2009, the primary structural deficit moved sharply toward deficit, indicating an anticyclical stance of policy. More controversially, the failure of the primary structural balance to move into surplus during the housing boom of the mid-2000s and the sharp movement toward surplus immediately after the cyclical trough of 2009 are seen by many economists as procyclical.

Data source: OECD, www.oecd.org, 2015

Bush administration in this time were inappropriate at a time when military spending for the Iraq and Afghanistan wars was rising rapidly. They say that the net effect of fiscal policy in this period was to contribute to a degree of overheating that then made the subsequent recession more severe than it needed to be.

The second episode that can be interpreted as procyclical occurs during the early years of the recovery from the Great Recession, roughly 2009 to 2013. Although proponents of countercyclical policy agree that it is appropriate to ease off on fiscal stimulus as the economy begins to recover, critics see the abrupt upward movement of the primary structural deficit as too much, too soon. A more gradual tapering of the fiscal stimulus, they say, would have sped the recovery of output and employment.

The conduct of fiscal policy in the early twenty-first century will undoubtedly remain a matter of controversy for some time. We will return to the subject of pro- and anticyclical fiscal policy in the next chapter, where we take a longer-term perspective that supplements this chapter's discussion of budget deficit, which has been largely focused on the short run, with a broader perspective that explores the long-run dynamics of government debt.

Summary

1. **How can the government use taxes and expenditures as tools of stabilization policy?**

   Fiscal policy means policy regarding government purchases and net taxes. If a decrease in private planned expenditure threatens to send the economy into a recession, an increase in government purchases or a cut in net taxes can help fill the output gap. When properly executed, such a policy can help the economy return more rapidly to full-employment equilibrium.

2. **What practical problems does the government encounter in implementing fiscal stimulus?**

   Lags and forecasting errors are one source of problems in implementing fiscal policy. In contrast to the ease of shifting curves in textbook models, several years may elapse in the real world between the onset of a recession and a return to full employment. A second problem is determining the proper size of a stimulus program, given uncertainties about the size of the multiplier and the crowding-out effect. Reversing fiscal stimulus once an expansion is underway is a third problem; failure to reverse a stimulus in time can lead to overshooting during the next expansion. Finally, it is difficult to align short-term fiscal stimulus with long-term budget priorities.

3. **How is the federal budget process supposed to work?**

   The federal budget operates on a fiscal year that runs from October through the following September. The budget process begins when the executive branch submits a budget proposal in January. In the spring, Congress passes a nonbinding budget resolution that sets out priorities. During the summer, these become the basis for specific appropriations bills. If Congress does not pass appropriations bills on time, the government must operate on the basis of continuing resolutions. A little over half of the budget consists of entitlements and the costs of debt service, which are not subject to the annual appropriations process.

4. **What role do tax expenditures play in the federal budget?**

   Tax expenditures means the use of tax deductions, credits, and other preferences to encourage households and firms to behave in a way that promotes a public purpose. Examples include encouraging home ownership with personal income tax deductions for home mortgage interest and encouraging investment with corporate tax credits. Tax expenditures have the same effect as ordinary cash expenditures, but they are less visible in the budget and they are not subject to the annual appropriations process. If tax expenditures were included, total federal expenditures would be about one-third larger.

5. **How can we measure the stance of fiscal policy?**

   The term *automatic fiscal policy* refers to the tendency for the government budget to move toward surplus as the economy expands and toward deficit as it contracts. That happens because of the operation of automatic stabilizers, like income taxes and unemployment benefits, that increase or decrease over the business cycle even if tax and spending laws remain unchanged. The structural budget balance removes the effects of automatic stabilizers, and the primary structural balance also removes the effect of net interest payments. Changes in the primary structural balance are a good indicator of the stance of fiscal policy. Observations of the primary structural balance in the United States suggest that fiscal policy has sometimes been anticyclical and sometimes procyclical

KEY TERMS

PROBLEMS AND TOPICS FOR DISCUSSION

1. **Disaster relief**   Suppose that, in response to an earthquake or hurricane, the government increases disaster relief spending by $5 billion. How would the increased spending affect the economy? How would the effects differ depending on the size and sign of the output gap when the crisis began? How would they differ depending on the size of the multiplier? Illustrate your answer with an aggregate supply and demand diagram.

2. **Kennedy tax cuts**   Use your favorite internet search engine to do a little historical research using the search term "Kennedy tax cut." How large were the tax cuts proposed by President John F. Kennedy in comparison with later tax cuts? How long were the lags involved in enacting them?

3. **Entitlement programs**   The Social Security Administration annually publishes a trustees report (look for it online at www.ssa.gov; from the homepage, enter "trustee report" in the search box). Look up the summary of the most recent available report. Do the trustees find that the Social Security and Medicare trust funds are in sound financial conditions? If not, what would need to be done to make them sound?

4. **New Air Force One**   The government has announced that it will replace Air Force One, the Boeing 747 that carries the president. The price of the new plane, including the special improvements needed for the president's use, is estimated to be more than $3 billion. Suppose that Congress does not want to add that much to the reported total of government spending, so it passes a law allowing the builders of the plane a $3 billion one-time tax credit in return for delivering the airplane to the government. Explain whether the fiscal policy impact of this "tax expenditure" would differ from purchasing the plane by issuing a government check for $3 billion.

CASE *for* DISCUSSION

Who Benefits from the Mortgage Interest Deduction?

One of the largest tax expenditures in the federal budget is the personal income tax deduction for interest paid on home mortgages. The deduction enjoys broad bipartisan support in Washington, DC. Politicians love to represent it as a key benefit for the middle class and working families. However, a study from the Urban-Brookings Tax Policy Center calls that claim into question. Instead, the study finds, the great bulk of the benefits go to higher-income households.

The most important reason is that mortgage interest relief benefits only those who itemize deductions on their personal income tax returns. Some 98 percent of tax units with incomes over $125,000 itemize compared with just 23 percent with incomes of $40,000 or less. A second reason is that the cap on the deduction, currently set at $1 million in mortgage debt, is much higher than the average value of debt. That means owners of more expensive homes gain more than those with homes that are more modest. A third reason is that higher-income households pay higher tax rates, so a dollar of tax deduction is worth more to them than to those in lower tax brackets.

The Tax Policy Center study concludes that the mortgage interest deduction is worth $5,393 a year for tax units in the top 1 percent of the income distribution (average income $1,302,188) but only $215 per year to those in the middle 20 percent (average income $43,678). For households in the bottom 20 percent of the income distribution, the deduction has almost no value.

The principal argument in favor of the mortgage interest deduction is the claim that home ownership would otherwise be unaffordable for a large segment of the population. For two reasons, that argument does not hold water.

First, as explained above, the mortgage interest deduction has little value for lower- and middle-income families, those most likely to be on the borderline between rental and ownership. A subsidy worth $215 a year is not going to move many $40,000 families out of rental housing into a home of their own. Neither would a tax increase of $5,000 a year likely induce many millionaires to move out of their own homes into rentals.

Second, the impact on the affordability of housing is less than it appears because the interest deduction helps to push up the market value of homes. Greater tax benefits cause buyers to bid up home prices. Conversely, elimination of those benefits would make home ownership less attractive, so home prices would fall. The effect on home prices does not fully offset the impact on home ownership because higher prices also encourage construction of new homes, but the effect is substantial.

Reformers have offered several ideas for what to do about the mortgage interest deduction. Some favor repealing it entirely. Others prefer a more gradual approach. One idea would be to switch from a deduction to a tax credit, which would be worth more to low-income families. At the same time, Congress could lower the cap on the value of the deduction to upper-income families. It could phase in either of the above ideas gradually over time and structure them to make a larger or smaller contribution to deficit reduction.

Sources: Eric Toder et al., "Reforming the Mortgage Interest Deduction," Urban-Brookings Tax Policy Center, May 26, 2010 (http://www.taxpolicycenter.org/publications/url.cfm?ID=412099). This case includes material from Ed Dolan's Econ Blog, "The Case Against the Mortgage Interest Deduction," February 6, 2010, used by permission of the author.

(Continues)

(Case for Discussion Continued)

Questions

1. Do you own a home with a mortgage? If so, by how much does the mortgage interest deduction reduce your taxes? If you don't own a home, assume you did and that you had a $150,000 mortgage with a 6 percent interest rate. Your income tax rate is 15 percent and you itemize deductions. What would be the value to you of the mortgage interest deduction?

2. Why would a tax credit for mortgage interest be worth more to lower-income families than a deduction? Would you favor changing the benefit from a tax deduction to a tax credit? What other changes might you want to make at the same time? Why?

3. Do you share the view that owning a home makes you a better citizen? Why or why not? In what ways would you expect owners and renters to behave differently as members of their communities?

From Ed Dolan's Econ Blog

Most of this chapter focuses on fiscal policy in the United States, but other countries have had their fiscal troubles, too. The post "Why Angry Greek Voters Backed a Change in Fiscal Policy. What Lessons for America?" shows the procyclical pattern of recent policy in that country and offers some lessons for the United States. Follow this link http://bvtlab.com/qK4c3 or scan the QR code.

Figure 12–3 shows that the mortgage interest deduction is the second largest US tax expenditure. "The Case Against the Mortgage Interest Tax Deduction" shows that, although this deduction is often portrayed as beneficial to the middle class, in fact, the great bulk of the benefits go to the very wealthy. The post also contains a link to a short slideshow on housing tax policy in the United States and other countries. Follow this link http://bvtlab.com/8T3Gr or scan the QR code.

The deduction for charitable contributions is another of the top ten tax expenditures. The two-part series, "The Charitable Deduction as a Tax Expenditure: What It Buys and What to Do About It," explains just what the deduction really buys and how it might be reformed. Follow this link http://bvtlab.com/tacG8 or scan the QR code.

BLOG POSTS

Endnotes

1. See the Appendix to Chapter 5 for details on the multiplier effect. In the simplest case, the multiplier is equal to 1/mpc, where mpc is the marginal propensity to consume.

2. Christina Romer and Jared Bernstein, "The Job Impact of the American Recovery and Reinvestment Plan," released January 10, 2009, by the Office of the President-Elect (http://otrans.3cdn.net/45593e8ecbd339d074_l3m6bt1te.pdf). Strictly speaking, the ratio of GDP change to change in government purchases estimated by Romer and Bernstein is not the same as the simple expenditure multiplier discussed in the Appendix to Chapter 5. The simple expenditure multiplier assumes that prices and interest rates remain constant as GDP increases, while most practical discussions allow for changes in prices, interest rates, bank reserves, and other variables. Loosely speaking, however, these estimates are often referred to as multipliers. We will refer to them with the informal term *effective fiscal multiplier*. For a thorough critique of the Romer and Bernstein estimates, see John F. Cogan et al., "New Keynesian vs. Old Keynesian Government Spending Multipliers," Center for Economic Policy Research, Discussion Paper DP7236, March 2009.

3. As reported by ABC News, October 17, 2013, http://abcnews.go.com/blogs/politics/2013/10/the-costs-of-the-government-shutdown.

4. Other data sources, including the quarterly estimates of the output gap from the Congressional Budget Office and the reports of the Business Cycle Dating Committee of the National Bureau of Economic Research, show slightly different timing and amplitude for the cyclical peaks and troughs, but the differences are not great enough to affect the general pattern of policy as discussed here.

CHAPTER 13

LONG-TERM FISCAL POLICY AND THE FEDERAL DEBT

AFTER READING THIS CHAPTER, you will understand the following:

1. The conditions for long-run balance in an economy
2. The conditions for sustainability of fiscal policy
3. The consequences of unsustainable fiscal policy
4. Whether US fiscal policy is sustainable
5. What kind of rules could be used to ensure sustainability of fiscal policy

BEFORE READING THIS CHAPTER, make sure you know the following concepts:

Automatic stabilizers

Structural balance

Primary structural balance

Entitlements

Tax expenditures

Balance sheets, assets, and liabilities

Solvency

Quantitative easing

Real interest rate

CHAPTER Outline

In Chapter 12, we looked at the fiscal policy in a short-run context. Now we turn to the role that fiscal policy plays in promoting a balanced and prosperous economy in the long run. Maintaining balance and prosperity requires more than budget procedures and policy adjustments that aim to moderate the business cycle. It requires a planning horizon that extends beyond the next election and a commitment to long-term rules.

13.1 ACHIEVING A BALANCED ECONOMY

Any doctor knows that a patient with a normal temperature can still have serious health problems. In much the same way, an economy that keeps the short-term business cycle within reasonable bounds can still have long-term structural problems. Structural problems can often be identified by examining the balance, or imbalance, among the four main components of GDP—consumption, investment, government purchases, and net exports.

13.1a Balance of Saving and Investment

Infrastructure

The shared physical systems, such as roads, power grids, and water systems, on which economic activity depends

One kind of balance to look for is that between saving and investment. At a bare minimum, just to keep the standard of living from decreasing, a country needs enough investment to replace housing and business equipment as it wears out. In the United States, that requires about 12 percent of GDP.

In addition to investment by individual businesses, the country needs to invest in basic **infrastructure** such as the roads, power grids, and water supplies that firms, households, and governments share. As *Applying Economic Ideas 13.1* explains, the United States has not done a very good job of maintaining its infrastructure in recent years.

Applying Economic Ideas 13.1

The Budget Deficit Versus the Infrastructure Deficit

Nearly everyone understands that deficits matter. But which deficits are most important? For people who are worried that they may be the first generation to leave their children a national balance sheet with a thinner margin between assets and liabilities than they inherited from their parents, the widely publicized federal budget deficit is not the only thing that matters.

The infrastructure deficit is no less important. The infrastructure deficit is the difference between what the country invests each year in new bridges, sewers, and power lines and the rate at which the old ones fall apart. If investment in infrastructure exceeds depreciation, the country is that much richer at the end of the year. If depreciation exceeds investment, it is poorer, as surely as if the Treasury were to borrow money and spend it on the most shortsighted programs you can think of.

Anyone who doubts that the infrastructure deficit is real should take a look at the *Report Card for America's Infrastructure,* published periodically by the American Society of Civil Engineers (ASCE). The **report card** assigns grades of "A" through "F" to various infrastructure categories. According to the latest report, real GDP grew by 11 percent over the first five years of recovery from the Great Recession. As it did so, the federal budget deficit shrank from 9.2 to 3.9 percent of GDP. Yet the condition of America's infrastructure barely improved, rising only from a dismal D to a pathetic D+. Dams, drinking water, wastewater, roads, and mass transit earned a grade of D. Rail transportation and bridges improved slightly, but still managed only a C+. The only category to do better than that was solid waste disposal, which managed a B–.

Consider dams, for example. There are some eighty-four thousand dams in the United States with an average age of fifty-two years. The report rates some four thousand dams as deficient, including some two thousand of the country's fourteen thousand high-hazard dams. (A dam is rated high hazard if its failure would cause loss of life.) Repairs and new construction are not keeping pace with the deterioration of existing dams. For every deficient high-hazard dam repaired in recent years, two more became deficient.

The same story repeats itself in one category of infrastructure after another. The previous report card estimated that $2.2 trillion in infrastructure spending would be needed over the five years from 2009 to 2013. Rather than catching up on its infrastructure, however, the country fell still further behind over that period. The latest report card estimates infrastructure spending needs for the coming five years at $3.6 trillion. Will that money be forthcoming? Not if Washington and the fifty states continue to ignore the infrastructure deficit.

The bottom line: we have to be very careful when cutting infrastructure spending. Cuts to essential repairs and upgrades will decrease the federal budget deficit only at the cost of increasing the infrastructure deficit. The trade-off is especially unfavorable when deferred maintenance leads to costly catastrophic failures. Realistically, just eliminating the infrastructure deficit isn't enough. Future economic growth will require an infrastructure surplus, so that

Aerial view of Shasta Dam, Northern California (Wikimedia Commons)

we can build wireless communication networks and renewable energy grids at the same time we make needed repairs to less glamorous elements of the infrastructure like aging sewers and bridges.

Sources: American Society of Civil Engineers, *2013 Report Card for America's Infrastructure*, March 2013 (http://www.infrastructurereportcard.org/grades/). This case includes material from Ed Dolan's Econ Blog, "Why Are Our Bridges Falling? The Economics of the Infrastructure Deficit," May 15, 2013. Used by permission of the author.

The financing for investment can come from several sources. Saving from household income is one possible source. Household savings rates vary widely around the world. Koreans and Italians save more than 20 percent of their disposable income. Canadians and Swedes save 10 percent or more. US households saved 8 to 12 percent of disposable income until the early 1990s, but after that, saving dropped sharply. By 2006, household saving was actually negative; on average, for the whole country, ordinary families spent more each year than they earned. The saving rate has recovered a bit since then; but as of 2013, it was still only 4 percent.

When household saving is low, we have to find some other way to finance investment. Business saving helps. Reinvestment of undistributed corporate profits amounts to about 3 percent of US GDP and constitutes the largest single component of private saving. By itself, however, business saving is not enough even to replace capital as it wears out.

A third possible source of saving would be a surplus in the government budget; however, in the United States, the combined federal, state, and local budget has been in surplus in only five of the past forty years. In many years, the deficit has been large enough to offset all business saving. When household, business, and government saving are all added together, then, the United States has a large, chronic imbalance between domestic saving and domestic investment.

13.1b External Balance

Even without an adequate source of domestic saving, a country can continue to invest by borrowing from abroad—that is, by drawing on the saving of other countries. In its international accounts, the borrowing will be reflected in a current account deficit (imports greater than exports), balanced by a financial inflow. As we explained in Chapter 5, an external imbalance between imports and exports is, in a sense, the twin of an imbalance between domestic saving and investment.

How seriously do low domestic savings and the large US current account deficit threaten the long-term prosperity of the US economy? Economists differ in opinion. Some take an optimistic view and see the ability of the US economy to attract foreign investment as a sign of strength. Others point out that the United States is not entirely at fault for the imbalance in its international accounts. To some extent, the accounts reflect opposite imbalances in the economies of trading partners.

Applying Economic Ideas 13.2 describes imbalances in the Chinese economy, which in some ways are the mirror image of those of the United States. Still, many observers warn that the United States as a whole has been living beyond its means. They warn that a day of reckoning could come if the oil-rich gulf states, the Chinese, the Russians, and others were to stop funding the deficit by buying US government securities at low interest rates. Without the cheap financial inflows on which the United States has become dependent, growth could slow, undermining living standards for future generations of Americans.

Applying Economic Ideas 13.2

Rebalancing the Chinese Economy

Americans are so used to dire warnings about trade deficits, budget deficits, spendthrift consumers, and underinvestment that we might easily see a country without those problems as an economic paradise. Consider China, which enjoyed growth averaging 10 percent or better for more than two decades. Its current account surplus reached 10 percent of GDP at one point, although it has recently fallen a bit. Investment, at 45 percent of GDP—or more, by some accounts—is the highest in the world. On top of that, the government budget, in most years, has shown a healthy surplus. What more could one want? Yet, economists both inside and outside China have long seen serious structural imbalances that posed a threat to the nation's seemingly unstoppable growth machine.

Take the question of saving versus consumption. While American families are among the world's most profligate, Chinese households are the world's thriftiest. Household savings run around 30 percent of disposable income. Consumption is extremely low—barely 40 percent of GDP—the lowest percentage anywhere.

What lies behind the high saving rate? Surveys suggest that high savings are, to a large extent, motivated by economic insecurity. China's social safety net is weak. Public financing of health care,

Year after year, China has had an economic growth rate of 10 percent or better. (iStock)

education, pensions, and unemployment benefits is minimal. Household access to credit is underdeveloped. As a result, Chinese families—even those with very low incomes—must scrimp and save to educate their children and be ready for their own illness or retirement.

What about all that investment? Yes, up to a point, high investment is one of the sources of China's rapid growth; but there is also a lot of wasted investment. Bloated state-owned steel mills and cement factories, with no shareholders to answer to, spend billions on expansion of low-tech, dirty, and relatively unproductive facilities. A study by the McKinsey Global Institute found that the amount of investment needed to produce one unit of additional output—the so-called incremental capital-output ratio—is lower in China than in neighboring Japan or South Korea, and it is getting worse, not better.

Surely, though, the huge trade surpluses are a blessing, are they not? Well, not entirely. When trade surpluses were at their height, China found it difficult to invest them profitably. Moreover, surpluses that were built on low-wage, labor-intensive industries brought meager benefits to Chinese workers.

Today, Chinese leaders are coming to the realization that Goldilocks may have been right. An economy may be healthiest when it is neither too hot nor too cold, when it has neither excessive surpluses nor excessive deficits, and when it gives its consumers a standard of living that is neither too far above nor too far below its real productive capabilities. Environmental realities like dirty air, poor water quality, and concerns over food safety are adding to political pressures to change the Chinese model. Growth is slowing. By 2015, it had dropped below 7 percent per year, a rate that would be a dream for many countries but is seen as a threat to political stability in China. The current account surplus had shrunk to around 2 percent of GDP.

The question facing China's leaders is no longer whether rebalancing is needed, but whether it will be manageable. Will it bring a slowdown from breakneck to moderate growth, in which economic gains are more widely shared by consumers? Or will there be a hard landing that could shake the Communist Party's monopoly on political power? Stay tuned.

Sources: Information on investment from McKinsey Global Institute, "Putting China's Capital to Work: The Value of Financial System Reform," May 2006. http://www.mckinsey.com/mgi/publications/china:capital/index.asp.

13.1c Balance Versus Cyclical Recovery

When a country with an imbalanced economy enters a recession, policymakers face a dilemma. Long-term imbalances like deficient household savings, procyclical fiscal policy, and persistent current account shortfalls may well have been part of the cause of the recession. However, the quickest way to eliminate the output gap and return to full employment may be to restore the economy to its state before the recession started, imbalances and all.

Suppose, for example, that household saving during the boom preceding a crisis had fallen to zero, whereas the economy would have a better long-run balance if saving rose to 5 percent of GDP. After rebalancing, the extra 5 percent formerly devoted to consumption would be available for additional government spending on national priorities like education or infrastructure, additional business investment, and reduction of the current account deficit.

If the circular flow of income and product were a set of pipes filled with some uniform substance like water, rebalancing the economy would be easy. We could adjust a few valves, and less would flow through the consumption channel while more flowed through the investment channel.

In reality, though, the circular flow contains a heterogeneous mix of donuts, building supplies, high school teaching, and tractors. It is not possible to change the ratio of the consumption flow to the investment or net export flow without moving specific workers and production equipment from one industry to another. However, retraining autoworkers as nurses or reconfiguring an assembly line to produce excavators rather than cars takes time. During a recession, when the highest priority is putting unemployed people back to work, such structural changes may actually slow recovery. There is a great temptation to restore the economy just as it used to be and put off worrying about restructuring until later. But when "later" comes and the economy is back at full employment, restructuring no longer seems like such a high priority.

13.2 Fiscal Sustainability

Chapter 12 discussed fiscal policy from a short-run perspective. In the short run, the most important question is whether fiscal policy tends to smooth the business cycle or destabilize it—that is, whether it is pro- or anticyclical. However, fiscal policy also raises long-term issues. Critics claim that fiscal policy will not be **sustainable** in the long run if it leads to a crisis such as uncontrolled inflation or accumulation of debt that the government cannot repay. This section will introduce some general principles regarding the long-run sustainability of fiscal policy and apply them to the debt of the federal government in the United States.

13.2a Sustainability as Solvency

The first and simplest perspective on sustainability equates it with solvency. Chapter 7 defined insolvency as a situation in which the net worth of a bank or other financial institution falls to zero. That kind of insolvency is not a concern for national governments, which typically have assets—including land, structures, and streams of future tax payments—that far exceed their liabilities. Instead, concerns over the sustainability of fiscal policy focus on a related concept, technically called *equitable solvency*, meaning the ability to meet payment obligations in full and on time. In principle, a government might find itself unable to meet payment obligations even if it had a positive net worth—for example, if it were unable to sell illiquid assets like bridges or national parks to raise the needed cash.

The risk of insolvency is greatest for a country (or a lower unit of government like a state or province within a country) that does not issue its own currency. Greece, a member of the Eurozone, is an example. The Greek government has debt equal to some 175 percent of GDP, all of it denominated in euros. It can obtain the euros it needs to service its debt only through borrowing or taxation, but those sources have reached their limit. Taxes are already high, and the tax collection system is inefficient. The government's credit rating is very low, making it almost impossible to borrow in private financial markets. As a result, Greece has not always been able to meet its debt payments in full and on time. Only government-to-government loans from EU authorities have kept it from outright default.

In contrast, a government that has its own currency can, at least in principle, always meet its financial obligations by issuing new money. In former times, that meant literally printing new paper money to hand out to civil servants, contractors, and creditors. In modern practice, where most money takes the form of bank balances, the treasury or minister of finance sells bonds to the central bank, which, in exchange, credits the equivalent amount to an account from which the government can write checks or make electronic transfers. When the treasury makes payments from this account, the funds enter the banking system, where, as explained in Chapter 8, they become part of the monetary base, which consists of bank reserves and currency. The amount of income the government derives is measured by the resulting increase in the monetary base. Economists refer to this procedure as **monetization**. If used without limit, monetization provides absolute protection against equitable insolvency.

Sustainability (of fiscal policy)

Fiscal policy is said to be unsustainable in the long run if it leads to a crisis such as uncontrolled inflation or an accumulation of debt that the government cannot repay

Monetization

Financing government operations or debt service by issuing new money through the central bank

In practice, however, many governments face self-imposed constraints on finance by monetization. One kind of constraint occurs in countries that have their own currencies but borrow by issuing bonds in dollars, euros, or another foreign currency. Such countries either must have sufficient export earnings to service their foreign debt or must maintain a high enough credit rating to sell new bonds to roll over old ones as they become due. The self-imposed constraints are even tighter for countries that both issue debt in foreign currencies and commit themselves to maintaining a fixed exchange rate. The Argentine debt crisis of 2001 is a case in point. During the 1990s, Argentina maintained a strictly fixed exchange rate of one US dollar per Argentine peso; but during that period, Argentina accumulated more debt than it could service. At the end of 2001, it was forced both to devalue its currency and to default on its dollar-denominated debt.

Even countries with floating exchange rates may face self-imposed limits on monetization. For example, laws in the United States and many other countries do not allow the government to borrow directly from the central bank. In addition, the US government is constrained by a congressionally mandated ceiling on the amount of debt it can issue. Those prohibitions are not absolute, however. The government can monetize the debt indirectly if it sells newly issued bonds to the public and, simultaneously, the central bank buys older bonds from the public through open market operations. Also, Congress can—and does—periodically raise the debt ceiling. With regard to these self-imposed limits, then, it is fair to say that any default by the US federal government would be the result of political choice, not of equitable insolvency.

13.2b Sustainability and the Debt Ratio

A second perspective defines sustainability of fiscal policy not in terms of solvency but in terms of the ratio of debt to GDP (the debt ratio, for short). According to this perspective, a pattern of fiscal policy is unsustainable if it leads to unlimited growth of the debt ratio.

The Mathematics of the Debt Ratio

Changes in the debt ratio over time are governed by some simple mathematical relationships. The first of these is the **government budget constraint**, which states the relationship between what a government spends and three sources of funds. Net taxes are the first source. (*Net taxes*, as explained in Chapter 5, means tax revenues minus transfer payments). The second source is borrowing. The US federal government borrows by selling securities, which are classified as bills (T-bills) if short term, notes if medium term, and bonds if long-term. It sells them in periodic auctions and pays a rate of interest determined by market conditions at the time. The third way for the government to finance purchases is with newly issued money—that is, by monetization.

If we let G stand for government purchases, T for net taxes, ΔD for borrowing (Δ stands for "change in" and D stands for debt), and ΔB for monetization (change in B, the monetary base), then the constraint is

$$G = T + \Delta D + \Delta B$$

In normal times, taxes and borrowing account for almost all of the funds available to finance government purchases, and monetization accounts for only a tiny share. Over the fifty-year period ending in 2007, the annual increase in the US monetary base

Government budget constraint

The relationship between what a government purchases and its sources of funds

The government has three sources of funds to pay for what it spends: taxation, borrowing, and issuing new money. (Shutterstock)

averaged about one-third of 1 percent of GDP, and only once did it reach one-half of 1 percent. For the remainder of this chapter, we will focus on that normal case, which allows us to simplify the budget constraint by dropping the term ΔB. In the next chapter, we will examine the exceptional circumstances under which the rate of money creation is much more rapid. (For example, from 2009 through 2014, during the height of the Fed's policy of quantitative easing, the growth of the monetary base was ten times faster than normal, averaging more than 3 percent of GDP.) Meanwhile, we can write the simplified budget constraint as

$$G = T + \Delta D$$

It follows from the simplified budget constraint that a government that spends more than the tax revenue it collects must have a constantly growing debt. To use a popular metaphor, borrowing builds a "debt pyramid." The bricks in the pyramid are bonds issued in past years to cover past deficits. Each year the government adds new bricks to the base of the pyramid to pay for this year's deficit, for the interest on debt issued in the past, and to roll over any previously issued bonds as they mature.

A growing debt is not a source of concern if the rest of the economy is growing too, but a debt that constantly grows faster than GDP could pose problems. We can determine whether the debt ratio will grow over time, remain stable, or decrease by looking at four variables:

- The primary structural balance (*PSB*) of the budget (As explained in the previous chapter, this is the budget surplus or deficit excluding interest payments and the effects of automatic stabilizers.)

- The initial ratio of debt to GDP (*DEBT*)

- The rate of interest on outstanding debt (*INT*)

- The rate of growth of GDP (*GROWTH*)

We can state the interest rate and GDP growth in either nominal or real terms, so long as both are stated the same way.

That brings us to our second important mathematical relationship: the steady-state primary structural balance—that is, the PSB that will hold the ratio of debt to GDP constant. This is equal to the initial debt ratio multiplied by the difference between the rate of interest and the rate of GDP growth. With all variables stated as a percentage of GDP, the equation looks like this:

$$PSB = DEBT \times (INT - GROWTH)$$

Some numerical examples will help make this clear (each of the examples assumes that debt is initially equal to 50 percent of GDP):

- Suppose the real interest rate and the growth rate of real GDP are both 5 percent. If so, the debt will remain constant as a percentage of GDP over time if the PSB is zero. The government must borrow enough each year (2.5 percent of GDP) to cover interest payments. The addition of new debt equal to 2.5 percent of GDP each year means that total debt, which is half of GDP, grows at an annual rate of 5 percent—just enough to keep the debt ratio constant. The overall structural balance, including interest payments, would be –2.5 percent of GDP—that is, there would be an overall structural deficit.

- Suppose, instead, that the interest rate is 5 percent but GDP grows by only 3 percent. New borrowing is now limited to 1.5 percent of GDP if we are to hold the debt ratio constant. Since total interest is 2.5 percent of GDP, the PSB must be in surplus by 1 percent of GDP. The overall structural budget balance would then be in deficit by 0.5 percent of GDP.

- Suppose, now, that GDP grows by 3 percent but the interest rate falls to 2 percent. With an initial debt ratio of 50 percent, interest expenses are only 1 percent of GDP. Government borrowing equal to 1.5 percent of GDP, the amount that will hold the debt ratio constant, permits a PSB of –0.5 percent of GDP—a primary structural deficit. The debt ratio would grow over time only if the primary structural balance were further in deficit. The overall structural balance would show a deficit of 2.0 percent of GDP.

These examples make it clear that, contrary to popular opinion, it is not always necessary to have a balanced budget in order to keep the debt ratio from growing. Even when a surplus is required for the primary structural balance, the overall structural balance, including interest, can be in deficit. When the interest rate on government debt is lower than the rate of growth, the debt can be stable when both the primary structural balance and the overall structural balance are in deficit.

The Consequences of a Growing Debt
Our discussion of the mathematics of the debt ratio raises some important policy questions. What happens if a country has a primary structural budget balance less than what it needs to stabilize its government debt? Would that mean an eventual crisis of some kind? What alternatives are available if a crisis does come? Let's look at each of these questions in turn.

Whether a rising debt ratio leads to an inevitable crisis depends, in part, on the relation of the interest rate to the rate of growth of GDP. Historically, interest rates have tended to be higher than GDP growth rates. For example, from 1980 to 2010, one benchmark of government borrowing costs, the interest rate on ten-year Treasury notes, averaged 1.3 percentage points higher than the growth rate of GDP. In contrast, from 2011 through 2015, while the Fed was engaged in quantitative easing, the ten-year Treasury rate averaged 1.2 percentage points lower than GDP growth. Most observers expect interest rates to rise above GDP growth again as the economy completes its recovery, but a minority think that low interest rates will become the new normal. Time will tell.

The relationship between the two indicators is important for sustainability because, as we have seen, the steady-state value of the primary structural balance is equal to the initial debt ratio times the difference between the interest rate and the rate of growth. A PSB below the steady-state value will cause the debt ratio to increase over time. However, if the interest rate is less than the rate of GDP growth, the debt ratio will not grow without limit. Instead, even if the PSB remains below its steady-state value, debt will grow toward, but not beyond, a new finite limit. Depending on the numbers, the new limiting debt ratio could be several times GDP, which some observers might think is dangerously high; but the approach of debt toward its limit would be gradual. It would not threaten any sudden breakdown of public finances.

If the rate of interest is higher than the growth rate of GDP, the dynamics of the debt work out differently. In that case, if the PSB were permanently at a level lower than the steady-state value associated with the initial debt ratio, the debt would grow at an ever faster rate. Eventually, outstanding debt would soar far past the level of 100 percent of GDP. As the supply of outstanding government debt grew without limit, the interest rates required to sell still more bonds and notes would begin to rise. Higher interest rates would slow economic growth. Those developments would further destabilize government finances. Major policy changes would become imperative.

What policy changes? Default would be one alternative. The government could simply tell bondholders, "Sorry, we can't pay the interest and principal we owe. You are out of luck!" Either the bondholders would get nothing, or they would have to settle for a fraction of the face value of their debt. Russia, in 1998, defaulted outright on its domestic debt, leaving creditors holding worthless paper. Argentina defaulted on

Irish finance minister Michael Noonan
(Wikimedia Commons)

foreign debt in 2002. In 2012, Greece arranged a so-called restructuring—a more orderly kind of default in which it, with the cooperation of other members of the euro area, strong-armed private creditors into exchanging their original bonds for new ones that were worth only a fraction as much.

A second alternative would be to monetize the debt. Instead of borrowing what it needs from the public, the treasury would begin selling its bonds directly to the central bank. The central bank, in turn, would add enough newly created money to the government's checking account to allow it to pay its bills. The big concern with this scenario is whether it would cause extreme inflation, a topic we will take up in the next chapter.

The third alternative for dealing with a runaway debt pyramid would be to raise taxes or cut spending by enough to bring the government's borrowing needs back within the limits of sustainability. Economists call this alternative **fiscal consolidation**; a popular term is **fiscal austerity**. Politically, fiscal consolidation can be the hardest of all the alternatives, but it is sometimes the one that does the least damage to the economy. Ireland and Denmark, in the 1980s, are examples of countries that once had unsustainable deficits but successfully achieved fiscal consolidation. (Ireland got into fiscal trouble once more after it joined the euro and had to go through the whole painful process of austerity again.)

Which Countries' Fiscal Policies Are Sustainable?

So much for sustainability in general. We can round out this section by taking a quick look at countries whose fiscal policies do or do not meet the mathematical requirements for sustainability. Figure 13–1 provides the numbers for a representative sample of developed countries. The numbers in the table are based on Organization for Economic Co-operation and Development (OECD) estimates that cover all levels of government, not central governments alone. International comparisons are meaningful only for all levels of government because of widely differing degrees of centralization.

In order for a country's ratio of debt to GDP to remain constant, the primary structural balance, expressed as a percentage of GDP, must be greater than the initial debt ratio multiplied by the difference between the interest rate and the rate of growth of GDP. The figure compares the actual PSB to two estimates of the steady-state PSB for eight high-income countries as of 2015. Estimate 1 for the steady-state PSB assumes that future interest rates will equal the average interest cost of debt currently outstanding. Estimate 2 assumes that future interest rates will equal current market rates on ten-year government securities.

Current fiscal policies in Germany and Italy meet the criterion for sustainability with room to spare, but for different reasons. Germany's net debt is a modest 44 percent of GDP and its interest rates are lower than its rate of GDP growth. It could maintain a stable debt ratio even with a small primary structural deficit, but instead it has a primary structural surplus of 2.4 percent of GDP. Italy's debt ratio is much higher, 138 percent of GDP and its interest rates are higher than its rate of GDP growth. However, it has a very substantial primary structural surplus of 4.1 percent of GDP, enough to bring its debt ratio down gradually over time.

At the other end of the scale, Japan, Canada, and the UK all currently have interest rates that are below their rates of growth, so that the steady-state value for their PSBs is negative. However, all three have PSBs that are further in deficit than the steady-state value permits. If current policies remain unchanged, their debt ratios will grow toward, but not beyond some new limiting value.

The situation in Greece is still different. Greece has the largest starting debt ratio of all the countries, shown at 141 percent of GDP. Market interest rates on Greek government debt are extremely high, and growth has been slow to negative. Evaluated at market

Fiscal consolidation (fiscal austerity)

The process of reducing government spending and increasing taxes by enough to make the deficit sustainable

FIGURE 13-1

Sustainability of Fiscal Policy in Selected High-Income Countries

	Primary Structural Balance	Steady-State PSB	
		Est. 1	Est. 2
Japan	-5.9	-2.2	-1.8
UK	-1.6	-1.4	-0.8
Canada	-1.0	-0.5	-0.7
USA	-0.6	-1.3	-0.6
France	-0.5	-0.4	0.6
Germany	2.4	-1.1	-0.3
Italy	4.1	1.0	2.5
Greece	7.2	14.3	7.3

The primary structural balance (PSB) is a key indicator of debt sustainability. This chart compares the actual PSB to estimates of the steady-state PSB for eight high-income countries as of 2015. The data indicate that the current fiscal policies of Germany and Italy are clearly sustainable; those of Japan, the UK, Canada, and Greece are clearly unsustainable; and those of the United States and France are close to sustainability.

Data source: Organization for Economic Co-operation and Development, www.oecd.org, 2015.

interest rates (Est. 1 in Figure 13–1), Greece would need a huge PSB surplus of 14.3 to stabilize its debt ratio. Its current PSB surplus of 7.2 percent is the highest of any developed country, but still not high enough. In practice, though, Greece does not have to pay market interest rates on all of its debt. Instead, it has been getting loans at reduced rates from EU authorities. Evaluated at the rates actually paid, Greece would need just a 7.3 percent PSB surplus to stabilize its debt—close to what it currently has.

Two countries in the table are near the borderline of sustainability. France's PSB is low enough to gradually shrink its debt if we measure interest costs at current market rates, but not if we measure them at the average interest cost of outstanding debt. Slow growth of GDP makes it more difficult for France to keep its debt ratio from growing beyond its current level of 75 percent of GDP.

The United States is in somewhat better shape than France, primarily because its economy has been growing faster. If market interest rates were to stay at their current low levels and growth were to continue at its 2014–2016 average, the current PSB deficit of 0.6 percent of GDP would be enough to ensure that the debt ratio would gradually decrease. The average rate of interest on outstanding debt is a little higher than current market rates, but even at those rates, the PSB is close to its steady-state value.

The numbers in the table are not definitive. Different sources provide different estimates because of different assumptions about interest rates, growth rates, and the output gap. In the United States, the Congressional Budget Office focuses on the federal budget alone and uses a methodology different from that of the OECD. The latest CBO projections show net US federal debt falling slightly from its current level of 74 percent of GDP until 2018 and rising gradually again through 2025 if current policies are unchanged.

Note that the numbers in Figure 13–1 only show whether a country's PSB is large enough to stabilize its debt ratio. They do not tell us whether that is a reasonable goal under current economic conditions. As discussed in the previous chapter, the theory of countercyclical policy suggests that a country's primary structural balance should move toward deficit when the economy is in recession and toward surplus as it approaches the peak of the business cycle. Keep in mind that countries like France, Greece, and the United States have had negative output gaps for years. None of them has fully recovered from the global financial crisis. That being the case, it can be argued that their fiscal policies have moved too strongly toward austerity too early in the recovery process in a premature effort to reach steady-state values for their PSBs. That issue will be the focus of the final section of this chapter.

13.2c Rules for Fiscal Policy

In Chapter 11, we discussed rules for monetary policy. Rules help overcome problems that discretionary policymaking encounters—especially the problems of lags, forecasting errors, and time inconsistency. Rules also help policymakers focus on the underlying goals of economic stability and prosperity, rather than short-term political goals that fail to look beyond the next election. This section examines possible rules for fiscal policy that integrate considerations of long-term sustainability, as discussed earlier in this chapter, with issues of fiscal stabilization over the business cycle, which were the subject of Chapter 12.

Why Not Just Balance the Budget Every Year?
The simplest fiscal policy rule would be to balance the budget every year. An annual w has immediate political appeal to voters, who see an analogy with their own household budgets. They know that they, as consumers, should not buy things they can't pay for. They know they can't run up credit card debt or mortgage debt beyond what their incomes will support. They know that the penalty for violating these rules is financial ruin and bankruptcy.

Capitalizing on this reasoning, many politicians have proposed one or another form of a **balanced budget amendment** that would require the government to limit its spending each year to the amount of tax revenue that it receives. Some variants add a maximum cap for expenditures, usually stated as a percentage of GDP. Some allow for temporary exceptions in times of war. The specific proposals put before Congress each year vary in detail, but they share the focus on strict annual balance.

Popular as the idea is among politicians, a requirement for an annually balanced budget finds little support among economists. The reason is that such a proposal would inevitably be procyclical. When a recession caused tax revenue to fall, such a rule would require cutting spending as well. That would reduce aggregate demand further and deepen the recession. In effect, an annually balanced budget would deactivate the automatic stabilizers that moderate the business cycle by allowing expenditures for items like unemployment compensation and support for low-income families to rise during recessions at the same time falling incomes reduce tax revenues.

At the same time, an annually balanced budget rule would provide little or no restraint on spending when the economy approaches the peak of a business cycle. As the output gap turns positive, rising output and incomes automatically raise tax revenues. Congress would be free to react by handing out favors to political supporters in the effect of special-interest tax breaks or pork barrel spending without putting the annual budget in deficit. The problem is not just that such moves would be unaffordable during the next

Balanced budget amendment

Any of a number of proposals to amend the US constitution in a way that would require the federal government to limit its spending each year to the amount of tax revenue that it receives

cyclical downturn. Rather, they would encourage overheating of the economy that would make the next downturn more severe than it would otherwise have been.

Another way to see the flaws in an annually balanced budget rule is to view it in terms of the primary structural deficit. Cutting taxes and increasing discretionary spending when the economy has a positive output gap moves the PSB toward deficit. Cutting spending when the output gap turns negative moves the PSB toward surplus. Such a procyclical pattern is clearly inconsistent with the goals of stability and prosperity.

A Structural Balance Rule   One way to overcome the procyclical properties of an annually balanced budget is to use the primary structural balance or overall structural balance as the fiscal policy target. If the government were required to keep the PSB at the steady-state value every year, it would control the growth of the debt over time while allowing full operation of automatic stabilizers to moderate the business cycle. If the debt were large to begin with, the target could be set somewhat above the steady-state value and held there until the debt came down to the desired level.

Chile, one of the most prosperous countries in Latin America, is an example of a country that uses a structural balance target for fiscal policy. Sound fiscal policy has helped Chile's economy grow steadily with moderate inflation and unemployment. Its total government debt has averaged under 10 percent of GDP over the last decade. The country uses the overall structural balance as its target rather than the primary balance. In the early 2000s, when the government first introduced the policy, it set its target at a 1 percent structural surplus in order to bring its debt ratio down. After the debt ratio reached 10 percent of GDP, the government changed the target to a structural balance of zero. The structural balance target, which began as an informal rule, was codified in law in 2006.

Among other benefits, the structural budget target helps Chile cope with the dependence of its economy on the world price of copper, its largest export. During the early 2000s, when commodity prices boomed, the structural target kept spending in check. By 2007, the ratio of debt to GDP had fallen to under 4 percent. When the copper price collapsed during the global financial crisis of 2008, the government was able to draw on reserves accumulated in good times to support incomes and speed recovery. More recently, slowing growth in China has again depressed copper prices, and Chile's output gap has again turned negative. The structural budget rule has allowed a larger current deficit and an increase in the debt ratio to help cushion the decrease in export demand.

Despite its apparent simplicity, implementing a structural balance rule is not completely straightforward. One problem is that policymakers cannot observe the structural balance directly. Instead, they first have to forecast the economy's output gap for the year ahead and use that, plus the estimates of interest rates and of the impact of automatic stabilizers, to forecast the structural deficit for the coming budget year. Estimating the output gap, in turn, requires estimating the long-term growth rate of potential GDP. If the forecasts show that current tax and spending laws would result in a structural balance less than the target, then taxes or spending must be adjusted.

Unfortunately, there is no foolproof way to measure the economy's output gap exactly, let alone forecast it in advance. A study by the Federal Reserve showed that three of the most common estimation methods produced results for the output gap that sometimes varied by more than 2 percent of GDP.[1] Purely technical errors in forecasts of the output gap would probably be tolerable if they averaged out over time. A greater danger is that political pressures would introduce a chronic bias toward overly optimistic forecasts, since a more favorable output gap would justify tax cuts or spending increases that would please voters ahead of an upcoming election. Political bias and time inconsistency could seriously undermine the effectiveness of a structural budget rule.

To guard against political bias, Chile leaves the job of forecasting and measuring the output gap to an independent committee of experts. So far, the system has worked reasonably well for that country. If the United States were to adopt a structural balance rule, the forecasting might fall to the Congressional Budget Office—which, by law, operates on a nonpartisan basis—or it might go to some new group created for the purpose.

Balance over the Business Cycle

A structural balance rule like Chile's is a big improvement over one requiring an annually balanced budget, but not all economists see it as the best possible system. Critics note that although a structural balance rule is cyclically neutral and allows automatic stabilizers to operate, it does not allow the government to pursue an actively countercyclical fiscal policy.

One kind of policy rule that combines the discipline of a structural target with the flexibility to pursue countercyclical policy is to require that the budget be in balance, on average, over the business cycle. Sweden's budget system is an example. The Case for Discussion at the end of the chapter explains how the rule helped Sweden recover from a serious fiscal crisis in the 1990s. In outline, the rule consists of four main elements.

First, the Swedish rule requires the budget to show a surplus equal to 1 percent per year, on average, over the business cycle. Neither the actual nor the structural budget needs to be in balance every year. During a recession, the government can allow a countercyclical structural deficit, provided it offsets that deficit with a structural surplus during the next expansion.

Second, each year the government sets a budget limit for three years ahead; thus, each year's taxes and spending are set under a cap set three years previously. The purpose is to counteract the universal tendency of democratic governments to spend extra tax revenue as it comes in during years of economic expansion, rather than running surpluses as required for proper countercyclical fiscal policy.

The third element is the idea of a budget margin—that is, each year's spending should not push all the way to the cap. The margin gives room during the year to adjust to unexpected changes in inflation or real GDP.

Fourth, the whole process operates under the oversight of the independent Swedish Fiscal Policy Council, which has the job of ensuring that the government's policies, in fact, conform to the rules it has set for itself.

Balancing the budget over the business cycle seems to have worked well in Sweden. Germany and Switzerland use a variant of the policy that they call a "debt brake." There has been some discussion of making the policy mandatory for all EU members, but that has not happened yet, partly for reasons discussed in the next section.

In Search of Functional Sustainability

We have now looked at the issue of sustainability from several perspectives. We have seen that, at a minimum, a government must maintain solvency—the ability to meet its financial commitments in full and on time. For countries that do not issue their own currency, that maintain a fixed exchange rate, or that borrow heavily in foreign currencies, the need for solvency can be a tight constraint on the government budget. For countries like the United States, which has its own currency in which it can borrow both at home and abroad, actual insolvency is not a concern.

We have also discussed the simple mathematics of sustainability, which tells us that the debt ratio will remain constant over time if the primary structural balance is equal to the initial debt ratio times the difference between the interest rate and the rate of GDP growth. The formula for the steady-state value of the primary structural balance is not a solution to the problem of fiscal policy, however—only a starting point for discussion.

What we really need is something we might best call **functional sustainability**. Functional sustainability of fiscal policy means having a set of rules and decision-making procedures that adjust fiscal parameters over time to serve the goals of long-run stability and prosperity. Unfortunately, that is just what the US government lacks. Many years ago Herbert Stein, then chairman of the Council of Economic Advisers, wrote, "We have no long-run budget policy—no policy for the size of deficits and for the rate of growth of the public debt over a period of years." Each year, according to Stein, the president and Congress make short-term budgetary decisions that are wholly inconsistent with their declared long-run goals, hoping "that something will happen or be done before the long-run arises, but not yet."[2] What Stein wrote remains very much true today.

Functional sustainability is partly a matter of institutions. It is hard to define an optimal budget rule, and the parameters of any workable rule—including output gaps and future interest rates—are impossible to estimate with precision. Successful implementation of fiscal rules requires institutions and advisory bodies that are insulated from short-term political pressures.

Functional sustainability of fiscal policy does not mean that politicians must agree on everything. Rules like annual balance of the structural budget or countercyclical activism constrained by balance over the business cycle have no inherent ideological content. They could equally well be adapted to a big government with a generous social safety net; a big government with a strong defense establishment; or a small government limited to protecting property and enforcing the rule of law. Whatever political goals are pursued, functional sustainability of fiscal policy requires a degree of political maturity and a shared commitment across political parties that places the long-run goals of economic stability and prosperity above the pursuit of short-run partisan advantage.

Functional sustainability

When a country's fiscal policy has a set of rules and decision-making procedures that adjust fiscal parameters over time to serve the goals of long-run stability and prosperity

Summary

1. What are the conditions for maintaining long-run balance in an economy?

Imbalances among the major sectors of the economy can become barriers to stability and prosperity. Areas of concern include the balance between saving and investment, the balance between government and the private sector, and the external balance of imports, exports, and financial flows.

2. What is required for fiscal policy to be sustainable?

One perspective on fiscal sustainability emphasizes solvency. Maintaining solvency is a particular concern for countries that do not issue their own currencies or that borrow heavily in foreign currencies. Another perspective focuses on the rate of increase or decrease in the ratio of government debt to GDP. The debt ratio will remain stable over time if the primary structural balance is equal to the initial debt ratio multiplied by the difference between the interest rate and the rate of growth of GDP.

3. What are the consequences if fiscal policy becomes unsustainable?

A government whose fiscal policy has become unsustainable has three choices. First, it can default on its debt—that is, declare that it will not repay money that it has borrowed. Second, it can monetize the deficit—that is, pay for spending by printing money instead of borrowing. Third, the government can undertake fiscal consolidation—that is, reform its tax and spending practices in a way that makes fiscal policy sustainable again.

4. Is US fiscal policy sustainable?

The United States has its own currency and is able to borrow in dollars from lenders throughout the world. It faces no risk of insolvency. At the time of writing (2015), the primary structural balance on the consolidated accounts of all levels of government is close to, or slightly above, its steady-state value. The ratio of net government debt to GDP is somewhat higher than its historical average, but not remarkably high compared to the situation in other developed economies. However, the United States lacks the institutions and rules that would be required to place a priority on long-run stability, prosperity, and fiscal sustainability.

5. What kind of rules could ensure the sustainability of fiscal policy?

One possible fiscal policy rule would be to require that the budget be in balance every year, regardless of the state of the business cycle. The disadvantage of such a rule is that it would disable the operation of automatic stabilizers and would lead to procyclical changes in taxes and spending. Another possible rule would require holding the primary or overall structural budget to its steady-state value in each year, while allowing automatic stabilizers to produce deficits during recessions and surpluses during expansions. A third rule would be to require the budget to be in balance on average over the business cycle, while allowing discretionary countercyclical policy to speed recovery from recessions and to cool booms.

KEY TERMS

PROBLEMS AND TOPICS FOR DISCUSSION

1.   **Military spending**   In your view, how should military spending be integrated into fiscal policy? In cases of war or a foreign military emergency, should we allow spending to add to the budget deficit without limit? Or should we maintain budget discipline at all costs, cutting civilian programs or raising taxes as needed to finance unexpected military expenditures? Discuss the issue in the abstract. Then use your internet research skills to explore the budget policies used to pay for World War II and the recent military intervention in Iraq.

2.   **A balanced budget amendment**   There have been many attempts over the years to enact some form of balanced budget amendment. Several candidates in the 2016 US presidential election favored some version of such an amendment. Enter the term "balanced budget amendment" in your favorite search engine. Look at the details of at least one such amendment that is currently under discussion. Under that version of a balanced budget amendment, would fiscal policy be procyclical, countercyclical, or neutral over the business cycle? Explain.

3.   **China's external balance**   In the early 2000s, China experienced enormous current account surpluses, sometimes more than 10 percent of GDP. Apply your internet research skills to find the current trend of China's current account surplus or deficit. Have the large surpluses returned? Has China's trade balance moved toward deficit? Discuss the implications for the health of both the Chinese and US economies.

4.   **CBO budget projections**   Each year the Congressional Budget Office issues a report called *The Budget and Economic Outlook*. You can find the most recent report online by entering the term "Budget and Economic Outlook" in your favorite search engine. Download the latest version. According to CBO projections, does US federal fiscal policy look more sustainable, less sustainable, or about the same as when this chapter was written?

CASE *for* DISCUSSION

How Smart Budget Rules Saved Sweden from Fiscal Crisis

Sweden today has one of the stronger economies in the European Union. However, at least as far as fiscal policy is concerned, that was not always the case. As the chart shows, Sweden faced a serious fiscal crisis in the early 1990s.

The chart also shows that Sweden has staged a remarkable fiscal consolidation since that time. Its debt has fallen to a third of its former level, and the budget is now regularly in surplus. Sweden's recovery took place under a set of budget rules that emphasize balance, on average, over the business cycle, as described earlier in this chapter.

Technicalities of fiscal rules aside, does Sweden's experience hold any lessons for the United States?

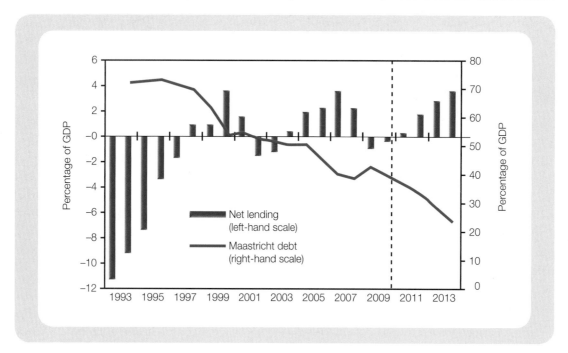

The first lesson is that the Swedish fiscal model in no way depends on a specific level of government spending. (Taking all levels of government together, government spending is about 52 percent of GDP in Sweden, compared to about 40 in the United States). Rather, the key is maintaining a rational balance between revenue and expenditure over the business cycle.

The second lesson is the need to strike a balance between flexibility and discipline. The appropriate balance may vary from one country to another. For example, Sweden's approach has a bit more flexibility in allowing for countercyclical policy and a bit less year-to-year discipline than Chile's, although both have met with success. A set of rules for the United States might need more of a tilt toward discipline, for two reasons.

One is the two-year US election cycle—the shortest among the world's major democracies. The short election cycle increases the pressure for government to spend increased revenues during an economic expansion rather than running the surplus needed for sustainable fiscal policy. It may be that the US political system is not mature enough to think three years ahead.

Another reason the United States needs to tilt toward discipline is the lower level of political consensus. In Sweden, the major political parties agree on the importance of following the rules. Look again at the chart of Sweden's debt and deficit since the fiscal reforms of the mid-1990s. The chart shows no sign of any disturbance as the government changed from social democratic to center-right and back again. Compare that to the radical change from the budget discipline of the Clinton years to the tax cuts and deficits of the Bush years. It would have taken a very strong set of chains indeed to prevent euphoric Republicans from squandering the once-in-a-lifetime budget surpluses they inherited after the election of 2000.

The third lesson is that, although the United States may need a stronger dose of fiscal discipline than Sweden does, discipline can also be too tight. Many critics fault the United States for being too aggressive in reducing its structural budget deficit at the expense of slowing recovery from the Great Recession. The proposed annual balance requirement favored by many US politicians would make the risk of procyclical fiscal policy considerably greater.

Finally, the most important lesson from the Swedish experience is a hopeful one: Fiscal consolidation is at least sometimes possible in a modern democracy. Sweden's position in the early 1990s had some striking parallels with that of the United States today. It had experienced a sharp recession following the collapse of a housing bubble. Its banking system had nearly collapsed and required a costly government rescue. The deficit reached 11 percent of GDP, and debt was around 70 percent, close to today's US numbers. Yet the country got back on track. It established a set of budget rules that all political parties could live with. The 2008 global crisis shook the Swedish economy, but Sweden recovered more quickly than most. It could happen here.

Sources: The chart is based on Convergence Program for Sweden, 2011 Update, Government Offices of Sweden (http://www.government. se/contentassets/082902bf1810471f863016acb882038c/convergence-programme-for-sweden---2011-uppdate). This case contains material from "How Smart Fiscal Rules Keep Sweden's Budget in Balance," Ed Dolan's Econ Blog, July 31, 2011 (http://bvtlab.com/7697q), used by permission of the author.

Questions

1. Do you think Sweden's fiscal policy was sustainable as of the early 1990s? Is it sustainable today? Discuss, based on the requirements for sustainability given in this chapter.

2. Are Sweden's fiscal policy rules procyclical, countercyclical, or neutral over the business cycle? Explain your answer based on material from this case and from the last section of the chapter itself.

3. Given the differences between Swedish and US politics, do you think the United States should look for more discipline and less flexibility than Sweden, or more flexibility and less discipline? Discuss.

4. Using a data source such as Eurostat, the OECD Statistical Annex, the IMF, or TradingEconomics.com, look for recent trends in GDP growth, the government budget deficit, and the ratio of debt to GDP in Sweden. Comment on those trends in light of this case study.

From Ed Dolan's Econ Blog

Ed Dolan's econ blog offers several posts and slideshows related to topics in this chapter.

For an overview, see the slideshow "Is the Government Debt Out of Control," which summarizes the mathematics of deficits and debts as given in this chapter and presents additional charts and numerical examples. Follow the link, http://bvtlab.com/563bJ, or scan the QR code.

For details on Chilean budget rules, see "How Intelligent Budget Rules Help Chile Prosper: Lessons for the US." Follow the link, http://bvtlab.com/93866, or scan the QR code.

Additional information on the Swedish experience with budget rules is given in "How Smart Fiscal Rules Keep Sweden's Budget in Balance." Follow the link, http://bvtlab.com/9JkCA, or scan the QR code.

For a critique of one variant of a proposed US balanced budget amendment, see "Yes, the US Needs Fiscal Policy Rules, but Not Hatch-Lee." Follow the link, http://bvtlab.com/Y727T, or scan the QR code.

Endnotes

1. Michael T. Kiley, "Output Gaps," *Financial and Economic Discussion Series* 2010-27, Federal Reserve Board, Washington, DC, March 18, 2010 (http://www.federalreserve.gov/pubs/feds/2010/201027/201027pap.pdf).

2. Herbert Stein, "After the Ball," *AEI Economist* (December 1984): 2.

CHAPTER 14

FIGHTING INFLATION AND DEFLATION

AFTER READING THIS CHAPTER,
you will understand the following:

1. The distinction between demand-side and supply-side inflation
2. The Phillips curve and its interpretation
3. Hyperinflation and how to combat it
4. Why demand-side deflation is harmful and what policies can prevent or reverse it
5. Supply-side deflation driven by productivity
6. The dangers of asset price bubbles

BEFORE READING THIS CHAPTER,
make sure you know the following concepts:

Aggregate supply and demand

Exchange rates

Accommodating monetary policy

Equation of exchange

Deflation

Real and nominal interest rates

Operating targets and intermediate targets

Taylor rule

NGDP targeting

Monetization

Quantitative easing

CHAPTER
Outline

There is no realistic way to eliminate the business cycle completely. The economy is subject to too many shocks from within and without, and, as we saw in Chapter 11, lags and forecasting errors make precise fine-tuning impossible. At best, by following preset rules and avoiding shortsighted policies that make matters worse, it is possible to avoid extremes of instability.

Unfortunately, policymakers do not always manage to avoid those extremes. They make mistakes that lead to booms and busts. The previous two chapters focused on the problem of recovering from recessions. This chapter turns to the problem of inflation. First, we look at some of the variants of inflation and policies to combat them. Then we turn to deflation, a problem that has reemerged as a topic of concern in the twenty-first century.

14.1 INFLATION

Inflation, in modern economics, means a sustained increase in the average price level. It is not an especially precise term. As Chapter 6 explained, there are many different ways of measuring inflation. The Fed currently considers anything above 2 percent annual inflation, as measured by the personal consumption deflator from the national income accounts, to be excessive—although some would draw the line at a higher or lower rate.

A few economists object in principle to defining inflation in terms of the price level. They prefer an older approach that defines inflation as a rapid increase in the quantity of money in circulation. As we will see later in the chapter, the rate of increase in the money stock can exercise a strong influence over the rate of increase of prices under certain conditions.

14.1a Inflation in the Aggregate Supply and Demand Model

Since Chapter 10, one of our main tools for understanding the macroeconomy has been the aggregate supply and demand model. We have shown how changes in the behavior of households and firms, and in fiscal and monetary policy, can shift the aggregate demand curve to the right or left. We have seen how the short-run aggregate supply curve shifts up or down with changes in expectations about the level of wages and other input prices. We have seen how the economy tends to move, with a lag, toward a long-run equilibrium at the natural level of real output—although new shocks may disturb it again before the adjustment is complete. In this section, we use the aggregate supply and demand model to identify types of inflation, and we look at the processes that set inflation in motion.

Demand-Side Inflation **Demand-side inflation** occurs when the aggregate demand curve shifts up and to the right while the short-run aggregate supply curve remains fixed or shifts upward at no more than an equal rate.

The simplest form of demand-side inflation begins with a one-time shift in the aggregate demand curve, starting from equilibrium. The economy first moves up and to the right along the aggregate supply curve to a new short-run equilibrium. Real output and the price level increase while the unemployment rate falls. After a lag, expectations regarding wages and other input prices begin to adjust, and the short-run aggregate supply curve starts to shift upward. If the aggregate demand curve remains in its new position, the economy moves up and to the left along it to a new long-run equilibrium, where real output returns to its natural level and unemployment returns to its natural rate.

Such a one-time shift in the aggregate demand curve is not the only form of demand-side inflation; nor is it even the most common one. Instead, as shown in Figure 14–1, sustained expansionary policy often allows aggregate demand to grow continuously. In

Demand-side inflation

Inflation caused by an upward shift of the aggregate demand curve while the aggregate supply curve remains fixed or shifts upward at no more than an equal rate

that case, as expectations of higher input prices shift the short-run aggregate supply curve upward from AS_1 to AS_2 and then to AS_3; the aggregate demand curve keeps pace with it moving to AD_2, and then AD_3. Real output does not fall back toward its natural level; rather, the economy moves straight upward along the path from E_1 to E_2 to E_3 and beyond.

The scenario shown in Figure 14–1 has major implications for economic policy. In the short run, starting from a state of long-run equilibrium, expansionary fiscal or monetary policy is effective in stimulating real economic growth and lowering unemployment as the economy moves from E_0 to E_1. The initial cost is only a little inflation. However, those initial gains in real output can be sustained only at the cost of ongoing demand-side

FIGURE 14–1

Demand-Side Inflation

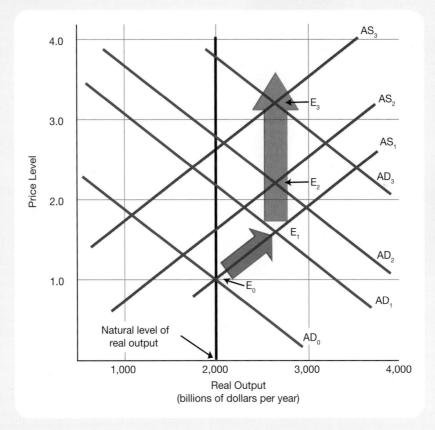

Demand-side inflation begins when a rightward shift in the aggregate demand curve moves the economy up and to the right along the short-run aggregate supply curve from E_0 to E_1. Soon, the short-run aggregate supply curve begins to shift upward as increases in final-goods prices filter through to cause expected increases in wages and other input prices. If expansionary policy continues to shift the aggregate demand curve as shown, real output can remain above its natural level for a sustained period. However, the cost of doing so will be ongoing inflation.

inflation. Although it is not directly apparent from Figure 14–1, a rate of inflation that is constant from year to year may not be enough to hold unemployment below its natural rate. Under plausible assumptions regarding the formation of expectations, inflation must accelerate to a higher rate each year to sustain a positive output gap.

Once the economy has achieved the initial gain in real output, policymakers face a dilemma. One choice is to stop the stimulus. If they do that, inflation will slow and eventually stop; however, output will fall back to its natural level, and unemployment will increase. The other choice is to continue expansionary policy. In that case, it is possible to maintain the positive output gap for an extended period. Choosing that path, however, will mean year after year of ever-faster inflation.

Supply-Side Inflation and Supply Shocks

Inflation can begin, instead, with an upward shift in the aggregate supply curve. The upward movement of the aggregate supply curve is the result of increases in expected wages and other input prices, which push up costs of production. We call the result **supply-side inflation**.

Supply shocks are one source of supply-side inflation. A supply shock is any event that changes the average level of expected input prices but does not arise from changes in aggregate demand. Increases in global commodity prices (oil, food, metals, and others) are examples of supply shocks. An increase in commodity prices affects expected input prices through two main channels. First, commodities like oil and metals are inputs for many firms, and their prices directly affect the expected costs of production. In addition, firms will expect that rising prices of commodities like food and fuel will affect the cost of living for their workers, so that they will sooner or later have to adjust nominal wages.

Commodity prices are one of the most common sources of supply shocks, but they are not the only one. Unusually bad weather raises expected costs in farming, construction, and transportation. Natural disasters, like earthquakes or hurricanes, raise costs of doing business in the affected areas and drive up prices of construction materials even outside those areas. Finally, changes in exchange rates affect the prices of inputs that a country imports. For example, a depreciation of the dollar relative to foreign currencies makes imported inputs (say, imported steel used by an appliance maker) more expensive. It may also increase demand for US exports of raw materials, farm products, chemicals, and other goods, thereby driving up their prices.

A natural disaster such as Hurricane Katrina can cause a supply shock. (Wikimedia Commons)

Supply-side inflation

Inflation that begins with an upward shift in the aggregate supply curve while the aggregate demand curve remains fixed or shifts upward more slowly

Supply shock

An event not arising from changes in aggregate demand that changes the average level of expected input prices

Supply shocks can work both ways. Just as increases in world commodity prices raise expected input prices, decreases in commodity prices reduce them. Similarly, unusually good weather that produces bumper crops or an appreciation of a country's currency would tend to cause decreases in expected input prices.

Figure 14–2 illustrates the short-run effects of a supply shock. In the figure, the economy begins in equilibrium at E_0. At that point, something—say a devastating hurricane—causes an increase in the expected level of input prices. As firms adjust their expectations, the short-run aggregate supply curve shifts upward from AS_0 to AS_1. With the higher expected level of input prices, but no matching increase in aggregate demand, firms must revise their production and pricing plans. As they raise prices to cover increased production costs, they find that it is no longer profitable to produce

FIGURE 14–2

Short-Run Effects of a Supply Shock

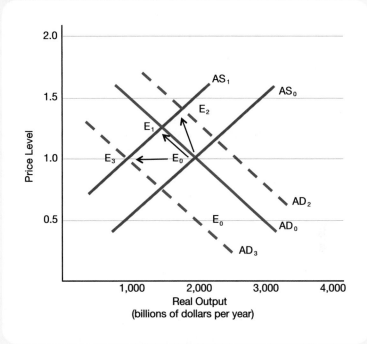

Beginning from E_0, suppose a supply shock shifts the aggregate supply curve from AS_0 to AS_1. If there is no change in aggregate demand, the economy will move from E_0 to E_1 along AD_0. The economy will experience supply-side inflation accompanied by falling real output. If the Fed uses expansionary monetary policy to partially accommodate the supply shock, shifting the aggregate demand curve to AD_2, the economy will instead end up at E_2. The supply shock will then have less impact on real output, but there will be more inflation. If the Fed follows a strict zero-inflation policy, it must shift the aggregate demand curve to AD_3. The economy will then end up at some place like E_3. There will be a greater loss of real output, but less inflation.

as much as before. The whole economy moves upward and to the left along aggregate demand curve AD_0 to E_1.

What happens next depends on how policymakers adjust aggregate demand. The hurricane has caused real damage to the economy. Even if people work just as many hours as before, the total quantity of goods and services available for consumption, investment, government purchases, and net exports will be less. If, as is likely, some people lose their jobs, there will be even more economic damage that no possible policies can fully offset. However, monetary policy can influence how much of the damage takes the form of lower real output and how much takes the form of inflation.

The movement along AD_0 from E_0 to E_1 assumes that the Fed does not use its policy instruments actively. That could happen simply through inaction or because the Fed consciously pursues a policy of targeting nominal GDP.[1] In either case, the damage of the supply shock is absorbed more or less evenly between inflation and unemployment.

Instead, the Fed could soften the effect on real GDP by using expansionary or monetary policy to accommodate the shock. Doing so would shift the aggregate demand curve to the right, to a position like AD_2 in Figure 14–2. In that case, the economy will move toward a point like E_2, where real output is higher but the price level is also higher than at E_1.

The accommodating policy does not undo all of the harm from the supply shock, but it changes the nature of its impact. There will be a smaller impact on output and employment. Firms outside the area affected by the hurricane can add shifts and increase output, creating jobs for some of the people thrown out of work by the storm; emergency government spending can put people to work repairing storm damage; and so on. At the same time, the accommodating policy produces a higher rate of inflation than there otherwise would have been.

Finally, the Fed could instead pursue a strict target of zero inflation. To do so, it would have to shift the aggregate demand curve leftward to AD_3. The economy would move to a point like E_3, where there would be no inflation but a larger loss of real output and higher unemployment. If the Fed had an inflation target that was greater than zero, the shift in demand would not be as strong and the economy would end up somewhere between E_3 and E_1.

Inflationary Expectations and Inflationary Recession

Supply shocks are not the only source of supply-side inflation. Prior experience with demand-side inflation can also cause supply-side inflation. To understand why, we need to look more closely at the way firms and workers form their expectations about input prices.

Up to this point, we have assumed that firms expect the level of input prices in the current year to be equal to the level of final-goods prices in the previous year. In practice, though, they may expect prices to continue rising in the future, instead of coming to a halt at the level they reached as a result of last year's inflation. If so, that will affect firms' pricing and production plans for the coming year.

A simple assumption that captures this behavior is that firms expect wages and other input prices in the coming year to increase by the same percentage as they did the year before. We call such a tendency of firms and workers to expect prices to continue rising in the future at the same rate as in the immediate past **inflation inertia** or **inflation momentum**.

Figure 14–3 shows what happens when inflation inertia becomes established. The story begins from a situation of ongoing demand-side inflation similar to the one shown in Figure 14–1. Expansionary fiscal or monetary policy has held output above its natural level for some time. The economy is moving upward along the arrow through E_1 and E_2. Because of past inflation, firms and workers expect more inflation in the future and have adjusted their plans to cope with it as best they can. The inflation momentum built into their plans causes repeated upward shifts of the short-run aggregate supply curve.

What happens if, after the economy has reached E_2, policymakers attempt to stop inflation by halting the growth of aggregate demand? The result, as seen in Figure 14–3, is to stop the upward shift of the aggregate demand curve, leaving it in the position AD_2.

Halting the growth of aggregate demand will not stop inflation in its tracks. Firms and workers have grown used to inflation and expect it to continue. Workers, expecting their costs of living to rise further, will have done their best to make contracts with their employers that give them compensating wage increases as the cost of living rises. Firms expect their input prices to rise further and will have become used to passing the increases along to their customers. As long as firms expect their input prices to continue rising and set their own prices and output plans on that basis, the short-run aggregate supply curve will continue to shift upward.

Inflation inertia (inflation momentum)

A tendency of firms and workers to expect prices to continue rising in the future at the same rate as in the immediate past

FIGURE 14–3

Inflationary Recession

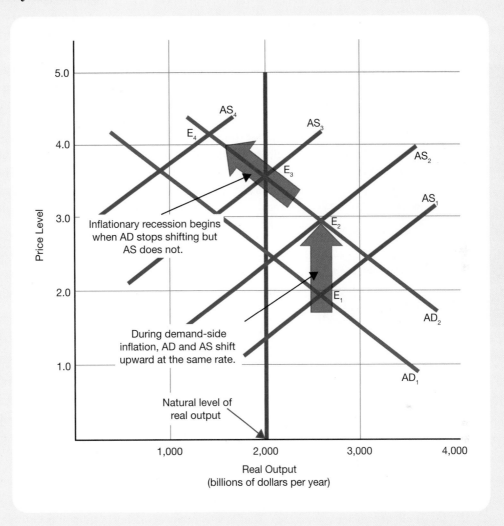

An inflationary recession occurs when aggregate demand slows or stops growing following a period of sustained inflation. In this figure, the aggregate demand curve stops shifting after the economy reaches E_2. Firms expect the level of input prices to continue to rise; thus, the short-run aggregate supply curve moves up to AS_3 in the next year and to AS_4 in the year after that. As it does, the economy enters a recession during which the price level continues to rise. For a time, the inflation rate may actually increase as real output falls.

With the aggregate supply curve moving upward while the aggregate demand curve stays put, real output starts to decrease and unemployment to increase. Meanwhile, the price level keeps rising. The economy will move along AD_2 toward point E_3 in Figure 14–3, where real output has returned to its natural level; but that is not the end of the story. Because firms and workers all saw inflation continue as the economy moved from E_2 to E_3, they will not expect inflation to stop now. As long as firms anticipate a further increase in the prices of final goods, they will continue to expect rising input prices. As a result, inflation momentum will continue to shift the aggregate supply curve further upward. As the economy moves along the aggregate demand curve toward a position like E_4, the economy experiences an **inflationary recession**—an episode in which inflation, rising unemployment, and a negative output gap all occur at the same time.[2]

What can policymakers do to bring the economy out of an inflationary recession? A "cold turkey" approach would be to sit tight and keep the lid on aggregate demand. At E_4, there is a negative output gap, accompanied by rising unemployment, declining sales, and an unplanned inventory buildup. The gap would, in time, cause firms and workers to revise their expectations about the rate of inflation for both inputs and final goods. Prices of raw materials would begin to fall. Workers, seeing first a slowing of the rise in the cost of living and then an actual decline, would accept lower nominal wages. Lower levels of expected input prices would cause the aggregate supply curve to begin shifting downward. Slowly the economy would slip back down along the aggregate demand curve toward equilibrium at E_3, but the experience would be a painful one.

Eliminating inflation, once it has become established, can be a painful process accompanied by high unemployment. (Shutterstock)

A more moderate approach would be to slow the growth of aggregate demand gradually rather than stopping it cold. With luck, this could bring the economy to a "soft landing" at the natural level of real output. It might take longer to slow inflation this way, but it might also be possible to avoid a severe recession.

In practice, there is a danger that politically driven time inconsistency will prevent smooth adjustment. Policymakers may first respond to pressures to "do something" about inflation by stopping the growth of aggregate demand altogether, and then react to pressures to "do something" about unemployment by renewing demand growth before inflation inertia has been broken. Such a "stop-go" policy would result in a highly unstable path for the economy over time. The instability of the US economy in the 1960s and 1970s, which we discussed in *Applying Economic Ideas 11.1* (Chapter 11), appears to fit this pattern of repeated inflationary recessions and time-inconsistent overreactions to them.

The truth is that no one knows a quick, painless way to stop inflation once it takes hold in public expectations. That is why many economists think it is better to keep inflation under control in the first place by using inflation targeting, NGDP targeting, or some other preset rule.

Inflationary recession

An episode in which real output falls toward or below its natural level and unemployment rises toward or above its natural rate while rapid inflation continues

Phillips curve

A graph showing the relationship between the inflation rate and the unemployment rate, other things being equal

14.1b The Phillips Curve

At several points, our examples have suggested an inverse relationship between inflation and unemployment. The initial effect of expansionary policy is to move the economy up and to the right along the short-run aggregate supply curve. As it does so, unemployment falls and inflation rises. Over a longer period, policymakers can keep unemployment below its natural rate by a policy of continuous expansion, but doing so has the side effect of accelerating inflation. On the down side, contractionary policy aimed at slowing inflation has the initial effect of reducing real output and raising unemployment.

We can represent this inverse relationship between inflation and unemployment by using a graph called a **Phillips curve**, named for A. W. H. Phillips, who first described it in a 1958 paper (see *Who Said It? Who Did It? 14.1*).[3]

Who Said It? Who Did It? **14.1**

A. W. H. Phillips and the Phillips Curve

The reputation of Alban W. H. Phillips, known to his friends as Bill, rests on a single paper he wrote on the right topic and published at the right time. In the late 1950s, the connection between inflation and unemployment was a major focus of macroeconomic theory. In an article in the journal *Economica* in 1958, Phillips presented a set of graphs that suggested a stable, inverse relationship between inflation and unemployment. The paper did not contain much by way of a theory to explain the relationship, but the

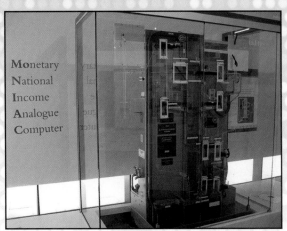

Monetary National Income Analogue Computer

(iStock)

author's curves became a peg on which future writers hung their discussions of the problem. Every subsequent article on inflation and unemployment discussed the shape of the Phillips curve that best served as a policy target, how best to shift the Phillips curve, and so on. Today the term is so familiar that Phillips' name enjoys a sort of immortality, even though Phillips left further development of the inflation-unemployment relationship to others.

Phillips was born in New Zealand in 1914. He moved to Australia at the age of 16, worked there as an apprentice electrician in a mine, and learned electrical engineering skills. In 1937, he immigrated to Britain. He served in World War II and spent time in a Japanese prison camp. After the war, he studied at the London School of Economics and later joined the faculty there. He stayed at LSE until 1967, when he moved to Australian National University.

Phillips's early hands-on engineering training seems to have influenced his approach to economic problems. One of his early projects at LSE was to construct a hydraulic analog computer called the Monetary National Income Analog Computer (MONIAC). The device simulated the circular flow of income and product in the economy. By adjusting valves on the computer, the operator could send flows of water representing saving, taxes, government spending, and other variables through a series of pipes and tanks. The MONIAC foreshadowed the widespread use of computers in modern economic research. Phillips made several copies of his machine, some of which are still in working order.

The Phillips Curve as a Policy Menu Figure 14–4 Part (a) shows a representative Phillips curve. During the 1960s, when the curve first attracted economists' attention, many viewed it as a menu of policy choices. Political liberals argued that policymakers should choose a point such as L on the Phillips curve; this point would "buy" full employment and prosperity at the price of a modest inflation rate. Conservatives objected to any but the slightest degree of inflation and argued for a point such as C, which would achieve price stability at the expense of some jobs.

FIGURE 14–4

A Representative Phillips Curve

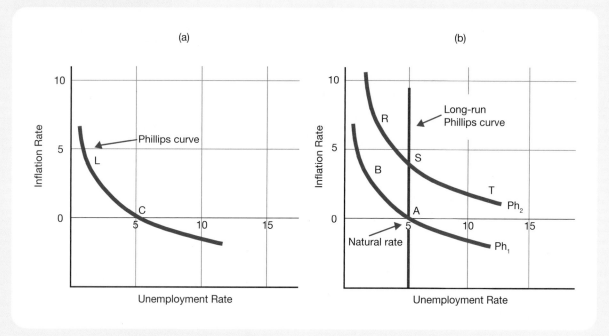

In the 1960s, many economists saw the Phillips curve as a policy menu, as shown in Part (a) of this figure. Political liberals could choose a point of permanent low unemployment with some inflation (L), while conservatives could choose permanent low inflation with higher unemployment (C). Later it became apparent that the Phillips curve could shift over time as inflation expectations adjust to past inflation. In Part (b), if inflation increased from 0 to 4 percent, the economy would at first move from A to B along Ph_1. Once people came to expect 4 percent inflation, the curve would shift up to Ph_2. Further changes in inflation would move the economy along Ph_2, in the short run, until expectations changed again.

Economists soon discovered a problem with viewing the Phillips curve as a policy menu: the choices it offered kept changing while the meal was in progress. As the 1960s unfolded, economists began to notice that inflation-unemployment points for recent years did not fit the curves they had plotted using data from the 1950s. It became common to speak of an upward drift of the Phillips curve. A given level of inflation would "buy" increasingly smaller reductions in unemployment.

If upward drift of the Phillips curve had been due to factors outside their control, policymakers could have chosen their preferred point on a new, higher Phillips curve. In the 1970s, however, perceptions of the Phillips curve started to change. It began to appear that the very policies that had sought to move the economy along the curve were causing it to shift.

The Phillips Curve in the Long Run   The key to this view of the Phillips curve lies in the distinction between long-run and short-run effects of changes in aggregate demand. A once-and-for-all rise in the level of aggregate demand leads only to a temporary reduction in unemployment. The reason is that expectations soon adjust to past inflation, causing an upward shift in the aggregate supply curve. Real output can rise above its natural level only as long as the short-run aggregate supply curve does not completely catch up with the shifting aggregate demand curve.

In the aggregate supply and demand model, unemployment is at its natural rate only when the expected inflation rate equals the actual inflation rate and when the inflation rate is neither accelerating nor decelerating. Those conditions can prevail when the expected and actual rates of inflation both are zero—but that is not the only possibility. Unemployment can also be at its natural rate when the economy is in a moving equilibrium with a constant, positive inflation rate to which everyone has become accustomed.

Figure 14–4 Part (b) shows this expectation-dependent view of the Phillips curve. The diagram includes two short-run Phillips curves, each corresponding to a different expected inflation rate. If the expected rate of inflation is zero, the Phillips curve takes the position Ph_1. The intersection of that Phillips curve with the horizontal axis occurs at the natural rate of unemployment, which we assume here to be 5 percent. If the actual inflation rate unexpectedly goes up to 4 percent, the economy will move upward and to the left along Phillips curve Ph_1 from point A to point B. We could show the same thing using an aggregate supply and demand diagram, where it would appear as a movement upward and to the right along the economy's short-run aggregate supply curve.

If the inflation rate remains at 4 percent per year, people will sooner or later adjust their expectations accordingly. We would show that in the aggregate supply and demand model as an upward shift in the aggregate supply curve. In Figure 14–4 Part (b), the same adjustment of expectations causes an upward shift of the short-run Phillips curve to Ph_2. As a result, the economy moves to point R.

Once the Phillips curve has shifted, the economy can make short-run movements upward or downward along it, depending on what happens to inflation. If inflation increases to 8 percent while people expect it to remain at 4 percent, the economy will, in the short run, move from R to S along Ph_2. If inflation slows to 2 percent while people expect it to remain at 4 percent, the economy at first will move from point R to point T. However, those movements along the short-run Phillips curve would not represent new points of long-run equilibrium. If some inflation rate other than 4 percent persists long enough for people to adjust to it, the short-run Phillips curve will shift again.

We can summarize the expectation-dependent view of the Phillips curve by saying that, in addition to a whole set of short-run curves, there is also a vertical long-run Phillips curve, as shown in Figure 14–4 Part (b). That conclusion follows from two familiar ideas. The first is that unemployment is at its natural rate whenever the actual and expected inflation rates are equal; the second is that people will expect any given steady rate of inflation to continue. The vertical long-run Phillips curve intersects the horizontal axis at the natural rate of unemployment. Each short-run Phillips curve intersects the long-run Phillips curve at the expected inflation rate for which the short-run curve is drawn. Unemployment will be at its natural rate only when the actual and expected inflation rates are equal.

What Has Happened to the Phillips Curve?   The expectations-dependent view of the Phillips curve appeared to provide a convincing explanation of the dynamics of inflation and unemployment during the 1960s and 1970s. After the mid-1980s, the average rate of inflation in the United States decreased. The negative relationship between inflation and unemployment became much less pronounced during the economic expansions of the 1990s and early 2000s. Then, during the long recovery from the Great Recession, the Phillips curve seemed to disappear altogether.

Figure 14–5 shows quarterly data for the period from the peak of unemployment in the fourth quarter of 2009 through the end of 2015. During this period, the unemployment rate decreased in all but one quarter, moving the economy from right to left along the curve and the trend line shown in the diagram. By the fourth quarter of 2015, inflation had fallen to just half its peak value. However, inflation did not increase, as the Phillips curve would predict. Instead, the inflation rate moved irregularly lower over the period, with a distinct downward trend.

What appears to have happened is a change in the behavior of inflation expectations. Despite the decrease in unemployment over the period, there is no sign that people expected any acceleration in future increases in the consumer price index (CPI). That, in turn, very likely reflects a change in expectations about the way the Fed would conduct monetary policy. In the 1960s and 1970s, the main driver of the upward-shifting Phillips curve appears to have been a belief that the Fed would hold off cyclical tightening of monetary policy until inflation was well underway. Now the expectation seems to be that the Fed will take its commitment to inflation at or below 2 percent seriously, and it will begin to tighten policy before inflation takes root. Congress reinforced the expectation of low inflation by tightening fiscal policy, as measured by the primary structural deficit, while unemployment was still high and real output was still well below its natural level. Until there is a change in the behavior of the makers of monetary and fiscal policy, the Phillips curve is likely to remain dormant.

FIGURE 14–5

Inflation and Unemployment in the Great Recession

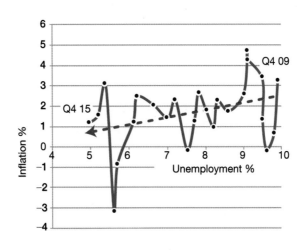

This figure tracks inflation and unemployment during the Great Recession. Each point on the curve represents the inflation and unemployment rates for a calendar quarter, beginning from the peak rate of inflation in the fourth quarter of 2009, near the upper right corner of the diagram. From there, the economy moved irregularly to the left as unemployment decreased in all but one quarter through the fourth quarter of 2015. The rate of inflation varied from quarter to quarter, but on average, it trended lower, not higher, as posited by the Phillips curve.

Source: Bureau of Labor Statistics.

14.1c Hyperinflation

The aggregate supply and demand model has proved useful to understanding the experience of economies with low to moderate inflation, but for more extreme inflation, or **hyperinflation**, we need a different approach. There is no precise cutoff between moderate inflation and hyperinflation. One classic study drew the line at an inflation rate of 50 percent per month, which, when compounded, is equivalent to about 14,000 percent per year. Others consider any rate of 1,000 percent per year or more to be hyperinflation. Some of the symptoms of hyperinflation begin to appear at rates as low as 100 percent per year. The upper limits of hyperinflation are extremely high, as discussed in *Economics in the News 14.1*.

Hyperinflation

Very rapid inflation

Economics in the News 14.1

Hyperinflation, Then and Now

One hundred trillion dollars for a loaf of bread? Impossible? Not if we are talking about Zimbabwe dollars. When Zimbabwe's inflation rate hit a high of 518 quintillion percent per year in 2008, the largest bill printed by the central bank, one hundred trillion dollars, was not quite enough to buy a loaf of bread.

At the peak of its hyperinflation, Zimbabwe's economy was in a state of total collapse. Production was at a virtual halt, and more than half the labor force was out of work. All countries that have experienced hyperinflation have shared that experience. Their economies, and often their governments, too, simply fall apart. With prices changing so fast, money loses its ability to function as a store of value and unit of account. Without money, any but the simplest economic activity is impossible.

Still, some economists argue that Zimbabwe's inflation was not an all-time record. They maintain that the record still belongs to Hungary, which, in 1946–1947, saw prices increase at a rate of … well, it is hard to put it in words. Most people don't even know what a "quintillion" is (it is a one followed by 18 zeros). Even fewer people would be able to properly express Hungary's inflation rate as "three octillion percent" (a three followed by 27 zeros).

Cases like Hungary and Zimbabwe make the 1993 hyperinflation in Yugoslavia, at 3 trillion percent, seem tame. The most famous hyper-inflation in history, 1923 in Germany, was a mere 300 million percent; but even that caused enough damage to help set the stage for the rise of Hitler's Nazi party a few years later.

In 2008, Zimbabwe saw an inflation rate of 518 quintillion percent. The largest bill printed, one hundred trillion Zimbabwe dollars, was not enough to buy a loaf of bread. (Shutterstock)

We don't need astronomical numbers for inflation to be harmful, however. Inflation of 2,000 percent per year in Argentina in 1991 brought down the government. Inflation at about the same rate in Russia in 1992, the year after the collapse of the Soviet Union, did not cause the fall of the government, but it undermined the credibility of the country's young democracy and market economy in ways that have not yet been forgotten.

More recently, Venezuela has been the world's inflation leader. In 2014, when the official inflation rate had not quite reached 100 percent, that country's government was sufficiently frightened to suspend the publication of official inflation statistics. However, it took no effective measures to actually slow increases in the price level. By the end of 2015, independent observers estimated that inflation was approaching 1,000 percent per year. The real economy, predictably, was in free fall.

We can be thankful that true hyperinflation is not common, but it is so frightening when it happens that central bankers around the world make avoiding even the possibility of hyperinflation one of their highest priorities.

The Dynamics of Hyperinflation

Hyperinflation, like any kind of inflation, begins when aggregate demand exceeds aggregate supply, putting upward pressure on prices; but the aggregate supply and demand model provides only a starting point to understand it. Instead, we need to look at the interaction of all the variables of the equation of exchange, $MV = PQ$.

Historically, war has often been the trigger to hyperinflation—World War I in the case of the German hyperinflation, World War II in the Hungarian case, and civil war in the Yugoslav episode. War puts a double squeeze on aggregate supply and demand. First, it increases aggregate demand, in that the government needs to spend more to buy military supplies and pay the salaries of its troops, shifting the aggregate demand curve to the right. At the same time, war disrupts production, shifting the aggregate supply curve to the left. The price level starts to rise.

When civilians see prices rising and goods disappearing from stores, they fear that the situation will only get worse. They try to protect themselves by spending whatever money they have as quickly as possible, before prices rise further and while there are still any goods at all to buy. When that happens, velocity—the V in the equation of exchange—begins to increase. Velocity means the number of times per year, on average, people use each unit of the money stock to make purchases. With prices rising daily, people learn that they should spend any money they earn as soon as they get it. The faster they run to the store to buy things, the less time they hold on to their money, and the more rapidly the money circulates through the economy.

If the nominal quantity of money in circulation were constant, inflation would eventually burn itself out because there are limits to how much velocity can increase. Suppose, for example, that the disruption of war cut real output in half and that velocity increased by a factor of fifty. A quick check of the equation of exchange shows that would only push the price level up by a factor of one hundred. The million and billion percent rates of inflation seen in real hyperinflations cannot take place without additional fuel in the form of additional money. Added to the increase in velocity and the decrease in output that is already underway, the increase in the nominal money stock adds even more fuel to the upward trend of the price level.

The entry point for most, if not all, of the new money is government spending. War and inflation disrupt not only the real economy but also the financial economy. The ability of the government to collect taxes cannot keep pace with the rise in prices, so the government's deficit increases. It covers the deficit either by simply printing paper money or by borrowing from the central bank and using the proceeds of the borrowing to make payments through the banking system.

As hyperinflation proceeds, the government adds more and more zeros to the currency, giving rise to collector's items like the trillion dollar bills printed in Zimbabwe. Paradoxically, though, the real quantity of money (M divided by P) *decreases* during hyperinflation. That is a simple arithmetic outcome of the fact that within the equation $MV = PQ$, V is rising and Q is falling at the same time that M is increasing. On the street, merchants and their customers are likely to complain of a shortage of currency to carry out everyday transactions.

Ending Hyperinflation

The good news about hyperinflation is that it does not go on forever. Sooner or later, suddenly or gradually, it ends. Most hyperinflations end in one of two ways.

It is sometimes possible to end moderate hyperinflation—for example, Russia's 2,000 percent inflation—with conventional tightening of monetary and fiscal policy. After 1993, the Russian government gradually stopped monetizing its deficit. It began to borrow more, both on domestic and foreign credit markets; and it printed less money. As inflation slowed, it became possible to reduce the deficit. By 1996, inflation was down to about 10 percent per year.

Conventional policy like Russia's is not the only way to end hyperinflation, nor is it always the best. Many countries have instead used an approach called **exchange-rate-based stabilization (ERB stabilization)**. Exchange-rate-based stabilization is an approach to the control of hyperinflation that emphasizes a fixed exchange rate relative to some stable currency, like the dollar or euro. The exchange rate acts as a "nominal anchor" that provides a fixed point of reference for everyone in the economy. People no longer have to deal with nominal values—nominal wages, nominal interest rates, nominal taxes—that increase by thousands or millions of percent each month and make it difficult to focus on the underlying real values when making production and investment decisions. Instead, ERB stabilization introduces a stable unit of account, based on the chosen stable currency, that allows everyone to get back to the real business of working, running a firm, or providing for a family.

An important part of the nominal-anchor principal is its impact on velocity. As long as the local currency is subject to rapid inflation, no one wants to hold on to paper currency or bank balances. Everyone tries to spend money as fast as possible, driving up velocity and making inflation worse. As soon as the government redefines money as having a fixed value relative to a reliable currency, people's attitudes change. There is now no "inflation tax" to pay if a person decides to hold on to some of Friday's pay to spend for groceries on Monday. As we can see from the equation of exchange, a decrease in velocity immediately slows—or even reverses—the rate of increase of the price level. During the period of a few weeks or months that it takes for velocity to return to normal, the government has a chance to bring the budget under control, and private firms have a chance to get their businesses in order and restore the growth of real output. If all goes well, the economy returns to stability.

There is more than one way to implement ERB stabilization. Some countries directly adopt another country's stable currency as their legal tender. For example, Ecuador adopted the US dollar as its currency in 2000 to end a hyperinflation, using a process called *dollarization*. Other countries keep their own currency in name only and peg it at a fixed ratio to a stable currency following an arrangement called a *currency board*. Argentina successfully ended a hyperinflation in 1991 using a currency board linked to the dollar; Estonia and Bulgaria used currency-board links to the German mark to end hyperinflation and later transferred the link to the euro when it replaced the mark.

Still other countries use less rigid forms of fixed exchange rates to accomplish the same purpose. For example, Latvia used a link to a weighted average of stable currencies. In the early 1990s, Poland did not rigidly fix its exchange rate, but instead followed a sliding scale that adjusted at a preannounced rate. Zimbabwe's recent hyperinflation finally came under control, not because of any decisive action by its government, but simply because people spontaneously quit using the nearly worthless Zimbabwe dollar and began using the US dollar or South African rand instead. Eventually the government gave up printing its own currency altogether.

14.2 DEFLATION

Exchange-rate-based stabilization (ERB stabilization)

A policy that uses a fixed exchange rate as the principal tool for ending hyperinflation

After the preceding discussion of the evils of inflation, it might seem that deflation—a prolonged period of falling prices—would present a lesser set of problems. If inflation is bad, shouldn't we expect its opposite to be good? Instead, we find that deflation can be just as much of a curse as inflation. Only under special circumstances can an economy remain healthy for long while prices of goods and services fall.

Like inflation, deflation has both demand-side and supply-side variants, as Figure 14–6 shows. Part (a) of the figure shows **demand-side deflation**. Suppose that, beginning from equilibrium at E_0, something happens to reduce aggregate demand—a slowdown in investment, a decrease in net exports, or a reduction in any other element of planned expenditure. As the aggregate demand curve shifts leftward, the economy moves down and to the left along its aggregate supply curve from E_0 to E_1. The price level and real output both decrease in the short run. If there were no further change in aggregate demand, expectations would eventually begin to adjust. As a result, the short-run aggregate supply curve would shift downward, and the economy would, with a lag, return to an equilibrium (not shown) at its natural level of real output.

Demand-side deflation

A period of falling prices caused by a decrease in aggregate demand

FIGURE 14–6

Demand-Side Versus Supply-Side Deflation

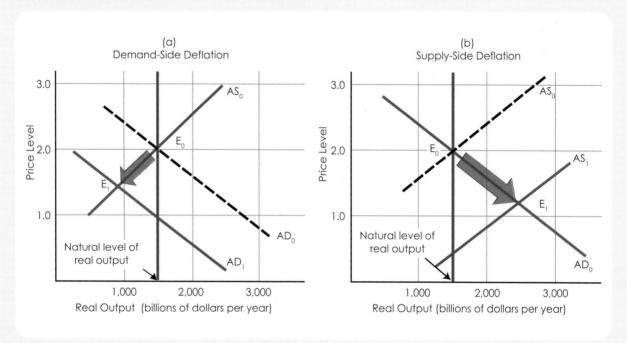

Deflation, like inflation, can exist in demand-side or supply-side variants. Part (a) shows demand-side deflation. Beginning from equilibrium at E_0, something happens to reduce aggregate demand (for example, a slowdown in investment or a decrease in net exports). The economy moves down and to the left along its aggregate supply curve from E_1 to E_2. The price level and real output both decrease. Part (b) shows supply-side deflation. A favorable supply shock (for example, a decrease in world commodity prices or an appreciation of the country's exchange rate) causes firms to expect a decrease in costs of production and shifts the short-run aggregate supply curve downward. The economy moves from E_0 to a new short-run equilibrium at E_1. Firms react to the expectation of lower production costs partly by increasing output and partly by passing along lower costs to their customers through price reductions. As that happens, real output increases and the price level falls.

Part (b) of Figure 14–6 shows **supply-side deflation**. Beginning from equilibrium at E_0, suppose a favorable supply shock occurs—for example, a decrease in world commodity prices or an appreciation of the country's exchange rate. Because inputs suddenly become cheaper, firms will expect a decrease in costs of production. This causes a downward shift of the short-run aggregate supply curve. If there is no change in aggregate demand, the economy moves from E_0 to a new short-run equilibrium at E_1. In the process, firms react to the expectation of lower production costs partly by increasing output and partly by passing along lower costs to their customers through price reductions. If the favorable supply shock is only temporary, the economy will later return to its starting point at E_0. The long-run effects of a lasting supply shock are more complex. We will return to them shortly.

Demand-side and supply-side deflation pose different problems for economic policy. We will begin with the more common, demand-side variant.

14.2a Demand-Side Deflation

In the aggregate supply and demand model, demand-side deflation looks like the mirror image of demand-side inflation, but the appearance is deceptive. The problem is that the economy is not perfectly symmetrical in its upward and downward movements. There are similarities between demand-side inflation and deflation, but there are important differences, as well.

Asymmetries in Labor Markets One of the differences concerns the ease with which labor markets adjust to increases and decreases in labor demand. Suppose, first, that demand for labor increases—say, because of an increase in demand for a country's exports. Export industries would step up production, partly by increasing workers' hours and partly by recruiting new workers. Wages in the export sector would start to rise. As workers switched jobs to the export sector, labor shortages would develop at firms that serve domestic markets, raising wages there, too. If workers were unionized, their leaders would take advantage of rising labor demand to negotiate better contracts. If workers were not organized, employers would still have to offer better wages to retain the workers they have and hire the new ones they need. Not all of this would happen immediately. It would take some time for employers to interview job candidates, workers to move to new job sites, and unions to negotiate new contracts. Still, the lags would not be long because everyone—workers and employers—would want to be among the first to take advantage of the changed situation.

If, instead, decreasing export demand caused labor demand to fall, the adjustment would not go so smoothly. Export industries would cut back output, shorten hours, and begin to lay off workers; but they would find it harder to lower wages. Union contracts would protect some workers. Even where workers were not unionized, it would be hard to get them to accept lower wages. People have a psychological resistance to losing something they already have that is greater than their appreciation of getting something they don't have. The psychological resistance to accepting nominal wage cuts persists even if deflation is lowering the cost of living, so that the lower nominal wage can buy the same real goods and services as before. Furthermore, any employer that attempted to cut wages would find

Supply-side deflation

A period of falling prices caused by a decrease in the expected costs of production

A country that exports beer will experience an increase in the demand for labor if world demand for beer increases. (Shutterstock)

BVT *Lab*

Visit **www.BVTLab.com** to explore the student resources available for this chapter.

its best workers quitting first because they would be the ones who would most easily find new jobs.

In a rising job market, workers who are just entering the labor market or who are temporarily unemployed will tend to enter expanding sectors where wages are high. In a falling labor market, it is harder for newly entering or unemployed workers to find jobs. In a world of pure economic rationality, unemployed workers might approach employers and offer to work for less than people who already have jobs; but in practice, social and cultural stigmas apply both to workers who propose undercutting their neighbors' wages and firms that agree to hire them on those terms.

When countries experience strong deflationary pressures, nominal wages do eventually begin to fall, but the process can be slow and painful. For example, in the United States during the first years of the Great Depression, nominal wages did decrease—but not as fast as the price level. That meant that real wages increased. With real wages increasing at the same time labor demand was decreasing, unemployment rose to nearly a quarter of the labor force.

Asymmetries in Financial Markets

Financial markets, too, react differently to deflation than to inflation. During the Great Recession in the United States, some of the most striking differences have been in markets for home mortgages.

During a boom, when jobs are plentiful and wages are rising, people are eager to move up to better housing. Banks willingly lend them the money to do so. When housing prices begin to rise, people begin to see a house not just as a place to live but also as a surefire investment. Lenders accommodate the eagerness of home buyers by offering loans with low down payments. If a banker extends a loan of 90 or even 100 percent of the value of a house, the collateral may at first be barely adequate. Both the borrower and lender expect, though, that rising prices will soon create a comfortable cushion of equity between the balance on the loan and the potential selling price. The equity will protect the bank in case the borrower becomes unable to pay. Expansion of the housing sector feeds on itself.

When the economy enters a recession, contraction of the market for home mortgages may feed on itself. (Shutterstock)

When the economy turns down, the dynamic of the mortgage market changes. As incomes level off and the increase in housing prices slows and then reverses, people who bought at the top find themselves in homes they cannot afford. Their financial situation is fragile. If they lose their jobs, or even see their hours cut, they may find it hard to keep up with mortgage payments. They find it hard to move down the market to a cheaper house because they can't sell the one they are in for enough to pay off the mortgage. Foreclosures begin to rise, and a glut of unsold houses begins to build.

As that happens, the construction industry grinds to a halt. More people lose their jobs. Lenders find they are no longer able to count on the collateral value of homes in case of foreclosures. Forced sales below loan values cause losses for banks, which then become unwilling or unable to make new loans even for people who have kept their jobs. Soon, tightening of credit markets spreads beyond the housing sector. Firms find it difficult to borrow to expand production and may not even be able to borrow the working capital they need to stay in business. Now it is the contraction that feeds on itself.

The Zero Interest Rate Bound

As financial markets begin to spiral downward, the economy runs into still another major asymmetry of deflation. This one concerns the way that interest rates behave during inflation and deflation. To understand this asymmetry, we need to draw on the distinction between real and nominal interest rates, first discussed in Chapter 4. Financial contracts use nominal interest rates—3 percent interest on a savings account, 6 percent interest on a home mortgage, 18 percent on a credit card bill, or whatever. We calculate real interest rates by subtracting the rate of inflation from the nominal interest rate. In equation form,

$$\text{Real interest rate} = \text{Nominal interest rate} - \text{Rate of inflation}$$

If the rate of inflation is, say, 5 percent, then the 18 percent nominal rate on the credit card bill becomes a real rate of 13 percent, the nominal 6 percent on the mortgage becomes a real rate of just 1 percent, and the 3 percent nominal rate on the savings account becomes a real rate of *minus* 2 percent. A negative real rate means that the holder of the savings account does not even get enough interest to compensate for the 5 percent per year loss in purchasing power of the money on deposit.

When inflation varies within a moderate but positive range, nominal interest rates tend to adjust to inflation automatically under the influence of supply and demand. For example, suppose the rate of inflation is at first 3 percent, at which time a bank is making auto loans at a nominal rate of 7 percent. The next year, the rate of inflation goes up to 5 percent. If both borrowers and lenders expect the new rate of inflation to last at least for the life of the loan, the nominal interest rate on auto loans will adjust upward to 9 percent by mutual consent. Borrowers will be willing to pay the extra amount because they expect their wages to rise 2 percent faster during the life of the loan. Bankers are willing to accept the extra 2 percent interest as compensation for the greater annual loss in the purchasing power of money. The real interest rate remains unchanged. At first, it was a nominal 7 percent minus 3 percent inflation for a real interest rate of 4 percent. Later it became a nominal 9 percent minus 5 percent inflation, still a real interest rate of 4 percent.

When deflation sets in, though, it can become impossible to adjust the nominal interest rates downward by enough to keep the real interest rate constant. Consider what would happen, in our example, if there were deflation of 5 percent per year (that is, inflation of minus 5 percent). To keep the real interest rate at 4 percent, the nominal rate would have to fall to minus 1 percent. As you learned in grade school, "minus a minus makes a plus," so the math would look like this:

$$(\text{Nominal rate of} -1 \text{ percent}) - (\text{Inflation rate of} -5 \text{ percent}) = (\text{Real rate of 4 percent})$$

The problem is that, although we can write out the equation, it is not really possible for a lender to offer a negative nominal interest rate. Think what would happen if you walked by your local bank and saw a sign advertising loans at minus 1 percent. That would mean you could borrow $1,000 today, and a year from now, you would owe the bank just $990. Good deal, right? You could borrow the $1,000, put aside $990 in cash to repay the loan when it comes due, and buy lunch with the remaining $10.

The minus 1 percent interest rate is such a good deal, why not borrow $10,000 or $10 billion? As the example shows, nominal interest rates can never fall below zero, because as they approach that level, the demand for loans becomes infinite. Economists call this principle the **zero interest rate bound (ZIRB)**. Because the ZIRB raises real interest rates during deflation, credit becomes more expensive. People become less willing to take out loans to build houses, buy cars, and upgrade production equipment. Falling investment reduces aggregate demand—still another reason why deflation, once started, feeds on itself.

Zero interest rate bound (ZIRB)

The principle that nominal interest rates cannot fall below zero

Policies to Fight Demand-Side Deflation

The zero interest rate bound is a source of trouble for the Fed and other central banks. As we saw in Chapter 8, when the Fed wants to tighten monetary policy, it raises its target for the federal funds rate. It then uses open market operations to withdraw reserves from the banking system until a reduced supply of reserves pushes the federal funds rate up to the new target. Doing so raises the opportunity cost to commercial banks of making loans, so they, in turn, raise their loan rates and tighten lending standards. Borrowing slows down; aggregate demand decreases; and, with a lag, real output growth and inflation begin to fall. When the Fed wants to loosen monetary policy, it does the opposite. It injects new reserves into the banking system, driving down the federal funds rate and making it cheaper for banks to make loans. Lending increases; aggregate demand strengthens; and, with a lag, inflation and real output speed up.

The interest rate operating target works well until deflation causes nominal interest rates to approach zero. Once that happens, injecting reserves has no further effect on interest rates. With nothing to gain by lending out reserves and no cost of holding excess reserves, banks have no incentive to lend reserves out to firms and consumers. As excess reserves accumulate in the banking system, lending slows down, investment falls, aggregate demand decreases, and the problem of deflation becomes worse.

The accumulation of excess reserves in the banking system is not the only problem. As nominal interest rates approach zero, the opportunity cost to firms and households of holding money decreases. There is no longer much incentive to manage cash carefully. Interest rates on alternative, safe, short-term investments are so low that firms and households simply allow funds to accumulate in transaction deposits or even as paper currency. Velocity slows. As we know from the equation of exchange, $MV = PQ$, a reduction in velocity, other things being equal, will cause either P, the price level, or Q, real output—or both—to decrease. The accumulation of excess money by firms and households thus makes deflation worse, once it is underway.

Together, the accumulation of liquid reserves by banks and money balances by households and firms reduces the effectiveness of monetary policy as nominal interest rates approach zero. Economists call this combination of circumstances a **liquidity trap**. The name comes from the fact that the economy is "trapped" in a state of low aggregate demand from which monetary policy cannot easily free it. Data presented in Figure 8A–2 (in the Appendix to Chapter 8) shows evidence of a liquidity trap during the Great Recession—namely, a decrease both in velocity and in the ratio of the M2 money stock to the monetary base.

As discussed in earlier chapters, policymakers in the United States and other countries did not sit on their hands as the threat of deflation developed during 2008 and 2009. They took vigorous measures, using both monetary and fiscal policies, to try to break out of the liquidity trap before full-scale deflation became established. In Chapter 8, we saw that the Fed undertook repeated rounds of quantitative easing in the form of massive open market purchases of mortgage-backed securities and other assets. Chapter 12 discussed the fiscal stimulus that Congress enacted in early 2009.

Economists disagree both about the effects of quantitative easing and the effects of the 2009 fiscal stimulus. Critics claim that neither program had much effect, whereas supporters say things would have been even worse without them. In any event, at least the US economy did not fall into full-fledged deflation. The consumer price index did fall for three consecutive months at the end of 2008; but after that, although inflation remained very low, the price level fell in only a few isolated months.

Because deflation is hard to stop once it takes hold, policymakers reduce the risk by setting an inflation target that is somewhat above zero. An inflation target of 2 or 3 percent gives a margin of error in case unexpected deflationary shocks hit the economy.

Liquidity trap
A situation in which monetary policy loses its effectiveness as nominal interest rates approach zero

14.2b Supply-Side Deflation

Just one topic—supply-side deflation—remains to be covered before we complete our survey of macroeconomics and stabilization policy. Although both involve a falling price level, supply-side deflation raises a very different set of issues than demand-side deflation. Both kinds of deflation turn out to be relevant, but in different ways, to the global economic crisis that began in 2008.

Deflation and Short-Term Supply Shocks   Supply-side deflation, as shown earlier in Figure 14–6, occurs when a favorable supply shock lowers expected production costs and shifts the short-run aggregate supply curve downward. Often such shocks are temporary, caused by a decrease in prices of imported commodities, unusually good weather, or an appreciation of the exchange rate. Temporary shocks of that kind are not likely to have major policy implications.

For one thing, the favorable short-run supply shock may occur during a period when the price level has already been rising, rather than during a stationary equilibrium, as was the case in Figure 14–6. That is especially likely to be the case if policymakers set a moderately positive inflation target for normal times. An example would be the fall in world oil prices in the second half of 2008, which followed an earlier oil price increase that had temporarily raised the inflation rate. Under such conditions, a deflationary supply shock only slows a previously established upward drift of the aggregate supply curve caused by inflationary momentum. Neither the aggregate supply curve itself nor the price level need actually fall.

Even if a temporary, favorable supply shock hits when inflation is already low or zero, so that prices do begin to fall, the effect may not continue long enough to bring nominal interest rates to zero. Financial markets tend to mark up nominal interest rates above real interest rates by an amount that reflects the rate of inflation expected over the life of loans they are currently making. Even if the price level decreases briefly, lenders and borrowers are likely to expect price stability or moderate inflation to return. Until prices fall for long enough that people come to see them as the norm, financial markets will be able to function without the danger of a liquidity trap.

Deflation and Long-Term Productivity Growth   Long-term productivity growth can cause a more problematic form of supply-side deflation. Figure 14–7 shows why. The story begins from a point of long-term equilibrium at E_0. Next, some improvement in technology or the organization of production begins to increase productivity.

The productivity growth has two effects. First, the economy's long-term natural level of real output increases because the existing stock of labor and capital can now produce more output than before. That effect appears as a rightward shift of the vertical long-run aggregate supply curve from N_0 to N_1. Second, improved productivity lowers the expected cost of production because it takes fewer units of inputs to produce any given quantity of output. That effect takes the form of a downward and rightward shift of the short-run aggregate supply curve from AS_0 to AS_1. If aggregate demand remains unchanged, the economy will move along the aggregate demand curve from E_0 to E_1. The price level will fall while real output increases. The unemployment rate does not need to change because real output stays at its natural level. Because of productivity improvements, the same number of labor hours as before now produces more output, more cheaply.

Supply-side deflation caused by productivity growth is less likely to have harmful consequences than demand-side deflation.[4] For one thing, it does not disrupt the operation of labor markets in the way demand-side deflation does. In demand-side deflation, nominal wage rates must fall in order to bring the economy to a new long-run equilibrium. Workers, whether unionized or nonunionized, are likely to resist nominal wage

FIGURE 14–7

Effects of Productivity Growth

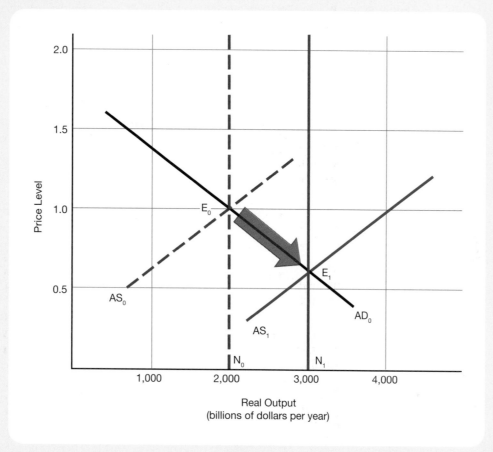

Beginning from equilibrium at point E_0, productivity growth has two effects. First, the economy's long-term natural level of real output increases from N_0 to N_1, shifting the long-term aggregate supply curve rightward. Second, improved productivity lowers the expected cost of production, shifting the short-run aggregate supply curve both downward and to the right, from AS_0 to AS_1. If aggregate demand remains unchanged, the price level will fall while real output increases; and the economy will move to a new equilibrium at E_1.

cuts, even if the price level is also falling. In contrast, productivity-driven supply-side deflation does not require a decrease in nominal wages. Productivity growth allows real wages to increase. The increase in real wages most often takes the form of a nominal wage that rises faster than the rate of inflation for goods and services. However, as in the case shown in Figure 14–7, it can instead take the form of a nominal wage that remains constant while falling prices reduce the cost of living. Either way, productivity growth makes workers better off. Deflation does not trigger either institutional or psychological disruption of labor markets.

Furthermore, productivity-driven deflation is less likely to disrupt financial markets. For one thing, productivity growth does not usually occur in sudden jumps, but rather at a rate of a few percent per year. If the price level were to fall by a steady 1 or 2 percent per year, nominal interest rates could remain positive—they would be lower than the real interest rate, but above zero. In addition, because productivity-driven deflation would not be accompanied by falling output, rising unemployment, and falling real incomes, there would be less danger of widespread loan defaults, foreclosures, and collapsing collateral values.

The most recent occurrence of prolonged productivity-driven deflation in the United States was in the 1920s, which was a decade of prosperity and growth until the stock market crash of 1929. During all of the nineteenth century, in both the United States and the UK, the price level fell, on average, one decade after another, interrupted only during periods of war. Both countries experienced steady growth and rising living standards. Economists sometimes cite these episodes to argue that supply-side deflation is benign, in contrast to the harmful demand-side variety.

Productivity Growth and Inflation Targeting   No country in recent years has experienced the kind of deflation shown in Figure 14–7, but that is not because there has been no productivity growth. On the contrary, productivity growth in the United States and many other countries was unusually strong in the 1990s and early 2000s. The reason there was no productivity-driven deflation during this period was that monetary policy did not allow it.

Figure 14–8 shows how monetary policy can prevent deflation even when productivity is growing. In the example, we assume that the central bank follows a strict form of inflation targeting that aims at complete price stability. As the long-run and short-run aggregate supply curves shift to the right, the central bank applies expansionary monetary policy to shift the aggregate demand curve from AD_0 to AD_1. The rapid growth of aggregate demand is enough to hold the price level constant at its original level of 1.0, despite shifts in the aggregate supply curves. In the process, real output grows even faster than in the case that was shown earlier in Figure 14–7. By the time the economy reaches E_2, real output is $3,600 billion. There is a positive output gap of $800 billion compared with the new natural real GDP of $2,800 billion ($N_1$).

Unintended Consequences: Asset Price Bubbles   At first glance, the circumstances produced by the combination of inflation targeting and productivity growth look like the best of all possible worlds. There is no inflation or deflation. Real output grows even more rapidly than it otherwise would. What is more, the unemployment rate falls as real output grows beyond its natural level and firms add shifts in a struggle to keep up with booming demand. However, as we all know, economists are a gloomy lot. They see unintended consequences and hidden trouble even in the sunny scenario shown in Figure 14–8.

The unintended consequences stem from the interest-rate policy that keeps demand growing fast enough to hold the price level constant. In order to prevent deflation, the central bank must push real output well above its natural level. To do that, it must keep interest rates very low. The banking system becomes awash with liquidity, credit becomes very cheap, and lending standards become lenient. Households and businesses are able to borrow as much as they want for almost any purpose.

The result of such a policy, say the critics, is the emergence of **asset price bubbles**. Remember, the price level shown on the vertical axis of the aggregate supply and demand diagram is an index of prices of final goods and services. Prices of assets—like real estate, stocks, and commodities—do not enter the index. Some of the easy credit available during the boom spills over into asset markets; and asset prices can rise to unsustainable levels, even if prices of final goods and services do not.

It is hard to predict just where asset price bubbles will first develop. In the United States in the 1990s, high-tech stocks were the most affected. In the course of the decade, the NASDAQ composite stock index, heavily weighted with stylish "dot-com"

Asset price bubble

A situation in which the prices of assets (stocks, real estate, commodities, etc.) rise to unsustainable levels in comparison to prices of goods and services

FIGURE 14–8

Preventing Deflation with Monetary Policy

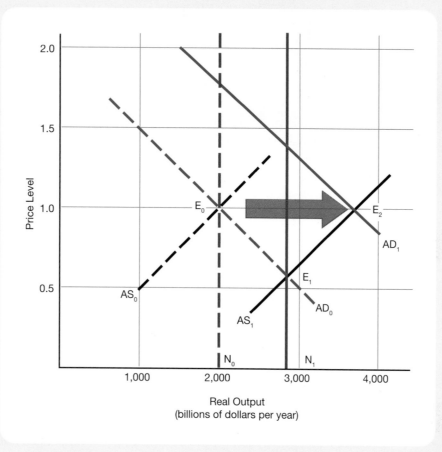

Expansionary monetary policy can keep the price level constant even while productivity growth is shifting the long- and short-run aggregate supply curves. In this example, the central bank follows a zero-inflation target. Strong expansionary policy shifts the aggregate demand curve from AD_0 to AD_1 as the aggregate supply curve moves from AS_0 to AS_1, so the economy moves from E_0 to E_2 instead of to E_1. The actual level of real output increases faster than the natural level of real output, a positive output gap develops, and there is no deflation.

companies, soared from under 500 to nearly 5,000 before it crashed again. In Japan in the 1980s and Thailand in the 1990s, the bubble was in commercial real estate; and in the United States in the early 2000s, home prices were the focus of the bubble, as we saw in Chapter 7.

Whatever particular asset is at the center of the bubble, people will invest in producing more of it. During the dot-com bubble, billions of dollars worth of capital flooded into investment in technology startups, a few of which were successful, but most of which failed. During the housing bubble, the investment poured into construction of new homes. People bought larger homes and second homes that they could not afford,

Google was one of the successful startups during the dot-com bubble.
(Shutterstock)

in the hope of quickly "flipping" them at higher prices to other buyers who would later arrive at the party.

When a bubble collapses, there is no smooth way to get the economy back to equilibrium. Much of the investment made during the boom turns out to have been a waste. It is not then possible to turn unwanted software code or subdivisions, produced at the cost of millions of labor-hours and billions of dollars, into something more useful, like shoes or schools. Borrowers default and banks find that the collateral that underpins their loans is worthless. Credit dries up, and the economy plunges from boom to bust.

What measures might counter the risk that a combination of inflation targeting, productivity growth, and asset price bubbles will lead to an unsustainable boom-bust cycle? The aggregate supply and demand model suggests an apparently simple answer: Rather than holding the price level constant as productivity grows, the central bank could follow a policy of planned, gradual deflation that is just sufficient to keep real output close to its natural level. The economy would follow a path closer to Figure 14–7 than to Figure 14–8. The economy would be prosperous and stable.

Some economists see NGDP targeting as the ideal way to balance the risks of excessively deflationary contractions against the risks of unsustainable bubbles and booms. They would set a target growth rate for nominal GDP a little above the long-term average growth rate of natural real output—say, 4.5 or 5 percent for the United States. Suppose the average growth rate of natural real GDP is 3 percent and the NGDP target is set at 5 percent. If natural real GDP does, in fact, grow at 3 percent, there will be 2 percent inflation. If productivity growth slows down, a positive output gap will develop and inflation will speed up a little, but not too much. If productivity growth speeds up, inflation will automatically slow down or even turn slightly negative. That will reduce the likelihood of asset price bubbles and a boom-bust cycle.

A more controversial idea for dealing with the danger of asset bubbles is to target asset prices directly. If policymakers saw something abnormal going on in the stock market or real estate or commodity prices, they could take that as a warning sign of overheating. To prevent the problem from getting out of hand, they could then try to deflate the bubble by raising interest rates. In the past, the Fed has resisted suggestions that it target asset price bubbles. Still, in the aftermath of the recent crisis, the idea that central banks should pay more attention to asset price bubbles is not likely to go away.

In retrospect, it is clear that housing price bubbles—not just in the United States but also in the UK, Spain, and other countries—were a key contributing factor to the global crisis. There is a strong argument that those bubbles grew out of control, in part, because central banks, including the Fed, kept interest rates too low for too long during the preceding expansion. Some observers argue that rather than "popping" the bubble with tight monetary policy, better financial regulation at the microeconomic level would have been enough to limit the damage. Our own discussion in Chapter 7 looked at several areas in which better regulation could have helped. All we can really hope for is that policymakers at both the microeconomic and macroeconomic level will be more vigilant next time, and that the current crisis does not repeat itself any time soon.

Summary

1. How does demand-side inflation differ from supply-side inflation?

Demand-side inflation is inflation that comes from an increase in aggregate demand. In the short run, an increase in aggregate demand will move the economy up and to the right along its short-run aggregate supply curve. As increases in final-goods prices come to affect expected input prices, the aggregate supply curve shifts upward. If continued expansionary policy shifts the aggregate demand curve upward at the same rate, the economy will stay above its natural level of real output for an extended period, although at a substantial cost in terms of inflation. If the short-run aggregate supply curve shifts upward while the aggregate demand curve stays in place or shifts upward more slowly, the economy will experience supply-side inflation. Real output will fall and the economy will enter an inflationary recession. One source of *supply-side inflation* is a supply shock, such as an increase in the price of a key input such as petroleum. Another is the momentum of inflationary expectations following previous demand-side inflation.

2. What is the Phillips curve, and how can we interpret it?

The short-run *Phillips curve* shows that, for a given expected inflation rate, lower actual inflation rates tend to accompany higher unemployment rates. When the Phillips curve first came to economists' attention, many interpreted it as a policy menu. Later, it became clear that an increase in the expected inflation rate tends to shift the short-run Phillips curve upward, so that the long-run Phillips curve is a vertical line at the natural rate of unemployment, and unemployment is at its natural rate only when the actual inflation rate equals the expected inflation rate. After the mid-1980s, the relationship between inflation and unemployment shown by the Phillips curve became less pronounced. During the recovery from the Great Recession, it disappeared altogether.

3. What is hyperinflation, and how can policymakers combat it?

Hyperinflation is very rapid inflation, in the thousands or millions of percent per year, or even higher. During hyperinflation, all the elements of the equation of exchange, $MV = PQ$, interact to cause the price level to increase. Velocity rises, real output falls, and monetization of fiscal deficits causes the money supply to grow. Conventional contractionary monetary policy and fiscal reforms can sometimes bring hyperinflation under control. Exchange-rate-based stabilization, which employs an exchange rate pegged to a stable currency, is another approach.

4. Why is demand-side deflation harmful, and what policies can prevent or reverse it?

Demand-side deflation is harmful because of three key asymmetries between inflation and deflation. First, labor markets do not function well because of resistance to cutting nominal wages. Second, financial markets run into trouble because of falling collateral values and increased loan defaults. Third, once the nominal interest rates hit the zero interest rate bound, real interest rates rise, further damping aggregate demand. Once demand-side deflation becomes established, it is hard to reverse. The economy enters a liquidity trap, which weakens the effectiveness of monetary policy. It may take a combination of super-expansionary monetary policy (*quantitative easing*) and fiscal stimulus to get the economy moving again.

Summary

5. How can productivity growth cause supply-side deflation?

When productivity increases, two things happen to aggregate supply. First, the economy's capacity to produce goods and services increases, so the long-run aggregate supply curve shifts to the right. Second, per-unit costs of production decrease, so the short-run aggregate supply curve shifts downward. If aggregate demand remains unchanged, the result will be a combination of deflation and growing real output, as was the case in the United States for much of the nineteenth century. Productivity-driven supply-side deflation is less likely to be harmful than demand-side deflation because it is less likely to disrupt the workings of labor and financial markets.

6. What are asset price bubbles, and what can we do about them?

Asset price bubbles develop when the prices of assets like real estate, stocks, or commodities rise to unsustainable levels, even while prices of goods and services remain under control. The sectors subject to asset price bubbles attract disproportionately large amounts of investment, some of which becomes worthless when the bubble collapses. The collapse of an asset price bubble can trigger an economy-wide contraction. One of the current controversies of monetary policy is whether central banks should try to "pop" asset price bubbles, try to lean gently against them, or do nothing about them.

KEY TERMS

Asset price bubble	378	Inflation inertia (inflation momentum)	360
Demand-side deflation	371	Liquidity trap	375
Demand-side inflation	356	Phillips curve	362
Exchange-rate-based stabilization		Supply shock	358
(ERB stabilization)	370	Supply-side deflation	372
Hyperinflation	367	Supply-side inflation	358
Inflationary recession	362	Zero interest rate bound (ZIRB)	374

PROBLEMS AND TOPICS FOR DISCUSSION

1. **Inflation or deflation?** Go to the website of the Bureau of Labor Statistics (www.bls.gov/cpi) and find the most recent information on the consumer price index. Has the United States experienced inflation, deflation, or a mix of the two over the most recent year? Two years? Do you think the inflation or deflation shown is of the demand-side or supply-side variety? What other information, from other data sources or news sources, might help you answer the supply-side/demand-side question?

2. **Phillips curve** Turn to the chart given in *Applying Economic Ideas 11.1* in Chapter 11. Look closely at the segment of the diagram that plots inflation/unemployment points for the years 1961 to 1969. Do you think that segment of the chart is best interpreted as a set of points from a single stationary Phillips curve, or do the points correspond to a Phillips curve that shifts over time? Explain the reason for your answer, based both on your understanding of the Phillips curve and on information contained in the text of the box.

3. **Phillips curve versus aggregate supply and demand** Now, look at another part of the chart given in *Applying Economic Ideas 11.1*—this time the segment that goes from 1976 to 1982. That diagram uses unemployment on the horizontal axis and inflation on the vertical axis. In contrast, the aggregate supply and demand diagram uses real output on the horizontal axis and the price level on the vertical axis. What do you think the pattern of year-to-year movements from 1976 to 1982 would look like if you plotted them on an aggregate supply and demand type of diagram? Try doing this. You will not be able to put exact numbers on your diagram or draw the exact positions of the curves—there is not enough information. However, you should be able to put points for each year in their correct relationship to each other (movement to the left or right, movement up or down), depending on whether the price level and real output increased or decreased from year to year. Of the various types of events described in this chapter (deflation, supply shock, inflationary recession, etc.), which one do you think best describes the pattern you have plotted?

4. **Supply shocks from oil prices** Visit the website oilprice.com, which provides current and historical data for world oil prices. Over the last six months, do you think the price of crude oil has produced an upward or a downward supply shock, or neither? How can you tell? Looking at historical data, when did the most recent oil-related supply shocks occur?

5. **The US housing bubble** The US Federal Housing Finance Agency publishes an index of home prices. You can find a chart using the St. Louis Feds FRED database: http://bvtlab.com/855W7. When did the US housing price bubble peak? Has the decline in housing prices ended? If so, when did it end?

CASE *for* **DISCUSSION**

Japan—One Lost Decade, or More?

From the 1960s through the 1980s, the Japanese economy was the envy of the world. As Japanese cars, consumer electronics, and industrial goods flooded the world and set new standards of quality, its economy boomed. Japan became the world's second-largest economy and the first Asian country whose living standards were on a par with those of North America and Western Europe. Books with titles like *The Japanese Century* became bestsellers.

Then, in the 1990s, all this began to fall apart. One of the first signs of change came from the consumer price index. Japan had never been a high inflation country; however, in the early 1990s, inflation slowed sharply from its already moderate rate. After dipping below zero in 1995 and rising slightly in 1996 through early 1998, the rate of inflation became persistently negative after 1999. Deflation continued for six more years.

People began to call this long period of deflation Japan's "lost decade." Performance of the real economy was very poor. One measure of this is the output gap—positive when real GDP is above its natural level, negative when the economy is performing below potential. The chart shows that the Japanese output gap was negative throughout the period of deflation. Although the unemployment rate remained at moderate levels by the standards of other countries, the weak labor market brought big changes to Japan. Among other effects, it undermined the "jobs for life" tradition that had been a hallmark of the Japanese economy.

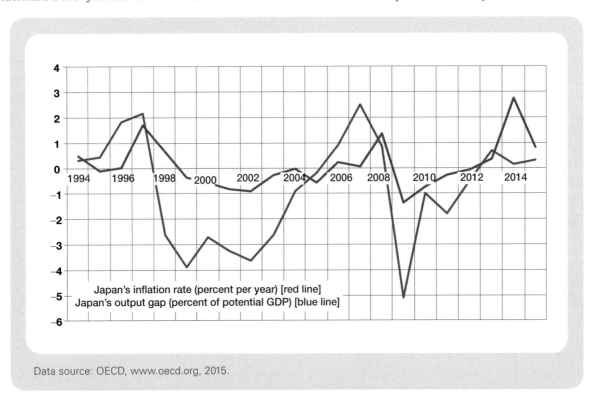

Japan's inflation rate (percent per year) [red line]
Japan's output gap (percent of potential GDP) [blue line]

Data source: OECD, www.oecd.org, 2015.

In 2006 and 2007, the Japanese economy finally showed signs of recovery. Few countries have ever been so happy to see consumer prices on the rise. Unfortunately, the recovery fell apart before it got far. In the second half of 2008 and over the next year or more, the spreading global recession undermined demand for Japan's exports. Sales of cars and consumer electronics fell by more than half, and the economy plunged back into renewed deflation. Then came the disastrous earthquake, tsunami, and nuclear incident of 2010. Pessimists began to worry that Japan's lost decade might become two—or more.

After his election in December 2012, Prime Minister Shinzo Abe was determined to slay the dragon of deflation once and for all. He proposed a program, which came to be known as "Abenomics," that consisted of three parts: monetary policy, fiscal policy, and structural reform.

Abenomics turned out to be a mixed success, at best. The monetary dimension of the policy was probably the most successful. The Bank of Japan announced a new program of quantitative easing and set an inflation target of 2 percent. In response, the yen depreciated on international markets, providing a boost to exports. The government also announced a fiscal stimulus package equivalent to 2 percent of GDP. However, in 2014, the fiscal dimension of the program was undermined by a boost in the value added tax, after which growth slowed sharply. Promised structural reforms were slow in coming and made little impact.

As this is written (in late 2015), Japan seems about to slip back into recession. Can renewed deflation be far behind?

Questions

1. Was Japan's deflation of the demand-side or supply-side variety? How can you tell from the information given?

2. From 1999 to the end of 2005, Japan's central bank held nominal short-term interest rates between 0.1 percent (one-tenth of a single percentage point) and 0.001 percent (one one-thousandth of a percentage point) per year. What happened to the real rate of interest over this period? In what year did the real interest rate reach its highest value, and approximately what was the value?

3. Check TradingEconomics.com, OECD.org, IMF.org, or another internet data source to find the latest data on the Japanese economy. Is the Japanese economy recovering, or has it slipped back into deflation?

Endnotes

1. See Chapter 11 for a discussion of NGDP targeting. To be precise, an NGDP target would give rise to an aggregate demand curve that is not a straight line, as shown in the figure, but instead is a unit elastic curve. Mathematically, we would describe such a curve as a rectangular hyperbola; it would have the property that $P \times Q$ would be the same at all points along the curve.

2. People sometimes call this situation "stagflation," but the term is not apt. The term *stagflation*—a combination of "stagnation" and "inflation"—was coined in the 1970s to describe a situation of slow or zero growth in real output, high inflation, and unemployment in excess of its natural rate. The term *inflationary recession* seems more suitable for periods that combine high inflation rates with decreasing real output.

3. A. W. H. Phillips, "The Relationship Between Unemployment and the Rate of Change of Money Wage Rates in the United Kingdom, 1861–1957," *Economica*, 25 (November 1958): 283–299.

4. For an excellent review of the literature on supply-side deflation, see David Beckworth, "Aggregate Supply–Driven Deflation and Its Implications for Macroeconomic Stability," *Cato Journal* (Fall 2008): 363–384. http://www.cato.org/pubs/ journal/cj28n3/cj28n3-1.pdf.

Glossary

A

Accommodating monetary policy   311
A policy in which the central bank holds interest rates constant in response to a fiscal stimulus

Actual budget balance   321
Total government revenues minus expenditures for a given period

Aggregate demand   256
Total real planned expenditure

Aggregate demand curve   256
A graph showing the relationship between aggregate demand and the aggregate price level

Aggregate supply   256
Total real output of final goods and services (real GDP)

Aggregate supply curve   261
A graph showing the relationship between real output (real domestic product) and the average price level of final goods

Appreciate   230
An increase in value of one country's currency relative to the currency of another country

Asset price bubbles   378
A situation in which the prices of assets (stocks, real estate, commodities, etc.) rise to unsustainable levels in comparison to prices of goods and services

Assets   175
All the things that the firm or household owns or to which it holds a legal claim

Automatic fiscal policy   313
Changes in government purchases or net taxes that are the results of changes in economic conditions, given unchanged tax and spending laws

Automatic stabilizers   315
Those elements of automatic fiscal policy that move the federal budget toward deficit during an economic contraction and toward surplus during an expansion

B

Balanced budget amendment   344
Any of a number of proposals to amend the US constitution in a way that would require the federal government to limit its spending each year to the amount of tax revenue that it receives

Balance sheet   174
A financial statement showing what a firm or household owns and what it owes

Bank   174
A financial institution whose principal business consists of accepting deposits and making loans

Base year   158
The year used as a basis for comparison when computing real GDP or a price index

Business cycle   103
A pattern of irregular but repeated expansion and contraction of aggregate economic activity

C

Capital   5
All means of production that are created by people, including tools, industrial equipment, and structures

Capital ratio   206
The ratio of a bank's capital (net worth) to its total assets

Central bank   174
A government agency responsible for carrying out monetary policy and often for regulating a country's banking system

Change in demand   46
A change in the quantity of a good that the buyers are willing and able to purchase that is caused by a change in some condition other than the price of that good; a shift in the demand curve

Change in quantity demanded   45
A change in the quantity of a good that buyers are willing and able to purchase that is caused by a change in the price of a good, other things being equal; shown by a movement from one point to another along a demand curve

Change in quantity supplied   52
A change in the quantity of a good that suppliers are willing and able to sell that is caused by a change in the good's price, other things being equal; shown by a movement along a supply curve

Change in supply   52
A change in the quantity of a good that suppliers are willing and able to sell that is caused by a change in some condition other than the good's price; shown by a shift in the supply curve

Circular flow of income and product   122
The flow of goods and services between households and firms, balanced by the flow of payments made in exchange for goods and services

Closed economy   123
An economy that has no links to the rest of the world

Comparative advantage   10
The ability to produce a good or service at a lower opportunity cost than someone else

Complementary goods   47
A pair of goods for which an increase in the price of one causes a decrease in demand for the other

Conditional forecast   22
A prediction of future economic events in the form "If A, then B, other things being equal"

Consumer price index (CPI or CPI-U)   159
A price index based on the market basket of goods and services for a typical urban household

Consumption   123
All purchases of goods and services by households for immediate use

Countercyclical policy   282
A pattern of monetary or fiscal policy that applies stimulus when the economy as at risk of falling into recession and restraint when it is in danger of overheating

Cross elasticity of demand   82
The ratio of the percentage change in the quantity of a good demanded to a given percentage change in the price of some other good, other things being equal

Crowding out effect   311
The tendency of expansionary fiscal policy to raise the interest rate and thereby cause a decrease in real planned investment

Currency   199
Coins and paper money

Currency union   237
Two or more countries that share a common currency

Current account balance   156
The value of a country's exports of goods and services minus the value of its imports of goods and services plus its net transfer receipts from foreign sources

Cyclical unemployment   108
The difference between the actual rate of unemployment at a given point in the business cycle and the natural rate of unemployment

D

Deflation   113
An episode during which the price level falls for a sustained period

Demand   44
The willingness and ability of buyers to purchase goods

Demand curve   44
A graphical representation of the relationship between the price of a good and the quantity of that good that buyers demand

Demand-side deflation   371
A period of falling prices caused by a decrease in aggregate demand

Demand-side inflation   356
Inflation caused by an upward shift of the aggregate demand curve while the aggregate supply curve remains fixed or shifts upward at no more than an equal rate

Depreciate   230
A decrease in value of one country's currency relative to the currency of another country

Direct relationship   32
A relationship between two variables in which an increase in the value of one variable is associated with an increase in the value of the other

Discount rate   207
The interest rate charged by the Fed on loans of reserves to banks

Discouraged worker   107
A person who would work if a suitable job were available but has given up looking for such a job

Discretionary fiscal policy   313
Changes in the laws regarding government purchases and net taxes

Disposable income   131
Income minus taxes

Domestic income   153
The total income of all types, including wages, rents, interest payments, and profits, earned by factors of production used in producing domestic product

E

Econometrics   22
The statistical analysis of empirical economic data

Economic efficiency   8
A state of affairs in which it is impossible to make any change that satisfies one person's wants more fully without causing some other person's wants to be satisfied less fully

Economics   4
The social science that seeks to understand the choices people make in using scarce resources to meet their wants

Efficiency in distribution   14
A situation in which it is not possible, by redistributing existing supplies of goods, to satisfy one person's wants more fully without causing some other person's wants to be satisfied less fully

Efficiency in production   8
A situation in which it is not possible, given available knowledge and productive resources, to produce more of one good without forgoing the opportunity to produce some of another good

Elastic demand   75
A situation in which quantity demanded changes by a larger percentage than price, so that total revenue increases as price decreases

Elasticity   74
A measure of the ratio of a change in one variable to a change in another, expressed as a percentage

Empirical   21
Based on experience or observation

Employed   105
A person who is working at least one hour a week for pay or at least fifteen hours per week as an unpaid worker in a family business

Endogenous   133
Any variable that is determined by other variables included in an economic model

Entitlements   318
Federal benefit programs such as Social Security and Medicare that are not subject to the annual budget process

Entrepreneurship   9
The process of looking for new possibilities, making use of new ways of doing things, being alert to new opportunities, and overcoming old limits

Equation of exchange   207
An equation that shows the relationship among the money stock (M), the income velocity of money (V), the price level (P), and real domestic product (Q); written as $MV = PQ$

Equilibrium   54
A condition in which buyers' and sellers' plans exactly mesh in the marketplace, so that the quantity supplied exactly equals the quantity demanded at a given price

Excess quantity demanded (shortage)   54
A condition in which the quantity of a good demanded at a given price exceeds the quantity supplied

Excess quantity supplied (surplus)   56
A condition in which the quantity of a good supplied at a given price exceeds the quantity demanded

Exchange-rate-based stabilization (ERB stabilization)   370
A policy that uses a fixed exchange rate as the principal tool for ending hyperinflation

Exogenous   133
Any variable that is determined by noneconomic considerations, or by economic considerations that lie outside the scope of a given model

Exports   127
An injection into the circular flow consisting of payments received for goods and services sold to the rest of the world

F

Factors of production   5
The basic inputs of labor, capital, and natural resources used in producing all goods and services

Federal funds market   208
A market in which banks lend reserves to one another for periods as short as twenty-four hours

Federal funds rate   208
The interest rate on overnight loans of reserves from one bank to another

Federal Open Market Committee (FOMC)   210
A committee within the Federal Reserve System that makes key decisions on monetary policy, including the target level of the federal funds rate

Federal Reserve System (the Fed)   174
The central bank of the United States, consisting of twelve regional Federal Reserve Banks and a Board of Governors in Washington, DC

Final goods and services   148
Goods and services sold to or ready for sale to parties that will use them for consumption, investment, government purchases, or exports

Financial inflow   127, 156
Purchases of domestic assets by foreign buyers and borrowing from foreign lenders; also often called *capital inflows*

Financial outflow   127, 156
Purchases of foreign assets by domestic residents or loans by domestic lenders to foreign borrowers; also often called *capital outflows*

Fine-tuning   282
An economic policy strategy that attempts to avoid even small, short-run departures from full employment and price stability

Fiscal consolidation (fiscal austerity)   342
The process of reducing government spending and increasing taxes by enough to make the deficit sustainable

Fiscal policy   260
Policy that is concerned with government purchases, taxes, and transfer payments

Fiscal year   316
The federal government's budgetary year, which in the United States starts on October 1 of the preceding calendar year

Fixed investment   126
Purchases of newly produced capital goods

Foreign-exchange markets   228
Markets in which the currencies of different countries are traded for one another

Frictional unemployment   108
The portion of unemployment that reflects the short periods of unemployment needed for matching jobs with job seekers

Functional sustainability   347
When a country's fiscal policy has a set of rules and decision-making procedures that adjust fiscal parameters over time to serve the goals of long-run stability and prosperity

G

GDP deflator   158
A measure of the average price level of goods and services based on the ratio of nominal GDP to year real GDP, stated relative to the prices of a chosen base year

Government budget constraint   339
The relationship between what a government purchases and its sources of funds

Government expenditures   125
Government purchases of goods and services plus transfer payments

Government purchases   125
Purchases of goods by all levels of government plus purchases of services from contractors and wages of government employees (The term "government consumption expenditures and gross investment" is used in the official national income accounts.)

Government-sponsored enterprises (GSEs)   179
Specialized intermediaries that operate like private firms but are backed and controlled by the government and that engage in the business of securitizing home mortgage loans and, sometimes, other loans

Great Recession   96
An informal term for the period of low economic activity that began in December 2007

Gross domestic income (domestic income)   122
The total income of all types—including wages, rents, interest payments, and profits—that is paid in return for factors of production used in producing domestic product

Gross domestic product (GDP) 96, 148
(1) A measure of the value of total output of goods and services produced within a nation's borders; (2) The value at current market prices of all final goods and services produced annually in a given country

H

Hierarchy 16
A way of achieving coordination in which individual actions are guided by instructions from a central authority

Hyperinflation 367
Very rapid inflation

I

Imports 127
A leakage from the circular flow consisting of payments for goods and services purchased from the rest of the world

Income elasticity of demand 81
The ratio of the percentage change in the quantity of a good demanded to a given percentage change in consumer incomes, other things being equal

Indexation 110
A policy of automatically adjusting a value or payment in proportion to changes in the average price level

Inelastic demand 76
A situation in which quantity demanded changes by a smaller percentage than price, so that total revenue decreases as price decreases

Inferior good 48
A good for which an increase in consumer incomes results in a decrease in demand

Inflation 110
A sustained increase in the average level of prices of all goods and services

Inflationary recession 362
An episode in which real output falls toward or below its natural level and unemployment rises toward or above its natural rate while rapid inflation continues

Inflation inertia (inflation momentum) 360
A tendency of firms and workers to expect prices to continue rising in the future at the same rate as in the immediate past

Inflation targeting 291
A strategy for stabilization policy that focuses on holding the rate of inflation within a target range

Infrastructure 334
The shared physical systems, such as roads, power grids, and water systems, on which economic activity depends

Injections 125
The government purchase, investment, and net export components of the circular flow

Input prices 261
A measure of the average prices of labor, raw materials, and other inputs that firms use to produce goods and services

Inside lags 284
Delays between the time a problem develops and the time policymakers decide what to do about it

Insolvency 176
A state of affairs in which the net worth (capital) of a bank or other business falls to zero

Intermediate goods 148
Goods and services that firms buy for use as inputs in producing other goods and services

Intermediate target 288
A variable that responds to the use of a policy instrument or a change in operating target with a significant lag

Inventory 54
A stock of a good awaiting sale or use

Inventory investment 126
Changes in stocks of finished goods ready for sale, raw materials, and partially completed goods in process of production

Inverse relationship 33
A relationship between two variables in which an increase in the value of one variable is associated with a decrease in the value of the other

Investment 9, 125
(1) The act of increasing the economy's stock of capital—that is, its supply of productive inputs made by people; (2) The sum of fixed investment and inventory investment

L

Labor   5
The contributions to production made by people working with their minds and their hands

Labor force   105
The sum of all individuals who are employed and all individuals who are unemployed

Labor force participation rate   97
The percentage of the adult population that is working or looking for work

Law of demand   44
The principle that an inverse relationship exists between the price of a good and the quantity of that good that buyers demand, other things being equal

Leakages   123
The saving, net tax, and import components of circular flow

Liabilities   175
All the legal claims against a firm by non-owners or against a household by nonmembers

Liquidity   177
An asset's ability to serve directly as a means of payment or be converted to cash without loss of nominal value

Liquidity trap   375
A situation in which monetary policy loses its effectiveness as nominal interest rates approach zero

M

M1   199
A measure of the money supply that includes currency and transaction deposits

M2   199
A measure of the money supply that includes M1 plus retail money market mutual fund shares, money market deposit accounts, and saving deposits

Macroeconomics   4
The branch of economics that studies large-scale economic phenomena, particularly inflation, unemployment, and economic growth

Marginal propensity to consume   130
The proportion of each added dollar of real disposable income that households devote to consumption

Market   16
Any arrangement people have for trading with one another

Merchandise balance   155
The value of a country's merchandise exports of goods (merchandise) minus the value of its imports of goods

Microeconomics   4
The branch of economics that studies the choices of individual units—including households, business firms, and government agencies

Model   18
A synonym for *theory*; in economics, often applied to theories that take the form of graphs or equations

Monetarism   289
A school of economic thought that emphasized the importance of the quantity of money and advocated the use of stable rules for monetary policy

Monetary base   202
The sum of currency and reserve deposits, the monetary liabilities of the central bank

Monetization   338
Financing government operations or debt service by issuing new money through the central bank

Money   198
An asset that serves as a means of payment, a store of purchasing power, and a unit of account

Money multiplier   205
The maximum amount of money that the banking system can create, stated as a multiple of reserves

Multiplier effect   135
The tendency of a given exogenous change in planned expenditure to increase equilibrium GDP by a greater amount

N

National income   153
The total income earned by a country's residents, including wages, rents, interest payments, and profits

National income accounts   148
A set of official government statistics on aggregate economic activity

Natural (potential) level of real output   102
The trend of real GDP growth over time, also known as potential

Natural rate of unemployment   105
The rate of unemployment that prevails when real output is at its natural level

Natural resources   5
Anything that people can use as a productive input in its natural state, such as farmland, building sites, forests, and mineral deposits

Negative slope   33
A slope having a value less than zero

Net exports   127
Payments received for exports minus payments made for imports

Net taxes   125
Tax revenue minus transfer payments

Net worth   175
A firm's or household's assets minus its liabilities, also called *equity* or *capital*

NGDP targeting   295
A policy under which the central bank adopts the rate of growth of nominal GDP as its principal intermediate target

Nominal   96
In economics, a term that refers to data that have not been adjusted for the effects of inflation

Nominal interest rate   112
The interest rate expressed in the usual way: in terms of current dollars, without adjustment for inflation

Non-accelerating inflation rate of unemployment (NAIRU)   105
The rate of unemployment below which inflation begins to rise

Normal good   48
A good for which an increase in consumer income results in an increase in demand

Normative economics   15
The area of economics that is devoted to judgments about whether economic policies or conditions are good or bad

O

Open economy   127
An economy that has links to the outside world in the form of imports, exports, and financial transactions

Open market operation   209
A purchase or sale of government securities by a central bank

Operating target   288
A variable that responds immediately to the use of a policy instrument

Opportunity cost   5
The cost of a good or service measured in terms of the forgone opportunity to pursue the best possible alternative activity with the same time or resources

Originate-to-distribute model of banking   178
A model of banking in which banks sell loans soon after they make them and use the proceeds from the sale to make new loans

Originate-to-hold model of banking   178
A model of banking that emphasized making loans and then holding the loans until maturity

Output gap   102
The economy's current level of real output minus its natural level of real output

Outside lags   284
Delays between the time policymakers reach a decision and the time the resulting policy action affects the economy

P

Perfectly elastic demand   76
A situation in which the demand curve is a horizontal line

Perfectly inelastic demand   76
A situation in which the demand curve is a vertical line

Phillips curve   362
A graph showing the relationship between the inflation rate and the unemployment rate, other things being equal

Planned expenditure   130
The sum of consumption, government purchases, net exports, and planned investment

Planned inventory investment   130
Changes in the level of inventory made on purpose, as part of a firm's business plan

Planned investment   130
The sum of fixed investment and planned inventory investment

Policy goal   288
A long-run objective of economic policy that is important for economic welfare

Policy instrument   288
A variable directly under the control of policymakers

Policy rules   288
A set of rules for monetary and fiscal policy that specifies in advance the actions that policymakers will take in response to economic developments

Positive economics   15
The area of economics that is concerned with facts and the relationships among them

Positive slope   32
A slope having a value greater than zero

Price elasticity of demand   74
The ratio of the percentage change in the quantity of a good demanded to a given percentage change in its price, other things being equal

Price elasticity of supply   82
The ratio of the percentage change in the quantity of a good supplied to a given percentage change in its price, other things being equal

Price index   158
A weighted average of the prices of goods and services expressed in relation to a base-year value of 100

Price level   158
A weighted average of the prices of goods and services expressed in relation to a base-year value of 1.0

Price stability   110
A rate of inflation that is low enough not to be a significant factor in business and individual decision making

Primary structural balance   321
The structural budget balance adjusted to remove government net interest payments

Procyclical policy   287
A poorly timed pattern of monetary or fiscal policy that applies restraint when the economy is already at risk of recession and stimulus when it is already beginning to overheat

Producer price index (PPI)   159
A price index based on a sample of goods and services bought by business firms

Production possibility frontier   20
A graph that shows possible combinations of goods that an economy can produce given available technology and factors of production

Purchasing power parity (PPP)   233
A situation in which goods cost the same in one country as in another when prices are compared using the market exchange rate

Q

Quantitative easing (QE)   212
A monetary policy strategy that uses open market operations to increase reserves of the banking system even after interest rates have fallen to or near zero

R

Real   96
In economics, a term that refers to data that have been adjusted for the effects of inflation

Real effective exchange rate (REER)   233
A weighted average of the exchange rate of a country's currency relative to those of all trading partners

Real interest rate   112
The nominal interest rate minus the rate of inflation

Real output   96
A synonym for real gross domestic product

Recession   103
A cyclical economic contraction that lasts six months or more

Required reserve ratio   205
The minimum level of reserves that the central bank requires a commercial bank to hold, stated as a percentage of deposits

Reserves   177
Cash in bank vaults and banks' deposits with the Federal Reserve System

Revenue   74
Price multiplied by quantity sold

S

Saving   125
The part of income that households do not use to buy goods and services or to pay taxes

Scarcity 4
A situation in which there is not enough of a resource to meet all of everyone's wants

Securitization 179
A process in which a specialized financial intermediary assembles a large pool of loans (or other assets) and uses those loans as a basis for issuing its own securities for sale to investors

Sequestration 318
A budget procedure that requires proportional, across-the-board spending cuts to meet a cap on total spending

Shadow banking system 174
Investment banks, mutual funds, hedge funds, and other institutions that provide bank-like services but do not fall under the full range of regulations that apply to depository institutions

Slope 31
For a straight line, the ratio of the change in the y value to the change in the x value between any two points on the line

Spontaneous order 16
A way of achieving coordination in which individuals adjust their actions in response to cues from their immediate environment

Structural balance 321
The balance of the government budget adjusted to remove the effects of automatic stabilizers

Structural unemployment 108
The portion of unemployment that reflects long periods out of work by people whose skills do not match those required for available jobs

Subprime mortgage 180
A mortgage with features like a low down payment, variable interest rate, and prepayment penalty that make it attractive to low-income borrowers

Substitute goods 47
A pair of goods for which an increase in the price of one causes an increase in demand for the other

Supply 44
The willingness and ability of sellers to provide goods for sale in a market

Supply curve 50
A graphical representation of the relationship between the price of a good and the quantity of that good that sellers are willing to supply

Supply shock 358
An event not arising from changes in aggregate demand that changes the average level of expected input prices

Supply-side deflation 372
A period of falling prices caused by a decrease in the expected costs of production

Supply-side inflation 358
Inflation that begins with an upward shift in the aggregate supply curve while the aggregate demand curve remains fixed or shifts upward more slowly

Sustainability (of fiscal policy) 338
Fiscal policy is said to be unsustainable if, in the long run, it leads to a crisis such as uncontrolled inflation or an accumulation of debt that the government cannot repay

T

T-account 202
A simplified version of a balance sheet that shows only items that change as a result of a given set of transactions

Tangent 33
A straight line that touches a curve at a given point without intersecting it

Target reserve ratio 205
The minimum acceptable quantity of bank reserves, stated as a percentage of deposits

Tax expenditure 319
A tax deduction or other tax preference that the government enacts to induce households or firms to behave in a way that serves some purpose of public policy

Tax revenue 125
The total value of all taxes that the government collects

Taylor rule 294
A rule that adjusts monetary policy according to changes in the rate of inflation and the output gap (or unemployment)

Theory 18
A representation of the relationships among facts

Time inconsistency 286
Tendency of policymakers to take actions that have desirable results in the short run, but undesirable long-run results

Total factor productivity 99
A measurement of improvements in technology and organization that allow increases in the output produced by given quantities of labor and capital

Transaction deposit   **176**
A deposit from which customers can withdraw funds freely by check or electronic transfer to make payments to third parties

Transfer payments   **110, 125**
Payments by government to individuals for pensions, unemployment compensation, and other payments that do not represent income from services that the recipients currently provide

U

Unemployed   **105**
A person who is not employed but is actively looking for work

Unemployment rate   **105**
The percentage of the labor force that is unemployed

Unit elastic demand   **76**
A situation in which price and quantity demanded change by the same percentage, so that total revenue remains unchanged as price changes

Unit labor cost   **242**
A measure of nominal wage rates adjusted for labor productivity

Unplanned inventory investment   **130**
Changes in the level of inventory that arise from a difference between planned and actual sales

V

Value added   **148**
The dollar value of an industry's sales less the value of intermediate goods purchased for use in production

Vault cash   **175**
Paper currency and coins held by banks as part of their reserves of liquid assets.

Velocity (income velocity of money)   **207**
The ratio of nominal GDP to the money stock; a measure of the average number of times that people use each dollar of the money stock each year to purchase final goods and services

Z

Zero interest rate bound (ZIRB)   **374**
The principle that nominal interest rates cannot fall below zero

Index